From Handaxe to Khan

From Handaxe to Khan

ESSAYS PRESENTED TO PEDER MORTENSEN
ON THE OCCASION OF HIS 70TH BIRTHDAY

Edited by

Kjeld von Folsach
Henrik Thrane & Ingolf Thuesen

AARHUS UNIVERSITY PRESS

From Handaxe to Khan

Copyright: Aarhus University Press and the authors 2004
Cover art: Bjørn Nørgaard
Cover design: Lotte Bruun Rasmussen
Typeset and printed in Gylling by Narayana Press
Typeface: Adobe Garamond
Paper: 115 g Arctic volume

ISBN 87 7934 107 1

AARHUS UNIVERSITY PRESS
Langelandsgade 177
DK-8200 Aarhus N

73 Lime Walk
Headington, Oxford OX2 7AD

Box 511
Oakville, CT 06779

Published with financial support by

C.L. David Foundation and Collection
Aarhus Universitets Forskningsfond
H.P. Hjerl Hansens Mindefondet for Dansk Palæstinaforskning

Contents

Preface   7

HENRIK THRANE
   From Jutland to Jordan   9

SULTAN MUHESEN
   An Introduction to the Palaeolithic of Syria 29

ROSE L. SOLECKI
   Cores Into Tools: A Technological Device
   Found in the Yabrudian Industry of The Levant 49

RALPH S. SOLECKI
   Footprints in the Sediments of Yabroud Rockshelter IV, Syria 51

HANS GEORG K. GEBEL
   Lithic Economic Systems and Early Sedentism 55

FRANK HOLE
   Campsites of the Seasonally Mobile in Western Iran 67

JOAN OATES
   Ubaid Mesopotamia Revisited 87

INGOLF THUESEN
   Messages in Stone:
   The Megaliths of the Nebo Region in Jordan 105

ERNIE HAERINCK & BRUNO OVERLAET
   The Chronology of the Pusht-i Kuh, Luristan:
   Results of the Belgian Archaeological Expedition in Iran 119

HANS J. NISSEN
   Elam's Backstage 137

D.T. POTTS
   The Numinous and the Immanent:
   Some Thoughts on Kurangun and the Rudkhaneh-e Fahliyan 143

ERIK HALLAGER
A Palace Without Sealings?   157

LISE HANNESTAD
Seleukos Nikator and Syria   165

ROSS BURNS
From Theatre to Temple   185

MICHELE PICCIRILLO
The Shaikh Zuwaydeh Mosaic on the Border of Palestine and Egypt   199

JØRGEN BÆK SIMONSEN
Muhammad's Letters   215

KJELD VON FOLSACH
Three Eastern Islamic Leather Wallets and Three Related
Stone Press-moulds in the David Collection   225

OLAF OLSEN & RIKKE AGNETE OLSEN
Saone – Sahyûn – Qalaat Saladin   241

ALISON MCQUITTY
The Architecture of Hospitality:
A madâfah in Northern Jordan   255

STEFAN WEBER
An Egyptian qa'a in 16th Century Damascus:
Representative Halls in Late Mamluk and Early Ottoman
Residential Architecture in Syria and Lebanon   265

JAKOB SKOVGAARD-PETERSEN
Illustrations of Islam:
Reflections on the Historical Role of Muslim Mass Media   297

ALAN WALMSLEY
Archaeology and Islamic studies:
The development of a relationship   317

CONTRIBUTORS   331

Preface

This book is dedicated to our friend and colleague, Peder Mortensen, on the occasion of his 70th birthday on May the 7th, 2004. The book contains a number of contributions dealing with such different topics as Palaeolithic stone tools, the remains of Early Man, and the study of Islamic history, art and archaeology. However, two common factors apply to all articles, namely the Near East and Peder Mortensen.

During his long career Peder has devoted much of his time and talent to the people and the culture of the Near East. Many countries have been regularly visited, numerous friendships have been made and many research projects with remarkable consequences have been initiated and accomplished. Besides being director of the Moesgård Museum for many years, Peder's work is also manifested in many extraordinary monuments which speak for themselves: a restored house in old Damascus, museums in Bahrain and Hama (Syria) – all masterpieces of superior quality. Not to mention several archaeological research projects, in Luristan, Bahrain, Syria and Jordan. Behind so many projects is Peder's sense for exploring and protecting culture, ancient as well as recent. Many are those who have benefitted from Peder's efforts and feelings for doing the right thing at the right time; indeed sometimes to a degree that made Peder look more anonymous than deserved, despite his being in many ways the founding father.

This book is a simple symbol of recognition of our debt to Peder for sharing with so many – formally and informally – his insight into and fascination with the people and culture of the Near East. The broad range of topics exemplify his extensive contribution. With this book the authors want to congratulate Peder for his achievements and at the same time express their gratitude to him for his extraordinary hospitality in sharing his projects with others.

The book was made possible by generous grants from the C.L. David Foundation and Collection, Aarhus Universitets Forskningsfond, and H.P. Hjerl Hansens Mindefondet for Dansk Palæstinaforskning. Thanks to Morten Hecquet and Aiysha Abu Laban who assisted in the editorial work.

Kjeld von Folsach   Henrik Thrane   Ingolf Thuesen

From Jutland to Jordan

HENRIK THRANE

Peder Mortensen's contribution to Near Eastern archaeology is, no doubt, familiar to the authors and readers of this volume. In order to fully appreciate his archaeological work, I find it necessary first to examine another aspect, namely what he has done for Prehistoric archaeology in Denmark.

His road from Jutland to Jordan has been neither straight nor narrow. His deep fascination with the Near East and his unquenchable quest for insight into its material culture have drawn him to research topics ever further from each other and from his original introduction to the Bronze Age of Bahrein.

Born and bred in Jutland, his home for the first 20 years, he began already in his student years to journey to the Near East. He worked in the Gulf with P.V. Glob 1956-62 and, in connection with trips home, took advantage of the opportunity to visit other Near and Middle East countries, finding his future love for their Prehistory and Islamic Past in this way. Iran, Iraq, Palestine and Syria became familiar environments; he lived for periods (with his family) in the village of Kahreh in Luristan and has studied at the various Foreign institutes in Amman, Baghdad, Beirut and Jerusalem, and with the Franciscans at Mount Nebo.

After an interlude in Copenhagen at the National Museum Peder returned to Jutland and stayed there for nearly 30 years, giving some of his best years to university teaching and to the Prehistoric Museum at Moesgård. The Near East was, however, always present in his mind and plans. Time and again he returned for fieldwork or periods of study. That Jordan should become the latest location for Peder's fieldwork was the result of having found a congenial environment (and of course because of the political development that he, as well as so many of his contemporaries, have had to cope with).

Peder began in Århus as a student of Prehistoric Archaeology in 1953 and has described his experience and first encounter with the charismatic if rather unorthodox professor (even by the standards of the time), P.V. Glob, who, having told the freshman what to read, disappeared immediately to the Gulf, only to return months later (Mortensen 1981a). And in this case the method worked!

Fig. 1. First dig abroad, at Kvamsöy, Norway 1954, unknown photographer.

This was indeed a somewhat 'special version' of how archaeology professors tended to receive their new (and few) students who had turned up at the beginning of term in early September with great expectations only to be told that September was for digging and that teaching would first begin in October.

Well, we either followed our masters into the field or busied ourselves other-

Fig. 2. The Danes are coming, albeit upheld en route. The Bahrein team of archaeologists waiting in the Oriental Palace Hotel, Kuwait in 1959, from left Knud Riisgaard, Harald Andersen, Hellmuth Andersen, Peder and at the far end P.V. Glob and the ethnographer Klaus Ferdinand, unknown photographer.

wise. Exams were only taken when student and professor agreed that now was the time – perhaps after eight years, but often after many more years. Peder set the record at seven years, taking his MA in June 1960.

During those seven years he managed to excavate a Neolithic barrow in Denmark with the by then earliest traces of ploughing with the ard – still used in the Near East when we began to work there. He typically let another publish this important novelty (Kjærum 1954). Poul Kjærum was in charge of another excavation in which Peder participated, the megalithic complex at Tustrup. Another excavation, in which Peder was in charge and directed a group of amateurs during three periods, was an Iron Age village that contained well-preserved house remains (Thomsen 1959). Bahrein, which entered Peder's 'constellation' in 1956 (Mortensen 1956), continued for decades to be the annual focus of a great number of Scandinavian archaeologists and artists. The Barbar temple, for example was where Peder did his main work with Hellmuth Andersen (Mortensen 1971b-c).

Peder Mortensen was exceptional in another way. He moved to the University of Copenhagen in 1956, and studied there for a couple of years. The collec-

Fig. 3.
Showing the
Barbar temple,
Bahrein.
December
1961, unknown
photographer.

Fig. 4.
Studying the
section in
the trench at
Tepe Guran,
a favourite
occupation. He
is wearing the
Luri felt coat
which had its
use in the wet
early spring.
Photographer:
Jørgen
Meldgaard,
April 1963.

Fig. 5. Tea on the mound, morning break on Tepe Guran, from left Peder, the author, Erik Ejrnæs and Erik Brinch Petersen. Photographer: Jørgen Meldgaard, May 1963.

Fig. 6. A contemplative Peder Mortensen above the Hulailan plain, enjoying the beauty of the Luristan landscape or planning future fieldwork? Photographer: Jørgen Meldgaard, May 1963. Note the bridge over the Saimarreh – the Kampsax road that brought us to Luristan.

Fig. 7. A rare occasion – not to be repeated – Peder mounted for the return trip from the excavation of Tepe Guran to the expedition house. Photographer: the author, May 16th 1963.

Fig. 8. Lecturing at Teheran University, 1977. Unknown photographer.

tions at the National Museum offered a much better opportunity for the study of artefacts than the provincial museums. He took his MA examination at the University of Aarhus with Professor Glob. After his exam he became an Assistant Curator at the Classical and Near Eastern department of the National Museum, but this proved not to be his happiest period.

When Peder finally returned to Århus in 1968, at the request of Glob's successor, Ole Klindt-Jensen, it was as a teacher of Theory and Near Eastern Prehistory at the University of Aarhus. This subject was obligatory for the students, who otherwise were taught European and, especially, Danish Prehistory. The introduction of agriculture was a favourite topic, after his own work on Tell Shimshara (Mortensen 1970) and his excavation at Tepe Guran 1963. In 1978 he became Reader in Near Eastern Archaeology – the first full time teaching post in this field in Denmark. When the Carlsberg Foundation asked this young Magister to publish the material from the Danish salvage excavation at Shimshara, it involved him in what was to become central to his research for many years – the incipient agriculture of the foothills of the Zagros mountains.

He was Dean of the Faculty of Humanities from 1978 – 1981 and for eight years represented archaeology in the Danish Research Council for the Humanities. In 1982 he succeeded Ole Klindt-Jensen as Director of the Prehistoric Museum at Moesgård (Mortensen 1981b).

During the period from 1979 – 1996 Peder also managed to keep the Near Eastern side going, working hard to ensure the publication of, among others the Danish expeditions to the Gulf. His ability and his connections – as well as his will to assist others, made him a valued fund-raiser and organiser for the Danish Hama excavations, the publication of which had been underway so lang that a serious impediment arose with regard to extra financial assistance from the otherwise generous Carlsberg foundation. Peder also did a lot of work to help Diana Kirkbride and further her work on Beidha (Bird 1989). He also began his latest fieldwork, the survey on Mount Nebo in Jordan (Mortensen 1995; Mortensen & Thuesen 1999).

His interests have gradually expanded – from the Neolithic to the Palaeolithic – the earlier the better! He seems to run across hand axes and chopper tools whenever he takes a stroll, be it in Jordan, Luristan or on Crete. Flintwork is indeed one of his special fields of interest, no doubt inspired by his Danish background (Mortensen 1971a & d; 1973b; 2002). It is a clear recognition from his colleagues that Peder has been asked to study the "chipped stone industry" of several of the great sites like Hacilar (Mortensen 1970b) Beidha (1971d), Chogha Mami (1973a) Tamerkhan (2002 – cf. Oates this volume). At the other end of the scale, Peder's fascination with Islamic art changed from the amateur to the professional level with his involvement with the board of the David Collection and with the Damascus Institute.

Moesgård

As director of the Moesgård Museum he managed to produce some spectacular exhibitions where his sense of coordination and cooperation served him and the exhibitions well. Just to name the most spectacular: The dresses and mosaics of Palestine and Jordan (Mortensen 1991), The Silk Road (Mortensen 1996) and the biggest, which joined three major museums in one project, on the Islamic world and involved the National Museum, the David Collection, and Moesgård, with three heavy catalogue volumes (v. Folsach, Lundbæk & Mortensen [eds.] 1991)

In this way he succeded, to an extent unknown before, in making Moesgård an international museum, in spite of it being a provincial museum – albeit with a special license to work all over Denmark and beyond.

Expeditions to the ever-widening field on the south shores of the Gulf continued to 1989 under the directorship of Karen Frifelt, one of the few Aarhus students from before 1953.

It was only natural that Moesgård should become involved in the creation

Fig. 9. The museum director in his office in the manor house Moesgård, before he surrendered to the PC, which took its time. Photographer: Jens Vellev, 1990.

of the National Museum of Bahrein, where Peder played a key role in the planning and coordination of this highly modern creation which was opened in 1988. Later, at a more modest level, he was able to repeat the success and collaboration with the local authorities when the Syrians asked the Danes to round off their early involvement with Hama with a new museum there – opening 1999 (Mortensen 1999).

Thus Peder managed to keep his interest in the Near East alive and to expand his own experience in later and earlier periods.

Being what is was, most of the daily activities at Moesgård were directly concerned with the archaeology of the immediate region, as well as selected excavations on Funen. University lecturers and the Museum archaeologists worked at Kjøkkenmøddinger, Neolithic causewayed camps, dolmens and Iron Age settlements. The Museum's archaeologists also transcended the national borders, excavating at Danevirke and Alt Lübeck. The dominant project was the resumption

Fig. 10. Dwarfed by classic Islamic architecture – Inge and Peder in Shakhrisabz, Uzbekistan. Photographer: the author, Oct. 3rd 1990.

of the excavation of the large complex weapon deposit of the Late Roman period in the valley of Illerup 26 km southwest of Aarhus, where Peder had participated in earlier campaigns under the great excavator Harald Andersen. Peder's father wrote a letter urging the field director to take his son on even before he entered university.

When the excavations finally ceased in 1985 because a solution had been found to the preservation of the water level, an even bigger project had its beginning. The magnitude of the problem will be realized by the fact that by 2003 10 volumes, 34 cm have been published and at least one more is still to come before the end of the project in 2004 when 50 years of Illerup work will come to an end. Peder has attended countless meetings and completed innumerable applications for funds in order to provide a situation of continuity for the researcher and draughtsmen employed.

That he also managed to do the same for the Gulf expeditions and to keep the publication work going can almost be taken for granted. Although this kind of operation may not appear as a major feature on a cv, it can exhaust even the most enthusiastic director. Now, fortunately, the books are coming, which is the main thing.

Danish Protohistory

The Danish Research Council for the Humanities had a tradition for research programmes designed by its individual members. Peder was a member for eight years and his project was rather different from those of his two archaeological predecessors. The first was the Settlement Research Programme and the second the Medieval Town Project. Both were directed at saving and studying chosen settlements and towns, very much in the Danish positivist tradition. Peder chose a field which he had become familiar with at Moesgård through the Illerup, Danevirke and the earliest Ribe and Aarhus excavations.

No doubt the idea stemmed from the renewal of archaeological theory of the 1960s, encountered for example, when Peder was Kevorkian lecturer in the U.S. in 1966. The orientation towards neo-evolutionism was a prominent feature in Danish Prehistory of the 1970s. Peder saw to it that prominent figures in the New Archaeology were invited to Moesgård for periods of teaching and debating: Lewis Binford, David Clarke, Patty Jo Watson, Bob Adams, and Kenneth Flannery were all here.

Thus, the renovation of archaeological theory was introduced to a Danish archaeology which had been completely a-theoretical, not to say anti-theoretical, at least in the generation of professors who taught Peder and me.

Out of this lively intellectual discourse, figures like Kristian Kristiansen and

Torsten Madsen, and several others, emerged who introduced new attitudes, new questions and new methods. The conflict between the university departments at Copenhagen and Aarhus, manifested mainly by the professors' personal dislikes and very different tempers, spread to their candidates with some rather silly antagonisms as a result.

Peder saw the opportunity of introducing the new theoretical frame to a wider Danish society and at the same time open up a fresh debate on issues which were simmering during the 1970s. The large scale mechanized area excavations had uncovered whole structures of complete villages and settlements, mainly Iron Age. Instead of spending money on new fieldwork, he used the money for a series of symposia held in an old manor run by modern nuns. The atmosphere was far from monastic though. It was highly enthusiastic and positive with lively discussions in fora with a broad range of disciplines and persons from all corners of the archaeological establishment.

At Sostrup Manor, Peder with his well developed tact gathered people who had not spoken with each other for years, and a new working climate was created. This in itself had a profound effect on research over the following years and may in itself be seen as a worthwhile investment. As a non-combatant in this field he was able to direct his colleagues – old and young – to a much more cooperative spirit.

The immediate product of the *Stamme – Stat* (tribe – state) project were two volumes containing the proceedings of a selection of lectures (Mortensen & Rasmussen 1988 & 1991). Modestly, he didn't even sign the forewords. The first volume was sold out completely and had to be re-printed – a rare success for an archaeological book in Danish.

Part of the reason was that the project was well timed. In Sweden and Norway people worked on similar lines and for them the *Stamme – Stat* volumes became a source of inspiration because of the inter-disciplinary and new theoretical approach.

I think these volumes perhaps were the first to employ this approach on such a national scale and without the authoritarian pressure which somehow marked similar German programmes – laudable as they were.

Thus, behind the scenes, as with Illerup, and on stage, as with the *Stamme – Stat* project Peder Mortensen has contributed significantly to research in Danish Pre- and Protohistory during his Moesgård years. This aspect should be remembered when we celebrate his other – main – field of interest.

As the first academic with a permanent job in Near Eastern Archaeology, and thanks to the foresight of Ole Klindt-Jensen at Aarhus University, it was inevitable that Peder was the person who carried enough clout to ensure the future of the discipline at the University of Copenhagen, and at the Carsten Niebuhr Institute which has proved so worthy of the trust placed in it in 1982. It seems historical justice that Peder was chosen on his retirement from the Damascus Institute in 2002 as the Institute's first *adjungeret professor* (Honorary Professor) in Near Eastern archaeology.

Fieldwork

Peder's list of publications is rather different from those of many of his contemporaries. That is not caused by any lack of enthusiasm or by declining energy. I see it rather as a result of his perfectionism – and as the result of his involvement in others' work, some of which I have mentioned above.

When, after many years of intense study he felt that he could not produce the new work on Childe and his Neolithic revolution that he had intended – partly because of the flood of books at that stage – he just dropped it, which is a pity. I am sure that his study would have been well worth reading (Mortensen 1973a; and 1978a give a glimpse).

Peder is a planner, his agenda is well prepared and the list of tasks is still long enough to keep him busy through a long otium. May he succeed. We look forward to important studies on Luristan, Jordan, and much else.

That same perfectionism explains two of his main contributions to Near Eastern Archaeology, as I see them.

The first was his approach to the Tepe Guran sounding. I think we were two days late compared to the original timetable, but virgin soil was reached and there was no lowering of the standard during those last hot weeks deep down in the mound.

The method of a trench that functioned as a guide to the layers and levels – and at the same time eased the disposal of the soil from the main square – was simple but elegant and efficient (Meldgaard, Mortensen & Thrane 1964). With the knowledge gained in the trench, the square could be documented in every detail, whereas the traditional approach does nothing to alleviate your doubts and difficulties because you have no idea of what is coming next.

I think that Kent Flannery at least will agree with me that it is a pity that many distractions have kept Peder from finishing his report on Tepe Guran. It became a *locus classicus* immediately and deserves the final monograph to keep this position.

The second example is Peder's Hulailan survey. I suppose that all of us who have ever tried a survey in the Near East, realized sooner or later how far from being complete our efforts were, regardless of whether air photography (satellite now) or other wide-cover were available or not. The representativity of certain types of (esp. non-tell) sites and periods was, mildly put, uncertain. No one ever had sufficient time to carry out a thorough survey, somewhat along the lines of what was seen as necessary and practical in temperate Europe where field walking at close and regular intervals had become the normal procedure during the immediate pre- and post-war period. Peder took his time over the Hulailan area, surveying the plain and its immediate surroundings with caves and open air sites and was able to demonstrate different settlement patterns for different periods. The differences reflected important changes in subsistence economy and are rather relevant for vital periods of the Stone and Metal Ages. His survey gave a solid background for the Tepe Guran sequence – being the reverse use of surveys from the normal one. It also carried knowledge of the settlement of the

Fig. 11. Peder Mortensen doing the field photography at his trench into the Neolithic Tepe Guran May 1963. No wonder archaeologists complain about their sore backs. Photographer: Jørgen Meldgaard.

Fig. 12. In the field again – Mount Nebo. Photographer: Ingolf Thuesen.

valley far beyond anything our half-hearted efforts in 1962 – 64 had ever led us to suspect (Mortensen 1974a – 1979).

Now Peder has continued this approach in the Mount Nebo area, with a very different environment and different cultures. The level of refinement and coverage is the same, as was his partner in the field – Inge (Mortensen & Thuesen 1993).

These two cases illustrate Peder's well prepared, carefully planned and scrupulously executed approach to archaeological fieldwork.

I hope that his example may inspire widely – beyond the immediate circle of contemporary field directors.

Damascus

That Peder should finish his career as a diplomat and creator and restorer of one of the fine old hidden palaces of Damascus must have been the fulfilment of a dream. He was familiar with the city from the 1950s. Here he was able to combine his inborn sense of diplomacy with his long standing knowledge of the

Fig. 13. With the indispensable attributes, at Mount Nebo monastery, 2003. Photographer: Ingolf Thuesen.

old city and its souk and treasures from the Islamic period. The result speaks for itself (Bredal & Lange 2003) but not about the meetings, set-backs and planning and waiting that were involved. That Peder Mortensen should finish his official (paid) career as the first director of the new Danish cultural institute in the Near East seems, in retrospect, somehow fitting.

Recent books bear witness to a lifelong love of the arts that is symbolically expressed in Bjørn Nørgaard's series of prints from Syria (Nørgaard 2002). Peder came from a home full of art and art talk. His father was a proliferous freelance art historian and critic, the author of a series of books on Danish artists, several of whom Peder met in his home. Peder no longer plays the violin but has kept

Fig. 14. The enthusiastic director explaining the restored Danish Institute in Damascus to i.a. the artist, Bjørn Nørgaard (left). Photographer: Steen F. Lindberg, May 2001.

his keen ear for music. The many colleagues who visited Peder and Inge in one of their hospitable homes will know that the visual arts play an enormous role in their daily lives, modern Danish Art hangs next to Islamic good bits, competing for the limited space. His membership of the board of that great Danish Oriental collection, David's Samling, unites his insight and knowledge in a fruitful way. In other words, Peder is a bit of a polyhistor combining very detailed research in special fields with a widely ranging encyclopaedic knowledge. His excellent memory and love of telling anecdotes and reminiscences from his travels is enjoyed by all of us, some of us with some envy. I have had the pleasure of having Peder as a close friend for nearly 50 years, and whether in the field, travelling, visiting, or discussing research policy it has been a very good time. There was always a cup of Nescafé, a piece of advice and fresh information available in his office.

All we have done is to scratch the surface of the vast range of Near Eastern Prehistory with which Peder has been involved. Peder's work has been continuous and successful, done with minimal resources, and in environments which were not always congenial to his ideas. I have only sketched some aspects of his work here, hoping that he will not disagree too much with my presentation.

References

Bird, B.F. 1989. *The Natufian Encampment at Beidha, Excavations at Beidha* I. Højbjerg.

Bredal, B. & B. Lange 2003. *Et hus i Damaskus*. København.

Folsach, K. von, T. Lundbæk & P. Mortensen (eds.) 1996a. *Sultan, Shah og Stormogul*. København.

Folsach, K. von, T. Lundbæk & P. Mortensen (eds.) 1996b. *Den arabiske Rejse*. Århus.

Folsach, K. von, T. Lundbæk & P. Mortensen (eds.) 1996c. *I halvmånens Skær*. København.

Ilkjær, J. 2002. *Illerup Ådal – Archaeology as a magic mirror*. Højbjerg.

Kjærum, P. 1954. 'Striber på kryds og tværs', *Kuml* 1954, 18-28.

Meldgaard, J., P. Mortensen & H. Thrane 1964. 'Excavations at Tepe Guran, Luristan', *Acta Archaeologica* XXXIV, 97-133.

Mortensen I. Demant & P. Mortensen 1989. 'On the Origin of Nomadism in Northern Luristan', *AIO* II, 929-51.

Mortensen, P. 1955. 'En billedsten med dyreslyng fra Borum Kirke', *Aarbog f. historisk samfund Aarhus Stift 1955*, Århus, 67-78.

Mortensen, P. 1956. 'Barbartemplets ovale anlæg', *Kuml* 1956, 189-98.

Mortensen, P. 1962a. 'To mykenske pragtsværd', *NMArbm* 1962, 120-22

Mortensen, P. 1962b. 'On the Chronology of Early Village-farming Comunities in Northern Iraq', *Sumer*, XVIII, 73-80.

Mortensen, P. 1964. 'Additional Remarks on the Chronology of Early Village-Farming Communities in the Zagros Area', *Sumer*, XX, 28-36.

Mortensen, P. 1965. 'Expeditioner til Luristan', *NMArbm* 1965, 141-43

Mortensen, P. 1970a. *Tell Shimshara. The Hassuna Period*, (Det kgl. Danske Videnskabernes Selskab Historisk-Filosofiske Skrifter 5.2), København.

Mortensen, P. 1970b. 'The Chipped Stone Industry'. In: J. Mellart (ed.), *Excavations at Hacilar*, Edinburgh, 153-157.

Mortensen, P. 1971a. 'Seasonal Camps and Early Villages in the Zagros'. In: P. Ucko, R. Tringham & G.W. Dimpleby (eds.), *Man, Settlement and Urbanism*, London, 293-97.

Mortensen, P. 1971b. *On the Date of the Temple at Barbar in Bahrein*, (Artibus Asiae XXXIII,4), New York.

Mortensen, P. 1971c. 'Barbartemplets datering', *Kuml* 1970, 385- 98.

Mortensen, P. 1971d. 'A Preliminary Study of the Chipped Stone Industry from Beidha', *Acta Archaeologica*, XLI,1-54.

Mortensen, P. 1973a. 'On the Reflection of Cultural Changes in Artefact Material with Special Regard to the Study of Innovation'. In: C. Renfrew (ed.), *The Explanation of Culture Change*, London, 155-69.

Mortensen, P. 1973b. 'A Sequence of Samarran Flint and Obsidian Tools from Chogha Mami', *Iraq*, XXXV, 37-56.

Mortensen, P. 1973c. Seasonal Camps and Early Villages in the Zagros. In: R. Tringhouse (ed.), *Ecology and Agricultural Settlements*, Andover, 1-5.

Mortensen, P. 1974a. 'A Survey of Early Prehistoric Sites in the Holailan Valley in Lorestan', *Proc. 2nd Ann. Symp*, 34-52, Tehran.

Mortensen, P. 1974b. 'A Survey of Prehistoric Settlements in Northern Luristan', *Acta Archaeologica*, XLV, 1-47.

Mortensen, P. 1974c. 'On the Date of the Barbar Temple, Dilmun'. *A Journal of Archaeology and History in Bahrein*, 6, 4-9.

Mortensen, P. 1975a. 'A Survey of Prehistoric Settlements in Northern Luristan', *Acta Archaeologica*, 45, 1-47.

Mortensen, P. 1975b. 'Survey and Soundings in the Hulailan Valley 1974', *Proceedings of the IIIrd Annual Symposium on Archaeological Research in Iran*, Teheran, 1-12.

Mortensen, P. 1975c. 'The Hulailan Survey', *Iran*, XIII, 190-91.

Mortensen, P. 1976. 'Det første agerbrug i den nære Orient'. In: H. Dehn-Nielsen (ed.), *Det daglige brød*, København, 15-21.

Mortensen, P. 1977. 'Chalcolithic Settlements in the Holailan Valley', *Proceedings of the IVth Annual Symposium on Archaeological Research in Iran*, Tehran, 42- 61.

Mortensen, P. 1978a. 'Kulturforandring eller periodeovergange?', *Hikuin*, 4, 135-44, summ. 163, Højbjerg.

Mortensen, P. 1978b. 'Mesopotamien i forhistorisk tid', *Lousiana Revy*, 18, No.3, København, 4-5.

Mortensen, P. 1979a. 'The Hulailan Survey: A Note on the Relationship Between Aims and Method', *Akten des VII. Internationalen Kongresses für iranische Kunst und Archäologie, München 7.-10. Sept. 1976*, München, 3-8.

Mortensen, P. 1979b. 'Det ældste nærorientalske landbrug', *Carlsbergfondets Årsskrift 1979*, 24-28.

Mortensen, P. 1980. 'Fortidens spor i Ådal og skove', *Århus '82*, 36-37.

Mortensen, P. 1981a. 'Carl Hillmans ledsager'. In: H. Andersen (ed.), *Kammerat Glob*, 75-79, Højbjerg.

Mortensen, P. 1981b. 'Ole Klindt-Jensen 1918 – 1980', *Kuml 1980*, 229-231.

Mortensen, P. 1981c. 'Ole Klindt-Jensen', *Aarhus Universitets Årsberetning 1981*, Århus, 17-21.

Mortensen, P. 1983. 'Patterns of Interaction between Seasonal Settlements and Early Villages in Mesopotamia'. In: T.C. Young, P.E.L. Smith & P. Mortensen (eds.), *The Hilly Flanks and Beyond (Braidwood Festschrift)*. Chicago, 207-29.

Mortensen, P. 1985. 'De ældste samfund'. In: O. Fenger & S. Jørgensen (eds.), *Skabelse, Udvikling, Samfund*. (Acta Jutlandica LX). Århus, 93-102.

Mortensen, P. 1986a. 'Ex oriente lux'. In: H.J. Madsen & J. Vellev (eds.), *Arkæologiske krøniker*. Højbjerg, 22-26.

Mortensen, P. 1986b. 'Forord'. In: Anon, *Fra Oldkammer til Forhistorisk Museum 1861-1986*. Århus, 5.

Mortensen, P. 1988. 'A note on a small box with flint blades and arrowheads from Beidha and its implications'. In: A.N. Garrard & H.G. Gebel (eds.), *The Prehistory of Jordan*, (BAR international Series 396), Oxford, 199-207.

Mortensen, P. 1990. 'Forord'. In: A. Damm (ed.), *Langs Silkevejen/Along the Silk Road*, Højbjerg, 7.

Mortensen, P. 1991a. 'The Brå Cauldron', *The Celts* (exhibition catalogue), Venezia, 375.

Mortensen, P. 1991b. 'Forord'. In: A. Damm (ed.), *2000 års farvepragt, Dragter og mosaikker fra Palæstina og Jordan*, Højbjerg, 7-8.

Mortensen, P. 1993. 'Palaeolithic and Epipalaeolithic Sites in the Hulailan Valley, Northern Luristan'. In: D.l. Olzewski & H.L. Dobble (eds.), *The Palaeolithic Prehistory of the Zagros – Taurus*, Philadelphia, 159-186.

Mortensen, P. 1995. 'Nebobjerget – danske arkæologer på bibelsk jord', *Sfinx*, 18, 3-8.

Mortensen, P. 1996a. 'Forord'. In: K. von Folsach, T. Lundbæk & P. Mortensen (eds.), *Den arabiske rejse*. Århus, 7.

Mortensen, P. 1996b. 'De danske arkæologiske ekspeditioner til Mellemøsten', *Ibid.* 121-29.

Mortensen, P. 1996c. 'Det Danske Institut i Damascus', *Sfinx,* 19, 39-41.

Mortensen, P. 1996d. 'Mount Nebo Survey', *AJA,* 100, 511.

Mortensen, P. 1997.'National or Religious Identification seen in a Local and Global Perspective'. In: O. Højris & S. M. Yürükel (eds.), *Contrasts and Solutions in the Middle East.* Århus, 14-17.

Mortensen, P. 1999. 'Det nye museum i Hama', *Sfinx,* 22, 172-75.

Mortensen, P. 2001a. 'Det romerske teater', *Sfinx,* 24, 132-33.

Mortensen, P. 2001b. *Arabesque. An Exhibition of Paintings by Nina Merra Kelivan and Pernille Moegaard at Khan Asyad Resta,* Damascus, 16pp.

Mortensen, P. 2002a. 'Speech for Hans J. Nissen'. In: A. Hausleiter, S. Kerner & B. Müller-Neuhop (eds.), *Material Culture and Mental Spheres.* Münster, 25-29.

Mortensen, P. 2002b. 'A Note on the Chipped Stone Industry of Tamerkhan', IA XXXVII, 219-227.

Mortensen, P. 2002c. 'A Note on the Theatre of Herod the Great in Damascus'. In: L. Al-Gailani Werr, J. Curtis, H. Martin, A. McMahon, J. Oates & J. Reade (eds.), *Of Pots and Plans.* London, 1-4.

Mortensen, P. 2003. 'Robert J. Braidwood', *Antiquity,* 77, 213-14.

Mortensen, P. (ed.) In prep. Bayt al-Aqqad, (*Publications of the Danish Institute in Damascus*).

Mortensen, P. & K.V. Flannery 1966. 'En af verdens ældste landsbyer', *NMArbm* 1966, 85- 96.

Mortensen, P. & B. Rasmussen (eds.) 1988, *Fra Stamme til Stat i Danmark. Jernalderens stammesamfund,* Højbjerg

Mortensen, P., M. Kervian & F. Hiebert 1987. 'The Occupational Enigma of Bahrain between the 13th and the 8th Cent. BC', *Paléorient,* 13, 77-93.

Mortensen, P. & B. Rasmussen (eds.) 1988, *Fra Stamme til Stat i Danmark. Jernalderens stammesamfund.* Højbjerg.

Mortensen, P. & B. Rasmussen (eds.) 1991. *Fra Stamme til Stat i Danmark 2. Høvdingesamfund og Kongemagt.* Højbjerg.

Mortensen, P. & P.E.L. Smith 1980. 'Three new "Early Neolithic" Sites in Western Iran', *Current Anthropology,* 21, 511-12.

Mortensen, P. & I. Thuesen 1999. 'The Prehistoric Periods'. In: M. Piccirillo & E. Alliata (eds), *Mount Nebo. New Archaeological Excavations 1967 – 1997.* Jerusalem, 85-99.

Nørgaard, B. 2003. *I de dage paven kom til Damaskus.* Viborg.

Thomsen, N. 1959. 'Hus og kældre i romersk jernalder', *Kuml* 1959, 13-27.

Young Jr., T.C., P.E.L.Smith & P. Mortensen (eds.) 1983. *The Hilly Flanks and Beyond,* (*Braidwood Festschrift*). Chicago.

An Introduction to the Palaeolithic of Syria

SULTAN MUHESEN

We begin by outlining briefly the commencement and development of research into the Palaeolithic of Syria, from the first activities until the present day. During the first three decades of the last century, information was limited to surface collections, which came from the valleys of the main Syrian rivers and which, to a large degree, were attributed to Acheulian, and Levalloiso-mousterian. The importance of finding early indications of Palaeolithic occupation was emphasized by the systematic excavation which took place at Yabroud (fig. 1), in the 1930s where a long sequence of prehistoric occupation covering the period form the lower Palaeolithic to the Neolithic was exposed (Rust 1950).

Further research took place in the 1960s, being the date of the excavation at the middle Palaeolithic cave site of Jerf Ajla (Coon 1957). This was followed by an excavation of the middle Acheulian open air site of Latamne (Clark 1966 a,b) and Solecki's re-excavation of Yabroud (Solecki & Solecki 1966).

The 1970s were marked by work on the middle Paleolithic cave, Douara, in the Palmyra region (Suzuki & Takai 1973). At the end of the 1980s, excavation took place at the upper Acheulian site, Gharmachi, in the Orontes Valley (Muhesen 1985).

Actually, five major Palaeolithic excavations which started mostly at the beginning of the 1990s are still going on. These are: the lower Paleolithic sites of Nadaouiyeh and Hummal, the middle Palaeolithic site Umm el Tlel, all of which are located in the region of El Kowm (Le Tensorer et al. 1993; Boeda & Muhesen 1993), the middle Paleolithic site Dederiyeh in the Afrin region (Muhesen et al. 1988b; Akazawa et al. 1993; Akazawa & Muhesen (eds.) 2002), and the Jerf Ajla middle Paleolithic site, which is under new excavation also (Richter et al. 2001).

Lower Palaeolithic

One of the major issues in Old World history is the human colonization of Eurasia. It seems that Homo-Habilis, first identified in Africa and linked with

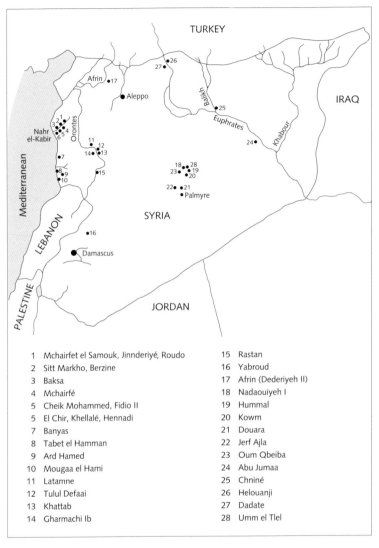

Fig. 1. Main Palaeolithic sites in Syria.

1	Mchairfet el Samouk, Jinnderiyé, Roudo	15	Rastan
2	Sitt Markho, Berzine	16	Yabroud
3	Baksa	17	Afrin (Dederiyeh II)
4	Mchairfé	18	Nadaouiyeh I
5	Cheik Mohammed, Fidio II	19	Hummal
5	El Chir, Khellalé, Hennadi	20	Kowm
7	Banyas	21	Douara
8	Tabet el Hamman	22	Jerf Ajla
9	Ard Hamed	23	Oum Qbeiba
10	Mougaa el Hami	24	Abu Jumaa
11	Latamne	25	Chniné
12	Tulul Defaai	26	Helouanji
13	Khattab	27	Dadate
14	Gharmachi Ib	28	Umm el Tlel

the oldest stone-tools attribuated to 'Oldwan', dated to some 2 million years ago, never left the African continent. Homo-Erectus, who is considered an evolutionary stage of Homo-Habilis, was the first hominid to spread out of Africa some 1.5 million years age. Discoveries from Ubeidiyah in the Jordan Valley, and Dmanise in Georgia, can be connected with this first wave of emigration, 'out of Africa 1': This wave is characterized by a core and flake industri as well as early Acheulian bifaces (Bar-Yosef 1998). The earliest traces of human presence in Syria are found in two regions: the coast, where Sitt Markho in the Valley of Nahr el Kebir yielded early Acheulian bifaces (fig. 2) (Sanlaville 1979). The

Fig. 2. Old Acheulian bifaces from Sitt-Markho. After Sanlaville (ed.) 1979.

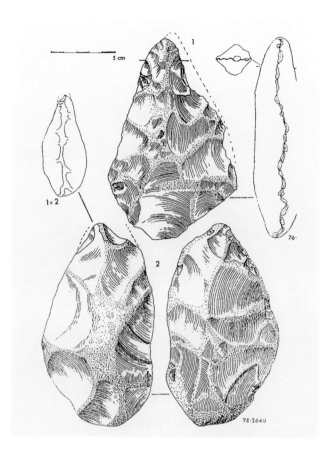

second region is the Orontes Valley, where Khattab 2 yielded the flake industry (fig. 3) (Sanlaville 1993). The sites of this early lower Palaeolithic phase are rare and poor, and they are geologically connected with QfIV (Quaternary fluviatile IV), 'Sitt Markho formation', of the late lower Pleistocene age. In the later period, which is the middle lower Palaeolithic, human occupation extended widely nd was more dense. This period was dominated by the middle Acheulian stone industry, for which a key site is Latamne in the Orontes Valley (fig. 4), which also yielded the oldest traces in Syria of open air constructions and use of fire (Muhesen 1988a). Human occupation spread to the Syrian desert, as shown by el-Meirah, in the region of el-Kowm (Boeda & Muhesen 1993). The limited excavation, 7 m², on this site yielded four hundred artifacts, among which were around 80 bifaces, belonging to a homogeneous middle Acheulian industry, resembling those found at the Latamne quarries in the Orontes Valley (fig. 5).

Some few bones from this site proved the presence of hippopotamus in this – actually steppic – region. Thus we can establish that in the middle Acheulian

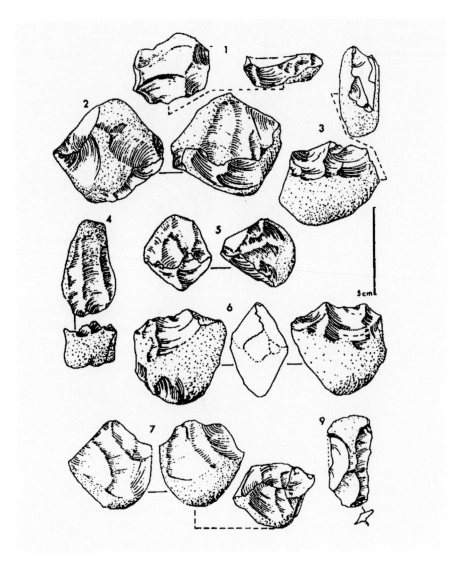

Fig. 3. Flake industry from Rastan. After Sanlaville 1993.

period the region was a savanna and humid. A stone industry was identified at several sites along the Syrian coast (Nahr el Kebir and Abrach Vallies), the Orontes Valley, the Syrian desert and perhaps also the Euphrates Valley. These sites are connected with Qm II (Quaternary Marine III) along the coast and Qf III in the inland. In addition to their own local original adaptations, early and middle Acheulian were clearly influenced by the African tradition, and this situation began changes in the late lower Palaeolithic, upper Acheulian, which is marked by a very dense, extended, and varied occupation (Muhesen 1993).

Fig. 4. Middle
Acheulian from
Latamné. After Clark
1966a.

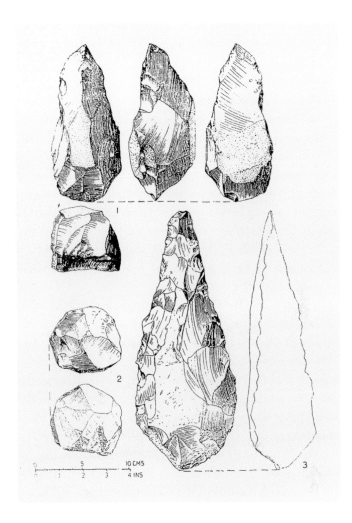

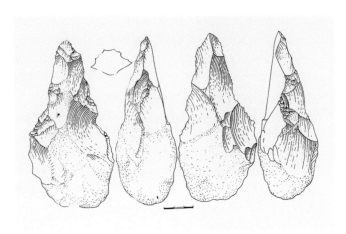

Fig. 5. Middle
Acheulian from el-
Meirah. After Boeda &
Muhesen 1993.

It is well represented in the arid zone of the country where the key site is Nadaouiyeh to which we will devote more information.

Nadaouiyeh

Nadaouiyeh is situated in the el Kowm region; it is an open air site, located near an old spring. The site was discovered in 1980 (Hours *et al.* 1983). It has been under excavation by a Syro-Swiss team since 1989, and has yielded rich archaeological, palaeonthological and anthropological data. More than 25 archaeological levels were exposed, included in lacustrine, fluvial and eolian deposits of about 20 m. thick. The major occupation is represented by a long sequence of stone making that covers a period from the late middle Acheulian to the final Acheulian. The archaeological levels are, from oldest to youngest, as follows:

– Nadaouiyeh F: the deepest and the oldest level, which gave a middle Acheulian material dominated by ovates and amygdaloïdes bifaces, very well manufactured.

– Nadaouiyeh E – D – C – B: are upper Acheulian levels, though the Acheulian of these levels is not the same. Levels E – D – C gave standarized bifaces of high quality, of different types: ovates, amygdaloïdes, cordiforms and lanceolates. Small bifaces, bifacial pieces, picks, choppers and chopping tools were also present. Nonstandarized bifaces, generally of large dimensions, came from level B. Yabrudian material came from a disturbed layer above level B. The Yabrudian is characterized here by side scrapers bearing a large stepped retouch; bifaces were present while chopping tools and the Levallois method were absent.

The Hummalian is dominated by the blade industry, which came also from eroded layers. The Yabrudian is known to precede the Hummalian in other sites, namely Hummal in the El-Kowm region. The latest level at Nadaouiyeh is level A, which is the final Acheulian 'living floor', posterior to Yabrudian and Hummalian. The lithic industry of Nadaouiyeh is generally dominated by small bifaces of different types, abundant bifacial pieces, small choppers, chopping tools, and a few flake tools. The Levallois method was absent. It is worth noting that the season of excavation in 2002 showed the presence of Mousterain level under the final Acheulien of level A. This proves the early appearance of middle Palaeolithic, preceding the final Acheulian, and the late persistence of the final Acheulian itself (fig. 6). Palaeontological data from Nadaouiyeh are rich, and indicate an open steppic environment. Bovidae were the most important, followed by Camelidae and Equidae. Antelope, gazelle, dog, birds, and rhinoceros were also present. The vegetation is dominated by pine and oak (Muhesen *et al.* 1998). The most remarkable discovery at Nadaouiyeh is a fragment of human skull, *os parietal*, which was found in level D, together with very rich and developed Acheulian artefacts, with abundant fauna of gazelles and antelopes (fig. 7).

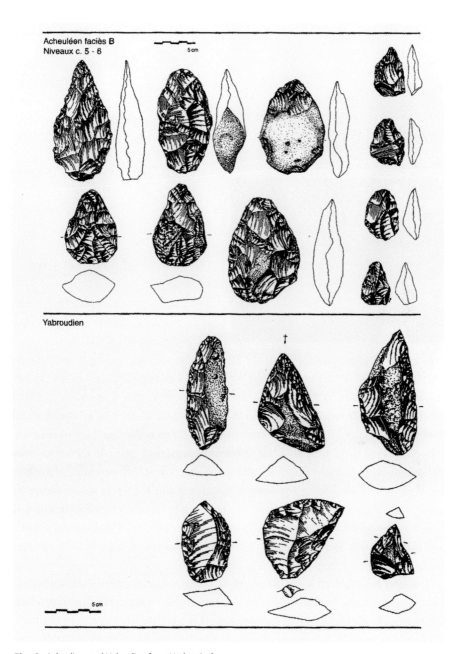

Fig. 6. Acheulian, and Yabrudian from Nadaouiyeh.

This *parietal* provokes many questions as to its archaic form and remarkable thickness, which place it closer to Asian Homo-Erectus than to african Homo-Ergaster (Jagher *et al.* 1997).

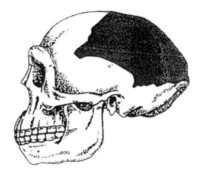

Fig. 7. *Os parietal* from Nadaouiyeh.
After Jagher *et al.* 1997.

The Acheulian sequence at Nadaouiyeh obliges us to review the classical evolutionary model of the Acheulian. We have to abandon the idea of progressive evolution, from simple forms toward more perfect ones. It seems that the Acheulian evolution was not so simple and linear. Clear differences were noticed between Acheulian levels. The most outstanding phenomen is the existence of more perfect industry in lower, older levels, while less developed industry was found in the upper younger levels. This goes against the standard known model, and indicates also frequent population changes, each producing its own cultural tradition (Jagher 2000).

Though Nadaouiyeh is not dated yet, it can be assumed that the site was occupied for almost the last half million years of human history. The late Acheulian industries are generally connected with QF II formation. By the end of the middle Pleistocene and the beginning of the upper Pleistocene (period of QM I), the Near East, including Syria, passed through crucial changes co-occurring with the intermediate period between the lower and middle Palaeolithic. The transitional industries are characterized by a variety of different facies and although these facies are more or less contemporary they are very different from each other.

The major transitional industries are: Yabrudian, a flake industry with a specific kind of scraper, 'dejeté' with Quina retouch. Hummalian, Pre-Aurignacian, are blade industries with upper Palaeolithic types of tools, but the use of the Levallois method is absent. Final Acheulian, Samoukian, and Defaian are characterized by having produced small bifaces, choppers and a frequent use of the Levallois method. These industries can reflect an uninterrupted evolution from lower to middle Palaeolithic, as they contain many elements of both periods (Hours 1992). But it has still to be checked if these facies, which are well restricted in time and space, being almost limited to central and northern Levant, are the reflection of cultural, ecological, chronological or other factors.

Hummal

Hummal is an open air site located near an old spring in el Kowm, about 100 km north of Palmyra. The site was discovered in the 1980s. It has been under excavation by a Syro-Swiss mission since 2000. Stratigraphic sequence, more than 25 m thickness, was exposesed. The lowest level revealed a 'pebble' industry, followed by Tayacian, which is followed by Acheulian, Yabrudian, Hummalian, Mousterian and upper Palaeolithic. This continuous archaeological sequence covers more than half a million years of prehistoric life, making Hummal a key site for understanding the Palaeolithic of the region.

Middle Palaeolithic

With this period we notice the return of a uniform tradition known as Levantine Mousterian. The industries are connected with QfI fluviatil formation. The sites are not limited to the open air, but also caves and rock shelters were inhabited. Human occupation in all geographical zones of the Near East became wider and denser than at any time before. Two human types represent the population of this period: the Neanderthal and archaic Homo-Sapiens. The unilinear model of the middle Palaeolithic industries, derived from evolution at Tabun cave, through D – C – B phases, cannot be applied to the whole Levant. Yabrud I is the only Syrian site where this model can be traced through its three successive phases.

Along the coast the middle Palaeolithic starts with phase C, marked by broad and ovate flakes, and finishes with phase B, with short broad-based points, while in the inland desert, including Douara cave, near Palmyra, the early middle Palaeolithic starts with a blade industry with long and narrow points, resembling Tabun D, which may derive from the preceding Hummalian (Copeland 1981). The middle Palaeolithic sites, actually under excavation, contribute largely to our knowledge of Syrian Palaeolithic. These are, Umm el-Tlel, at el Kowm and Dederiyeh in the Afrin valley.

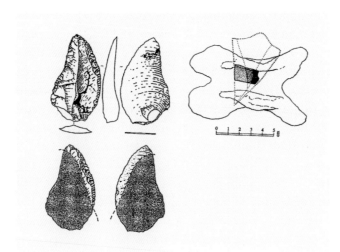

Fig. 8. Silex with bitumen traces and point projectile in the vertebra of an ass. After Boeda *et al.* 2000.

Umm el-Tlel

This is an open-air site, situated near an old spring in el Kowm region. It has been under excavation since 1991 by a Syro-French team. Different sections of the excavation produced around 100 archaeological levels of c. 30 m deposits of palustre, lacustre and eolian origin. They extend from the Neolithic to the lower Palaeolithic period, but, with more than 70 levels, the middle Palaeolithic was the major occupation period yet to be exposed. Umm el-Tlel was also one of the very rare Syrian sites (after Yabrud II, III and Jerf Ajla) to produce upper Palaeolithic in about 30 levels, while four levels produced 'intermediate' industry between middle and upper Palaeolithic. Very rich archaeological and Palaeonthological data were also obtained from this site. As indicated, the major occupation in the site is middle Palaeolithic, with all levels exposed from this period being of recent Mousterian phase. The archaeological material is Levantine Mousterian, corresponding *grosso-modo* with the Tabun B phase, based on the frequent utilization of Levalloise methods to produce short projectiles on a large base. The number of archaeological levels are well distinguished from each other, though some are different and others are identical. The density varies from several tens to several thousands of artefacts, which indicate that the function and the duration of the occupation had varied very much through time. Some levels show real occupation floors, others were knapping workshops, while some were butchering places, and so on. The archaeological levels reflect different groups of people who represent different cultures adapted to an environment that was changing from a steppic to desertic one. Umm el Tlel revealed some unusual evidence for this period, *i.e.* was the use of bitumen in hafting stone artefacts. As far as we know, bitumen was not known to be used before Neolithic time. The excavation of Umm el-Tlel showed

Fig. 9. Symbolic disposition of artifacts and incised stone from Umm el-Tlel. After Boeda *et al.* 2001 & 2002.

traces of bitumen in all Palaeolithic levels, but the most surprising were those from the middle Palaeolithic levels. The bitumen was found here in two main forms, either in small bullae, 1-3 cm, or in the form of bitumen remains on archaeological objects. Several such traces were collected, many from middle Paleolithic levels dated to c. 70,000 years age. This is good proof of heating and using this material in the hafting of stone artefacts, some of which also show traces of preparation for such hafting, and of course the remains of bitumen on the artefacts themselves. Many of them were Levallois points (Boeda *et al.* 2000).

The bitumen quarries were situated some 50-100 km away in the Buchri mountains northeast of the site. This shows a special control of resources not only in the near areas but also in the far environment of Umm el Tlel. The site yielded also a broken Levallois point in the vertebra of a wild ass, a direct indication of the hunting techniques of the Neanderthal (fig. 8). Some very well preserved remains of poplar and willow leaves were found, indicating Neanderthal living and sleeping places. Several indications of symbolic behaviour were also found: A small limestone, carved with parallel and crossing lines. Some lines form very schematic shapes, 'human?' There was also a concentration of stone artifacts and animal bones accorded an organized shape. Whatever the explanation for such behaviour, it must be considered as one of the earliest manifestations of symbolic art since the middle Palaeolithic (fig. 9). A fragment of a Neanderthal occipital was found. The palaeontological data indicate that middle Palaeolithic levels of the site were dominated by the dromedary camels, which indicated a steppic arid environment, while the upper levels are dominated by Equid and show a savanna ecology (Boeda *et al.* 2001 & 2002).

Dederiyeh

Dederiyeh is a cave located in the valley of Afrin, north of Aleppo; here some small vallies cut the chain of Jabal Samaan toward the river itself. The site is situated in one of these vallies, 'Dederiyeh'. It is at 500 meters above sea level. This cave has two doors, the normal entrance is from the side of the valley, while the second – additional – 'door' is in the form of a chimney, resulting from the collapsing of the roof of the cave, and that is situated on the plateau side. It is a large cave, with dimensions 60x15x10 m. The site was discovered by a Syro-Japanese mission (Muhesen *et al.* 1988b); sondages took place in 1989 and 1990. Systematic excavations have taken place since 1993, mainly yielding important anthropological and archaeological remains (Akazawa *et al.* 1993 and 1995; Akazawa & Muhesen (eds.) 2002).

About 15 archaeological layers were distinguished in a section of five meters thickness. The archeological levels were included in four Stratigraphical Units. Stratigraphic Unit I (layers 15-12) S. U. II (layers 11-7) S. U. III (layers 6-4) S. U. IV (layers 3-1). The main deposits of these units are sediments of sand, gravels and stones. All archaeological layers yielded Mousterian artefacts. The most important anthropological finds came from layer 13 (S. U. IV) and layer 3 (S. U. I). The stone industry is generally poor when compared with other middle Palaeolithic sites in Syria and the Near East. The methods used are Levallois with uni-directional, bi-directional, convergent and centripetal preparation. The dominating tools are side-scrappers, of different types: simple, double, convex, concave. Mousterian points, and retouched pieces are common and upper Palaeolithic type tools: scrappers, burins, also exist. The industry from all archaeological layers presents similar techno-typological traits of the Levantine Mousterian of the Tabun B phase, with short large-base points (fig. 10). The entrance of the cave, from the valley side, yielded a natufian material.

The most remarkable finds from Dederiyeh are the Neandertalian skeletal remains. Since 1989-1990 many skeletal fragments were found, and all of them, except the left humerus of a six months old baby, came from disturbed layers. Actually the skeletal fragments of about 16 individuals were excavated. About half of this number are children, with two skeletons Dederiyeh 1 and Dederiyeh 2 (Akazawa *et al.* 1999; Akazawa & Muhesen (eds.) 2002). Dederiyeh 1 (burial 1)

Fig. 10. Levantine Mousterian from Dederiyeh. After Akazawa *et al.* 1993.

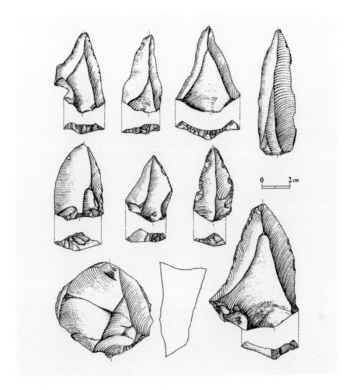

was found in 1993 in layer II, together with Mousterian artefacts and hearths. The skeleton was at 1.5 m below the surface, just under a historic pit of 2.5 m diameter, in square D-6. It is almost complete; it is the skeleton of a child of about two-and-a-half years old. The child was buried in what seems to be a natural pit, lying on his back, the hands straight, the legs flexed, rectangular limestone beside the head, presumably it was under the head, and a piece of a flint artifact on the chest, beside the heart. All these conditions indicated an intentional burial. The morphological features show the classical Neanderthal characteristics of a child of about 84 cm tall. It may represent a boy judging by the thickness of his bones (fig. 11). Dederiyeh 2 (burial 2) was found in 1997, at 50 cm below the surface of D-8 square, in layer 3, together with Mousterian artefacts. It was buried in a pit of 70x50 cm and 25 cm deep. It was fragmented and less complete than burial 1. But all the fragments belong to the same individual which is also a child of about two-and-a-half-years old. Fourteen Mousterian artifacts, about 100 wastes, and the back of a tortoise, accompanied the child. Morphologically it is gracile, and less robust than burial 1; it may belong to a girl. But the differences between these two skeletons may also be a result of individual features, chronological and/or environmental factors (fig. 12). The stone artefacts, found

Fig. 11. Dederiyeh 1 Child. After Akazawa *et al.* 1995.

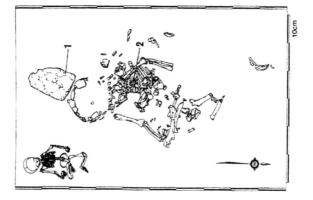

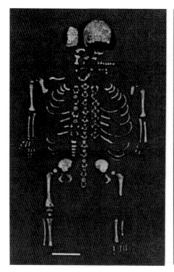

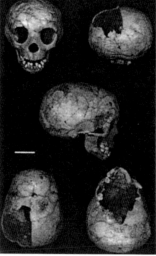

Fig. 12. Skeleton of Dederiyeh 1 and head of Dederiyeh 2 child. After Akazawa *et al.* 1999.

together with the two skeletons, reflect the same typo-technological features of the Levantine Mousterian of the Tabun B phase that are characterized by the frequent use of the Levallois method, with unidirectional, bi-directional and radial preparation. Side-scrapers are the most common tools.

The fauna of Dederiyeh in the lower levels 15-12 is dominated by wild goat and sheep. In level 11-7, gazelle, rhinoceros, horse, elephant, ox, dama, and bear, were present. In layers 6-1, goats and sheep dominate again. The repartition of the fauna is an indication of the climate changing between humid, dry and then humid again. The bones found in the sites were mainly the skeleton parts, rich in meat, which means that animals were butchered outside the site. Some bones showed traces of cutting or breaking, others had traces of use or retouch tools. The grains *of celtis* hackberry were the main floral palynological remains (Griggo 2000).

The dating of Dederiyeh has not yet been achieved. TL dating of a dozen flint pieces showed that dates from layers 1-4 varied between 50-70 kA, which seems to be coherent for the late Mousterian of the Levant, known from sites like Kebara, Amud, and Tabun (Bar-Yosef 1989), while dates from levels 6-9 varied between 70-90 kA. In fact, we need more samples to be measured in order to verify these results.

Dederiyeh, became one of the key sites for the middle Paleolithic of the Levant. It was proof of a connection between Tabun B industry and the Neanderthal. The discovery of the site threw new light on the Neanderthals of the region, and their relation to the modern human. They existed at an earlier date as shown by Qafzeh and Skhul, dated to c. 100,000 years ago, and connected with Tabun C industries (Bar-Yosef 1994).

Upper Palaeolithic

The Upper Palaeolithic, compared with the middle and lower, is a poor period in Syria and in the Levant generally. The sites are rare and the finds are limited almost to stone artefacts. There are no, or very few, bone tools, constructions or art. The sites of reference here are: Yabroud III and II, excavated since the 1930s, Jerf-Ajla, and Umm el-Tlel recently under excavation. Through these sites it is possible to follow the upper Palaeolithic stone industries from their early appearance. The lower level of Yabroud II yielded transitional industry from the middle to upper Palaeolithic, comparable to that known from Ksar Aqil phase A and B which is characterized by the presence of both Mousterian and upper Palaeolithic tools, and some chamfered pieces (Ohnuma 1988). The upper levels of Yabroud II were described as Levantine Aurignacian B, while the lowest levels of Yabroud III are assigned Levantine Aurignacian C.

Transitional and middle/upper Palaeolithic industry came from the upper level of Jerf-Ajla (Brown I) and from the surface site of Qalta in El-Kowm region. This industry is characterized by a very particular type of Levallois core, of flat triangular shape, carinated burins and end-scrappers. Early upper Palaeolithic industries came also from Umm el-Tlel, 'intermediate' levels II and III, comparable to Ksar Aqil phase B. While levels I and II of Umm el Tlel were characterized by blades, bladelets, and twisted bladelets, in addition to very few projectile points (fig. 13); these levels were described as Levantine Aurignacian B (Bourguignon 1998). Similar material come from site 74 near Palmyra, while site 50 yielded a bladelets-dominated industry, with carinated end-scrapers and burins described as Levantine Aurignacian C (Fujimoto 1979). In fact, the actual evidence of early upper Palaeolithic industries from Syria is not enough to compare them to major, key, upper Paleolithic sites in the Levant, such as Ksar Aqil on the Lebanese coast (Tixer 1974) and Boker Tachtit in Negev (Marks 1983). In spite of their typological differences these two sites are blade-dominated industry, designated Ahmarian (Nishiaki 1998). The final part of the upper Palaeolithic is marked by an evident increase in sites, characterized by the appearance of microlithic tools, assigned Kebaran, whose traces came from several parts of the country, and announcing the end of the upper Palaeolithic and the start of the Epi-Palaeolithic.

Conclusion

By mainly examining stone industries the aim of this presentation of the Palaeolithic of Syria has been to show cultural and historical development during this very long period, and to show a synthetic image of the period, with special emphasis on recent excavations (fig. 1). We wanted to situate the sites that have been under excavation within the general Palaeolithic framework known since the beginning of the 20th century. The techno-typological and spatio-temporal approach used to study human occupation showed the high cultural variability of the Palaeolithic period from its very beginning. From the early lower Palaeolithic we can ascertain the presence of two different facies, one characterized by a pebble culture, while the other is Acheulian. The middle lower Palaeolithic was evident along the coast with an ovate bifaces tradition and in the Orontes Valley with a trihedral picks tradition. Relative uniformity came in the upper Acheulian time, with the domination of lanceolate, ovate, amygdaloïd and cordiform bifaces. During the transitional period, a 'mosaic' of cultures Yabrudian, Pre-Aurignacian, Hummalian and final Acheulian coexisted in the same region at the same time. Cultural uniformity returned again in the middle Palaeolithic with the Mousterian. The Upper Palaeolithic seems to have been of local origin

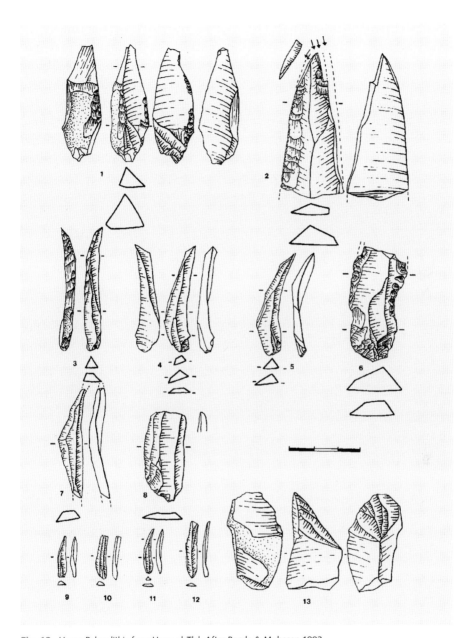

Fig. 13. Upper Palaeolithic from Umm el-Tlel. After Boeda & Muhesen 1993.

and was characterized by Ahmarian and Aurignacian, which occupied the major part of this period before the arrival of Kebaran by the end of this period.

With regard to population, it seems that Homo-Erectus was the first inhabitant in Syria. However, the parietal bone of Nadaouiyeh still requires further analysis to ascertain its character and its relation to African Homo-Ergaster or Asian Homo-Erectus. If we accept the hypothesis of two human species: one Neanderthal of European origin, the other archaic Homo-Sapiens of African origin, coexisting in middle Palaeolithic time, then the Dederiyeh Neanderthals will be of European origin. The upper Palaeolithic is largely connected with Homo-Sapiens (Cro-Magnon) although skeletons have not yet been found from the beginning of this period. In this way it will be possible to gain further insight into human behaviour with regard to climatic changes, and to understand how culture and man changed through time. The data coming from the Syrian sites that are under excavation right now can answer many of these questions.

References

Akazawa, T., S. Muhesen, Y. Dodo, A. Abdul Salam, Y. Abe, O. Kondo & Y. Misoquchi 1993. 'The Neanderthal Remains from Dederiyeh Cave in Syria: Interim Report', *Anthropology*, 101 (4), 361-387.

Akazawa, T., S. Muhesen, Y. Dodo, O. Kondo, Y. Mizoquchi, Y. Nishiaki, S. Ohta & J. Haydal 1995. 'Neanderthal Infant Burial from the Dederiyeh Cave, Syria', *Paléorient*, 21 (2), 77-86.

Akazawa, T., S. Muhesen, H. Ishida, C. Kondo, & C. Griggo 1999. 'New discovery of a Neanderthal Child Burial from the Dederiyeh Cave, Syria', *Paléorient*, 25 (2), 127-140.

Akazawa, T. & S. Muhesen (eds.) 2002. *Neanderthal Burials: Excavation of Dederiyeh Cave, Afrin, Syria*. Kyoto: Japanese Centre for International Research.

Bar-Yosef, O. 1989 'Geography of the Levantine Middle Palaeolithic'. In: P. Mellars & C. Stringer (eds.), *The Human Revolution*. Edinburgh: Edinburgh University Press, 589-610.

Bar-Yosef, O. 1994. 'The lower Palaeolithic of the Near East', *Journal of World Prehistory*, 8 (3), 211-265.

Bar-Yosef, O. 1998. 'Jordan Prehistory: a view from the west'. In: D.O. Henry (ed.), *prehistoric archaeology of Jordan*. (BAR International Series). 705, 162-178.

Bar-Yosef, O. & D. Pilbeam 2000. *The Geography of Neanderthals and modern human in Europe and the Greater Mediterranean*. Harvard University.

Boeda, E. & S. Muhesen 1993. 'Umm el-Tlel (El-Kowm Syrie): etude préliminaire des indurtries lithiques du Paléolithique moyen et supérieur 1991-1992', *Cahiers de l'Euphrate*, 7, 47-92.

Boeda, E. *et al.* 2000. 'Le site d'Umm el-Tlel (Syrie Centrale)', *Orient Express*, 2000 (2), 36-38.

Boeda, E. *et al.* 2001. *Comportements socio-économiques et territoires de l'homme du Paléolithique moyen et inférieur en milieu climatique instable (Proche-Orient, Syrie Centrale)*. (Rapport de mission archéologique Umm el Tlel/El Meirah, Bassin d'El Kowm, Syrie). Paris: Université Paris X-Nanterre.

Boeda, E. *et al.* 2002. *Analyse comportementale des hommes fossiles du paléolithique dans le désert syrien*. (Rapport de mission archéologique Umm el Tlel/El Meirah, Bassin d'El Kowm, Syrie). Paris: Université Paris X-Nanterre.

Bourguignon, L. 1998. 'Les industries du Paléolithique intermédiaire d'Umm el Tlel: nouveaux éléments pour le passage entre le Paléolithique moyen et supérieur dans le Bassin d'El Kowm'. In: Otte M. (dir.) *Préhistoire d'Anatolie. Genèse de deux mondes.* Eraul 85, 709-730. Liège.

Clark, D. 1966a. 'The middle acheulean occupation site at Latamné, Northern Syria', *AAAS*, 16 (2), 31-74; *Quaternaria*, 9, 1-68.

Clark, D. 1966b. 'The middle acheulean occupation site at Lataamné, Northern Syria, further excavation (1965)', *AAAS*, 16 (2), 75-120; *Quaternaria*, 10, 1-76.

Copeland, L. 1981 'Chronology and distribution of the Middle Paleolithic as known in 1980 in Lebanon and Syria'. In: J. Cauvin & P. Sanlaville (éd.), *Préhistoire du Levant.* Paris: Editions du CNRS, 239-263.

Coon, Ch. 1957 *The seven caves. Archaeological exploration in the Middle East.* New York: A. Knopf.

Fujimoto, T. 1979. 'Upper Palaeolithic and Epi-Palaeolithic assemblages in the Palmyra basin: site 50 and site 74'. In: K. Hanihara & T. Akazawa (eds.), *Paleolithic site of Douara cave and Palaeogeography of Palmyra Basin, in Syria.* Museum of the University of Tokyo, Bulletin 16, 77-130.

Griggo, C. 2000. 'Adaptations environnementales et activités de subsistence au Paléolithique moyen en Syrie'. *Annales de la Fondation Fyssen*, 15, 49-62.

Hours, F., J.-M. Le Tensorer, S. Muhesen & I. Yalcinkaya 1983. 'Premiers travaux sur le site acheuléen de Nadaouiyeh 1', *Paléorient*, 9 (2), 5-13.

Hours, F. 1992. *Le Paléolithique et l'pipaléolithique de la Syrie et du Liban.* Beyrouth: Dar el-Machreq.

Jagher, R. 2000. *L'Acheuléen de Nadaouiyeh.* (PhD.). Institut de la Préhistoire, Université de Bâle.

Jagher, R., J.-M. Le Tensorer, Ph. Morel, J. Miiskowski, S. Muhesen & P. Schmid 1997. 'Découvertes des restes humains dans les niveaux acheuléens de Nadaouiyeh Aïn Askar (El-Kom, Syrie centrale)', *Paléorient*, 23 (1), 45-76.

Le Tensorer, J.-M., S. Muhesen & R. Jagher 1993. 'Nadaouiyeh I, Aïn Askar: Une Grande Séquence Paléolithique du Bassin d'El-Kowm (Syrie), premiers résultats, fouilles 1989-1992', *Cahiers de l'Euphrate*, 7, ERC, 11-36.

Marks, A. (ed.) 1983. *Prehistory and paleoenvironments in the Central Neguev, Israël* III. Dallas: SMU Press.

Muhesen, S. 1985. 'L'Acheuléen Récent Evolué de la Syrie' (BAR International Series, 248). 261.

Muhesen, S. 1988a. 'Le Paléolithique Inférieur de la Syrie', *L'Anthropologie*, 93 (3), 963-882, Paris.

Muhesen, S. 1993. 'L'Acheuléen Récent Evolué de l'Oronte'. In: P. Sanlaville (ed.), *La Géomorphologie et la Préhistoire de la Vallée de l'Oronte* (BAR International Series, 587). 145-146.

Muhesen, S., T. Akazawa & A. Abdul-Salam 1988b. 'Prospection préhistorique dans la region d'Afrin (Syrie)', *Paléorient*, 142, 145-153.

Muhesen, S., R. Jagher & J.-M. Le Tensorer 1998. 'Nadaouiyeh, Aïn Askar et Hummal (El-Kowm, Syrie centrale 1997)', *Chronique archéologique en Syrie*, II, 109-120.

Nishiaki, Y. 1998. 'The Palaeolithic and Neolithic of Syria: an overview with reference to jordanain Prehistory'. In: D.O. Henry (ed.), *Prehistoric archaeology of Jordan.* (BAR International Series, 705). 195-207.

Ohnuma, K. 1988. *Ksar Aqil, Lebanon: A technological Study of the Early Upper Palaeolithic levels XXV-XIV.* (BAR International Series, 426). Oxford.

Richter, D., H.B. Schroeder, P.L. Rink & H.P. Schwarez 2001. 'The Middle to Upper Palaeolithic Transition in the Levant and New Thermoluminescence dates for a Late Mousterian Assemblage from Jerf al-Ajla Cave (Syria)', *Paléorient*, 27 (2), 29-46.

Rust, A. 1950. *Die Höhlenfunde von Jabrud (Syrien).* Neumünster.

Sanlaville, P. (éd.) 1979. *Quaternaire et Préhistoire du Nahr el Kebir septentrional: les débuts de l'occupation humaine dans la Syrie du Nord et au Levant.* Paris: Ed. du CNRS.

Sanlaville, P. 1993. *La géomorphologie et la préhistoire de la vallée de l'Oronte.* (BAR International Series, 587).

Solecki, R.S. & R.L. Solecki 1966. 'New data from Yabroud, Syria', *AAAS*, 16 (2), 121-154.

Suzuki, H. & F. Takai 1973. *The Palaeolithic site of Douara cave in Syria Part.* Museum of the University of Tokyo, Bulletin 1.

Tixier, J. 1974. 'Fouille à Ksar 'Aqil, Liban, 1969-1974', *Paléorient*, 2, 183-185.

Cores Into Tools

A Technological Device Found in the Yabrudian Industry of The Levant

ROSE L. SOLECKI

The tool type described in this paper was found in the pre-Mousterian (Yabrudian) deposits of Yabroud Rock Shelter I, Syria. They resemble the miniature handaxes but they do not have bifacial retouch. A similar tool from the site of Bezez, Lebanon, Level C has been illustrated by L. Copeland (2000, fig. 5b). Copeland (ibid) referred to this tool as a 'partial biface or bifacial racloir', it is reproduced in this paper as fig. 1b. Three examples of this tool type have been found in the excavations at Yabroud Shelter I, all from the upper or later deposits of the Yabrudian occupation.

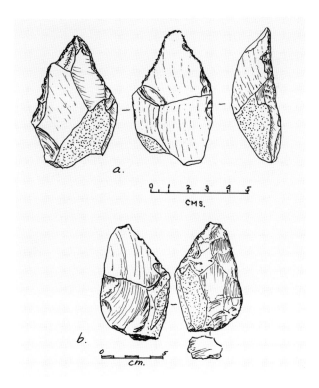

Fig. 1a. A transverse side scraper.
By Rose L. Solecki.
Fig. 1b. A fragmentary scraper – possibly transverse.
By Rose L. Solecki.

The unique feature of these tools is that they are made on exhausted unidirectional cores. Cortex is still present on the back face of the core blank and the flake removal face still exhibits the scars of unidirection flake removals. The knapper took advantage of the thickness of the remnant cores to create a scraper with Quina or half Quina retouch along the edges. The scraper retouch is always present on the cortex or back face of the original core. The four specimens available for this study have been made into side scrapers. As there is no butt end on a core to orient the scraper edge, I have used the striking platform end as the orientation plane. Two of the scrapers are definitely transverse side scrapers (fig. 1a); one fragmentary one is possibly transverse, and the fourth (fig. 1b) is dejete. All have Quina or half Quina retouch. Two complete tools from the Yabroud Shelter I collection have similar dimensions (6.2 cm x3.2 cm x2.3 cm and 6.7 cm × 4.3 cm × 2.6 cm). The Bezez specimen (fig. 1b) is larger.

At the site of Yabroud Shelter I, raw material was an important factor in the size and type of cores, blanks, and tools manufactured there (Solecki & Solecki, n.d.). The occupants of that site picked up Acheulian handaxes from long abandoned surface sites and recycled them into cores. Perhaps raw material scarcity also resulted in the recycling of not completely exhausted cores into stout edged tools when such were needed for specialized tasks.

References

Copeland, Lorraine 2000. 'Yabrudian and Related Industries: The State of Research in 1996'. In: A. Ronen & M. Weinstein-Evron (eds.), *Toward Modern Humans. The Yabrudian and Micoquian 400-50 K Years Ago.* (BAR International Series, 850).

Solecki, R. L. & R. S. n.d. 'The Use of Raw Material at Yabroud Rockshelter I, Syria'. Paper prepared for a volume on raw material use in the Near East.

Footprints in the Sediments of Yabroud Rockshelter IV, Syria

RALPH S. SOLECKI

At Yabroud, Syria, one of the foremost prehistoric archaeological sites in the Near East, footprints were found in the silty/clay deposits of Rockshelter IV. It is one of five rockshelters in the Skifta (cave) valley of Yabroud. Among these mainly animal tracks were found a number of footprints believed to be of hominid origin, probably Neanderthal. The occurrence of these footprints was noted briefly at the time of discovery (Solecki & Solecki, 1966; Solecki, 1968).

Alfred Rust (1950) excavated in three of the Yabroud rockshelters (Yabroud Shelters I, II, III) in the 1930s. He aborted a small sondage in the Shelter IV proper area, being unaware of the deep 11.5 deposits at the foot or apron of Shelter IV. Fronting the bottom of the shelter are giant boulders, which J. de Heinzelin (1966) thought formed a protective baulk to the archaeological deposits laid behind this barrier. The stratigraphy of Shelter IV was clear cut, evidencing much fluvial action. De Heinzelin (1966: 159, 163) characterized it as 'rhythmic graded bedding'. Twenty two major layers were recognized in the stratigraphy. No clear traces of habitation such as hearths were found in the layers. The comparatively few flints recovered are demonstrably pre-Mousterian in type. A date of about 195,000 years was obtained on burned flints from a pre-Mousterian level in Shelter I (Huxtable, 1990). From this we infer a date of over 200,000 years for Shelter IV and its contents.

The footprints were found in two layers, layers K and Q. Eight imprints were identified as rhinoceros, seven in the top of layer K5 (fig. 1), and one in layer Q. Five fairly good plus one vague imprint of what we identified as hominid footprints were found in association with rhinoceros hoofprints in layer K5. Uncovered in layer K2 were fourteen imprints of what appear to be those of an equid, a couple of long turtle tracks, and numerous bird tracks. The rhinoceros hoofprints in layer K5 looked like shallow bowl shaped depressions about 25 cm across. They were about 3.5 cm deep. The decisive clue to their identity was the discovery of a beautiful three-toed rhino hoof impression in layer Q, and a number rhinoceros bones and teeth. These were identified in the field by D. Hooijer (1966) as belonging to "Dicerorhinus hemitoechus." D. Perkins, Jr.

(1968) also field identified rhinoceros bones in the deposits of Shelter I, just across the valley from Shelter IV.

A letter dated May 5, 1992, from Dr. Edward Maruska of the Cincinnati Zoo and Botanical Garden of Cincinnati, to whom I had sent photographs of the Yabroud hoofprints, said that he was in complete agreement that the hoofprints are of a rhino. I would also agree that the rhino was probably in a hurry.

The footprints identified in the field as likely hominid were charted together with the associated rhino hoofprints (fig. 1). The hominid prints were numbered 6, 7, 8, 11 and 12. There was an additional imprint, no. 13, vague, but in the proper position of association with the others. The rhino hoofprints were numbered 1-5, and 9, 10.

Fig. 1. Chart of foot prints. By R. S. Solecki.

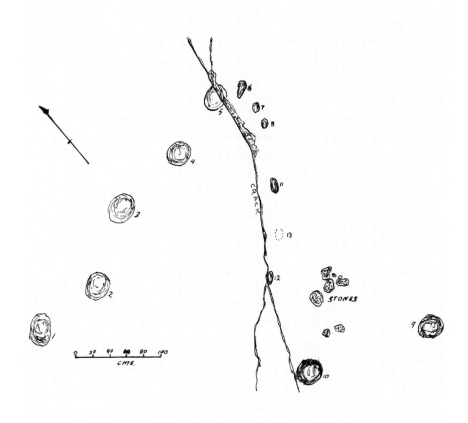

Photographs of the suspected hominid footprint casts were sent to Dr. Louise M. Robbins, of the University of North Carolina (Greensboro). In a communication from her dated June 29, 1981, she stated that 'the footprints in the casts do indeed appear to be human footprints according to the morphological contours that I can isolate in the regions of the heel, ball and toes.' Using her formula for calculating the height of the individual from the maximum foot length (Robbins, 1985, xi), the Yabroud individual's height from imprint no. 6 (length 23 cm.) was 153.3 cm or about 5 feet. Using her calculations for obtaining the weight of the individual from the foot length, we get a weight of about 126 (+/- 10) pounds (Robbins, 1985, 204-5). Using John Napier's (1972, 119) method of calculating the height of the individual, we get a stature of about 58.5 inches, or about 4.9 feet, which agrees closely with Robbin's measurement.

The height and weight of the Yabroud individual appears to be in close agreement with other reported hominids from the lower palaeolithic age. The more ancient pre-hominid footprints of Laetoli, Tanzania (Hay & Leakey, 1982) were of individuals shorter in stature.

From the orientations of the imprints of the hominid and the rhino, we infer that the hominid was not in close pursuit of the rhino, traversing in roughly the opposite direction. However, since the tracks were laid in the same layer of plastic silty/clay, the incidents were fairly close in time. There can be no doubt that the hominid was very much aware of his close encounter with the rhino.

References

Hay, Richard L. & Mary D. Leakey 1982. 'The Fossil Footprints of Laetoli', *Scientific American*, 246(2), 50-57.

de Heinzelin, Jean 1966. 'Revision du site de Yabroud', *Les Annales Archéologiques Arabes Syriennes*, XVI(II), 157-165.

Hooijer, D.A. 1966. 'The Dicerorhinus Hemitoechus (falconer) at Yabroud', *Les Archéologiques Arabes Syriennes*, XVI(II), 155-156.

Napier, John 1972. *Big Foot, The Yeti and Sasquatch in Myth and Reality*. London: Johnathon Cape.

Perkins, Dexter Jr. 1968. 'The Pleistocene Fauna from Yabrudian Rockshelters', *Les Annales Archéologiques Arabes Syriennes*, XVIII(1-2), 123-130.

Robbins, Louise M. 1985. *Footprints, Collection, Analysis, and Interpretation*. Illinois: Charles C. Thomas, Springfield.

Rust, Alfred 1950. *Die Höhlenfunde von Jabrud (Syrien)*. Neumünster.

Solecki, Ralph S. & Rose L. 1966. 'New Data from Yabroud, Syria', *Les Annales Archéologiques Arabes Syriennes*, XVI (II), 157-166.

Solecki, Ralph S. 1968. 'The Shemsi Industry, a Tayacian-Related Industry at Yabroud, Syria, Preliminary Report'. In: Denise de Sonneville-Bordes (ed.), *La Préhistoire, Problemes et Tendances*. (Éditions du Centre National de la Recherche Scientifique). Paris, 401-410.

Lithic Economic Systems and Early Sedentism

HANS GEORG K. GEBEL

Introduction

When Peder Mortensen in 1988 for the first time spoke about the 'domestication of flint', it was neither a metaphoric issue nor a tongue-in-cheek argument (Mortensen 1988). Referring to a flint box with selected blade materials from a MPPNB house in Beidha (Middle Pre-Pottery Neolithic B, c. 8000-7600 BC), he tried to guide us towards a new understanding of Early Neolithic chipped stone behaviour: that of the hitherto most complex management of flint by man, practiced in the framework of the new domestication economies of sedentary life. Some of those who read these words 'domestication of flint' found them either odd or inadequate, but at the same time not really to be ignored. This contribution tries to continue along the thoughts of a great scholar.

Since 1988, Neolithic chipped stone research has moved towards approaches that can result in meaningful historical information on Neolithic lithic behaviour and its social and techno-economical contexts beyond the dull data that often were and still are produced without a 'historical translation' by chipped lithic analysts. Among the leading experts able to interpret such data into socio-economic meaningful patterns are Philip Wilke and Leslie Quintero, who derive much support for their insights from replicative/experimental approaches (*e.g.* Quintero 1996, 1998; Quintero & Wilke 1995; Wilke & Quintero 1996). They also have stressed that we must deal with entire lithic economic systems rather than just parts of them, such as the chipped lithic tchnologies or the tool kits. The framework of our understanding should be all contexts of mineral use, and that the 'decipherment' of Neolithic life modes with the help of lithic information has to implement these new levels of interpretation that can scarcely be achieved by using only traditional techno-typological and statistical methods.

Sedentism brought substantial changes for the conditions of lithic behaviour and the management of the abiotic resources. Surplus factors (such as 'time' and 'labour force' in communities with progressive population dynamics), a fixed territoriality (with an intensifying concentration on a specific mineral resource), and long-distance exchange helped to create new products and markets both within and outside a region. 'Lithic identities' began to characterize resource areas and production sites (*e.g.*, obsidian, sandstone rings, chocolate flint; but also 'lithic styles'), and the mineral-rich geology of an area could promote the material culture and the importance of an area with all its social, economic and cognitive consequences.

Lithic Behaviour and Abiotic Resources

Abiotic resources generally are understood as 'passive' elements of lithic land-scapes; they are simply present and become the subject of human procurement only when innovation processes have prepared their exploitation. Little observa-tion has been invested in the understanding of man's permanently alert cognitive 'interaction' with the stone resources of his habitats and the innovative behaviour triggered by deposits or minerals. The term 'interaction with nature' is generally accepted as a concept – and as a crucial matter for the establishment of Neo-lithic life modes – when dealing with biotic resources (*e.g.*, ungulate herds, cereal stands). Biological resources 'react' to human manipulation, while abiotic mate-rials don't appear to do so. This 'dead-stone-understanding' of research has long hindered insights into the vital relationship that developed between humans and abiotic resources, especially when practiced under the conditions of resident life modes. One might mention just a few resources and minerals that became crucial for Neolithization: layered stone deposits, exchanged exotic minerals, quality flint deposits, alluvial silt and arable soil, gravel drainages (Gebel n.d. a), etc.

All these were subjects of an interaction dominated by the complexity of tech-nological experience, experiment, and expertise, and certainly even ideological or metaphoric interpretation. Even today one can observe with traditional inhabit-ants of rural or arid Near Eastern environments this very basic and immediate interest in mineral materials and their contexts; local residents are always trying to find out how – and for what purpose – a material could be used, and what the physical and even the metaphoric nature of the material is. These relics of a natural attitude to comprehend the mineral/abiotic worlds and their contexts may be testimony to a vanished part of human ethology, one that disappeared under the conditions of industrial lithic behaviour that started to prevail in the Late Stone Age periods. The Near Eastern Early Neolithic appears to be a culmin-ation of experimental complexity in lithic behaviour, which later became reduced (through alternative techniques and materials) into a few lithic sectors with a high degree of specialization (such as the so-called Agro-Standards in chipped lithics, the ateliers of polished igneous rock products, and the like). Seen from the Palaeolithic, the Neolithic geological and geomorphological knowledge and observations on stone and other abiotic resources reached cognitive levels hith-erto not touched. This does not necessarily refer to chipped lithic skills, which already reached very sophisticated levels in Upper Palaeolithic industries.

Lithic behaviour can be interpreted as part of a larger abiotic resources be-haviour, at least as long as the activities are related to the procurement levels (Gebel 1996) and their environmental contexts. As some of the above mentioned examples show, in many cases the two behaviours cannot be distinguished.

Also, as a lithic researcher, one cannot define a basic difference between Neolithic biotic and abiotic/lithic behaviour. Both are fields of an intensified interaction with and control of resources, each of which demanded their own methods of retrieving the relevant information under the given local conditions to allow their management. But the abiotic resources did require another type of investigative behaviour, one that is typical for 'passive resources'. But this does not mean that the abiotic resources were not as crucial for the establishment of early village life as the biological elements were (*cf.* Gebel n.d. a).

Domestication economies are characterized by their capability to manipulate or modify species, materials, landscapes, and non-material concepts (such as land tenure, vertical space) for their existence in domestic environments. It should not be ignored that the ethology of man – and here especially his territoriality – also had to change socially and ritually in order to manage a domestic life based on reliable subsistence practices. For the lithic systems, sedentary life had to create the specific conditions and means for the procurement, technological development, use, exchange, and 'meaning' of the products. These, and their social and cognitive consequences, formed the innovative milieu in which the chipped lithics behaved as one of the driving forces or 'pillars' of domestic life. In that sense we do deal with domesticated flint.

Transformation and Dichotomy in Lithic Behaviour (Epipalaeolithic – Neolithic)

In the course of socioeconomic developments from the Epipalaeolithic to the Late Neolithic in the Near East, stone management shifted, as a general trend, from a restricted choice of minerals exploited for personal needs to an extended or specialized use of more mineral varieties increasingly produced and exchanged in new and more complex contexts outside the sphere of personal needs. Local surplus production co-existed with a diversifying spectrum of production modes (including opportunistic, household, and *ad hoc* modes), before a kind of techno-logical and tool kit 'devolution' in the Pottery Neolithic agropastoral economies focussed lithic behaviour in certain regionally different sectors only. This general trend should be seen as an evolutionary and regionally diversified, jerky transformation of lithic behaviour over millennia and not as dichotomies between periods (except for the PPNB-PN transitions in the southern Levant). Dichotomies in lithic behaviour are instead the subject of diversity within individual periods, regions, or interaction spheres, when different lithic economic systems co-existed under the different conditions that promoted (or did not promote) early sedentism and food production.

Lithic skills or technological developments are difficult matters when investigated under transformation or dichotomy aspects. We can assume that the Neolithic specialists knew and understood the techniques and lithic behaviour found in the Palaeolithic and Epipalaeolithic remains in their environments, and they used such insights in their behaviour when they supported their needs. Interpretive approaches that qualitatively try to differentiate between Neolithic skill levels and those of previous periods (or of marginal or unfavourable zones contemporary to the Neolithic) may result in misleading evaluations of dichotomies.

Lithic dichotomies and transformations in the Near Eastern Neolithic come under the realm of conditions that were created by a new quality in lithic territoriality. Resulting from the various processes of sedentarization, these patterns of (a more aggressive) lithic behaviour show a vast array of new frames in which they functioned: from the permanent (and defended?) claim on stone resources and networks to real property built of stone tothe marking of territories on bedrock (rock art, petroglyphs). Arrowheads are not only good for hunting animals, and indigenous war might have resulted from limited abiotic sources. Good quality mineral resources must have promoted the wealth and innovative progress in certain sites or areas, and they may have triggered action in others. Dichotomies of lithic economies within Neolithic settlement patterns or between regions could have driven lithic competition, and this may have been resolved by accepted new patterns of specialization in lithic production and distribution during the formation of new levels in the settlement systems and interaction spheres.

Lithic dichotomies and transformations in theNear Eastern Neolithic for the first time involved craft specialization that developed along the local and regional supplies of lithic sources and the corresponding social and innovative frameworks forcing their development. Craft specialization in wall paintings, obsidian mirrors, or white ware stood at the end of a longer experience with pigment sourcing and processing, raw material selection, and the experimental study of marls, gypsum and limestone. One would hesitate to link the earthen technologies (pottery, clay figurines, mudbricks/*pisé*) too close to the 'hard rock' technologies, but with respect to the craft specialization they seem to have developed and flourished under similar behavioural patterns because they belonged anyhow to the abiotic resources family.

The expansion of the bidirectional/naviform technologies in the PPN is a superb area to study lithic dichotomies and transformation as well as lithic stagnation. These technologies marked (or not) technological participation in a main stream production, observable even with neighbouring contemporary sites. For example, Basta was a major bidirectional blade production site, but nearby Ba'ja was basically without this technique, although it 'imitated' it (*cf.* below; Gebel n.d. b). Lithic transformations become most obvious when such an efficient, technologically dominating reduction technique migrated into a region that hitherto had not used these techniques, especially if it could take advantage of tabular raw material that did not necessarily demand the trimming of a crest. With a rich flint source (Jiththa) nearby and an established technology without any innovative pressure for alternatives, the surplus production of Basta also witnessed technological stagnation, or conservatism. It was most probably terminated by the collapse of chipped lithic markets in southern Jordan in the course of the social disintegration of the mega-sites at the end of the PPNB.

A Digression: Lithic Ecofacts

Odd-shaped flint nodules, Tertiary fossils, coloured stones, etc., were collected in all periods and appear very often in Neolithic contexts, many times showing traces of wear (sometimes paint) but not revealing their function. Even though they are sometimes not mentioned in publications, they have to be considered as a very basic part of lithic behaviour, most probably connected to sociobiological and metaphoric/symbolic functions. While their collection seems to belong to a universal possessive behaviour (probably related to the 'effectance of competence motivation', *cf.* Furby 1978, 331), their use could have occupied the whole range of (mixed) functions between possessing something attractive/meaningful/symbolic/magical and objects used in socially motivated giving/taking/sharing. The study of lithic ecofacts in the Near Eastern Neolithic is an ignored field of social information; this digression was inserted here to explain how far the definition of 'lithic behaviour' may reach.

The following essay discusses only general aspects of transformations in the sedentary lithic subsystems of the Near Eastern Neolithic, with regard to their environmental, exchange, technological, social, socio-economic, and cognitive contexts, or subsystems (*cf.* Hermansen & Gebel 2003; Gebel 1996; for the social change backgrounds *cf.* Gebel 2002). Needless to say, several other abiotic resources, belonging particularly to the sedimentary environments (*e.g.* soils, aquifers), are of course closely related to, or part of, lithic economic systems, but for the sake of this chapter's required brevity, the stone economies are the focus of the presentation.

Developments in the Sedentary Lithic Environmental Subsystems: Local, Regional and Long-Distance Resources

In the Near Eastern core and corridor areas that maintained and transferred the Neolithic trajectory, the human relation to abiotic resources experienced a gradual shift from casual/opportunistic patterns in procurement towards determined and purposeful behaviours in the confined frameworks of sedentary territorialism (10,000-7,000 BC). Mineral-rich environments began to influence or even generate the various sectors of the shifting lithic interaction spheres through which the transfer of raw materials, technological know-how and stylistic diction flourished. Local and regional markets were established for raw materials, for which mineral resources, pre-forms and later finished products entered into long-distance networks on the basis of local exchange or even direct trade.

This general evolutionary trend under the conditions of ongoing sedentarization, however, can scarcely characterize the functioning of the fundamental variability and complexity in the formation and devolution of regional procurement processes. They are an important part of the complex interrelations that form this polycentric Early Neolithic trajectory, and the individual contribution of a resource or resource area to broader developments can only be understood by studying the regionalism of the accompanying conditions and parameters. Certainly from the later 8th millennium BC onwards, resources and resource areas had the strong potential to influence the socioeconomic and demographic conditions of the local communities (as well as along the routes of the network), around the regional population centers that flourished. During the PN (Pottery Neolithic, 6,900-5,000 BC), the interregional importance of lithic resources seems to have diminished with the exception of obsidian.

In the Late Neolithic the socioeconomic restructuring (first pastoral and hydraulic economies, locally confined agricultural societies) in the Near Eastern interaction spheres led to regionalizations that terminated or altered the former routes and markets of the resources. A non-geographical but 'internal' reason for what appears to be a decline of supra-regional material culture identities could be the specialized economies of the 7th and 6th millennium BC, which no longer promoted the broad spectrum lithic consumption of the PPN, and triggered 'lithic impoverishment' and technological concentration in some sectors only, with all the pertinent consequences for the patterns of raw material acquisition.

These specialized economies of the PN seem to have had qualitatively reduced demands on resource varieties, although the demands must not necessarily have been reduced quantitatively. In addition, much of the procurement innovation in these periods must have been absorbed by a new concentration on the earthen resources (white ware and pottery technologies).

Among the most prominent resources (other than the tool stone resources of flint, quartzite and obsidian) gaining cross-regional importance in the PPN were the colored marble varieties, possibly pigment minerals, amber, 'green stones' or copper-bearing minerals, certain igneous rocks, fossil corals and mollusks, pumice, bitumen, for example). Other resources, such as layered stone in general, marls, (quartzitic and bituminous) limestone, dolomite, basalt, clays and silts, always retained local importance and formed the stable elements in the procurement techniques of an area.

Much competent investigation has to be devoted in the future to the field of Neolithic mining, quarrying, and resource selection strategies. Tool-stone and other stone is found everywhere outside the alluvial lands, but it was not necessarily used for the artifacts or processed materials found in archaeological layers. This field only appears approachable by a proper combination of replicative and mineralogical studies devoted to the individual question. All that we presently know is that the Neolithic extracting, mining, and quarrying efforts were steered by the selective behaviour of the producers (*e.g.*, Quintero 1996). Resource management in the later PPNB and PN periods could have had three main patterns: the opportunistic extraction for individual personal needs; the workshop-controlled selective acquisition for blanks, pre-forms or ready-made items; and the miners'-controlled selective acquisition to supply local and non-local markets. The miners and stone traders became part of the Early Neolithic craft specialization.

Developments in the Sedentary Lithic Technological Subsystems: Household, Workshop, and Community Sectors

The economic organization of tool, building material, and prestige goods production underwent substantial changes from the Late Epipalaeolithic to the Late Neolithic in the Near East. Established as parts of the domestication economies, the various sectors of production tended to develop towards surplus fabrication, operational chains characterized by error-control, and self-innovative technological behaviour. The 'driving' industries (especially flint production, building technologies, and certain prestige-goods sectors) created work hierarchies of producers, and consumers who could or could not afford products; these impacts must have been responsible for several shifts in the PPN-PN family and social structures. It appears most probable that linear models of family-type development (*e.g.*, 'macrobands', corporate core families, extended families, nuclear families in the south) are problematic, since social structures are co-influenced by many other, even stronger socio-economic and environmental factors than the conditions of production and consumption. For example, extended families would not have been promoted by the establishment of operational chains that require larger social units: they could have been first formed by the needs of economic efficiency in an increasingly competitive socioeconomic micro-environment, even then helping to promote production modes like operational chains. Family structures must be understood more as shifting (even reversible) adaptations to the regionally different, complex interrelations between temporary environmental, subsistence, and symbolic conditions.

There is much evidence for the broad development of dualistic production modes in the technological subsystems during the PPN periods, which continued only in certain regionally relevant sectors during the PN. Specialized production, if not to say professional work, forced the establishment of unspecialized and opportunistic production; they might also be called the household levels of production. These dual patterns are ingredients of all producing economies since the Neolithic; sectors shifted, but such structures did not become extinct during the Late Neolithic or some time in the Bronze Age!

The lithic surplus production beyond personal needs did not occur with the more isolated or autonomous band communities of the Late Epipalaeolithic, and it also did not characterize Late Neolithic households. It is linked to the central part of the Near Eastern Neolithic trajectory, when the expansion of economic activities created demands far beyond the traditional structures of lithic procurement and production. By the beginning of the PPNB, settlement sizes and their social pressures would have made self-sufficient communities impossible without the momentum developed by a new behavioural lithic regime that both exploited suitable previous experience and forced standardized and predictable work hierarchies (in technological, economic, and social senses). Still, this might not have been enough to satisfy the immense market needs, and it is herein that another cause of complementary production, or dualistic lithic economy, may rest.

These complementary elements demonstrated by the informal technologies of the Near Eastern Neolithic are not restricted to tool-stone use. They can be found in the repair measures of buildings, in the imitation of prestige goods, and in the recycling of materials from earlier archaeological periods. Household or opportunistic, *ad hoc* levels of production are closely related to (the earlier) non-domestic production modes, in which work success was heavily influenced by the competence to react to unforeseen or unpredicted factors in the production and use processes. It might be taken as a general pattern that the mobile economies demanded a high competence in informal technologies or improvisation competence, whereas the technological success of the sedentary communities was based on predictable technological strategies. Occasional or *ad hoc* behaviour in stone and soil technologies would not have developed the high skill levels reached in the bidirectional, pottery or plaster technologies, for example. The lithic behaviours (including the relation to the lithic landscape) required for these skills needed permanent training, innovative approaches, and transfer through generations of craft specialists. A good example of a shift from formal to informal technologies during a shift from sedentary to partial mobile life are the PPNC and Yarmoukian flake-based industries of 'Ain Ghazal, which followed the PPNB naviform-dominated technology (Quintero 1998).

The development of lithic tool kits and lithic technologies (both fabrication and use) also mirrors the previously described culmination of broad-spectrum advanced lithic activities during the PPNB, replaced by sectorial advanced lithic activities in the PN. This is also reflected in the prestige goods inventories. It is visible in the distinction to be made between the formal and non-formal tools and technologies, as well as in the degree of standardization. The high skill standardization of the Early Neolithic kind not only standardized the products (*e.g.* blanks and thus the final products) but also the work processes. While standardization efforts could also be an ingredient of Paleolithic stone work, this combination of standardization of product and process must be called the hallmark of the Near Eastern Neolithic, or to put it another way, the lithic efficiency of domestic life.

An interesting example of opportunistic and specialized blade blank production in the LPPNB of the Petra area should illustrate a contemporary diversity in sedentary lithic technological subsystems on the household, workshop, and community levels. In Ba'ja, two major blade-core technologies exist: single platform blade-cores and informal bidirectional blade-cores, which very much give the impression that the knapper had only an inkling of bidirectional core reduction. In neighboring Basta, with the resources of the excellent brownish and grayish flint varieties in its catchment, the number of single-platform and 'imitated' bidirectional blade cores is limited, whereas almost hundred per cent of the blade production stems from standardized bidirectional blade core technologies. Their waste and the few preserved ateliers were not found in the houses, but in the site's open areas and fringes. The Basta products could be found traded to nearby Ba'ja and al-Baseet and further down to the Wadi Araba, if not further.

One question needs to be raised on the common-sense understanding that specialized production in the Later PPN and PN was based on the competence of selected sedentary families (houses). Discussion seems to exclude the possibility of multifamily co-operatives. This understanding is possibly triggered by the evidence concentrating in intra-mural workshops; but we should be aware that open settlement ateliers are more difficult to find (settlement fringes, at resource locations) or whose integrity was not easily maintained in communal spaces. However, some of the social structures in the later Neolithic could well have allowed such cooperative lithic production.

Acknowledgements

This essay benefited greatly from the discussions I had with many members of the chipped lithics family who gather during workshops on PPN Chipped Lithic Industries since 1993. In recent years much of my understanding and approaches were influenced by the works of Philip Wilke and Leslie Quintero, which helped me to leave the tracks and traps of a 'measurementalist'. But it was Peder Mortensen's love of chipped stones that infected my interests in 1978; he taught me chipped lithic thinking.

NOTE: The term PPN is used in this contribution always in its meaning: PPN and contemporary cultures.

References

Furby, L. 1978. 'Possessions. Toward a Theory of Their Meaning and Function Throughout the Life Cyle'. In: *Life Span Development and Behavior*, 1, 297-336.

Gebel, Hans Georg K. 1996. 'Chipped Lithics in the Basta Craft System'. In: Stefan K. Kozlowski & Hans Georg K. Gebel (eds.), *Neolithic Chipped Stone Industries of the Fertile Crescent, and Their Contemporaries in Adjacent Regions.* (Studies in Early Near Eastern Production, Subsistence, and Environment, 3). Berlin: ex oriente, 287-297.

Gebel, Hans Georg K. 2002. *Subsistenzformen, Siedlungsweisen und Prozesse des sozialen Wandels vom akeramischen bis zum keramischen Neolithikum, Teil II: Grundzüge sozialen Wandels im Neolithikum der südlichen Levante.* http://www.freidok.uni-freiburg.de/volltexte/466. Freiburg: Universitätsbibliothek.

Gebel, Hans Georg K. n.d. a. 'The Domestication of Water. Evidence from Early Neolithic Ba'ja'. In: Hans-Dieter Bienert & Jutta Häuser (eds.), *Men of Dikes and Canals. The Archaeology of Water in the Middle East.* (Orient-Archäologie 10). Rahden: Marie Leidorf.

Gebel, Hans Georg K. n.d. b. 'Technological Dualism in Ba'ja and Basta'. Contribution to the 5th Workshop on PPN Chipped Lithic Industries (Fréjus, 29th Feb- 5th March, 2004).

Hermansen, Bo Dahl & Hans Georg K. Gebel 2003. 'Towards a Framework for Studying the Basta Industries'. In: Hans-J. Nissen, Mujahed Muheisen & Hans Georg K. Gebel (eds.), *Basta* I. *The Human Ecology.* (bibliotheca neolithica Asiae meridionalis et occidentalis). Berlin: ex oriente. (in press).

Mortensen, Peder 1988. 'A Note on a Small Box with Flint Blades and Arrowheads from Beidha, and its Implications'. In: Andrew N. Garrard & Hans Georg Gebel (eds.), *The*

Prehistory of Jordan. Status of 1986. (BAR – International Series, 396:1). Oxford: British Archaeological Reports, 199-207.

Quintero, Leslie A. 1996. 'Flint Mining in the Pre-Pottery Neolithic: Preliminary Report on the Exploitation of Flint at Neolithic 'Ain Ghazal in Highland Jordan'. in: S.K. Kozlowski & H.G.K. Gebel (eds.), *Neolithic Chipped Stone Industries of the Fertile Crescent, and Their Contemporaries in Adjacent Regions*. (Studies in Early Near Eastern Production, Subsistence, and Environment, 3). Berlin: ex oriente, 256-266.

Quintero, Leslie A. 1998. *Evolution of Lithic Economies in the Levantine Neolithic: Development and Demise of Naviform Core Technology*. Riverside: University of California: unpublished Ph.D. dissertation.

Quintero, Leslie A. & Phil J. Wilke 1995. 'Evolution and Significance of Naviform Core-and-Blade Technology'. *Paléorient*, 21(1), 17-33.

Wilke, Phil J. & Leslie A. Quintero 1996. 'Near Eastern Neolithic Millstone Production: Insights from Research in the Arid Southwestern United States'. In: Stefan K. Kozlowski & Hans Georg K. Gebel (eds.), *Neolithic Chipped Stone Industries of the Fertile Crescent, and Their Contemporaries in Adjacent Regions*. (Studies in Early Near Eastern Production, Subsistence, and Environment, 3). Berlin: ex oriente, 267-285.

Campsites of the Seasonally Mobile in Western Iran

FRANK HOLE

Introduction

In western Iran, where there is a long tradition of transhumant pastoralism, an intriguing question is when this way of life began. If we can identify archaeological sites of transhumant people, then we may be able to assess their importance and role throughout prehistory. For practical purposes, pastoral nomads have no indigenous written history, and they were only occasionally written about by other people so that archaeology is the only means to recover their past. The problems of discovering transitory sites stem from their short-term use, the perishable nature of much of the building material, and the similarly perishable artifact inventory that are usually thought to characterize this way of life.

In an attempt to begin to understand what is entailed in living a life following herds, I spent some months in 1973 traveling with one tribe and visiting many others in Luristan (Hole 1978; Hole 1979). This experience provided much information on how these people travel, what the geographic and social constraints are, how the territory is used, and what the various campsites look like. This paper addresses how to identify nomad camps and compares them with village houses in the same region. Although there are nomadic people throughout the Near East, the focus here is on people of the central Zagros and may not pertain in all respects to other regions. In his book, *Nomads in Archaeology*, Roger Cribb referred extensively to an unpublished paper of mine, the substance of which is contained in this article, and which provides the opportunity to clarify some points (Cribb 1991a).

The Archaeological Issues

Let us first dispel a semantic issue, the distinctions among mobile, transitory, or nomadic. The main question is whether a site was occupied temporarily during seasonal visits, or whether it was occupied continuously, in the sense of being permanent. The latter characterizes village houses, even when people live in them only part of the year. On the other hand, campsites have short-term and often not repeated use, and have little or no 'permanent' structural modifications to them. This is not to say that mobile people never make structural modifications, only that any modifications require little skill or resources, and the people usually do not retain exclusive rights to their repeated use.

The regional and situational variability of dwellings used by herders in the Near East ranges from houses to the most ephemeral camp sites (Cribb 1991a). Given this variability, as archaeologists we may ask, do the structures of settled farmers differ in recognizable ways from those mobile herders? The answer, as I discuss in this paper, is yes.

The territory

Transhumant pastoralists in the Central Zagros move twice a year between winter pastures in the warmer lowlands and summer pastures in the uplands. Within each of the main pasture zones they may move horizontally from time to time and they may camp for longer or shorter periods during their longer semi-annual treks. The precise circumstances vary according to local environments as well as the presence of non-nomadic people and tribal interactions. For herders the imperative is to find pastures for the goats and sheep. The territory is the land that is, or can be, grazed by a particular group and it has features that dictate routes of travel as well as places to camp. Travel in Western Iran is often constrained because of mountain ridges and lack of surface water, which is particularly serious during the summer, and may render much of a territory unsuited to camping.

To discover sites we need to be able to assess the potential of a region to support transhumance. Where are the water sources? Where are there good routes between valleys? Where is the good pasture? Where is there shelter from wind? We can deduce some of these from topographic maps as well as from the accounts of military, political and tourist travelers early in the 19th and 20th centuries, some of whom traveled with, and by leave of, nomadic tribes.[1] Finally we can use the more recent experiences of archaeologists and ethnographers.[2] An archaeologist preparing in this way could find the most probable camp locations, but not necessarily the camps themselves.

Structures of pastoralists

The signature dwelling of Iranian nomadic groups is the black tent, a structure woven from goat hair and supported with poles and ropes (fig. 1), yet seasonally other forms of shelter prevailed. The tent cover may stand alone or be used

Fig. 1. The tent of Murad Khan, leader of a camp of Luri pastoralists in spring 1973.

to cover stone or mud walls during times of the year when it is cold and added protection from the wind and rain is desired. During more clement weather, when the tribe is on the move, the campsite may consist only of an area screened by hand-made, portable reed walls with no covering. During the summer it was traditional for mobile groups to construct shelters with branches covering them, called by British travelers, 'bowers' and *kulas* by the Lurs. Pens or corrals for the lambs and kids were commonly built of low stone walls or brush in the early spring, especially where the group planned to stay for some time. Alternatively animals might be kept in an annex to the tent. Grain and straw might be stored in bins dug along routes of migration or placed in natural sink holes, caves or even archaeological sites. Ordinarily nomads make little physical modification of the land except, perhaps, to construct a small dam where a water seep might create a pool for the herds to drink. Wells might be dug into the bottoms of wadies and, if so, there might be a watering trough close by. Routes of travel were not heavily modified, if at all, despite rough terrain and difficult passage.

In areas where oaks grow there are kilns to roast the nuts and boulders on which they were crushed with heavy rocker stones. Mangers for the horses, built of clay and stone, are sometimes seen at campsites. Sometimes herders make use of caves and shelters in which they may erect stone walls to pen their animals or even dwellings for themselves (Solecki 1998).

Tents

A tent site is a rectangular plot within a tent camp that is occupied by a single family and ordinarily is covered with some kind of perishable material. For convenience in discussion I use the term 'tent' whether or not the space was actually covered with fabric and it may not be possible to tell from the floor plan remaining after people have departed whether fabric or some other material covered the space.

My ethnographic study and other sources indicate that tents are invariably rectangular, with a length/width ratio of 1.4 to 3.3 (Table 1). The length of a family tent is commonly 6-10 m and each tent is separated from other similar structures.

Pastoral Camp	# Tents	Tot. Area	Avg. Tent	Largest	Smallest	L/W Ratio
Murad Khan	5	104	6.1 x 3.4	7.0 x 4.0	5.3 x 3.0	1.8
Chin-i-Zal	5	270	8.8 x 6.2	10.5 x 6.0	6.5 x 5.5	1.4
Deh Luran	4	153	7.6 x 5.0	8.0 x 5.0	7.5 x 5.0	1.5
Kurd	6	257	8.1 x 5.3	9.4 x 5.8	7.5 x 5.0	1.5
Bakhtiari I	11	335	9.4 x 3.2	16.5 x 3.3	7.0 x 3.0	2.9
Bakhtiari II	11	252	9.7 x 2.9	15.0 x 4.0	6.0 x 2.5	3.3
Bakhtiari III	9	341	9.7 x 3.8	18.0 x 5.0	7.0 x 3.3	2.6

Village Rooms	# Rooms	Tot. Area	Avg. Rm	Largest	Smallest	L/W Ratio
Hassuna IV	10	49	2.8 x 1.6	4.0 x 2.75	1.8 x 1.0	1.8
Hassuna V	11	96	3.6 x 2.0	6.7 x 3.2	1.6 x 1.5	1.8
Matarrah I	13	43	2.2 x 1.4	4.2 x 2.0	1.3 x 1.0	1.5
Matarra 2	4	17	2.8 x 1.5	3.5 x 2.0	2.1 x 1.0	1.9
Um Dabaghiyah	13	79	3.4 x 1.8	6.0 x 1.8	1.0 x 1.0	1.9
Es Sawwan I:2	20	206	4.4 x 2.5	7.2 x 3.5	2.0 x 1.8	1.8
Es Sawwan IIIA:2	12	55	3.2 x 1.5	3.0 x 2.5	1.8 x 1.1	2.1
Es Sawwan IIIA:4	10	45	3.1 x 1.5	3.2 x 3.1	1.5 x 1.2	2
Es Sawwan IIIA:6	10	31	2,5 x 1,3	2,8 x 2.8	1.3 x 1.0	1.9
Es Sawwan IIIA:7	11	36	2.4 x 1.3	2.7 x 2.7	1.0 x 0.8	1.8
Es Sawwan IIIA:8	12	40	2.3 x 1.4	3.0 x 3.0	1.2 x 2.0	1.6
Es Sawwan IIIA:10	12	55	3.1 x 1.4	3.8 x 3.8	1.5 x 0.8	2.2
Es Sawwan IIIA:13	12	51	2.6 x 1.6	3.8 x 2.9	1.2 x 1.0	1.8
Choga Mami 011-12	12	30	1.8 x 1.5	2.0 x 1.5	1.5 x 1.3	1.2
Choga Mami H8	9	23	1.8 x 1.4	2.0 x 1.8	1.5 x 1.1	1.3
Choga Mami H9	8	21	1.7 x 1.6	1.8 x 1.6	1.3 x 1.5	1.1

Table 1. Dimensions and areas of tent camps and archaeological villages. Data from my field notes and Digard 1981, Feilberg 1966-67, and Watson 1978.

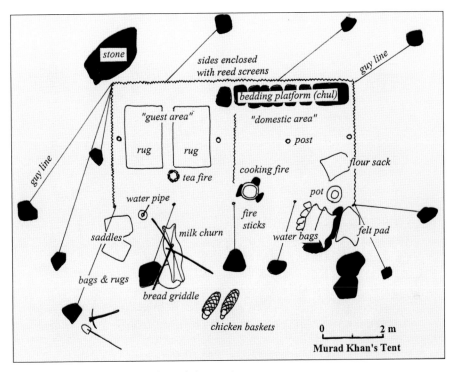

Fig. 2. Drawing of the furnishings of Murad Khan's tent.

There is usually one fireplace inside the rectangle and perhaps another outside, as well as a rectangular bed of stones along the rear of the tent on which bedding is placed. Often the tent area is outlined with rocks or has been ditched to divert water. These features of a tent site are not found in mud-walled village houses where typical rooms are smaller and often contiguous with other roofed areas.

Apart from the cover, a tent is composed of poles to support the roof and it is enclosed with tent fabric, reed screens or even stone or mud walls on three or four sides depending on the weather. Once this form had been adopted, a customary ratio between length and width emerged, along with characteristic dimensions, although those do vary with ethnic group and certainly with status (Table 1) (Cribb 1991a). The three Bahktiari camps are close to one another and to Murad Khan's camp, but they are distinct from the Deh Luran, Kurd and Chin-i-Zal camps. These distributions suggest that relatively subtle differences, which are greater than the within-camp variability, exist between camps used during different seasons or by different ethnic groups.

The widths of Luri tents tend to be more standardized than the lengths because width is determined by the number of strips of cloth that make up the cover. I was told that an average Baharvand tent is made of 12 strips, 10-12 m

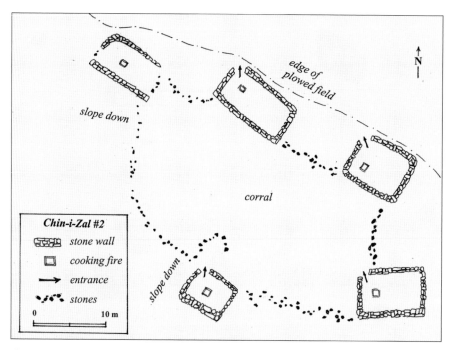

Fig. 3. Winter camp site in Chin-i-Zal where tents were enclosed with stone walls.

long, whose average width is 30-40 cm. Thus, depending on whether the tent is used for sides as well as roof, it may cover an area from 6-10 m long and 2.5-5.0 m wide. People tend to cover the area they need, subject to the limitations of wealth, the number of people who live in the tent, and their ability to carry the cover from camp to camp. Unless compelling circumstances warrant, people tend to use smaller rather than larger tents. Large families do not necessarily constitute compelling circumstances, but the need to protect young animals or to entertain guests may. Winter sites, which are outlined with stone or mud walls, are often somewhat broader than open tents, in part because it is not necessary to pull the cover down along the sides (fig. 3).

The interior arrangement of a tent is highly structured. Among the nomadic groups of western Iran, the norm is that the right half of each tent (when entering from the outside) is the domestic or family side, whereas the left side is reserved for male activities and the entertaining of guests. Kurds, Lurs and Bakhtiari all follow this practice but the layout may be reversed with other groups (Edelberg 1966-67, 384; Digard 1975, 122). Typically, the guest area is undeveloped except in the tent of the tribal or camp leader. When there is a fireplace in the guest area one can infer that the family has duties as hosts. This is true even if the tent possesses no other distinctive features such as greater size or difference in artifacts.

Most domestic activities take place around the fireplace where the women prepare food. A great deal of domestic work, such as churning, baking bread, and other cooking is done outside so that traces of these activities may be scattered. I was told that most activities could take place anywhere inside the tent. For example, people sleep wherever they choose, sometimes filling the entire interior of a tent; and animals may wander through the tents at night or may seek shelter there during stormy weather.

There is a great deal of variation in the placement of artifacts within a tent. People shift their belongings from campsite to campsite even though they retain the basic organization of space outlined above. An example of how the tent both frames and fails to contain the people and goods is seen in figs. 1 and 2, a campsite occupied for three days during April 1973. We see the scatter of household goods immediately in front of the tent. The saddles, pick axe, shovel and water pipe are outside the men's area. The water bags, firewood and pack for animals that carry bedding are close to the domestic side. The churn and bread griddle are also within the domestic sphere which is more extensive than the guest area since the latter is entirely under the cover of the tent. The arrangement of belongings is typical of Murad Khan's tent but it changed somewhat at each camp. Murad Khan, the leader of the camp, has two wives and five children. His status is seen in the guest area with its fireplace for keeping the teapot warm and the somewhat longer tent, but it is not evident in other respects as compared with other tents in the same camp.

Unlike village houses, tents can be adjusted with little, if any archaeological trace whenever the need arises. Village homes are constantly renovated but the mud walling makes such changes more likely to stand for archaeological investigation. Tents, on the other hand, can be closed, opened to give access to corrals, and moved from place to place to deal with changing needs through the year and years. Any particular campsite is likely to contain one specific type of tent site rather than many, since pastoral activities depend largely on the season.

Camps

Camps vary in size from four to as many as 16-20 tents, except in unusual circumstances when even more tents may be grouped. The lower limits on size relate to the number of people and livestock who are required to maintain a livelihood and, at the upper end, to the number of people and animals a particular area can support. In the part of Luristan where I worked, 4-5 tents was normal in the spring, but in the fall, following the sale of livestock, 10-12 tents was not uncommon. In prehistory we need not expect autumn sale, but faunal

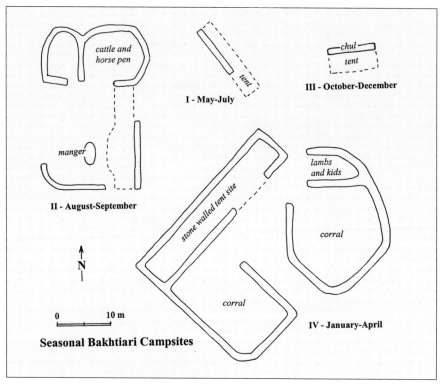

Fig. 4. Seasonal changes in Bakhtiari tent sites. After Digard 1975.

studies show that even then young males were selectively killed at the onset of the lean winter season (Zeder 2001).

The lower limit of camp size is also determined by the requirements of security. In Western Iran, nomads fear attack by wolves and other nomads, a fear that is partly expressed as terror of isolation. Tents are spaced closely enough that normal conversation can be shared among them, and adjacent tents are seldom more than 10 m apart and the distance between them is often much less. Close proximity is so pervasive that an isolated tent signals something unusual. Camp layout is discussed in Cribb and follows topography, social organization and need to pen animals at night. It is common for Luri tents to be arrayed around a central corral, but Kurdish camps are often in one or more lines with a common corral in front.

The seasonal specificity of sites is especially important for archaeological interpretation. In pastoral camps changes are expressed in separate, distinct, successive specialized campsites throughout the territory of a people. Figure 4 shows successive camps of one Bakhtiari family that was studied by Digard (1975). Although the differences between the occupied camps are striking, particular abandoned tent sites may not show these differences clearly because people return to them annually with somewhat different group composition and immediate needs. As a result the tents sites are scavenged for materials and reoccupied with renovations for untold numbers of times and thus are most revealing of the last occupation. In places where there is little deposition it is possible that modern nomads may be reusing materials first assembled at the site by pastoralists of the 7th millennium BC. Clearly we have little hope of charting successive occupations in a case like that, except through the finding of artifacts of previous periods. If it is a modern camp site occupied seasonally it is likely to have been used in similar ways in previous eras.

Pastoral Camps versus Villages

The sizes and layouts of tents contrast so sharply with village rooms that ethnographers have remarked on how the houses erected by newly settled nomads may be similar to the layout of tents (Aurenche & Desfarges 1983; Watson 1979). According to Cribb (1991, 376) there is a 'house-like' quality to the tent, but this does not consider that prehistoric village houses have multiple small rooms rather than a single large room (Table 1). That modern tent layouts are as old as the prehistoric houses is shown by the site of Tula'i (in northwest Khuzistan) where distinctively tent sites were in use by 6000 BC (Hole 1974). We note, however, that camps of nomadic hunters and gatherers are invariably circular, as were the first village houses (Aurenche 1982) and the modern yurts of Turkomen herders (Irons 1975). It is apparent from this that there is nothing obvious in either migration or the keeping of animals that dictates the use of rectangular tents, and from our modern vantage point it seems most likely that a combination of available materials and climate give rise to the particular form used for a dwelling. In the case of tents, the major innovation allowing (or perhaps suggesting) a shift from round to rectangular may have been weaving. The fabric, woven in narrow strips of variable lengths, lent itself to rectangular structures and it is portable.

Although the layout of village houses tends to be quite different from tents, there is a transitional form. For example, Watson (1979, 280) says,

At Hasanabad, (where) all food preparation is done on or around a stone-lined firepit in the same room where the family sleeps, eats and entertains. The Hasanabadis, in this respect as in various others, give every indication of being more similar to people like Hole's Baharvand than to the longtime peasants Kramer studied.

Watson's description (1978, 140) of the contents of a 'living room' supports this statement even though the layout of the village is quite different from a pastoral camp. However, since the living rooms in Hasanabad average more than 18 m², they more closely approach the sizes of tents than do most village rooms (Watson 1978, 294, Table 7.11). This similarity in arrangement and size raises the interesting point that lingering pastoral traditions, even in a village context of mud-walled architecture, may be detectable archaeologically.

Tents are usually considerably larger than village rooms, although not necessarily larger than village houses. Watson (1978) provides a number of tables listing the dimensions of rooms in early prehistoric sites whose average sizes and proportions are in Table 1. The two populations are entirely different: only exceptional village rooms are as large as a nomad tent. However, if we compare the sizes of village houses – which are composed of several rooms – with the area of nomad tents, we find essential overlap between the two populations. Cribb (1991, 145) rightly observes that one needs to recognize that tents do not encompass all of the space used by a family; rather he estimates that a combined inside-outside area of 10x20m is needed. What he does not say is that a similar space is used in much the same way outside a typical village house.

The data leave no doubt that nomad tents stand apart from village rooms and houses in both their overall dimensions and lack of solid partitions under the common roof, as least in the central Zagros. On the other hand, the length/ width ratios of the rooms and tents vary little except at one archaeological site, Choga Mami, where tiny, nearly square rooms are the norm, possibly to be understood as storerooms rather than dwellings.[3] It is striking, in fact, how small many rooms are in most prehistoric sites.

Criteria of Campsites

Although I shall not discuss villages in detail, implicit in the following discussion is that, in western Iran, we should be able to distinguish between camps and villages whenever we encounter them. Moreover, we should also be able to identify a tent site if it occurs in a village amongst the mud-walled houses. I believe that we can do these things with great reliability once we understand the criteria that characterize pastoral camps. Broadly speaking, location of the sites, floor plans, and evidence of seasonal specialization are the chief criteria.

Location refers to two characteristics: geographic locale and specific orientation and placement of a tent. For the most part, pastoral camps are situated away from the best arable land, although it is customary for nomads to camp on agricultural fields after the harvests so that siting of camps is not necessarily mutually exclusive with villages. In general, villagers have preempted the most desirable arable land near springs or other water and pastoralists take what is left over. Travelers in Luristan have noticed that foundations of seasonal camps are often located on slopes just above arable land.[4] Where irrigation can be practiced, villagers carefully maintain control over the water sources, but in pastureland only herding camps are to be found even where isolated arable patches exist.

Wherever nomads camp, their sites are placed to take advantage of flat land, shelter from prevailing winds, access to good pasture and reasonable sources of water. The latter two considerations are less important than the former. As these criteria run contrary to conventional wisdom, it deserves explanation. Flat land is desired, as anyone who has spread his bed on uneven ground will appreciate. Digard (1975, 120) reports that the Bakhtiyari build level mud platforms on which to pitch their tents, a custom the nomads I traveled with did not practice but which I have seen. The people camp where they can find comfortable space and men make the decisions about where to camp. Shelter from the wind is another obvious criterion at any season.

The weather also has a bearing on the location and orientation of the sites. My informants were quite specific that winter sites had to be in protected positions, with the axis of the tents placed against the prevailing winds and these depend on local topography. Normally storms come from the west, whereas dry weather (often very cold) comes from the east. Winter sites are likely to have solid stone walls entirely or partly enclosing the tent, although mud may also be used. Among the Lurs that I observed, the highest stone walls are on the south sides where they serve as passive solar collectors to provide radiant heat during the night. Figure 3 shows some tent sites with these characteristics, as well as protection from winds provided by hills.

Pastoral people in an arid land where rain falls during only half the year, use rain-fed pools and seasonal seeps, as well as springs, rivers and sometimes wells for their water sources. It is not uncommon today for villagers to make treks of several kilometers to fetch water. Cribb suggests that this may be true during migration but probably not at more settled camps because pack animals are seldom used by nomads to carry water; rather, women and girls carry water, usually on their backs. Pasturage is for the use of animals who can take themselves to it; hence only general proximity to good grazing is required in a camp. The one need is to have enough pasture to feed the herds – too little pasture and the group will not linger. Unless one knows an area intimately and its qualities in different seasons and years, one might not recognize the combination of features required for a good campsite.

Because the seasonal migrations correspond with different parts of the economic cycle, successive sites are likely to show evidence of special activities. In turn, this evidence is a clue to the season that a site was occupied as discussed by

Digard (1975) and Edelberg (1966-67). Digard's data are especially valuable in a consideration of intrasite variation because he mapped four successive seasonal sites used by the same group of people in the course of one year. His sketches, more vividly than words, portray the essential differences in these sites in response to changing seasonal needs (fig. 4).

Tents in Prehistoric Sites

The excavation of Tula'i, a site in northwest Khuzistan, was the first test of principles learned in the ethnographic study (Hole 1974). The site lies at the northern edge of the arable part of the Khuzistan plain. Although agriculture is practiced there today with the aid of machinery, the locale of the site is some 4 km from a permanent source of water on a somewhat rolling landscape. We have found no early agricultural villages in this particular part of the plain. For the past several hundred years, the region has been occupied by transhumant pastoralists of various tribal affiliation within the Lur group (Amanolahi-Baharvand 1975). Government policies initiated in the 1930s required many of the pastoralists to settle into villages, several of which are within walking distance of the site.

I excavated at Tula'i over a ten-day period in May 1973, using reluctant workers in temperatures that rose well over 110 degrees daily. Although conditions were far from ideal, I was able to establish the outlines of a chronology for the site and to test various parts of its wide extent.[5]

Just prior to my working at the site, the entire area had been leveled as part of a massive agricultural scheme intended to bring tens of thousands of hectares under irrigation. The leveling had exposed concentrations of ash and discontinuous lines or groups of large stones. Before leveling, there seems to have been no surface evidence of a site over most of the terrain, although early pottery and flints were found by Henry Wright during his examination of a Sasanian irrigation canal. The canal had been cut down into the earlier site and sherds were in the spoil banks.

A cursory examination of the leveled part of the site indicated that ash and stones extended over perhaps as much as a kilometer east-west. North-south limits have not been established. The site was something clearly different from the typical compact, mounded village. Indeed, it looked exactly like the remains of a dispersed tent camp although we first found sherds in a small mound that was part of the canal bank.

The workmen whom we hired from a nearby village had been pastoralists before their enforced sedentism and they were quick to point out that Tula'i was a tent camp. They were also able to give cogent reasons why this was the case and to help explain some of the features that we found. What we found were alignments of stones along with more compact rectangular clusters of stones, fireplaces, ash pits, and trash piles. One of the older workmen, Sayid Ali, was particularly interested in the site and he gave us a running commentary as features were exposed.

He said that his tribe had used this particular area nearly the year round, but that in winter cloth-covered tents were used, whereas in the summer, a shelter (*kula*) made of poles and branches was preferred. Either material covers the same floor space but during the summer the firepit is generally just outside the branch-covered *kula* whereas it is always inside the tent in winter. He also volunteered that tents face south during winter but that in spring they may face either direction and in summer, the tent or *kula* faces north. He then pointed out that site D4 faces south whereas D3 faces north (Fig. 5). If the two tents were used at the same time, it follows that the season must have been spring, but there is no reason why the tents would necessarily have been used at the same time. The reason for this is that the camping area is quite large (there are probably hundreds of tent sites) and when people return to a specific locale they move stones from one tent site to another to create the conditions they desire. Some tent sites which remain unoccupied within a particular camping area during one season will be used the next time the area is occupied. Thus there is a constant shifting of the stones from tent sites in order to accommodate the unique needs of the latest occupants.

Along the rear wall of a tent or *kula* is the *chul*, a layer of stones on which bedding is placed during the day. This feature appears to be universal among the people of Luristan and it provides a convenient point of reference from which to deduce the remainder of the shelter. As a test of this notion, I asked Sayid Ali, who had announced in no uncertain terms that we were digging a tent site, to find the fireplace. He oriented himself on the *chul*, took two quick steps and said, 'here' I told him to dig, whereupon he turned up the telltale ash. I then asked him to show me where the ash had been dumped when the fireplace was cleaned. He strode to the imaginary front of the tent, turned an oblique left, took about 5 steps and said, 'here.' Again I asked him to dig and this time he turned up the shallow depression of water-layered ash. By that time I was convinced that he understood the logic of the site.

The other matter of concern about tent site D4 was the scatter of broken mortars, rocks, and a small cup-shaped mortar just north of the presumed back wall of the tent. Sayid Ali said that it was probably a trash pile, the rocks having been discarded out of the way of traffic. I then asked him whether he had any ideas about the function of the little cup-shaped mortars. He replied that in his day the nomads had used similar objects to grind salt and spices, a suggestion that we have not been able to verify archaeologically.

Sayid Ali also told us that suitable river stones for the *chuls* and tent outlines could be obtained in the bed of the Karkheh River, some 4 kilometers distant. There is no other nearby source. Reeds for tents as well as poles and branches for the *kulas* were likewise obtained in the river bottoms. When I inquired about the sizes of tents, he gave me the same answer that I had heard elsewhere: camp leaders generally have the largest tent sites. He then pointed to D3 and said that it belonged to the leader. For reasons beyond my control, I was unable to dig that site extensively enough to search for evidence of two fireplaces.

Had Tula'i been a village like many contemporary sites in Khuzistan, it would have been built of mud and taken on the characteristics of a typical compact, mounded village like Choga Bonut (Alizadeh 1997). That it did not testifies to its essential difference in spite of the close similarity of artifacts in the two types of sites. The suggestion that Tula'i was a pastoral camp thus seems well supported. Additional lines of evidence point in the same direction. For example, contemporary Chagha Sefid, a village in Deh Luran, contains a much greater variety of artifacts, especially those used in reaping and grinding grain. Few sickles were among the artifacts of Tula'i, nor were there grinding slabs which are common in villages. On the other hand, Tula'i has pottery, figurines, spindle whorls, and other domestic objects that are no different from those found in villages. What is lacking at Tula'i is precisely those artifacts that pertain to agriculture.

The analysis of faunal remains, one of the better studied aspects of the early settlements allows us to compare Ali Kosh, Chagha Sefid, and Tula'i. Ali Kosh is a 'typical' mixed agricultural-stock raising settlement where a great deal of hunting and collecting supplemented the domestic diet (Hole, Flannery & Neely 1969). Contemporary Chagha Sefid, only 15 kilometers distant from Ali Kosh, exhibits entirely different patterns: a consistent and nearly exclusive preoccupation with domestic sheep and goats (Hole 1974). Tula'i conforms most nearly to this pattern, 91 per cent of the bones being sheep and goat. Based on her analysis (Wheeler Pires-Ferreira 1975-1977, 279), suggested that Tula'i was a 'fallow herd' camp rather than a 'true pastoral nomad camp.' Because Tula'i contained virtually no hunted animals and had no very young specimens, it must have been a fallow herd camp – a camp of animals which, because they are not currently involved in reproduction or nursing of the young, are detached from the village herd. In other words, she sees Tula'i as a specialist appendage of a village.

It is hard to refute this notion. In fact, it is not possible to tell, based on present ethnographic and archaeological information, whether Tula'i or similar sites were closely tied to a village. The fact that, with the exception of harvesting and grinding tools, a full complement of village artifacts is present at Tula'i suggests that a viable and complete life was carried on in the tent sites with all members of the nuclear family present. In other words, Tula'i is not just a camp composed of male herders living in tents.

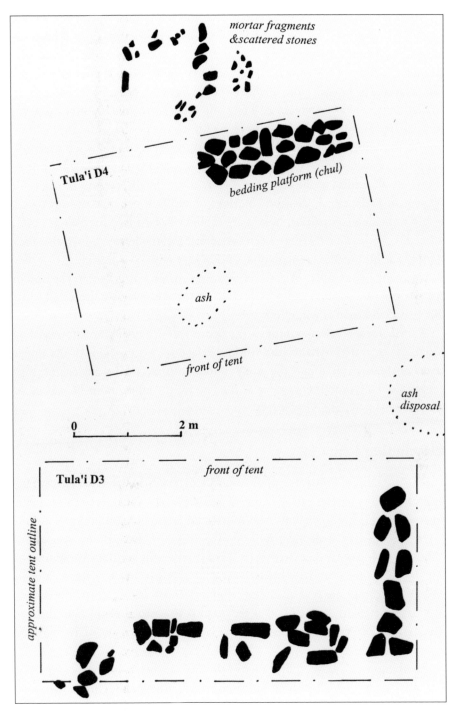

Fig. 5. Two archaeological traces of tent sites at Tula'i in Khuzistan.

There are two archaeological village sites in Deh Luran which may contain examples of pastoral tent sites or houses of settled pastoralists. The clearest example was found during surface survey at a site called Ashrafabad where the stone foundation of a Mehmeh Phase house had been exposed through erosion. The plan of this house (Hole, Flannery & Neely 1969, fig. 17b) shows striking similarities to the arrangement of a tent. At Tepe Sabz, a nearby site, a portion of what appears to be a similar floor plan of the same period was excavated in a narrow sounding (Hole, Flannery & Neely 1969, fig. 17a). The wide rear wall, platforms of stones for bedding and other goods, and the encircling outline of stones are all similar to the layout of a tent, as are the dimensions of nearly 10 by 5 m. At Farukhabad, the stone footings of an Uruk structure measuring 5.0 by 2.9 m, with a central post hole, were thought to be a tent site (Wright 1981, #623, 78). At the time these structures were first recorded, we assumed that they were village houses, but ethnographic studies have raised the possibility that they may actually be examples of pastoral tent sites within villages or, in the case of Ashrafabad, of a pastoral camp itself. That this should not be unexpected is the fact that Deh Luran is winter pasture.

A final archaeological example is the site of Kunji, a cave near Khorramabad where we excavated remains of a Middle Paleolithic occupation. In the upper layers of the cave we found the stone foundations of circular enclosures, suggesting use by pastoralists as early as the late fourth millennium BC (Hole & Flannery 1967; Wright, *et al.* 1975).

Concluding Remarks

There is a wealth of information, diverse and scattered though it may be, on intrasite variability among pastoral and village people of western Iran. This paper is an attempt to begin to exploit these sources for archaeological interpretation.

In western Iran, pastoral people move seasonally, establishing specialized camps in each part of their territories. In this sense, the territory is the unit of investigation – the site whose internal variability we seek to understand. Within each of the camps are tent sites that belong to individual families. These tent sites have spatial arrangements that are peculiar to pastoral people and distinct from settled villagers. The camps also have layouts related to season, topography and social organization.

An ability to read the significance of the sparse remains of these camps and tent sites can be gained through judicious use of ethnography. Immediate testing of the ideas can be implemented in selected areas so that there will be rapid and beneficial feedback between archaeology and ethnography.

Acknowledgements

My profound thanks go to (now) Dr. Sekandar Amanolahi, my former student, who introduced me to the Luri groups and provided companionship, served as an intellectual sounding board, and helped me elicit information in the Luri dialect that would have been impossible for me alone. It would be unforgivable too, not to extend my gratitude to the late Murad Khan and members of his camp who graciously put up with endless questions about things considered by them to be too mundane for discussion.

I should also like to recognize Kent Flannery, with whom I had my first experiences in recording transitory campsites, and later Henry Wright, Melinda Zeder, and Richard Redding, who accompanied me on one or another nomadic adventure and added their insights to our accumulating knowledge. I first became aware of the potential for studying transhumant people when Patty Jo Watson carried out her ethnoarchaeological project during our first year in Iran. Finally, our projects were sanctioned and aided through the kind offices of the Ministry of Art and Culture and the Iranian Center for Archaeological Research whose representative at Tula'i was Mr. Mohammad-Jaffar Nikkah.

Funding for the various projects was provided by Rice University, and National Science Foundations grants GS-67, GS-2194 and GS-35818.

References

Ainsworth, W.F. 1842. *Travels and Research in Asia Minor, Mesopotamia, Chaldea and Armenia.* (2 vols). London: J. W. Parker.

Alizadeh, Abbas 1997. 'Excavations at Chogha Bonut, an aceramic Neolithic site in lowland Susiana, Southwestern Iran', *Neo-Lithics,* (1/97), 6-8.

Aurenche, Olivier 1982. 'Les premières maisons et les premières villages', *La Recherche,* 13, 880-889.

Aurenche, Olivier & P. Desfarges 1983. 'Travaux d'ethnoarchéologie en Syrie et en Jordanie. Rapport préliminaires', *Syria,* 60, 147-185.

Cribb, Roger 1991a. *Nomads in Archaeology.* Cambridge: Cambridge University Press.

Cribb, Roger L.D. 1991b. 'Mobile villagers: the structure and organization of nomadic pastoral campsites in the Near East'. In: C.S. Gamble & W.A. Boismier (eds.), *Ethnoarchaeological Approaches to Mobile Campsites,* 371-393. (*Ethnoarchaeological Series,* Vol. 1). Ann Arbor: International Monographs in Prehistory.

Digard, Jean-Pierre 1974. *Techniques et culture des nomades: Baxtyari d'Iran.* Paris: Institut d'Ethnologie.

Digard, Jean-Pierre 1975. 'Campements Baxtyari. Observations d'un ethnologue sur des materiaux interessant l'archéologue', *Studia Iranica,* 4 (1), 117-129.

Digard, Jean-Pierre 1981. *Techniques Des Nomades Baxtyari d'Iran.* Cambridge: Cambridge University Press.

Edelberg, Lennart 1966-67. 'Seasonal dwellings of farmers in North-western Luristan', *Folk,* 8-9, 373-401.

Edelberg, Lennart & S. Jones 1979. *Nuristan.* Graz: Akademische Druck.

Feilberg, C.G. 1941. *La Tente Noire. Contribution Ethnographique à l'Histoire Culturelle des Nomades.* (Etnografisk Række, 2). Copenhagen: Nationalmuseets Skrifter.

Feilberg, C.G. 1952. *Les Papis, Tribu Persane de Nomades Montagnards du Sud-Ouest de l'Iran.* (Etnografisk Række, 4). Copenhagen: Nationalmuseets Skrifter.

Goff, Claire L. 1971. 'Luristan before the Iron Age', *Iran,* 9, 131-152.

Hole, Frank 1974. 'Tepe Tula'i, an early campsite in Khuzistan, Iran', *Paléorient,* 2, 219-242.

Hole, Frank 1978. 'Pastoral nomadism in western Iran'. In: R.A. Gould (ed.), *Explorations in Ethnoarchaeology.* University of New Mexico Press, 127-167.

Hole, Frank 1979. 'Rediscovering the past in the present: ethnoarchaeology in Luristan, Iran'. In: C. Kramer (ed.), *Ethnoarchaeology: Implications of Ethnography for Archaeology.* New York: Columbia University Press, 192-218.

Hole, Frank, & Kent V. Flannery 1967. 'The prehistory of Southwestern Iran: a preliminary report', *Proceedings of the Prehistory Society,* 33, 147-206.

Irons, William 1975. *The Yomut Turkmen: a study of social organization among a central Asian Turkic-speaking population.* Museum of Anthropology, Anthropological Papers, University of Michigan 58.

Ker Porter, R. 1821. *Travels in Georgia, Persia and Armenia,* Vol. 1. London.

Kramer, Carol 1982. *Village Ethnoarchaeology: Rural Iran in Archaeological Perspective.* New York: Academic Press.

Löffler, Reinhard, & Erica Friedl 1967. 'Eine Ethnographische Sammlung von der Boir Ahmad, Sudiran', *Archiv für Volkerkunde,* 21, 95-207.

Mortensen, Inge Demant 1993. *Nomads of Luristan.* New York: Thames and Hudson.

Mortensen, Peder 1974. 'A survey of prehistoric settlements in northern Luristan', *Acta Archaeologica,* 45, 1-47.

Schmidt, Eric F. 1940. *Flights Over Ancient Cities of Iran.* Chicago: University of Chicago Press.

Schmidt, Erich F., Maurits N. van Loon, & Hans S. Curvers 1989. *The Holmes Expeditions to Luristan,* Vol. 108. Chicago: The Oriental Institute of the University of Chicago.

Solecki, Ralph S. 1998. 'Archaeological survey of caves in northern Iraq', *International Journal of Kurdish Studies,* 12(1,2), 1-70.

Stark, Freya 1933. 'The Pusht-i-Kuh', *The Geographical Journal,* 82, 247-59.

Sykes, E.C. 1898. *Through Persia on a Side-Saddle.* London: Innes and Co.

Watson, Patty Jo 1979. *Archaeological Ethnography in Western Iran.* Tucson: University of Arizona Press.

Wheeler Pires-Ferreira, Jane 1975-1977. 'Tepe Tula'i: faunal remains from an early camp site in Khuzistan, Iran', *Paléorient,* 3, 275-280.

Wilson, Sir A.T. 1926. 'The Bakhtiaris', *Journal of the Royal Central Asian Society,* 13, 171-178.

Wilson, Sir A.T. 1941. *S.W. Persia: a political officer's diary 1907-1914.* Oxford University Press.

Wright, Henry T., *et al.* 1975. 'Early fourth millennium developments in Southwestern Iran', *Iran,* 13, 129-148.

Zeder, Melinda A. 2001. 'A metrical analysis of a collection of modern goats (*Capra hircus aegagrus* and *C. h. hircus*) from Iran and Iraq: Implications for the study of caprine domestication', *Journal of Archaeological Science*, 28 (1), 61-79.

Notes

1 Ainsworth 1842; Sykes 1898; Wilson 1926; Wilson 1941
2 Cribb 1991a; Cribb 1991b; Digard 1974; Digard 1975; Digard 1981; Edelberg 1966-67; Edelberg and Jones 1979; Feilberg 1941; Feilberg 1952; Goff 1971; Ker Porter 1821; Kramer 1982; Löffler and Friedl 1967; Mortensen 1993; Schmidt 1940; Schmidt, *et al.* 1989; Stark 1933; Watson 1979
3 When I last saw Tula'i in 1977, it was under maize cultivation and appeared to have been substantially disturbed as a result of plowing. Whether it will ever be possible to expand the excavations there is questionable, but since its discovery a number of other probable tent camp sites have been reported. The material from Tula'i has never been analyzed in detail and it remains in Tehran where I have not had access to it since the excavation.
4 Goff 1971; Mortensen 1974; Schmidt 1940; Schmidt, *et al.* 1989
5 Although the specific locale of Tula'i might have been used in any season, summers in upper Khuzistan are extremely hot and most pastoralists move to the nearby mountains where living conditions are more salubrious.

Ubaid Mesopotamia Revisited

JOAN OATES

It is with the greatest pleasure that I dedicate this paper to Peder Mortensen, a distinguished prehistorian and a close friend and colleague over many years, whom I first knew in the context of the prehistory of the Near East but most recently within the compelling beauty of Bayt al-Aqqad, the Mameluke house now the new Danish Institute in Damascus, of which Peder was not only the first Director but the Director responsible for overseeing its restoration.

Twenty-five years ago I wrote in a Festschrift for another distinguished prehistorian that:

> in the many years since I first worked in Iraq, the early prehistory of the Near East has altered beyond recognition. At the same, the later prehistoric periods, Ubaid and Uruk, have attracted relatively little interest, at least in terms of excavation, despite an increasing focus on the theoretical aspects of the rise of urbanism and the state, for the study of which, in Sumer, both periods are of major significance ... As a broad generalisation it remains true that during the past thirty years the later prehistory of Mesopotamia has not been a major focus of archaeological research and that Eridu, dug just after the last war, and Tepe Gawra, excavated some fifty years ago, still provide the basis for any assessment of Ubaid materials.
>
> (1983, 251)

It was also remarked that the only discoveries in recent years that had increased our understanding of the prehistory of Sumer had lain outside southern Mesopotamia, that is, the identification of Ubaid sites along the Arabian Gulf and the excavation of substantial Late Uruk 'colonies' on the Euphrates in northern Syria.

Published in 1983, this paper was actually written at the time of the first excavations in the Hamrin, an area also peripheral to southern Mesopotamia but one in which our knowledge and understanding of Ubaid settlement was substantially to increase. The Hamrin Ubaid sites were relatively small. Nonetheless, these rescue excavations provided the most extensive information then

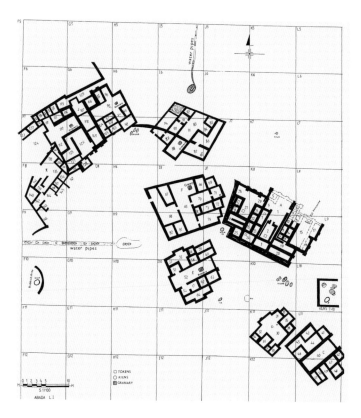

Fig. 1a. Plan of Levels 1 (fig. 1a) and 2 (fig. 1b) of the Ubaid village at Tell Abada; the small square symbols indicate the distribution of jars containing tokens. After Jasim 1989, figs. 13, 25.

available concerning the nature and structure of village settlement at this time. Of especial importance was the site of Abada, excavated in 1977-78 by Dr Sabah Abboud Jasim (1985; 1989). This provided the first coherent Ubaid village plan, distinguished in particular in its latest level by its complex water systems, including at least two pipe drains (fig. 1a), and by one unusually large and elaborate building from which were recovered a variety of vessels containing groups of relatively complex clay 'tokens', a discovery not as yet paralleled elsewhere (Jasim & Oates 1986), and beneath the floors of which were some 57 infant burial urns. Further knowledge of Ubaid Sumer at this time came from Warka, where the presence of two large and impressive Ubaid 'temples' was identified in the area of the *Steingebäude*. These appeared to have been associated with an Ubaid version of the 'high terrace', but direct stratigraphic connection with the foundations of the Anu Ziggurrat had been cut in the construction of the *Steingebäude* itself (Schmidt 1974).

It was not until 1978 that investigations within Sumer began to reveal new evidence of major significance to our understanding of its prehistory. This was of course the work of Jean-Louis Huot and others at the small site of Tell el Oueili,

Fig. 1b.

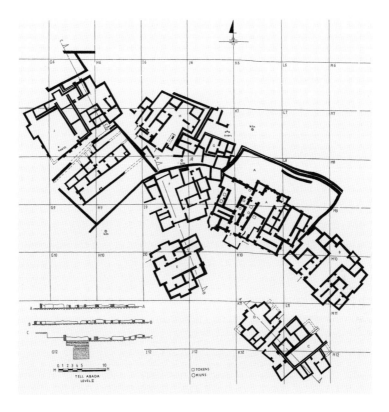

3.5 km from Larsa.[1] A second event of importance to our understanding of the Ubaid contribution to the prehistory of Sumer was a symposium organised by Elizabeth Henrickson and Ingolf Thuesen at Elsinore in 1988 and promptly published the following year; this brought together both evidence from the Hamrin and Oueili investigations and commentaries on recent research over many aspects of Ubaid society, not only in Mesopotamia but on its periphery.

It is Oueili, however, which has undoubtedly provided the most important new evidence with respect to Ubaid Sumer. Indeed, Oueili is without question one of the most important prehistoric sites ever to have been excavated in Iraq. This importance derives from the presence there of an early phase of occupation, clearly related to but stratigraphically preceding the Ubaid 1 phase and stretching back to sometime before 6000 BC. These early levels have been referred to as the 'Oueili phase' or 'Ubaid 0 (zero)', the latter both a term reflecting the demonstrable continuity from this early phase throughout the later sequence of Ubaid occupation as represented also at Eridu, and a whimsical joke at my expense, reflecting a classification (Ubaid 1-4) of which the original intention was to emphasise a comparable continuity among the Eridu materials themselves, in particular in the context of the so-called Sumerian problem (Oates 1960), an observation of some significance at a time when the apparent changes in pottery style between Ubaid 2 ('Hajji Muhammad') and Ubaid 3 (Ubaid I) were widely thought to signal the arrival of 'new people'. The validity of the proposed continuity, argued on the evidence of Eridu, was later clearly confirmed at the site of Ras al Amiya where, as at Eridu, the so-called Hajji Muhammad style of Ubaid 2 was found to continue in levels also characterised by conventional Ubaid 3 material (Stronach 1961).

At Oueili the prehistoric occupation has been explored to a depth of 4.5 m below modern plain level, where the presence of the modern water table has prevented further investigation. Here radiocarbon determinations attest the presence of an Ubaid 0 village well before 6000 cal BC. The earliest architecture yet excavated at Oueili would appear to consist of the foundations of a large 'granary' covering an area of at least 80 m² (Huot 1994, 118; Huot et al. 1996, fig. 48). Even more remarkable are the houses of subsequent Ubaid 0 levels, built on the tripartite principle identified also in the earliest Samarran architecture and perhaps as large as 330 m² (Forest 1983; 1996). Especially impressive are their central hypostyle halls, up to now unattested elsewhere (fig. 2). At present the Ubaid 0 phase is known solely from Oueili, but no such settlement can exist in isolation. Indeed Oueili provides not only a particularly striking illustration of our ignorance of the antiquity and complexity of prehistoric Sumer but also of the difficulties inherent in its investigation.

The closest parallels to Ubaid 0 material culture lie with the so-called Choga Mami Transitional, itself closely related to that of Samarran Mesopotamia where the architectural comparisons are also to be found. CMT pottery and indeed aspects of the associated building traditions and economy, including possibly the use of irrigation as attested at Choga Mami, appear in Khuzistan in the Sefid phase at Chaga Sefid (Oates & Oates 1976, 128-33; Hole 1977, 12; see also the section on the Choga Mami Transitional in Huot 1987b). Before the excavation of Oueili the arrival in Khuzistan of Mesopotamian black-on-buff pottery together with a new range of plants and animals and the use of elongated ('cigar-shaped'), impressed bricks was interpreted as an extension of central Mesopotamian (CMT) influence and perhaps the earliest convincing evidence for the actual movement of people. The new Oueili evidence introduces at least the possibility of an early and more direct connection between Sumer and Khuzistan. Certainly at the time of this early village the Gulf coastline would have been considerably south of its present position. Recent estimates place sea level in the Gulf during the sixth millennium BC some 10 m below that of the present day, with a coastline therefore some 100-150 km south of its modern

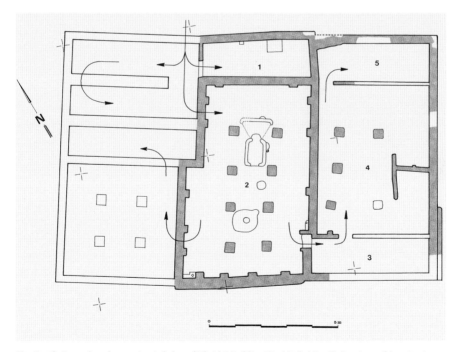

Fig. 2. Photograph and reconstructed plan of Ubaid 0 Building 37 at Tell el Oueili. Courtesy of Jean-Louis Huot.

position (Zarins 1992, 57, and fig. 5). Thus land access may have been easier than in subsequent periods.

Elements of the *Samarran* component of the CMT pottery, found not only at Choga Mami but also just to the north in the Hamrin (Matsumoto 1987), are however distinctly rare at Oueili. Thus the presence of Samarra-related materials at Choga Sefid (Hole 1977, figs. 50, 51[2]) suggests that this earliest visible connection between Mesopotamia and Khuzistan may already at that time represent the traditional route along the foothills via Badra. Certainly the earliest direct connection between Sumer and Iran appears in the sherds found on the surface of Halilih, a small site on the Bushehr Peninsula, which seem to fall exclusively within the Eridu/Hajji Muhammad range, that is, Ubaid 1-2 (I am indebted to Martha Prickett for information about this site).

We lack evidence from Sumer by which to judge the level of interaction, if any, between the earlier Zagros and Khuzistan cultures of Iran and southern Mesopotamia. Indeed Tamerkhan, a small 'Jarmo-type' site along the Zagros foothills near Choga Mami from which the chipped stone material has recently been published by Peder Mortensen (2002), remains at present the sole site on the Mesopotamian plain of which the material repertoire clearly belongs within the 'Zagros Group' (Mortensen 2002, 223); there is also one tiny fragment of Sefid red-on-cream ware (Hole 1977, 114). Such evidence clearly illustrates the view long held by Peder (see 1964 paper in *Sumer;* also Oates 1960, 1973) that the cultural traditions of the Zagros were clearly distinct from those of lowland Mesopotamia, that is, that there is no evidence to support the once widely held view that the prehistoric cultures of Mesopotamia derived from those of Iran.

Important new work by Jennifer Pournelle (2003), based on satellite imagery and the archaeological data from the various surveys carried out there (e.g. Adams & Nissen 1972; Wright 1969), promises to throw new light on early landscapes and patterns of settlement within Sumer itself. Also important is her return to an emphasis on the significance in general, and in the specific context of southern Mesopotamia, of marsh and riverine resources to early sedentary economies. We have no way of calculating the number of sites that have been lost beneath the alluvium. Those that are visible, however, appear to have been situated on relict river terraces ('turtlebacks'). These include large sites like Telloh and much smaller ones such as Warka survey site 298, the sole site on which surface sherds of possible Ubaid 0 date have been found and which is situated on a turtleback facing a levee backslope (Pournelle 2003b, 178-9). Indeed the early settlement at Oueili is itself situated on such a surface, revealed only by excavation as a buried turtleback, while the four metres of alluvial deposition in the deep sounding would initially have surrounded and eventually buried the channels that carried water past the Ubaid 0 foundations (ibid. 179). Thus surface sherds of Ubaid o attribution were not found here, nor have such sherds been identified as yet among surface collections elsewhere in Sumer with the possible exception noted above (WS-298, Adams & Nissen 1972, 174-5). Closely related surface sherds have, of course, been recovered in the Mandali area (Oates 1968) but here, at the eastern edge of the Mesopotamian plain, alluvial deposition has been relatively shallow. Thus, for the moment at least, only the evidence of Oueili provides a window into the period of early neolithic settlement in Sumer.

Regrettably, since the publication of the Elsinore seminar further archaeo-logical work in Sumer has been impossible. This is not to say that Ubaid research has stagnated. On the contrary. Ubaid sites have been investigated in Kuwait, in the Khabur region to the northwest and further to the west along the Euphrates in northern Syria. As in the Hamrin, much of this research has been the result of rescue excavations, in particular associated with the construction of dams on the Tigris, the Euphrates and the Khabur.

In Kuwait, following the work of Abdullah Masry (1974) on Ubaid-related sites along the western coast of the Gulf and pottery analyses demonstrating direct connections with Sumer (Oates *et al.* 1977), further evidence of Ubaid-related settlement has been found, in particular a small site (H3) on the north side of the bay opposite Kuwait City, discovered by Dr Fahad Al Wohaibi, Director of the National Museum, and subsequently excavated by a Kuwaiti-British expedi-tion (Carter *et al.* 1999, Carter & Crawford 2000, 2001). Part of this continu-ing project involves further survey of the area (in which a second Ubaid-related site was identified) and investigation of the ancient shoreline. Among the more unusual finds are stone architecture, the presence of a shell bead workshop and impressed and barnacled bitumen slabs providing clear evidence of the use of bitumen-coated, reed-bundle, sea-going vessels (Carter 2002, 22-3; also Vosmer 2000), evidence that certainly resolves, if such proof were needed, a recent debate in *Antiquity* concerning the contemporary boat models from Eridu (Bourriau & Oates 1997). At H3 the evidence that the material assemblage reflects elements of both Arabian Gulf and Mesopotamian Ubaid traditions is particularly clear. In recent years Ubaid sherds have also been found much further south along the western shores of the Gulf than was previously known, but in quantities far smaller than on major sites to the north such as Dosariyah and perhaps repre-senting no more than interaction among the Ubaid-related sites themselves (for example, Uerpmann & Uerpmann 1996; Beech *et al.* 2000).

In northern Iraq, following the important Russian excavations at Yarim Tepe where a sequence of Ubaid settlements was revealed on mound III, a number of sites of this date have been identified, and some excavated, in the rescue operations associated with the construction of the Eski Mosul dam (*inter alia*, Khirbet Derak, Breniquet 1996; Abu Dhahir, Ball 2003, 10). Further to the west,

Fig. 3. Distinctive Hajji Muhammad style bowl type of Ubaid 2/3 attribution. After Oates & Oates 1976b, 56 (*cf.* Safar *et al.* 1981, figs. 73, 90:3-5; Stronach 1961, pl. 49:2).

in the Khabur plain of Northeastern Syria, Ubaid levels have been excavated in rescue operations both north and south of Hasake, for example at Tell Ziyade (Buccellati *et al.* 1991) and Tell Mashnaqa (Thuesen 2000). The material culture at these sites closely resembles that of the south including, at Mashnaqa, the presence of a model boat of the same reed and bitumen type recently identified in Kuwait. North of Hasake an Ubaid cemetery has been excavated at Kashkashok II (Matsutani 1991) and Ubaid pottery found on mound III and at Tell Kuran (Hole 1999; 2000, 22). Ubaid levels have been reached in two deep soundings at Tell Brak (Area CH), and Ubaid pottery has been reported from other large sites such as Tell Leilan.

A number of Ubaid sites have been identified on surveys along the various rivers and in the northern plain (*inter alia*, Wilkinson & Tucker 1995, 43 sites; Meijer 1986, 25 sites; Lyonnet 2000). In the first season of an intensive survey begun in 2002 in the area of Tell Brak some 22 Ubaid sites were mapped within a 7 km radius of Brak itself, including the seven identified in the Eidem and Warburton survey (1996); in the 2003 season a further 49 sites were identified within a 15 km radius of Brak, though these are very preliminary figures. The latter included a small, ploughed-out site near Tell Grezil, a major but previously unidentified third/second millennium site some 10 km north of Brak. On the small Ubaid site a virtually complete and beautifully made 'tortoise vessel' was recovered, a surprise discovery on what appears to have been a relatively insignificant settlement.[3]

Tell Brak itself has produced, unfortunately out-of-context, the earliest examples of Ubaid pottery as yet known outside southern Mesopotamia, including a sherd from one of the most distinctive 'Hajji Muhammad' type fossils, otherwise unknown in the north (fig. 3, and Oates 1987, pl. 45a:4, from a decayed brick in the Eye Temple platform) and a single sherd that belongs unquestionably within the Ubaid 1-2 range (Oates 1987, 193, fig. 1:b). Such early connections with the south almost certainly reflect Brak's 'gateway' position on one of the main routes from the Tigris Valley to the north and west, and raise the question of the method of transmission of Ubaid material culture, a problem returned to below.

Ubaid sites are attested further west, along the Balikh River. Of especial interest are two Euphrates sites at which remarkable evidence for pottery production has been discovered, Tell al Abr and Tell Kosak Shamali (Hammade & Koike 1992; Nishiaki & Matsutani 2001, 2003). Pottery workshops, storerooms and horseshoe-shaped pottery kilns have been found in Ubaid levels at both sites. A reconstructed kiln from Kosak together with potters' tools from the workshops can now be seen in the Aleppo Museum. As in the Khabur area many southern types are found but distinctive local traditions seem also to be well represented, for example the emphasis on the 'eye motif' found from the Euphrates to Brak but rarely in Sumer (*inter alia*, Hammade & Koike 1992, fig. 20; the only southern example known to me is from Uqair, Lloyd & Safar 1943, pl. 21b:13). This common and essentially northern motif would seem to have been one of many Halaf legacies: *inter alia*, Halaf examples at Ras Shamra and Shams ed-Din on the Euphrates (Aleppo Museum).

Undoubtedly the most important northern Ubaid settlement to have been excavated in recent years lies, however, in Anatolia, the site of Değirmentepe, situated on an ancient Euphrates terrace northeast of Malatya, in the area of the Karakaya dam, and excavated by Ufuk Esin in 1978-86. Levels 6-11 belong to a chalcolithic phase closely related to the Mesopotamian Ubaid, not only in its painted pottery and house type but also other objects such as figurines, clay nails and seals. Even clay sickles are found, despite the ready accessibility of both flint and obsidian (Esin 1989, 136). A thick mud-brick wall surrounded the settlement and, as well as the typical Ubaid tripartite, *Mittelsaal* house (fig. 4), there were numerous workshops in which microlithic flint engraving tools were manufactured. Copper slags and ovens indicate also the smelting of that metal. Indeed the material remains strongly argue that Değirmentepe was an Ubaid colony,

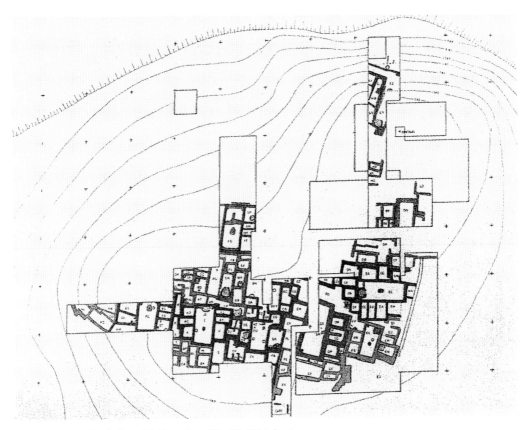

Fig. 4. Plan of Değirmentepe. After Esin 1994, fig. 4.

engaged at least partly in the acquisition of copper, almost a millennium before the Uruk colonies of the later fourth millennium.

Also of especial significance at Değirmentepe are the numerous seals and impressions (Esin 1994), closely reminiscent of those from Tepe Gawra (*inter alia*, fig. 5, and see also the sealings of Khirbet Derak, Breniquet 1996). Perhaps surprisingly, such objects have rarely been recovered in Sumer, where a few possible stone seals are known but as yet not a single impression. The contrast in the north is striking. Here there is extensive evidence for the use of seals already in the Samarran phase, while the first known sealings date back at least to the earliest ceramic neolithic (for example at Bouqras, P.A. Akkermans *et al.* 1983). Extensive evidence from Sabi Abyadh, recovered from a heavily burnt village dating to c. 6000 cal. BC, provides an early example of a system that must have been far more widespread, at least in Northern Mesopotamia (Akkermans & Duistermaat 1997). Indeed, on present evidence, many of the components of the Sumerian administrative system seem to have originated in the north where seals

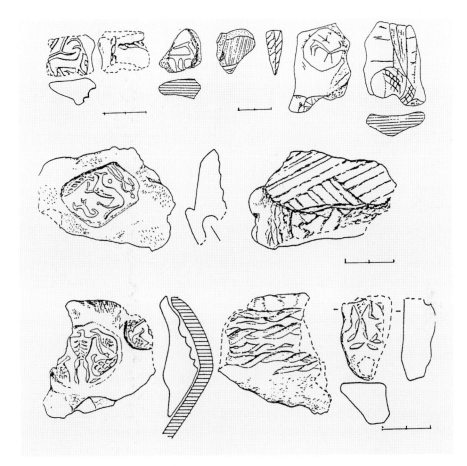

Fig.5. Sealings from Değirmentepe. After Esin 1994.

and other *aides mémoires* were in common use from an early date; by 4000 BC, moreover, a settlement of urban proportions with monumental secular architecture is clearly attested at Brak (Oates 1996; 2002; in press, fig. 2). Even earlier, a number of northern Ubaid sites are estimated to occupy areas of up to 10-15 ha, certainly comparable with known sites in the south (*inter alia*, Nieuwenhuyse 2000, 191, site T.70 at ancient Nisibis, c. 13 ha, and Tell al Hawa, Wilkinson & Tucker 1995, 40, estimated area 15 ha, compared with Uqair and Eridu, Wright 1981, 338, at around 12 ha).

Ubaid pottery is reported also at a number of sites in the Değirmentepe area (including Norşuntepe, Tepecik and Tülintepe, see Esin 1983, 187), but without more detailed publication it remains difficult to judge this evidence. Pottery long ago described as Ubaid from sites like Mersin and others in the Amuq and Jabbul plains is for the most part no more than possibly Ubaid-related or, more commonly, related to so-called 'developed Halaf'. There is, however, more persuasively Ubaid material at sites such as Kurdu and Tell al-Shaikh (Lines 1953, 139;[4] Braidwood & Braidwood 1960). In general, however, there is little true Ubaid west of the Euphrates, while some of the Ubaid-related material in the Amuq and Cilicia is almost certainly post-Ubaid in date (Lines 1953; see also Thuesen 1989, 435, with reference to Hama). Certainly there are no sites known to me comparable with Değirmentepe which, with its *Mittelsaal* houses, is difficult to see other than as a genuine colony site.

Opinions differ as to the appropriate interpretation of the Ubaid phenomenon, one of the most striking features of which is the great distances to which its influence spread. Current opinion tends to favour the acculturation for which there seems to be clear evidence at sites like Tell Mefesh in the Balikh and Tepe Gawra (*inter alia*, Breniquet 1989, 1996). Perhaps not surprisingly, this explanation seems most convincing at sites with earlier Halaf occupation. At most northern Ubaid sites there is little if any evidence of the tripartite *Mittelsaal* plan, perhaps a reflection only of lack of lateral exposure, but even at Yarim Tepe this plan is not attested. That the apparent absence of the *Mittelsaal* house type is not true of all sites with a 'transitional' phase can of course be seen clearly at Tepe Gawra.

At other sites the evidence seems more strongly to favour some movement of people from the south or, at the least, very close southern contact (*inter alia*, Mashnaqa on the Khabur (Thuesen 2000)). On the basis of the sealings, however, the 'colonisation' at Değirmentepe would seem to have been an entirely northern phenomenon. Further chemical and physical analyses of pottery and sealings would be highly relevant here, as would more lateral excavation to reveal the types of house plan. A programme initiated by the author some years ago provided clear evidence that the majority of Ubaid ceramics were made at the sites on which they were found. That is, there was no evidence for central production centres despite the identical, indeed indistinguishable, nature of much of the pottery. In this regrettably unpublished research 240 sherds from 15 sites were examined by petrographic and NAA analysis and the paint on 100 of the south and central Mesopotamian samples was further analysed by electron microprobe. Of these some 50 sherds had been deliberately selected in groups of *identical* shape, design and visible fabric from sites including Eridu, Ur, Ras al Amiya, Choga Mami, Hassuna and Tepe Gawra. Unfortunately the NAA results were lost owing to the illness of one of the collaborators, but that evidence had been said to conform to that of the paints which showed that, for the most part, these superficially identical vessels had been made locally. Only in a very few cases was there evidence for possible non-local production.[5] 'All the technological data point to manufacture of Ubaid ceramics by specialised craftsmen, but on each individual site' (Kamilli *et al.* 1982, 50). On the basis of these studies there is no evidence whatsoever for centralised production centres at this time.

It is not until the empire of the Late Assyrians that a comparable geographical area is brought within a single influence and at this time, unlike the Ubaid phenomenon, Late Assyrian material culture was not adopted to a similar degree; in fact rather the reverse was true. As Thuesen remarks, in the context of the Ubaid-related materials of Western Syria, 'it is striking how powerful the Mesopotamian Ubaid cultures were in setting standards' (1989, 435). With this I return to the point of the earlier Festschrift paper, which was not only to emphasise the significance of the Ubaid phase in the growth of the earliest complex urban society but also to lament the apparent lack of interest in its further investigation. The recent focus on the Uruk 'colony phase' has brought much illumination into the fourth millennium, and I am certain that a comparable focus on the preceding millennium would prove equally, if not more, rewarding. Until the day when a large Ubaid site is *extensively* excavated in the south, however, 'we shall undoubtedly continue to underestimate the achievements of the people whose activities almost certainly provided the initial stimulus to the growth of Sumerian society' (Oates 1983, 263). The new evidence from the north, however, shows clearly that not all innovation was of southern origin, and that the prehistoric north played a greater role in later social and economic development than is usually acknowledged.

Thus Ubaid studies have not been quiescent over the past 25 years, either in the field or on the theoretical side. Indeed there have been a number of papers treating the origins of 'civilisation' in Sumer. Among these Gil Stein (1994) focuses on small scale, irrigation-based Ubaid polities using 'inclusive ideologies emphasizing group membership through a strategy of ritually mobilized staple finance' rather than overtly hierarchical principles, while Algaze (2001; in press) looks back from his Uruk stance to the unique ecology of the alluvial lowlands, with their resource resilience and transportational advantages. The unique ecology of the alluvial lowlands and in particular the importance of littoral resources in this economy are also emphasised by Pournelle (2003).

For the moment, however, it is Oueili that provides the only true window into Sumer's past, with its extraordinary evidence for an underlying continuity in southern Mesopotamia from the earliest village yet excavated to the temple sequence at Eridu and, in my own view, throughout the Uruk phase as well. Moreover, the evidence from Oueili reinforces a view expressed long ago by Peder Mortensen (1964) and myself (1960, 1973), but slow to be generally adopted, that the cultures of lowland Mesopotamia owed little to their highland, or even their lowland, neighbours to the east, a perspective that now seems irrefutable (for the latest comment, see Mortensen 2002, 223).

I close not only in wishing Peder a very happy 70th birthday and congratulating him on a long and successful career, but in wishing both Peder and Inge a happy and successful future, for many years to come.

Acknowledgements

I would like to thank both Jean-Louis Huot and Jean-Daniel Forest for the photograph from the Oueili excavations, and for their kind permission to publish it. I would also like to thank most warmly both Guillermo Algaze and Jennifer Pournelle for permission to refer to unpublished manuscripts.

References

Adams, R. McC. & H.J. Nissen 1972. *The Uruk Countryside*. Chicago: University Press.

Akkermans, P.A., J.A.K. Boerma, A.T. Clason, S.G. Hill, E. Lohof, C. Meiklejohn, M. LeMière, M.L.F. Molgat, J.J. Roodenberg, W. Waterbolk-van Rooyen & W. van Zeist 1983. 'Bouqras revisited: preliminary report of a project in Eastern Syria', *Proceedings of the Prehistoric Society*, 49, 335-72.

Akkermans, P.M.M.G. & Kim Duistermaat 1997. 'Of storage and nomads: the sealings from late neolithic Sabi Abyad', *Paléorient*, 22(2), 17-44.

Algaze, Guillermo 2001. 'Initial Social Complexity in Southwestern Asia, The Mesopotamian Advantage', *Current Anthropology*, 42, 199-233.

Algaze, Guillermo 2003. 'The Sumerian Takeoff'. In: E. Stone (ed.), *Settlement and Society: Ecology, Urbanism, Trade, and Technology in Ancient Mesopotamia and Beyond. Festschrift in Honor of Robert McCormick Adams*. Los Angeles: Cotsen Institute of Archaeology.

Ball, Warwick (ed.) 2003. *Ancient Settlement in the Zammar Region*. (BAR International Series, 1096).

Beech, Mark, Joseph Elders & Elizabeth Shepherd 2000. 'Reconsidering the Ubaid of the southern Gulf: new results from excavations on Dalma Island, U.A.E', *Proceedings of the Seminar for Arabian Studies*, 30, 41-7.

Bourriau, Janine & Joan Oates 1997. 'Spinning or sailing?: the boat models from Eridu', *Antiquity*, 71, 719-21.

Braidwood, Robert & Linda S. Braidwood 1960. *Excavations in the Plain of Antioch I. The Earlier Assemblages. Phases A-J*. OIP, 61. Chicago: University Press.

Breniquet, Catherine 1989. 'Les origines de la culture d'Obeid en Mésopotamie du nord'. In: Henrickson & Thuesen (eds.), 325-36.

Breniquet, Catherine 1996. *La disparition de la culture de Halaf*. Paris: ERC.

Buccellati, G., D. Buia & S. Reimer 1991. 'Tell Ziyade: the First Three Seasons of Excavation (1988-90)', *Bulletin of the Canadian Society for Mesopotamian Studies*, 21, 31-62.

Carter, Robert 2002. Ubaid-period boat remains from As-Sabiyah: excavations by the British Archaeological Expedition to Kuwait', *Proceedings of the Seminar for Arabian Studies*, 32, 13-30.

Carter, Robert & Harriet Crawford 2001. 'The Kuwait-British Archaeological Expedition to as-Sabiyah: Report on the second season's work', *Iraq*, 63, 1-20.

Carter, Robert & Harriet Crawford 2002. 'The Kuwait-British Archaeological Expedition to as-Sabiyah: Report on the third season's work', *Iraq*, 64, 1-13.

Carter, R., H. Crawford, S. Mellalieu & D. Barrett 1999. 'The Kuwait-British Archaeological Expedition to as-Sabiyah: Report on the first season's work', *Iraq*, 61, 43-58.

Eidem, Jesper & David Warburton 1996. 'In the Land of Nagar: a Survey around Tell Brak', *Iraq*, 58, 51-64.

Esin, Ufuk 1983. 'Zur Datierung der vorgeschichtlichen Schichten von Değirmentepe bei Malatya in der östlichen Türkei'. In: R.M. Boehmer & H. Hauptmann (eds.), *Beiträge zur Altertumskunde Kleinasiens*. (FS Kurt Bittel). Mainz: von Zabern, 175-90.

Esin, Ufuk 1989. 'An Early Trading Center in Eastern Anatolia'. In: K. Emre, B. Hrouda, M. Mellink & N. Özgüç (eds.), *Anatolia and the Ancient Near East, Studies in Honor of Tahsin Özgüç*. Ankara, 135-41.

Esin, Ufuk 1994. 'The Functional Evidence of Seals and Sealings of Değirmentepe'. In: P. Feriola, E. Fiandra, G.G. Fissore & M. Frangipane (eds.), *Archives Before Writing*. Rome: Scriptorium, 59-81.

Forest, Jean-Daniel 1983. 'Aux origines de l'architecture obédienne: les plans de type Samarra', *Akkadica*, 34, 1-47.

Forest, Jean-Daniel 1996. 'Oueili et les origines de l'architecture obeidienne'. In: Huot (ed.), 141-50.

Forest, Jean Daniel 1997. 'Maison, Maisonnée et Structure Sociale en Mésopotamie Préhistorique (6ᵉ – 4ᵉ Millénaire)', *Al-Rafidan*, 18, 81-91.

Forest, J.-D., R. Vallet & C. Breniquet 1996. 'Stratigraphie et architecture de 'Oueili Obeid o et 1. Travaux de 1987 et 1989'. In: Huot (ed.), 19-102.

Gianessi, Deborah 2002. 'Tell Afis: the Late Chalcolithic Painted Ware', *Levant*, 34, 83-97.

Hammade, Hamido & Yayoi Koike 1992. 'Syrian Archaeological Expedition in the Tishreen Dam Basin, Excavations at Tell al-'Abr 1990 and 1991', *Damaszener Mitt.*, 6.

Henrickson, Elizabeth F. & Ingolf Thuesen (eds.) 1989. *Upon This Foundation – the Ubaid Reconsidered*. (CNI Publ., 10). Copenhagen: Museum Tusculanum Press.

Hole, Frank 1977. *Studies in the Archeological History of the Deh Luran Plain, The Excavation of Chagha Sefid*. Ann Arbor: Memoirs of the Museum of Anthropology, 9.

Hole, Frank 1999. 'Preliminary Report on the Joint American-Danish Archaeobiological Sampling of Sites in the Khabur Basin (1990)'. In: *Misc. Papers of the Yale University Khabur Basin Project, Northeast Syria, 1986-1997*. (Unpublished MS).

Hole, Frank 2000. 'The Prehistory of the Khabur', *Subartu*, 7, 17-27.

Huot, Jean-Louis 1971. 'French Archaeological Mission at Larsa, Tell El 'Oueili: surface Exploration', *Sumer*, 27, 45-58.

Huot, Jean-Louis (ed.) 1983. *Larsa et Oueili, travaux de 1978-1981*. Paris: Editions Recherche sur les Civilisations.

Huot, Jean-Louis (ed.) 1987a. *Larsa et Oueili. Rapport préliminaire (1983)*. Paris: Editions Recherches sur les Civilisations.

Huot, Jean-Louis (ed.) 1987b. *Préhistoire de la Mésopotamie*. Paris: Editions de la CNRS.

Huot, Jean-Louis 1989. 'Ubaidian villages of lower Mesopotamia'. In: Henrickson & Thuesen (eds.) 1989, 19-40.

Huot, Jean-Louis 1994. *Les Premiers Villageois de Mésopotamie*. Paris: Armand Colin.

Huot, Jean-Louis 1996. *Oueili. Travaux de 1987 et 1989*. Paris: Editions Recherches sur les Civilisations.

Huot, J.-L. & R. Vallet 1990. 'Les habitations à salles hypostyles d'époque Obeid 0 de Tell el Oueili', *Paléorient*, 16/1, 125-30.

Jasim, Sabah Abboud 1985. *The Ubaid Period in Iraq. Recent Excavations in the Hamrin Region*. (BAR International Series, 267).

Jasim, Sabah Abboud 1989. 'Structure and Function of an Ubaid Village'. In: Henrickson & Thuesen (eds.) 1989, 79-88.

Jasim, S.A. & J. Oates 1986. 'Early tokens and tablets in Mesopotamia', *World Archaeology*, 17, 348-61.

Kamada, Hiroko & Tadahiko Ohtsu 1991. 'Second Report on the Excavations at Songor A – Ubaid Graves', *Al-Rafidan*, 12, 221-38.

Kamilli, Diana, Arthur Steinberg & Rita Wright 1982. 'An Early Pottery Industry: Development and distribution of Ubaid Wares'. Unpublished manuscript.

Lees, G.M. & N.L. Falcon 1952. 'The Geographical History of the Mesopotamian Plains', *Geographical Journal*, 118, 24-39.

Lines, J.L. 1953. *The Al Ubaid Period in Mesopotamia*.(unpubl. Ph.D. dissertation), University of Cambridge.

Lyonnet, Bertille (ed.) 2000. *Prospection Archéologique Haut-Khabur Occidental* I. Beyrouth: Institut Français d'Archéologie du Proche-Orient.

Masry, A.H. 1974. *Prehistory in Northeastern Arabia: The Problem of Interregional Interaction*. Miami: Field Research Projects.

Matsumoto, Ken 1987. 'The Samarran Period at Tell Songor A'. In: Huot 1987b, 189-95.

Matsutani, Toshio (ed.) 1991. *Tell Kashkashok, The Excavations at Tell No. II*. Tokyo: Institute of Oriental Culture.

Meijer, Diederik J.W. 1986. *A Survey in Northeastern Syria*. Istanbul: Nederlands Historisch-Archaeologisch Instituut.

Mortensen, Peder 1964. 'Additional Remarks on the Chronology of Early Village-Farming Communities', *Sumer*, 20, 28-36.

Mortensen, Peder 1973. 'A Sequence of Flint and Obsidian Tools from Choga Mami', *Iraq*, 35, 37-55.

Mortensen, Peder 2002. 'A Note on the Chipped Stone Industry of Tamerkhan', *Iranica Antiqua*, 37, 219-27.

Munchaev, R.M. & N.Y. Merpert 1981. *Earliest Agricultural Settlement of Northern Mesopotamia*. Moscow: Nauk.

Nieuwenhuyse, O. 2000. 'Halaf Settlement in the Khabur Headwaters'. In: Lyonnet (ed.) 2000, 151-205.

Nishiaki, Y. 2000. 'An Ubaidian burnt building from Tell Kosak Shamali'. In: P. Matthiae, A. Enea, L. Peyronel & F. Pinnock (eds.), *Proceedings of the First International Congress on the Archaeology of the Ancient Near East*. Rome: University of Rome, 1213-23.

Nishiaki, Y. & T. Matsutani 2001. *Tell Kosak Shamali* I. *Chalcolithic Architecture and the Earlier Prehistoric Remains*. Tokyo: University Museum, University of Tokyo Monograph 1.

Nishiaki, Y. & T. Matsutani 2003. *Tell Kosak Shamali* II. *Chalcolithic Technology and Subsistence.* Tokyo: University Museum, University of Tokyo Monograph 2.

Oates, David & Joan Oates 1976a. 'Early Irrigation Agriculture in Mesopotamia'. In: G. de G. Sieveking, I.H. Longworth & K.E. Wilson (eds.), *Problems in Economic and Social Archaeology.* (Grahame Clark FS). London: Duckworth, 109-35.

Oates, David & Joan Oates 1976b. *The Rise of Civilisation.* Oxford: Elsevir Phaidon.

Oates, Joan 1960. 'Ur and Eridu, the Prehistory', *Iraq*, 22, 32-50.

Oates, Joan 1968. 'Prehistoric Investigations near Mandali, Iraq', *Iraq*, 30, 1-20.

Oates, Joan 1969. 'Choga Mami, 1967-68, a preliminary report', *Iraq*, 31, 115-52.

Oates, Joan 1973. 'The Background and Development of Early Farming Communities in Mesopotamia and the Zagros', *Proceedings of the Prehistoric Society*, 39, 147-81.

Oates, Joan 1983. 'Ubaid Mesopotamia Reconsidered'. In: T. Cuyler Young, Jr, P.E.L. Smith & Peder Mortensen (eds.), *The Hilly Flanks, Essays on the Prehistory of Southwestern Asia.* (Braidwood FS). Chicago: SAOC 36, 251-66.

Oates, Joan 1987a. 'The Choga Mami Transitional'. In: Huot 1987b, 163-95.

Oates, Joan 1987b. 'A Note on Ubaid and Mitanni Pottery from Tell Brak', *Iraq*, 49, 193-8.

Oates, Joan 1996. 'A Prehistoric Communication Revolution', *Cambridge Archaeological Journal*, 6, 165-76.

Oates, Joan 2002. 'Tell Brak: the 4th Millennium Sequence and its Implications'. In: J.N. Postgate (ed.), *Artefacts of Complexity.* Warminster: Aris & Phillips, 111-22.

Oates, Joan, in press. *Monumental Public Architecture in Late Chalcolithic and Bronze Age Mesopotamia, with particular reference to Tell Brak and Tell al Rimah.*

Oates, Joan, T.E. Davidson, D. Kamilli & H. McKerrell 1977. 'Sea-faring Merchants of Ur?', *Antiquity*, 51, 221-34.

Pournelle, Jennifer R. 2003a. 'The littoral foundations of the Uruk state: Using satellite photography toward a new understanding of 5th/4th millennium BCE landscapes in the Warka Survey Area, Iraq'. In: Dragos Gheorghiu (ed.), *Chalcolithic and early Bronze Age hydrostrategies.* (BAR International Series, 1123). 5-23.

Pournelle, Jennifer R. 2003b. *Marshland of Cities: Deltaic Landscapes and the Evolution of Early Mesopotamian Civilization.* (Ph.D. dissertation), University of California, San Diego.

Safar, Fuad, Mohammed Ali Mustafa & Seton Lloyd 1981. *Eridu.* Baghdad: Ministry of Culture and Information.

Schmidt, J. 1974. 'Zwei Tempel der Obed-Zeit in Uruk', *Baghdader Mitteilungen*, 7, 173-87.

Stein, Gil 1994. 'Economy, Ritual, and Power in Ubaid Mesopotamia'. In: G. Stein & M. Rothman (eds.), *Chiefdoms and Early States in the Near East.* Prehistory Press: Monographs in World Archaeology 18, 35-45.

Stronach, David 1961. 'The excavations at Ras Al Amiya', *Iraq*, 23, 95-137.

Suleiman, Antoine & Olivier Nieuwenhuyse 2002. 'Tell Boueid II, A Late Neolithic Village on the Middle Khabur', *Subartu*, 11.

Thuesen, Ingolf 1989. 'Diffusion of Ubaid Pottery into Western Syria'. In: Henrickson & Thuesen (eds.) 1989, 419-37.

Thuesen, Ingolf 2000. Ubaid Expansion in the Khabur. New Evidence from Tell Mashnaqa', *Subartu*, 7, 71-79.

Tobler, A.J. 1950. *Excavations at Tepe Gawra,* Vol. 2. Philadelphia: University Museum.

Uerpmann, H.-P. & M. Uerpmann 1996. Ubaid pottery in the eastern Gulf – new evidence from Umm al-Qawain (UAE)', *Arabian Archaeology and Epigraphy*, 7, 125-39.

Vosmer, Tom 2000. 'Ships in the ancient Arabian Sea', *Proceedings of the Seminar for Arabian Studies*, 30, 235-42.

Wilkinson, T.J. & D.J. Tucker 1995. *Settlement Development in the North Jazira, Iraq.* (Iraq Archaeological Reports, 3). Warminster: Aris & Phillips.

Wright, Henry T. 1969. *The Administration of Rural Production in an Early Mesopotamian Town.* Ann Arbor: Museum of Anthropology, University of Michigan.

Wright, H.T., E.S.A. Rupley, J. Ur, J. Oates & E. Ganem 2003. 'Preliminary Report on the 2002 Tell Brak Sustaining Area Survey', Presented to the Director General of Antiquities and Museums, Damascus.

Zarins, Juris 1992. 'The Early Settlement of Southern Mesopotamia: a Review of Recent Historical, Geological, and Archaeological Research', *JAOS*, 112, 55-77.

Ziegler, Charlotte 1953. *Die Keramik von der Qal'a des Haggi Mohammad.* Berlin: Gebr. Mann Verlag.

Notes

1 The site was discovered by André Parrot in 1967 (Tell el-Oualy, 1967, 43); a surface examination was carried out by Jean-Louis Huot in 1970 (Huot 1971). The site was subsequently recorded as Tell Awayli in the Warka survey (Adams & Nissen 1972, site 460). Excavation reports are listed in the bibliography; see also the Huot paper in the Elsinore publication (1989, 19-42) and Huot 1994, 107-31.

2 Note that the incised sherd identified as 'Hassuna' in Hole 1977, fig. 51:g is in fact Samarran; no Hassuna pottery has as yet been identified at Choga Mami or in Khuzistan, although there are possibly some painted and incised Hassuna sherds at Tell es-Sawwan.

3 These distinctive vessels are known from Eridu from 'temples' XIII to VIII, that is, end of Ubaid 2 and Ubaid 3 (Safar *et al.* 1981, fig. 73) and from Ubaid 3 levels at Tepe Gawra (Tobler 1950, 136); more recently they have been found at small sites such as Ras al Amiya (Stronach 1961, pl. 56) and Songor A in the Hamrin where one was recovered from an Ubaid grave (Kamada & Ohtsu 1991, pl. 7). The Gawra and Ras al Amiya examples do not come from ritual contexts but from occupation debris.

4 Observations made on the basis of sherds available in the 1950s in Antioch, Adana, London and Cambridge, and on the then unpublished Braidwood 'Amuq volume plates.

5 These analyses included the very distinctive type illustrated in fig. 3, sherds of which proved largely of local manufacture, including examples from Choga Mami and Ras al Amiya. Sherds from the very distinctive tortoise vase type and from bowls with an internal rosette pattern (as in Stronach 1962, pl. 48:2) were also analysed, of which one Choga Mami example and one of three from Ras al Amiya showed some non-local characteristics. A number of the analysed vessel types have recently been found at H3 in Kuwait (Carter 2002, fig. 6).

Messages in Stone

The Megaliths of the Nebo Region in Jordan[1]

INGOLF THUESEN

Back in the 1950s a remarkable archaeological discovery was made at the small village, Tustrup, in central Jutland. On a terrace next to a small brook the remains of three megalithic structures were located, two dolmens and one passage grave, dating to the neolithic period. While such stone monuments already were well known from Danish prehistory – dolmens have as a matter of fact become a national symbol – in this case they were associated with a horse-shoe shaped building placed in the centre of the megalithic complex. Inside the structure was found a large amount of offering vessels, and consequently the site was understood as a place for rituals associated with megalithic burial rituals (Kjærum 1955 and 1957).

Several thousands of kilometres separate Tustrup from the dolmen fields in the Gebel Nebo region in central Jordan. Despite this geographical distance there are links other than between how people during the late 4th and early 3rd millennia expressed their concern for death. One of the young archaeologists working at Tustrup was Peder Mortensen, who about forty years later again took up his interest for megalithic monuments. This time he did so by directing a field project in the major wadi systems surrounding Gebel Nebo located southwest of Madaba, where the plain drops into the Jordan rift valley (fig. 1). While the Tustrup monument in many ways fell within archaeologically well-known neolithic traditions in Denmark, the existence of large megalithic fields in central Jordan were only provisionally documented and far from well understood. This was probably one good reason for Peder Mortensen to take up the challenge. Therefore, in 1992 he initiated a survey in the region, which should shed light on these picturesque relics of the past. The survey has now been terminated, but the project still continues as some of the discovered monuments need a detailed recording and study in order to improve our understanding of their function and date. For instance, in these years the impressive and enigmatic site known as Conder's circle is being measured, drawn and partly excavated.

Fig. 1. A general view of the Nebo region.

This contribution presents some observations made in connection with the study of megalithic traditions in the Nebo region, following the result generated by Peder Mortensen's devoted commitment to investigate the area. It should be mentioned that the survey not only recorded megalithic structures, but any remains of human activities from the very early Lower Palaeolithic stone tools to Ottoman architecture of the 18th and 19th century AD.[2] It has revealed a long tradition in the region for building megalithic stone structures of which dolmens are only one main type. From working in the region it soon became obvious that megaliths were erected with attention to the topography of the surrounding landscape and therefore in most instances built to be seen by the living, despite their primary function as burial monuments for the dead. It is therefore argued here, that the megaliths can be perceived as a segment of an ancient regional communication system as they in many cases are highly visible from a distance. It is also emphasized that the dolmen is understood as reflecting a complexity of functions ranging from the practical needs for burying the physical remains of a human being through communicating symbolic messages of cultural identity.

The megaliths and dolmens of the Nebo region

Dolmen is a word used in Bretagne for a certain type of megalithic monument with the shape of a table. Dolmen means table, and the structures actually look very much like huge stone tables. A subsequent association to ritual activities was logical: according to tradition they were gigantic offering tables of the past. For people living in a dolmen district these peculiar monuments, based as they were on their direct appeal to fantasy, could be explained in many ways. But also artists and writers have been attracted by the romantic and eternal nature of the monuments, seeing them as an expression of our ancestors way of sculpturing the landscape with stones. And not least the dolmens have generated a number of speculations and interpretations from archaeologists who, on the other hand, felt they needed to tell the 'true' cultural history of the megaliths. All in all, dolmens have, due to their monumental character in the landscape, generated a high amount of speculation and interpretation. That fact in itself underscores the meaning of the monuments as visual communicating systems, perhaps even surpassing their funerary function.

Dolmens therefore were built to be seen in the landscape. Not only were they large structures, but also they were located in a way which tended to alter the surrounding landscape. The position was a deliberate attempt to remodel and to add cultural meaning to nature. For the archaeologist it has also been puzzling that the tradition is distributed over an enormous geographical region – from the Middle East (dolmens are reported as far southeast as Yemen) to Scandinavia – within a rather limited time horizon. At a point the phenomenon led many archaeologists to accept them as an expression of an 'Old World' culture stretching from the Levant through Sardinia over the Iberian Peninsula and Bretagne to Ireland and England, where they became associated with the druids. They occur frequently in northern Germany and Scandinavia. In particular, the tradition has flourished in Denmark and southern Sweden. However, this diffusion of a tradition was not accepted by the positivist school of archaeologists developing during the 60s and 70s as there was no obvious explanation for such a large scale distribution of cultural tradition.

Cultural diffusion is, however, much more than migrating human groups. It is indeed axiomatic that people learn and that knowledge is communicated. We can therefore accept cultural diffusion in an archaeological explanation which contains, in particular, a broader definition including the diffusion of more than people or materials. The diffusion of ideas and concepts including all possible alterations and local adaptations is, as a matter of fact, one of the strongest tools in archaeological explanation of cultural process.

The dolmens and megaliths in the Nebo region offer another chapter to the book on dolmens and megaliths worldwide and contribute another example of our ancestors' way of communicating with large boulders and stone structures. In addition, the systematic recording of dolmens and megaliths in the Nebo region has given us an important and needed understanding of the dating of these monuments which, due to thousands of years of exposure, are almost void of associated artifacts and therefore lack secure dating criteria.

The survey of the Nebo region

A Danish team has carried out a survey since 1992 in the Mount Nebo Region. During five campaigns of recognisance in a 64 km² large area around the Siyagha (the Moses memorial) all archaeological remains have been visited and mapped. In total, 747 sites of interest have been recorded.

The topography of the survey area is complicated and impossible to cover intensively in a systematic way. Steep slopes and deeply cut wadies characterise the area with an elevation ranging from 800 metres above sea level in the east, on top of the plateau, to 100 metres below sea level on the western outskirts of the survey area in the Jordan valley. Main features are the two important wadi systems, Wadi Jadidah and Wadi ʿAyun Musa. Between them rises the plateau in a formation that is known today as Gebel Nebo.

The survey was carried out by walking through the landscape in areas which might contain remains of archaeological importance, for example, terraces and plateaus along the slopes of the wadies. Also the tops of hills and adjacent slopes were visited. All known sites and newly discovered sites were mapped in order to produce a complete map of the region.

A major part of the 747 sites identified were stone built graves or megalithic structures, and of these the dolmens made up a substantial part. One dolmen field alone comprised almost 200 dolmens or megalithic monuments, namely the Jadidah dolmens field, which already was recognized by Colonel Conder in his survey of the region in the early 1880s (Conder 1889). The dolmen field is located on the southern side of the wadi close to the spring. Another dolmen field is located on the southern slopes of the hills adjacent to ʿAjun Musa, between the modern road leading to the Dear Sea and the spring. In the landscape the dolmens can be seen as structures crawling up the hills in some planned pattern, the logical explanation of which still remain a puzzle.

A typical dolmen consists of 3-4 vertical side stones, ca. 1.5 meter tall, carrying a larger horizontal cap stone measuring 2-3 metres in diameter (fig. 2). The dolmen normally opens to one side. The floor is a large flat stone, which perhaps is covering the burial place. This, however, has to be demonstrated by future excavations. Today the dolmens stand empty in the landscape. They were probably

Fig 2. Dolmens in the Jadidah dolmen field.

left open and accessible already in the past and have consequently been a target for looting and secondary use, turning archaeological dating into a nightmare. Sherds of basalt and pottery vessels found scattered around the dolmens were the only finds which indicated that offerings had taken place inside or at the dolmens. The few fragments that were found support a dating of the dolmens within the Late Chalcolithic-EBA period, which is also suggested from observations on the contextual position of the dolmen fields in the region.

Another megalithic structure which associates to the dolmens is the so-called menhir. This structure was encountered in the same area as the dolmens and appeared as large upright standing limestone. It normally measures 2-3 metres in height and consists of one large, free-standing, monolith placed so that a flat front side faces the wadi (fig. 3).

A third megalithic structure also connected to the dolmens are rows of stones. They are often very difficult to identify in the landscape. Either are they fragmentary and inconclusive as stones have been removed or reused for later building activities. Or they may resemble terrace walls for fields, which often are dating to much later periods. But there are some clear indications that in some

Fig. 3. Menhir at the Ma'in dolmen field.

cases they indeed are old and associated with menhirs and dolmens. First of all they are not built as walls but rather as lines of boulders. While terrace walls tend to follow the horizontal contours of the hill slopes, the ancient stone lines often follow vertical or oblique patterns. And an even much more clear indication of their meaning is, that in some instances they are integrated parts of a megalithic complex, which comprises dolmens and menhirs. Typical rows of boulders form connecting lines between dolmens (fig. 4). This confirms the proposed contextual dating of this group of megalithic structures. Dolmens, menhirs and rows of stones are contemporary.

Fig. 4. Row of stone connecting dolmens in the Jadidah dolmen field.

The last group of megalithic monuments are circular tombs which occur frequently throughout the entire region. They may consist of several concentric circles of stones with a burial chamber in the centre often constructed with larger boulders (fig. 5). The structure may measure several metres in diameter and be delimited by a circle of upright standing stones. Smaller types can measure less than two metres in diameter and be places together in groups on plateaus or terraces.

The circular tombs are also placed with attention to the topography, but in a different way than the dolmens. The larger well-built monuments are often placed on prominent hill tops or on plateaus and expressing an individual and dominating character. If the dolmens express group affinity, the larger stone circles express individuality. In some cases the structures were covered with stones which must have given them a different appearance in the landscape in the past. Today, unfortunately, most of the monuments have been looted. This sad fact has left us with only a few potsherds or fragments of bones and another extremely difficult dating situation. But there are reported finds of pottery which support a dating of these circular tombs to the 2nd millennium BC (Palumbo 1998).

Fig. 5. Circular tomb in the Nebo region.

The chronology of Megalithic structures in the Nebo region

Some stray finds of potsherds and fragments of basalt vessels around the mega-liths have provided us with some dating hints. For the dolmens the date would fall within the 4th millennium in what should be the equivalent of very Late Chalkolithic and EBA and most likely the EBA I. As the menhirs and stone lines are features in the landscape that relate to the dolmens, a similar date is suggested for those monuments. However, the circular tombs and mounds of stones are clearly later and date after 2000 BC or MB IIC according to a pub-lished find (Palumbo op.cit.).

Compared to the dating suggested by other authors, our dating is in com-plete agreement with the dates of dolmens north east of the Dead Sea given by Kay Prag (Prag 1995), but is in conflict with the dates suggested by Epstein and Zohar, who place the related or similar dolmens in Galilee and Golan in the EB/MB transitional phase, that is late 3rd millennium BC (Epstein 1985; Zohar 1989 and 1992). Epstein reached her conclusions based on an attempt to set up a typology for any megalith structures observed here. However, the suggested typology does not compensate for temporal variations, and also the typology does not clearly discriminate dolmens from circular tombs in the way it has been observed in the Nebo region. The Zohar type A, and perhaps variations D, E, and F, resembles the Nebo dolmens, while types B and C could be circular tombs (Zohar op.cit.). Zohar's dating of the structures to the late 3rd millennium sup-ports the date of the corresponding Nebo circular tombs.

The case exemplifies the danger of applying typological dating for non-lin-ear and non-continuous sequences. In this case dolmens and circular tombs are two different and non-connected traditions separated in time by more than one thousand years. Any general megalithic typology should therefore be avoided before we have access to a secure alternative dating criteria, e.g. pottery, C-14 etc.

Function or meaning of the Nebo megaliths

In particular two authors have approached the question of function or mean-ing of the megaliths, first Zohar (1992) and shortly hereafter Prag (1995). Both scholars apply analogy to contemporary *bedu* tribes in order to explain the tra-dition. Prag's hypothesis is in particular of interest as it introduces important contextual observations by analysing the dolmens within the cultural landscape of the region. One conclusion is that these monuments were not alone associ-ated with a non-sedentary population, but more likely with a pastoral lifestyle practising seasonal migration between the highland and the valley. Zohar, on

Fig. 6. Conder's circle at the Jadidah dolmen field.

the other hand, emphasizes the location of the monuments in territories with little agricultural value, placed on hill slopes in order to facilitate the construction of the monuments. Also the location of the megaliths at passageways of transhuman cultures has been suggested as an explanation. Other speculations concern the tendency of sedentary agriculturalist to bury their dead underground while nomads are afraid to hurt the soil and also lacking the resources to dig out underground tombs. Also it is mentioned that the size of the dolmens allow for the suggestion that they belonged to a pastoral elite.

The situation in the Nebo region, and particularly around Wadi Jadidah, has added useful information to the discussion. First of all it is clear from the survey that the dolmen fields are not isolated but rather part of a complex system of settlements and some other large structures that we still do not understand, for instance, a large circular rampart, ca. 100 m in diameter, which already was recognized by Conder in his survey in the 1880s. It is located on a lower elevation than the dolmens on a small plateau above the spring (fig. 6). This is the structure which now is being studied in detail by the survey team. Potsherds and other materials found on the surface date to the EBA I-II. Test trenches and excavations in the central part of the structure reveal that the central wall crossing the structure, and shown on Conder's rendering of the monument, did not belong to the original structure but was built during the Byzantine period, and that the circular rampart is enclosing a large building on stone foundations. Conder already pointed out the relation between this structure and the dolmens, and the new investigations confirm this observation. There is a match of the small finds collected in the dolmen field and finds excavated *in situ* in the circular monument.

Even more surprisingly, a rather large settlement from the EBA contemporary to the dolmens and the large circle was discovered during the survey. It is extended over several hectars on both sides of the wadi close to the spring, but without any visual fortification wall or tell formation. The EBA I period in this region therefore includes a large settlement, a large circular structure and a dolmen field. Inspired by a well-known terminology for large non-urban neolithic settlements in Jordan, it is tempting to call this phenomenon a mega-town phase in order to distinguishing it from the well-known pristine urbanism in Mesopotamia.

In the light of these new discoveries we can now say that the dolmens at Ain Jadidah were part of a complex settlement pattern of a rather sedentary character. The dolmens were built with attention to the topography following the slopes of the hillside, radiating from the town in the valley toward the top of the hill. Sometimes they were connected with lines of stones and free-standing menhirs.

This pattern may reflect some basic socio-ideological structures of the society. The dolmens can be understood as a collective burial tradition erected according to lineage or kinship structures. For instance, the lay-out in the landscape may symbolize family trees. But, as mentioned above dolmens should not be interpreted as burial sites only. They were built primarily to be seen, placed on hill slopes radiating from town centres. Such monuments would communicate a visual message to all people passing by or living in the vicinity, in the past as they still do today. They communicated this message, as did their counterparts in Denmark or other places – a message more which it is impossible, however, to translate into a concrete concept. On a small scale they may express symbolic messages to a community, as do the pyramids of Egypt or the temple platforms in Iraq. In that respect it is remarkable that the dolmens in Jordan tie into a global old world mental system which can be followed all the way from Jordan to Scandinavia. Without saying that there existed a physical contact through this vast area we may gain insight by analysing the dolmens and megalithic structures as a whole – in a worldwide context – if we want to approach there

Fig. 7. Dolmens at the Ma'in quarry.

true meaning. A world system theory should not only apply to economic and social institutions, but may as well concern mental templates. Such a template was probably active during the 4th millennium. The dolmens and 4th millennium megaliths are an obvious topics for such a project and may improve our analytical approach and understanding of the dolmens in Jordan, where they tend in some ways to differ from the traditions we normally encounter in the region, e.g. rock-cut or underground tombs.

To return briefly to the ritual building found in Tustrup in Jutland: It would not be surprising to find the remains of a similar and even more sophisticated ritual installation in central Jordan. There are candidates for such a monument, namely the dolmen field at the Ma'in quarries located ca. 20 km south of Nebo. Here the pattern known from the Ain Jadidah field is repeated: dolmens, menhirs and rows of stones (fig. 7). When the survey team visited the site during the 1990's we found a high concentration of menhirs set up in structures that resembled building foundations or complex ritual installations on a plateau at the foot of the slopes containing dolmens. Dolmens sometimes connected with rows of stone radiated up the surrounding hills from this plateau. When we visited the place some years later the site was used as a camp for three or four *bedu* families, which prevented us from making any detailed investigations, but in some way the setting had a strange resemblance to the situation known from Tustrup in Jutland.[3]

Conclusion

Due to the initiative by Peder Mortensen we have today a much better understanding of the megalithic traditions of central Jordan. Some of the major observations can be summarized as follows:

- dolmens and circular tombs are two chronologically separate traditions, dating to different and unconnected periods
- megalithic structures can be characterized as elements of a visual communication system. Dolmens reflect group identity consisting of many similar structures connected with rows of stones and placed in the vicinity of a town. Large circular tombs reflect individuality being located at hill tops or plateaus and have no clear association to settlements. They appear rather to symbolize an elite burial.
- dolmens are associated with sedentary settlements located around perennial springs. That does not mean that they may not be associated with a pastoral life style, but rather that they tie into a complex subsistence pattern with interrelated pastoral and sedentary subsistence strategies
- dolmens are placed with attention to the landscape and to other dolmens and with connection to ritual installations such as menhirs.
- dolmens are highly communicative, but the message today is most likely not the same as in the past.

References

Conder, C.R. 1889. *The Survey of Eastern Palestine*. London.
Epstein, C. 1985. 'Dolmens Excavated in the Golan', *Atiqot English Series*, XVIII, 20-58.
Mortensen, P. & I. Thuesen 1998. 'The Prehistoric Periods'. In: M. Piccirillo & E. Alliata (eds.), *Mount Nebo. New Archaeological Excavations 1967-1997*. (Studium Biblicum Franciscanum. Collectio Maior 27). Jerusalem, 85-99.
Kjærum, P. 1955. 'Tempelhus fra Stenalderen', *KUML*, 7-35.
Kjærum, P. 1957. 'Storstensgrave ved Tustrup', *KUML*, 9-23.

Palumbo, G. 1998. 'The Bronze Age'. In: M. Piccirillo & E. Alliata (eds.), *Mount Nebo. New Archaeological Excavations 1967-1997*. (Studium Biblicum Franciscanum. Collectio Maior 27). Jerusalem, 100-109.

Prag, K. 1995. 'The Dead Sea Dolmens: Death and the Landscape'. In: S. Campbell & A. Green (eds.), *The Archaeology of Death in the Ancient Near East* (Oxbow Monograph, 51). 75-84.

Zohar, M. 1989 'Rogem Hiri: A megalithic Monument in the Golan', *IEJ*, 39, 18-31.

Zohar, M. 1992 'Megalithic Cemeteries in the Levant. In: 'Bar-Yosef, O. & Khazanov, A. (eds.), *Pastoralism in the Levant*. (Monographs in World Archaeology, 10). Madison: Prehistory Press, 43-64.

Notes

1 A version of this paper was presented at the Eight International Conference on the History and Archaeology of Jordan, Sydney 2001. I am grateful to Peder Mortensen for generously allowing me to draw on the results of the Mt. Nebo survey in this paper.

2 A preliminary report has appeared in 1998 (Mortensen & Thuesen). The survey team included Peder Mortesen, Inge Mortensen, Francesco Bennedetucci and the author.

3 Recently a recording of the Ma'in monuments has been initiated by the Canadian group of archaeologists working in Madaba (Harrison, personal communication).

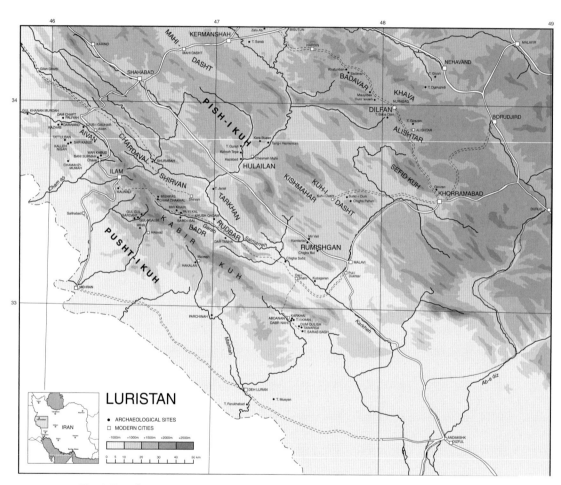

Fig. 1. Map of Luristan

The Chronology of the Pusht-i Kuh, Luristan

Results of the Belgian Archaeological Expedition in Iran

ERNIE HAERINCK & BRUNO OVERLAET

Luristan remains one of these enigmatic regions of Iran where only a small number of archaeologists were able to pursue innovative fieldwork. Peder Mortensen is certainly one of them. Therefore, we felt it was an appropriate idea, on the occasion of his seventieth birthday to contribute a paper which discusses the chronology of the Pusht-i Kuh region, based on the fieldwork of the Belgian Archaeological Mission in Iran.

The geography and the Belgian research

The Luristan region is located in W-Iran and belongs to the Western part of the Zagros chain (fig. 1). The area can be subdivided into the Pusht-i Kuh ('behind the mountain' from the perspective of the Central Iranian Plateau) and the Pish-i Kuh ('before the mountain'). The Zagros chain and particularly the area of the Pusht-i Kuh creates the geographical border between the Iranian plateau and the Mesopotamian lowlands.

The Pusht-i Kuh belongs to the modern province of Ilam and is usually seen as the area confined to the West of the NW-SE running Kabir Kuh mountain ridge (literally 'the big mountain'). The Saimarreh is the main river, which runs further South into the Khuzistan lowland were it changes name to Karkheh. Rather than the Kabir Kuh mountain range, the Saimarreh river can be considered as the real north-eastern frontier of the Belgian research in W-Iran.

The Pusht-i Kuh is characterised by intra-mountainous small plains or valleys and a rugged countryside. Larger plains are extending towards the Khuzistan province in the South and the Pish-i Kuh in the East. One of the problems of Pusht-i Kuh archaeology is the fact that permanent dwellings are seemingly very rare. Only extensive burial-grounds represent the main archaeological testimonies, which allow for the elaboration of a chronological framework and regional distribution patterns. This could of course reflect that most inhabitants were semi-nomadic or nomadic and moved around with their herds and lived in tents made of goathair or reedmats. However, we should be careful and realise that geomorphologic conditions largely dictate the present landscape. The build-up of sediments in the valleys, or other processes, may have largely obliterated settlement sites under thick layers of soil. A renewed study with a more pluridisciplinary approach is therefore badly needed.

As to historical geography, there exists no written evidence on the populations which inhabited the region, although some cuneiform texts refer to mountain tribes living to the East of Mesopotamia. Only from the Iron Age onwards do we have some more information, although the interpretation of regional names and toponyms remains a matter of debate.

We assume that the area remained largely uncontrolled by its mighty neighbours, due to the difficult terrain which prohibits easy access, though Mesopotamian and – to a lesser degree – Elamite influences are attested. This observation, however, does not necessarily imply that the Pusht-i Kuh was subdued by lowland populations.

The Belgian research in the Pusht-i Kuh was the initiative of the late Louis Vanden Berghe (1923-1993). He was Professor of Near Eastern Art and Archaeology at Ghent University and responsible for the section 'Iran' at the 'Royal Museums of Art and History' in Brussels. Vanden Berghe's interest in the Luristan problem was largely due to the important collection of Luristan Bronzes kept in the Brussels Museum. Since all these objects were the result of clandestine excavations, however, their mysterious beauty was its main value. For research purposes, such as the elaboration of a chronological framework, they offered little information. To tackle this problem, Vanden Berghe decided that the only solution was to go out in the field and try to solve some of the problems before everything disappeared due to ongoing illegal digging or modernisation.

During fifteen yearly seasons (between 1965-1979) of 3 months each, a small Belgian research team was active in the Pusht-i Kuh. Although the field conditions were rough, the tenacity and perseverance of its director and its team resulted in a wealth of information. However, many questions still remain unanswered and further fieldwork is badly needed.

The prospections and excavations allow us to distinguish three major phases, dating from the 5th millennium BC to the 7th century BC.

The Chalcolithic Period

In the Pusht-i Kuh, the oldest tombs excavated by the Belgian team belong to the Middle Chalcolithic era and are to be dated to the second half of the 5th/first half of the 4th millennium BC. Two burial grounds were excavated. At Hakalan 36 tombs were researched, while at Parchinah more than 160 were found. At the

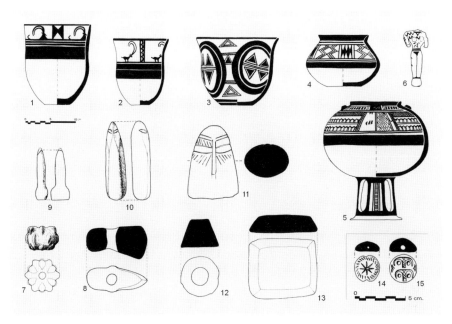

Fig. 2. Middle Chalcolithic burial goods

latter site many tombs remain to be excavated. Both graveyards must have been in use for a considerable time span and for several generations.

The tombs are stone-built and 1.60 to 2.40 m in length. The four sides are constructed with upright standing stone slabs. Most tombs were intended for individual burials. Skeletons had mostly disappeared, although some were still preserved. Usually, the buried person lay in an outstretched position, apparently on the back, with the arms extended along the body, the hands resting sometimes on the abdomen. A hole in some of the skulls indicated that trepanation occurred. Some tombs contained no burialgoods, but usually the deceased was accompanied by a couple of objects for the afterlife. These objects included unpainted and painted pottery (fig. 2: 1-5), stone vessels, button-seals (fig. 2: 14-15), maceheads (fig. 2: 7), axes and hammer-axes (fig. 2: 8), handstones and grinding slabs, presumably for cosmetics (fig. 2: 12-13), pestles (fig. 2: 9-10) and some tools. Beads were very rare. Only one copper macehead was recovered. At last, two pottery figurines were found. One represents a standing woman (fig. 2: 6), the other shows an acephalic bovid. The decoration on the stone seals is mostly geometrical or floral. Some show animals (e.g. a snake, a lizard or stylised bucrania, fig. 2: 15).

Pottery was by far the most represented object. Common was a buff coloured pottery with black painted decoration. The painted motifs were rich and varied.

Besides purely geometrical motifs, stylised heads of goats and complete goats also occurred.

The Uruk period, of the second half of the 4th millennium BC, is not attested in the Pusht-i Kuh, which could be explained by the fact that the population may have been attracted by the wealth of the growing cities and villages in the Mesopotamian and SW-Iranian plains. On the other hand, this might also be mere chance of research. Maybe the locals changed their burial practices and buried their dead in simple pit burials, which are very difficult to detect.

The Bronze Age

The Bronze Age represents a long period of more than 1500 years and is usually subdivided into three periods: the Early, Middle and Late Bronze Age. However, even the Early Bronze Age must be further subdivided into an Early, Middle and Late phase, in view of changes in the tomb structures and in the material culture, particularly in the ceramics and the metal objects. This phenomenon is further complicated by the distinction of three cultural regions within the Pusht-i Kuh. One of the main problems which remain is the lack of sufficient representative finds from all three regions in all the chronological phases, thus leaving us with a rather blurred and incomplete picture.

The Early Bronze Age

The *earliest phase* of the Early Bronze Age dates back to the late 4th/early 3rd millennium BC and is represented by small, mainly individual graves at Mir Khair and some graves at Kalleh Nisar. This phase is of the same chronological horizon as the Djemdet Nasr period and the early Early Dynastic I period in Mesopotamia. In this phase, the graves are stonelined and usually have a flat cover consisting of several slabs. Some tombs have a gabled roof, however. Usually these graves are between 0.80 to 1.40 m in length, but some larger tombs do occur as well. The floor is made of flat slabs on which the body and objects rested. The preserved skeletons all lay in a flexed position, on their left or right side. The number of burial gifts was mostly very limited. The pottery consists of a rather coarse, handmade common ware of a brownish-black colour containing large grits (fig. 3: 1-2). These vessels represent the daily cooking recipients. Another group is the fine common ware, most of which is wheelthrown. Finally, a limited number of vessels belong to a painted group, whether monochrome or polychrome (fig. 3: 3-4). They usually have a carinated profile. The geometrical motifs are mainly painted on the shoulder. Usually, these are repeated cross-hatched triangles bordered by black lines filled in with red, and sometimes

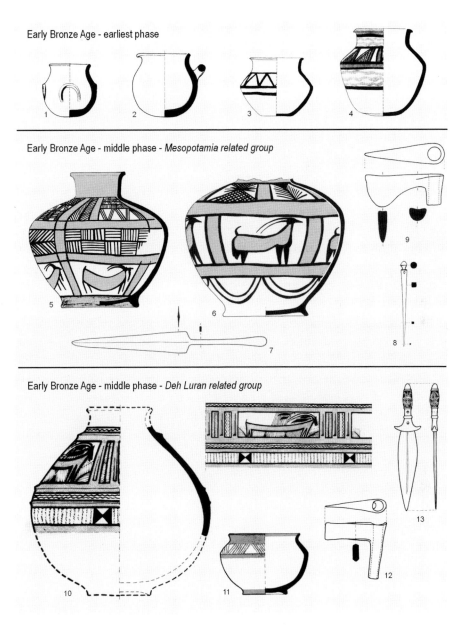

Fig. 3. Early Bronze Age burial goods from the Pusht-i Kuh.

separated by vertical lines equally filled in with red paint. Below the carination, painted wavy bands sometimes occur.

Besides a couple of carnelian beads, some marine shells and microliths, there were also simple copper items. There are awls, flat axes, some coiled bracelets and finger rings of copper wire and some simple tanged knives.

Middle Phase

For a large part of the 3rd millennium BC (from Early Dynastic I/II to the Akkadian period in terms of Mesopotamian chronology), we have to make a distinction between three regions, clearly identified by their painted pottery. The associations of this painted pottery allows us to distinguish a Mesopotamia related group, a Deh Luran related group and a Pish-i Kuh related group. The remainder of the burial goods, however, particularly the copper/bronze objects, are largely identical throughout these three regions.

a) The Mesopotamia related group (fig. 3: 5-9)

The tombs at Bani Surmah (fig. 4) and Kalleh Nisar, belong to the largest ever built in the Pusht-i Kuh. The smallest ones are some 5 m. long, most are 9 to 14 m. One tomb at Bani Surmah even measured 16 m. in length and was 3.10 m. wide and is thus by far the largest ever found in Luristan. The graves are very well built with large boulders and are covered by a flat roof of big stones, each often weighing several hundred kilos. The efforts to built these tombs must have been considerable. Unfortunately most of the skeletons had fully decayed and it was impossible to establish how many interments had taken place, or how precisely the deceased had been deposited in the tomb.

The main problem with these tombs is the fact that they have often been disturbed and have been re-used for a very long time, sometimes even until the Old Babylonian period. Therefore, it is difficult to distinguish separate clusters of objects which could be attributed to an individual. Also it is difficult to work out which inhumation was the earliest and which one the latest. The absence of clearly distinguishable skeletons complicates the attribution. All possible associations of objects have to be carefully analysed.

A lot of pottery recovered from the graves is badly broken and fragmentary and consists largely of coarse common ware vessels of a broad necked type. There is also a fine common ware, mainly jars with carinated shoulder, a broad straight or concave neck and a ring base. These are imports or local imitations of Mesopotamian types. A characteristic group are the locally produced polychrome painted vessels. The whole body of the vessel is decorated and bulls or goats, often with birds on their backs, are depicted on the lower part of the vessel (fig. 3: 5-6). They usually have rounded shoulders. It is clear that this group, although inspired by the production in the Hamrin and Diyala regions in Eastern Mesopotamia, is clearly of local manufacture. The presence of an unpierced lug on the shoulder of some vessels points to an Early Dynastic I date, or eventually to Early Dynastic II.

That the tombs remained in use during the Early Dynastic III and Akkadian periods, is evidenced particularly by several Mesopotamian cylinder seals which

Fig. 4. View of the collective Early Bronze Age tombs at Bani Surmah.

were discovered in the tombs. Also metal objects, such as copper/bronze flat or shafthole axes (fig. 3: 9), daggers, saws, needles, cosmetic sets, bronze rings and vessels are represented. Identical items have been found in the famous Royal Tombs of Ur, in Southern Iraq and at several other sites. Whether Luristan imported these objects, or produced them on a large scale as export products, remains unanswered. For the moment we favour the idea that they are mainly Mesopotamian or SW-Iranian products which found their way into mountainous West-Iran. These imports could be the result of commercial activities, but it cannot be ruled out either that the mountain people acquired them by raids into the lowlands. Anyhow, shell beads from the Persian Gulf also reached the backward and isolated region of Luristan and may testify to the existence of long distance trade.

b) The Deh Luran related group (fig. 3: 10-13)
Megalithic tombs were also built in the Southern part of the Pusht-i Kuh. Several of them were excavated in the area of Abdanan, bordering the Khuzistan plain where the Elamite culture developed. These tombs were 6 to 10 m long and were covered with a flat roof. They have straight sides built in horizontal layers or with upright standing slabs. Metal artefacts are very rare. Also these tombs remained in use for several generations.

Besides some common ware, there is a fine, light-brown to light-orange coloured pottery. Of interest are mono- and polychrome painted vessels. The monochrome ones have a simple geometric decoration and are mostly small (fig. 3: 11). The most characteristic shape among the polychrome vessels are large jars with a rather broad but low concave neck, and a bulbous or oval body on a ring base (fig. 3: 10). Also typical is the common presence of a ridge on the transition from neck to shoulder, and a single or double plastic ridge on the transition from shoulder to body. Painting is usually of a bright red, black is used mainly for some geometrical patterns. Very characteristic for this pottery is that the shoulder between the ribs is decorated in metopes with goats having an elongated body on which birds are sitting (fig. 3: 10). Sometimes there are trees with large extending and finely painted branches instead of animals. The painting is usually finely and carefully executed. The dating of these vessels remains a matter of debate. Only a few bronzes, such as shaft hole axes (fig. 3: 12) were found, as well as a beautiful dagger of mid-3rd millennium BC date (fig. 3: 13).

c) The Pish-i Kuh related group (fig. 5: 1-5)

The few excavated graves which belong to this group are in all aspects similar to most Pish-i Kuh ones. They have a gabled roof and were equally made for multiple interments. They are between 6 to 8 m long and also remained in use over a long period. Particularly the tombs from Dar Tanha are representative for this period.

Burial gifts consist mainly of painted monochrome pottery (fig. 5: 1-2), but also include some copper/bronze weapons and tools. There are flat and shaft-hole axes (fig. 5: 4) and daggers, saws and awls. Exceptional was the discovery of a small cast sculpture of a wild boar (fig. 5: 5). Jars with monochrome painted decoration and with a rounded or sharply carinated shoulder are clearly related to the central Pish-i Kuh (fig. 5: 1-2). A few vessels with polychrome decorations link this region also to the western group (fig. 5: 3). Most likely the monochrome pottery originated in Luristan and spread later to the North (e.g. Godin Tepe III: 6, in the Kangavar area) and the South (Susa, Ville Royale I, period IVA (?)).

Late Phase

In the last centuries of the 3rd millennium BC, no large tombs were built anymore. The graves of this period are small and individual. The most characteristic feature of these graves is the fact that they have three walls only and are c. 1.20 to 1.70 m long. Usually these tombs do not contain many objects (fig. 5: 6-12). Typical are painted, small monochrome jars with a quite large concave neck and slightly carinated or rounded shoulder and rounded bottom (fig. 5: 6-7). This pottery is largely inspired by Pish-i Kuh types, but the decoration is

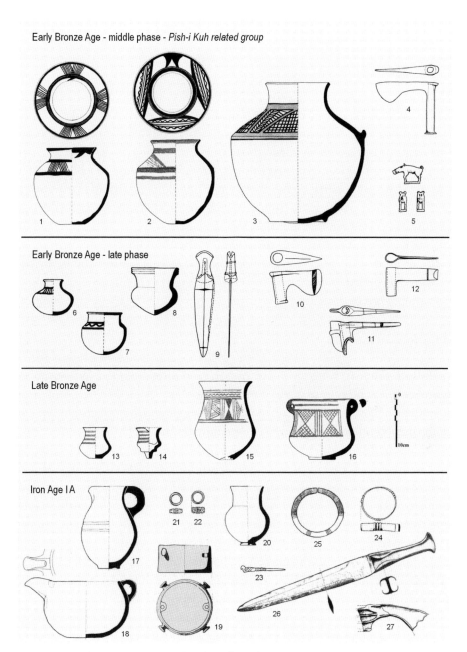

Fig. 5. Bronze and Iron Age burial goods from the Pusht-i Kuh.

simpler and confined to triangles and groups of vertical lines. Some fine buff vessels are undecorated but are clearly of Mesopotamian origin (fig. 5: 8). Metal is rare although small shaft-hole axes do occur (fig. 5: 10-12). Quite specific are the axes made of sheet metal (fig. 5: 12). Simple daggers are equally present (fig. 5: 9). One tomb contained an etched carnelian bead of Indian origin. A few cylinder-seals are typical of the so-called Gutian-style and have crudely executed and hardly recognisable representations.

The Middle and Late Bronze Age (fig. 5: 13-16)

Both periods are badly represented in our records and this could point to an important population reduction in the area. Almost no remains have been recovered in the Pusht-i Kuh. The first centuries of the 2nd millennium BC are only illustrated by some burial goods, mostly unpainted pottery, which were found in re-used graves of the Early Bronze Age. A bronze tankard equally belongs to that phase, as well as some Old Babylonian seals.

The late Bronze Age, around the middle of the 2nd millennium is even more badly documented. Only one tomb at Sarab Bagh could eventually be attributed to that period. It contained some painted pottery (fig. 5: 13-16) and some very simple bronze pins.

The Iron Age

A distinct cultural change with the preceding Bronze Age can be observed in Luristan at the beginning of the Iron Age (ca. 1300/1250 – 650/600 BC). The Late Bronze Age population had a sedentary lifestyle which made maximum use of the natural resources of the region. Agriculture was possible in the wide fertile plains of the Pish-i Kuh, which could sustain a large population. Many important settlement sites are known from the Pish-i Kuh. However, these Bronze Age settlements appear to have been massively deserted at the beginning of the Iron Age around 1300/1250 BC. At that moment, a new culture, the *Luristan Iron Age culture*, appears to have made its appearance. This culture is mostly known because of its 'bronzes' which come from plundered cemeteries and sanctuaries ending up in many museums and collections. The characteristic Luristan bronzes, with their specific and complex figurative iconography, can now be dated more precisely to the Early Iron Age (c. 1300/1250 – 800/750 BC).

The detailed study of the excavations has allowed us to reconsider some of the dating and assumptions that have been made about the Iron Age Luristan population. It made it possible to obtain a better understanding of the chronological evolution of the region and its role in the general cultural and socio-economical events which took place in the ancient Near East. The present knowledge does allow us to advance a number of hypotheses which will have to be put to the test, however, by more and focused field research. At the same time, it also demonstrates the limits of our understanding of the Luristan culture.

The Iranian Iron Age is traditionally divided into three phases, but this system is inadequate in the case of the Pusht-i Kuh. The Iron Age in the Pusht-i Kuh can at present best be discussed in four chronological phases: the Iron IA, the Iron IB-IIA, the Iron IIB and the Iron Age III phase.

The Iron Age IA (ca. 1300/1250-1150 BC)

Habitation sites and tombs from the Late Bronze Age in the north-western Pusht-i Kuh are lacking. However, some of the pottery from Early Iron Age tombs, such as pitchers with pinched spout (fig. 5: 17) and some rare painted vessels, are closely related to the pottery from Late Bronze Age sites in the Pish-i Kuh. This suggests that the Late Bronze Age in the Pusht-i Kuh may not have differed much from that in the Pish-i Kuh where a local Giyan III-II related culture was present (= Godin III, post III-2 graves and III:1). Based on the comparison of pottery shapes with Mesopotamian and Elamite examples, the start of the 'Iron Age' in the Pusht-i Kuh is situated in the beginning of the 13th century BC. The earliest stage is best illustrated by finds from the graveyard at Duruyeh. It is an 'extra-muros' cemetery with individual tombs. Characteristic burial goods are toggle pins and pitchers with a pinched spout (fig. 5: 17). Both types of objects are a continuation of Bronze Age traditions, be it that the pitchers are no longer painted but are made in buff ware. Although a distinctive class of painted ware continues to be found in Iron Age levels in the Pish-i Kuh (so-called 'trickle paint ware' at Tepe Guran), it seems to be completely replaced by buff ware in the Pusht-i Kuh.

The continued occurrence of certain Bronze Age pottery shapes and objects suggests we are not confronted with a radical change as one could, or would, expect with the arrival of a totally new population, replacing that of the Bronze Age. We may rather have to think along the lines that certain changes in the living circumstances (caused by climatological/ecological changes) may have brought about the necessity to adapt to a new lifestyle. It may have favoured the expansion of minorities in the region whose way of life may have been more suited to the new situation. One may think of semi-sedentary or even nomadic groups already present in the region. They could have more easily survived a collapse of the agriculturally oriented food production of the sedentary Bronze Age population.

The presence among the Early Iron Age burial goods of 'Iron IA carinated beakers' (fig. 5: 20), related to Late Kassite pottery from Mesopotamia, points to the existence of commercial relations. Similar beakers occur at Tepe Guran in the Pish-i Kuh. At Duruyeh it was noticed that pitchers were being replaced by teapots (fig. 5: 18), which will remain the distinctive pottery shape throughout the rest of the Iron Age. The Iron IA tombs at Kutal-i Gulgul seem to be slightly younger than those at Duruyeh. They are no longer conceived as individual tombs but are built somewhat larger and are destined to receive a number of consecutive burials. Apart from the Iron IA carinated beakers, other objects such as faience vessels (fig. 5: 19) and particularly a group of decorated shell finger rings of Kassite manufacture (fig. 5: 21-22), indicate continued contacts with Mesopotamia. The geometrically decorated Kassite rings, which were once colourfully inlaid, can in their Mesopotamian context be dated to the last quarter of the 13th century and the first half of the 12th century BC. The end of the Iron IA phase in the Pusht-i Kuh, a phase which is characterised by the presence of imported objects from Kassite Mesopotamia, can be situated around 1150 BC. The military campaign of the Elamite army of Shutruk-Nahhunte around 1160 BC, which resulted in the destruction of the Kassite townships in the Diyala, may have cut off the Pusht-i Kuh from its suppliers. As a result, the deposition of Kassite objects in tombs may have ended not long afterwards.

Although the occurrence of iron, particularly for jewellery, in the Iron Age IA phase is a possibility, it is certainly not distinctive. Anklets, bracelets and finger rings are still made of bronze. Distinctive for the Iron Age I-II phase in the Pusht-i Kuh is the occurrence of bronze bracelets and anklets with incised geometric decorations (fig. 5: 25). Also distinctive for both the Iron Age I and II phases are bronze arrowheads with incised herringbone patterns. Bronze flange-hilted daggers are common among the Iron Age I to IIA burial goods and one specific sub-type seems to be characteristic for the Pusht-i Kuh (fig. 5: 26, 6: 5).

The first elements of the typical Luristan decorative style date back to the Iron Age IA phase. The association with Kassite shell rings made it possible to date a fragmentary spiked axehead and a 'swimming duck' headed pin (fig. 5: 23, 27). Other canonical bronzes such as spiked axes with animal decorations (fig. 6: 4), whetstone handles with naturalistic animal decorations (fig. 6: 3), bracelets with terminals in the shape of a 'swimming duck' and idols in the shape of naturalistically rendered rampant animals (fig. 6: 6) may also belong to the Iron Age IA phase but could be slightly younger, belonging to the Iron Age IB phase.

The Iron Age IB – IIA (ca. 1150 – ca. 900 BC)

After the Iron Age IA phase follows a less well-documented period. Due to the absence of imports from neighbouring regions, it is not possible to propose accurate dates within the Iron Age IB-IIA phase (ca. 1150 – ca. 900 BC). Minor climatic variations are thought to have plunged Mesopotamia in a cascade of extreme droughts, failing crops and epidemics, leading eventually to migrations and wars. The population density in some areas, such as in the Diyala, seems to have dropped dramatically. In the Pusht-i Kuh, only a few tombs can be dated with

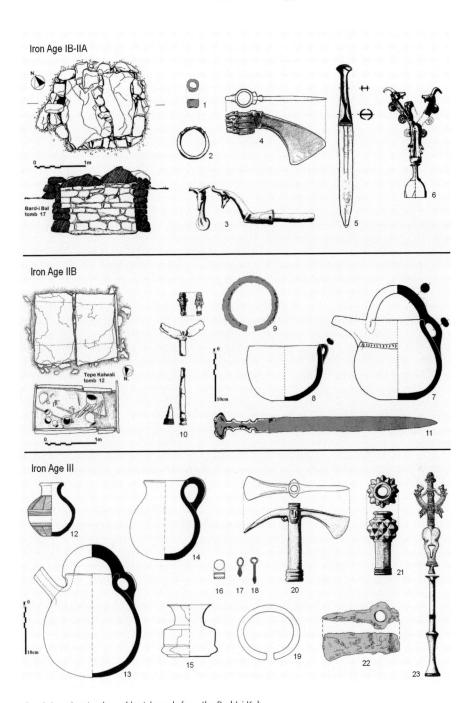

Fig. 6. Iron Age tombs and burial goods from the Pusht-i Kuh.

some certainty to this phase. This may be purely accidental but may also point to a comparable demographic evolution as in some areas of Mesopotamia.

During the Iron Age IB-IIA, the Luristan decorative style further developed. Tombs with decorated spiked axes (fig. 6: 4), whetstone handles in the shape of naturalistically rendered animals (fig. 6: 3), bracelets with terminals in the shape of a 'swimming duck', and idols in the shape of naturalistically rampant animals (fig. 6: 6) must probably be dated to this phase, although as said before, such objects may already have occurred in the Iron Age IA.

The Iron Age IIB (ca. 900-800/750 BC)

In the Iron Age IIB distinctive pottery shapes can again be distinguished (fig. 6: 7-8). Tepe Kalwali is the most important site that belongs to this period. Pusht-i Kabud and Darwand B are other examples but are already to be dated on the transition to the Iron Age III. At Tepe Kalwali, individual tombs were discovered with only a small number of relatively poor burial goods (fig. 6: Tepe Kalwali tomb 12). Metal objects were limited to some iron daggers, bracelets (fig. 6: 9) and rings. In view of this, Tepe Kalwali is not likely to provide a complete and representative picture of the Iron Age IIB in the Pusht-i Kuh.

During this phase there is a return to individual tombs, a concept which will continue in the Iron Age III phase. Teapots with basket handles (fig. 6: 7) and/or double grooved vertical handles, and plates or bowls with one small vertical handle (fig. 6: 8) or knob on the rim are distinctive shapes. Ceramic ladles with vertical stem can be dated to the transition from Iron Age IIB to III. The use of iron is no longer limited to jewellery. Daggers are now also produced in iron (fig. 6: 11). Not all of the weaponry is made of iron, however. Arrowheads continue to be made of bronze and will only be made of iron from the Iron Age III onwards. There were no axes excavated in any of the IIB tombs and it remains uncertain whether bronze spiked axes were still used or whether another type of (iron) axe, which is known from Iron Age III cemeteries (fig. 6: 22), had already been introduced. A unique find at Bard-i Bal (fig. 7) has demonstrated that the idols have evolved from the naturalistically rendered rampant animals into a more complicated iconography (fig. 6: 10). Other canonical bronzes were, however, not found.

In the Pish-i Kuh, several Late Bronze Age habitation sites are settled again by a population that is characterised by its painted 'Baba Djan III' ware.

The Iron Age III (ca. 800/750 – ca. 650 BC)

Whereas only a small number of Iron Age IIB tombs are known from the Pusht-i Kuh, a much larger number of Iron Age III cemeteries and tombs are documented. Our knowledge of the material culture is now much more representative.

Fig. 7. View of the Iron Age graveyard at Bard-I Bal.

New wares and pottery shapes occur. Distinctive are fine buff and particularly fine grey ware (fig. 6: 12). Certain new shapes seem to have been adopted from the Pish-i Kuh, since not only the shapes but also the incised decorative patterns on them imitate painted patterns of Baba Djan III ware (fig. 6: 12). Still, important differences continue to occur between both regions. Teapots with a bridged channel spout and base-pouch are characteristic among the Baba Djan III ware but are almost absent in the Pusht-i Kuh. In the Pusht-i Kuh, jugs with one handle (fig. 6: 14) and teapots with tubular spout and basket handle (fig. 6: 13) are among the distinctive shapes.

Iron is in the Iron Age III phase no longer a material which is identified with value or prestige. Consequently, iron jewellery has become rare and instead, bronze is used again. Iron is generally used for numerous weapons as well as for utensils (fig. 6: 22). Bronze vessels, which were exceptionally rare during the Iron Age I-II, are common among the Iron III burial goods (fig. 6: 15).

Canonical Luristan bronzes are rare among the Iron Age III Pusht-i Kuh finds, which may indicate either that the height is passed or that the centre is located in the Pish-i Kuh, the Pusht-i Kuh being merely the border area of the Luristan culture. At Tattulban, an idol with its bronze support was found in a tomb which must be dated to the very beginning of the Iron Age III (fig. 6: 23). Simple iron shaft-hole axes occurred at several sites (fig. 6: 22). They have replaced the bronze spike-butted axes of the Iron Age I and II. In three of the cemeteries, there still occurred a bronze axe-adze, only two of which were decorated with bearded human faces (fig. 6: 20). It is, however, a simple naturalistic human face that has little left in common with the complicated iconography of the Luristan imagery.

The large number of Iron Age III tombs in the Pusht-i Kuh and the resettlement of the habitation sites in the Pish-i Kuh, suggests a noticeable increase in population size. The burial goods reflect renewed contacts with the surrounding cultures, such as the Elamites to the south-west and the Assyrians in Mesopotamia. The Assyrian annals regularly mention military conflicts with the Luristan populations. The historical proof of this was provided when the BAMI discovered a Neo-Assyrian rock-sculpture at Shikaft-i Gulgul in the Pusht-i Kuh.

Final remarks

The field research of the BAMI created for the first time the opportunity to study the archaeological cultures of the Pusht-i Kuh region of Luristan, based on scientifically excavated material. It has been possible to place some of the 'Luristan bronzes' in their cultural and chronological context and to evaluate the relations of the Pusht-i Kuh with its Mesopotamian and Iranian neighbours. However, important lacunae still remain. We have, for example, virtually no information on the Late Bronze Age in the Pusht-i Kuh. Settlement sites remain to be studied. Important tepes are known to exist in the plains of Aivan, Shirvan and Chardaval but none has been excavated or studied. More, and particularly interdisciplinary, field research in both the Pusht-i Kuh and the Pish-i Kuh is necessary to complement our present data. One of the key issues in future research will have to be the relation between the Pusht-i Kuh and the Pish-i Kuh.

References

The late Prof. Louis Vanden Berghe, regularly published preliminary reports on his excavations in the scientific periodical *Iranica Antiqua*. A synthesis of his research was published as an exhibition catalogue in 1982:

L. Vanden Berghe, in collaboration with Chr. Langeraert-Seeuws, B. Overlaet & E. Haerinck 1982. *Luristan, een verdwenen bronskunst uit West-Iran*, Gent.

An ongoing project to prepare the final excavation reports on the BAMI Luristan expeditions started in 1996:

Haerinck, E. & Overlaet, B. 1996. *The Chalcolithic Period, Parchinah and Hakalan. (Luristan Excavation Documents* I*)*. Brussels.

Haerinck, E. & Overlaet, B. 1998. 'Chamahzi Mumah. An Iron Age III Graveyard'. (*Luristan Excavation Documents* II). *Acta Iranica*, 33, troisième série, XIX, Leuven.

Haerinck, E. & Overlaet, B. 1999. 'Djub-i Gauhar and Gul Khanan Murdah, Iron Age III Graveyards in the Aivan plain'. (*Luristan Excavation Documents* III). *Acta Iranica*, 36, troisième série, XXII, Leuven.

Haerinck, E. & Overlaet, B. 2004 (in print). 'Tepe War Kabud, an Iron Age III Graveyard in the Chavar district, Pusht-i Kuh, Luristan'. (*Luristan Excavation Documents* V). *Acta Iranica*, troisième série, Leuven.

Haerinck, E. & Overlaet, B. (in preparation). 'The Early Bronze Age Graveyard of Bani Surmah, Chavar district, Pusht-i Kuh, Luristan'. (*Luristan Excavation Documents* VI). *Acta Iranica*, troisième série, Leuven,

Overlaet, B. 2003. 'The Early Iron Age in the Pusht-i Kuh, Luristan'. (*Luristan Excavation Documents* IV). *Acta Iranica*, 40, troisième série, XXVI, Leuven.

Elam's Backstage

HANS J. NISSEN

From whichever point you approach the history of Mesopotamia, sooner or later you will come across Elam, either as an integral part, ally, or enemy. More than once, Elam will turn out to be a power exercising direct influence on the history of Mesopotamia, and in particular, its southern part, Babylonia. This implies a power and strength that according to our sources does not seem to be justified. At the same time, there is a marked difference regarding such neighbouring areas of Mesopotamia like Syria or Anatolia, which rarely, if at all, ever interfered actively with Mesopotamia's history, though throughout the history of the Ancient Near East they remained parts of the same larger koine. However, in this respect, also our sources do not offer an easy explanation.

At first glance it would seem that insufficient and unbalanced sources are the cause of our difficulties. This is true. Writing was employed only during limited periods, and if a piece of written information is only available from internal sources in a particular area, there could be a considerable amount of bias involved. Also, there were periods with internal and external information – primarily Mesopotamian – alternating with periods where external information was only available to a limited extent, if at all. Therefore, a history of Elam based exclusively on internal sources, cannot be written, and the result remains unsatisfactory even if all available information is used.

The situation is equally dismal when we look for archaeological evidence. It is not plentiful and first and foremost does not encompass enough information to enable us to reconstruct a picture of its own, let alone help us to fill those gaps left by the written material. Part of the problem is that the extent of the research dedicated to Elam has been unduly restricted by our general picture which – following most Mesopotamian sources – saw Elam most of all as lowlands formed by the lower courses of the rivers Karun and Kerkha with the principal site of Susa. Except for the excavations at Tell Malyan, in ancient Anshan, north of the modern town of Shiraz, the eastern part of Elam has hardly attracted any investigation. Consequently, there is very little information available, either from written sources or from archaeology for the hilly and mountainous parts of Elam.

In spite of the poor information available, an attempt will nevertheless be made here to emphasize the role of Elam's eastern parts as its virtual backbone, and as the source of its stamina and the reason for it being different from the other neighboring regions of Mesopotamia.

First, however, a word about the imbalance in the written sources. There is a widespread prejudice that only written material qualifies for 'history', and that consequently, aliterate societies are less complex than those in possession of the written word. Since Elam has gone through longer periods when writing was not employed, it tends to be overlooked as a major player in the history of the Ancient Near East and to be attributed a somewhat lower level of complexity. As a result of this misunderstanding we are surprised to see Elam entering as a fully established power on various occasions. However, even after centuries of 'silence', these situations lose their peculiarity when seen in the context of the use of writing in Mesopotamia. Even there, which could be called a 'writing culture' par excellence, writing was only used to a limited extent. In fact in all periods – and almost exclusively in its early phases – writing was used only in cases when it was unavoidable *i.e.*, mainly economic matters. Considering the bulk of our written material we get the impression that writing was used primarily to prevent improper use of any kind: in public life to prevent the diversion of public property for private use; in private life to render security to economic settlements by establishing the possibility of verification.

Only rarely, and differing from one period to the other, has writing been employed in other fields. The best example is an uneven coverage in the field of legal procedures, but in spite of this fact we can be sure that justice was administered and was a normal and important part of Mesopotamian society. Then, in most periods, royal or private correspondence is almost non-existent.

This is an after-effect of the situation prevailing at the time when writing was invented. It was used very sparingly in that only those elements were written down which were too complicated to be remembered, and which diverged from the common knowledge of the time. All common knowledge would be assumed to be 'inserted' when 'read'. This reservation with employing the written word included the retention of older, less complicated systems of information storage even after writing was already known.

The possibility to avail oneself of a number of recording systems, including writing, meant that intermittent it was felt that media, other than the demanding writing system, would suffice. Incidentally, this may have been one reason for the relative paucity of records in Mesopotamia itself during part of the second millennium.

Such phases have apparently occurred more often in the neighbouring regions of Mesopotamia, resulting in longer or shorter periods completely without, or with very little, written material. From the aforesaid it should be clear, however, that these periods should by no means be called 'dark', or periods of decline, by virtue of the absence of the written word. Until further evidence is forthcoming, they should rather be defined as periods of total – local – continuity on all levels, except for the use of writing.

Applied to Elam this enables us to see Elam as a thoroughly stable political unit through the millennia, with occasional periods of weakness which, however, never jeopardized the overall continuity. This primarily applied to the mountainous parts of Elam which, contrary to the low-land parts, were able to escape being incorporated into the quarrels of low-land Mesopotamia. The highlands, therefore, were always the one constant factor that in politically difficult times constituted an area of retreat, but also represented a power reserve which enabled a swift presence even after political or military defeats.

One of the main reasons for the uneven course in Elam's history is the fact that its western part always belonged to the core area of the Ancient Near East. It felt to be – itself and was seen as – a normal partner. Equal to Mesopotamia, but that, because of its limited size and different conditions of production – rainy areas without the possibility of intensifying agricultural production – always remained the smaller partner who had to make an effort to be recognized.

From early times it was the apparent goal of Elam to extend its power into the area of the western neighbor Babylonia, following a pattern which becomes clearly visible at the end of the period of the so-called Third Dynasty of Ur, around 2000 BC. At the end of this phase, Babylonia is left weakened as a result of the constant inner tensions between the central government in Ur and the Pretender to the Throne belonging to the new invading group of the Amorites. Taking advantage of this situation, Elam invades Babylonia, occupies part of it, and takes the last King of Ur prisoner. Significantly, this prisoner is brought to Anshan instead of Susa, to the eastern center of Elam, thus disclosing its identity as the main stronghold.

A similar situation arose shortly before 1800 BC when we see one of the old and prestigious cities of Babylonia, Larsa, being governed by an Elamite dynasty. Too strong to be defeated militarily by Hammurapi of Babylon, Hammurapi had to recourse to the diversion of part of the Euphrates creating a famine in 'the land of Larsa' which swept away the Elamite ruler.

And again, the conquest of Babylonia around 1160 BC by the Elamite ruler Shutruk-Nahhunte follows this pattern, as obviously it was meant to be more than a short raid because he left his son Kutir-Nahhunte to be King of Babylon. This was preceded by a weak phase in Babylon when after the death of the powerful ruler Mardukapaliddina in 1161 the Assyrian ruler Assurdan had invaded Babylonia. In spite of Elam's intentions, the incursion turned out to be but a short affair since already in the following year we see a local ruler re-installed in Babylon. By the way, an interesting side view is offered by the fact that on his return to Elam Shutruk-Nahhunte collected all standing monuments from Babylonian cities and replacing the original inscriptions with his own and installed them in a part of his palace – where they have been found by the French excavators c. 3000 years later! Apparently, these wars were also fought on the level of ideology because this move certainly was not intended for the embellishment of the palace, but to transfer the prestige attached to these monuments to the new owner.

All these long and – more often – shorter phases of incursion ended in the expulsion of the Elamites, and in most cases in the destruction of Susa, the main site of lowland Elam. We never hear of the victorious forces following the enemy into the highlands, leaving that part essentially unharmed. It is understandable, therefore, that the eastern areas were a sanctuary for any regenerating efforts, and to build up military strength in order to be ready whenever the chance came again.

Whether the Babylonians never intended to enter the eastern parts, or whether this would have been beyond their means, remains unanswered. At any rate, however, it seems to have been the Assyrians who first developed the idea that Elam was even more vulnerable once attacked in its own backyard. This may be the explanation for the constant attempts of the Assyrians to use their holdings in the mountains east of their core area as bases for incursions into the southernmost parts of the Zagros. Eventually they did get dangerously close to the eastern parts of Elam. This may be the reason for the strangely close alliance to Babylonia still being adhered to even after Assurbanipal of Assyria had conquered Babylonia, and had demanded the extradition from Elam of the Babylonian ruler who had sought refuge there. Either misjudging the danger, or clinging to a defeated Babylonia as the last possible support in view of the Assyrian's potential of attacking from two sides, Elam rejected the request – with far-reaching consequences. In retaliation, Elam was conquered and Susa destroyed to such an extent that it did not recover for a long time. Although there is no explicit information about highland Elam, it seems feasible that Assyrian forces also attacked via the mountains, thus eliminating Elam's area of retreat.

This pattern over the millennia demonstrates on the one hand the important part played by its geo-political setting in the political survival of Elam, in spite of all difficulties. On the other hand, this setting reveals the reason for the differences between Elam and the other political units in the areas bordering Mesopotamia, none of which showed the relative consistency of Elam as political entities. It certainly is more than coincidence that only Elam encompassed both lowland and highland regions, while none of the other political units covered more than an ecologically/topographically defined unit, as they were all limited to either a lowland or a highland region.

Obviously this sketch cannot be more than a hypothesis; too much basic information is lacking. There is hope, however, that in the wake of recovering archaeological research in Iran the highland parts of Elam will also receive proper attention.

The Numinous and the Immanent

Some Thoughts on Kurangun and the Rudkhaneh-e Fahliyan

D.T. POTTS

Introduction

The road from Shiraz to Ahwaz via Kazerun and Behbehan crosses an archaeologically rich landscape with evidence of occupation from the Neolithic through the later historical periods. While the modern highway heads south from Shiraz via Dasht-e Arjan towards Kazerun, before turning north again and resuming a mainly westward trajectory, the traditional Anshan-to-Susa or Persepolis-to-Susa routes (Koch 1986; McDermott & Schippmann 1999) ran along a different set of tracks through the mountains via Pol-e Murd (Stein 1940, 15) towards Fahliyan, Kupun and the west. Although Bishapur is undoubtedly the most famous site in the district, well over fifty mounds and more than half-a-dozen prominent sites, all of which have long been known, are found here. These include the Sasanian rock relief of Sarab-e Bahram on the outskirts of Nurabad-e Mamasani (Herrmann & Howell 1983); the early Sasanian tower of Dum-i Mil (Huff 1975); the *imamzadeh* of Darb-e Ahanin (Mostafavi 1978, 86); the royal Achaemenid way-station at Jin-Jin/Tepe Suruvan (Atarashi & Horiuchi 1963); the mound of Tul-e Spid, where a stamped Elamite brick was found recording the erection of a temple to Kilahshupir by Shilhak-Inshushinak (König 1965, §41A); the 17th century BC Elamite rock relief of Kurangun (Seidl 1986; Vanden Berghe 1986); and the (probably) post-Achaemenid, rock-cut tomb of Da-u Dukhtar (Stronach 1978, 304). As Ernst Herzfeld observed when he visited the region in 1924, 'Die Ruinen oder alten Reste des Mamaseni-Gebietes übertrafen alles was mir der Amir i Humayun [son of the district's "owner", Mu'in at-Tuddjar] davon erzählt hatte' (Herzfeld 1926, 258), and most modern visitors would probably agree with him.

In this study, I shall focus on the Elamite rock relief at Kurangun and, in particular, its water imagery and relationship to the Rudkhaneh-e Fahliyan or Fahliyan river which, when viewed from the relief itself, forms such a dramatic part of the landscape (fig. 1). Almost thirty years ago, Peder Mortensen com-

Fig. 1. The Rudkhaneh-e Fahliyan or Fahliyan River, viewed from the Elamite rock relief at Kurangun.

menced the Introduction to his own report on the Hulailan survey, published in *Acta Archaeologica* 44 (Mortensen 1974, 20), with a description of the Saimarreh river. I hope that the following reflections on the numinous quality of rivers; the immanence of divinity in them; and the resonance of these perceptions in Elamite art, religion and law will kindle fond memories of field seasons spent in the awe-inspiring Zagros mountains of western Iran.

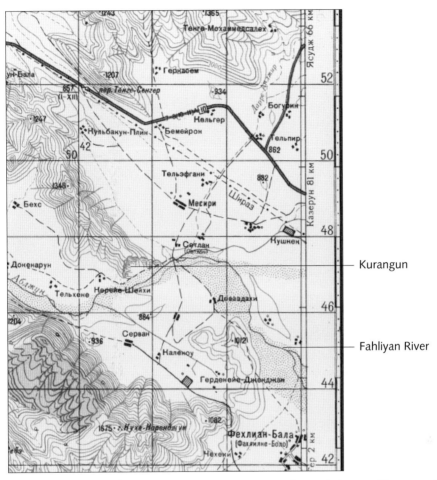

Kurangun

Fahliyan River

Fig. 2. Detail of a Russian military 1:100,000 map of the Fahliyan area showing the location of Kurangun and the Fahliyan River.

The setting and the problem

Leaving Nurabad-e Mamasani and driving towards the north and west, in the direction of Behbehan, one reaches Pol-e Fahliyan, a small town clustered along the road just before it reaches a bridge over the Fahliyan river. All year round the cool waters of the Fahliyan river flow rapidly in a wide bed of white river cobbles heading towards the northwest until they strike the easternmost end of the Kuh-e Pataweh. There the river bends sharply to the southwest, skirting the southeastern edge of the mountain. At precisely this point, roughly 80 m above the river (Kleiss 1993, 358), on the southern face of the rock outcrop, sits the rock relief of Kurangun (fig. 2).

Fig. 3. Mr. Hassan Habibi Fahliyani, native of the village of Fahliyan, inspecting the Kurangun relief from the ledge in front of it.

Discovered by Ernst Herzfeld in 1924 (Herzfeld 1926, 259), the early Elamite rock relief at Kurangun has been fully published and described in detail (esp. Vanden Berghe; 1986, Seidl 1986 with earlier bibliography). Carved into the rock at the top of the lowest, easternmost spur of the Kuh-e Pataweh is a roughly 3.5 m long gallery approximately 2 m high (max. 2.5 m), accessed by a series of steps. The relief can be examined closely by climbing down the steps onto a narrow ledge in front of it (fig. 3) which overlooks the Fahliyan river (Seidl 1986, 7). The central focus of the relief (figs. 4-5) is a bearded, male deity wearing horned headgear. He is seated on a throne formed by the body of a snake, coiled back upon itself over and over again, and he grasps the tail of the snake in his left hand. In his right he holds the divine rod and ring (Spycket 1998, 656), from which two streams of water flow in opposite directions. One branch flows to the left, seemingly into the hands of a bearded male worshipper, who stands before the god, accompanied by a female (unbearded) and male (bearded) attendant. A second branch flows towards the right, where a similar set of three worshippers/attendants can be seen. Beneath the flowing water to the right of the god sits a seated female (unbearded) deity, likewise wearing horned headgear. In front of the male deity is what appears to be a large stand, perhaps an altar with flames (Seidl 1986, 9; *cf.* Wiggermann 1997, 46). Beneath the figures at Kurangun is a narrow frieze depicting fish in a stream. That this portion of the relief is original, *i.e.* not added afterwards (*e.g.* in the 1st millennium BC when the files of worshippers on the lefthand side of the scene were carved) has been demonstrated by Vanden Berghe (de Miroschedji 1981, 9). As Seidl, Amiet and others have shown, there are clear similarities between the iconography of the Kurangun relief – particularly the snake-throne, long robes worn by the figures depicted and horned headgear – and Elamite glyptic of the *sukkalmah* period (Seidl 1986, 9; Potts 1999, 182 with earlier refs.).

In addition to scholarship focusing on the iconography of Kurangun and its dating, considerable energy has been expended on the identification of the deities depicted. As this literature has been well-summarised by Vanden Berghe (1986, 159 n. 6) and Seidl (1986, 20-21), it is unnecessary to do so again here. For Hinz the pair represented the Elamite deities Humban (m.) and Kiririsha (f.) or Parti (f.) (Hinz 1972, 52); for Amiet the male deity was Napirisha ('chef du panthéon, honoré particulièrement au pays d'Anshan') and his spouse (Kir-irisha, see Grillot & Vallat 1984, 27), or else two related deities (Amiet 1973, 17; 1979, 349-350); while for de Miroschedji the male deity was Inshushinak, the city-god of Susa (de Miroschedji 1980, 139; 1981, 15).

To a large extent the identifications proposed for the deities depicted at Kurangun are founded upon a species of theological logic which consists of looking at the Elamite pantheon and nominating a suitably important male deity, after which, in some but not all cases, a female consort is identified. In contrast, de Miroschedji's approach to the 'dieu au serpent et aux eaux jaillissantes' hinged on adducing the well-known, if highly fragmentary stela of Untash-Napirisha from Susa where a seated deity with horned headgear, holding a rod and ring in the right hand, and the neck of a dragon-headed serpent in the left, faces the dedicant (Vallat 1981, 27-28). The accompanying, albeit fragmentary inscription identifies the deity in question as Inshushinak and, because of the similarity of this deity to the one shown at Kurangun, de Miroschedji has suggested that the Kurangun god is Inshushinak (de Miroschedji 1981, 15ff).

In fact, although de Miroschedji paid considerable attention to the iconography of both Kurangun and the Untash-Napirisha stela, none of the evidence marshalled unequivocally confirms his identification (Hinz 1976-1980, 118, has suggested without further elaboration that Inshushinak's emblem was an eagle with outspread wings) and de Miroschedji himself has enumerated several important reasons why one might prefer to identify the deity with Napirisha (de Miroschedji 1981, 23-25). Given the presence of the snake throne at Kurangun and the fact that the snake's tail is grasped by the seated deity, much attention has been paid to the snake associations of the Kurangun god (*cf.* Vanden Berghe 1984,

Fig. 4. The central panel of the Kurangun relief. After Seidl 1986, Abb. 1.

26; Trokay 1991; Wiggermann 1997, 44-46; Calmeyer 1994, 7-10 for a fascinating discussion of the incorporation of the twisted snake seen on the throne of the Middle Elamite relief [re-cut by Bahram II] at Naqsh-e Rustam (Seidl 1986, 14-19) in the depiction of Ahriman in the investiture relief of Ardashir at the same site), but many ancient Near Eastern deities have been associated with snakes (Wiggermann 1997). Similarly, the rod and ring, symbols of divinity clasped by the god at Kurangun, are not specific attributes of one deity alone (Spycket 1998, 657), nor are flowing streams of water (Amiet 2000, 2).

As alluded to above, I propose to take a different approach to the identification of the deity at Kurangun, focusing in particular on the god's association with water and the Fahliyan river.

Water resources of Nurabad-Fahliyan

While later visitors to the region of Nurabad-e Mamasani and Fahliyan, as mentioned in the Introduction above, were impressed by the antiquities of the district, it is notable that when Baron Clement Augustus de Bode reported on a journey between Kazerun and Behbehan undertaken in January, 1841, he came back again and again to the area's water resources.

As soon as he entered the Fahliyan district, de Bode 'passed a spring of water' (de Bode 1843, 77). At Sarab-e Bahram, he discovered 'the source of the river of Behrám', describing the Sasanian relief there as 'surrounded by trees, water,

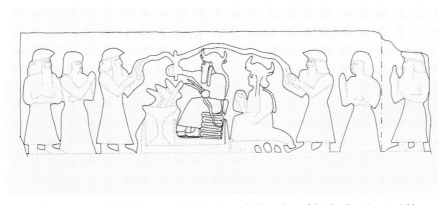

Fig. 5. The central panel of the Kurangun relief showing probable outlines of details otherwise not visible. After Seidl 1986, Abb. 2a.

and verdure…a very picturesque spot' (1843, 78), as it continues to be today. Leaving Nurabad and heading north along a high ridge, he 'looked down upon the beautiful valley which disclosed itself below, watered by a river and enamelled with flowers' (1843, 79). At Fahliyan he found the town 'supplied with water by a canal cut through the hills from the snow-capped chain beyond Kal'eh Sefid' and although the 'water of the Ab-shúr' was, 'as its name implies, brackish', it was used for irrigation and described as 'abundant' (1843, 80). Continuing westward, de Bode entered a valley which he called 'Ser-abi-Siyáh (Black Water Head)', observing, 'Many springs here burst forth from the ground and the rocks'. A little further on he observed that, 'We crossed many springs, bursting out almost under our feet, and soon afterwards augmenting the volume of the neighbouring lakes and pools, which appear to have no outlet, and are very deep' (1843, 81).

These descriptions contrast markedly with the perception which many scholars probably have of Fars province, particularly those more familiar with the Marv-Dasht, where so many of Iran's most important sites are located (*e.g.* Persepolis, Tal-e Malyan, Istakhr, Qasr-e Abu Nasr, Naqsh-e Rustam), or the even more arid southeast, around Firuzabad, Fasa or Darab. In addition to the wealth of springs just alluded to, the Nurabad-Fahliyan region enjoys the highest rainfall in Fars, averaging 600 mm annually (Ministry of Agriculture, Nurabad, pers. comm. K. Roustaei). It is this richness of water resources which, today, makes the Nurabad-Fahliyan area one of the few in Fars where double cropping is possible (wheat and barley in the winter; rice in the summer).

The vast majority of archaeologists working in Western Asia are, of course, acutely aware of the importance of water since so much of the region in which we work is arid. No discussion of the Neolithic Revolution and the origins of dry-farming can take place without reference to rainfall and isohyets. Similarly, no discussion of the Urban Revolution, at least in the case of Mesopotamia, can fail to examine the importance of canal irrigation and the roles of the Euphrates, and increasingly the Tigris, river regime. Thus, water is far from a neglected topic in our field, at least in its fundamental role in agriculture. Water, however, has other, symbolic associations and socio-religious as well as legal roles which may be relevant to an understanding of the Kurangun rock relief and its deities.

Water categories and their significance

In the same way that linguists discuss the semantic range of verbs and grammatical constructions, thereby denoting the breadth of contexts in which they function and different shades of meaning implied, we may use an analogous approach in considering what might be called the 'cultural range' of water. That all water was not alike or symbolically equal is amply demonstrated in the mythic/epic and religious literature of the cuneiform-using Near East. In addition, legal and economic texts attest to further contexts in which water took on a specific function.

In the Babylonian *Epic of Creation*, the very origin of the gods is attributed to the mingled union of Tiamat, 'who bore them all', and Apsû, 'their progenitor' (Foster 1993(I); 354). As Bottéro has observed,

In the beginning...when Heaven and Earth did not yet exist, in other words, in the absence of all things in the universe, including the gods, there existed, not one, but two gigantic divine liquid masses: the salty water of the sea and the freshwater (they were believed unchangeable and dissimilar)....the first member, set forth as the most important, the Mother, was 'Sea', or Tiamat (a Semitic name), the distant doublet of Nammu; playing the masculine role, here understood as secondary, was Apsû, 'freshwater'. The two were intertwined, as if in a formidable and motionless coupling, thus giving birth to the first divinities.

(Bottéro 2001, 75)

Yet Apsû did not encompass all freshwater (Horowitz 1998, 307-309). Rather, as Lambert has stressed, 'Apsû was a lower level of cosmic water' (Lambert 2000,75), deeper than the freshwater of springs and rivers found on the earth's surface. In a hymn to Enlil from the Ur III period, Enlil's Ekur at Nippur is compared to 'the Apsu which no one can understand/ Its interior is a distant sea which "Heaven's Edge" cannot comprehend' (Horowitz 1998, 308). Lambert has oberved, 'The idea that the earth is an earth-laden raft floating on the cosmic water explains how there is water beneath the earth, and simultaneously sea around the earth' (Lambert 2000, 77). While it is normally assumed that Ea/Enki resided in the Apsû – *cf.* the Babylonian *Epic of Gilgamesh* XI.42, 'I must go down to the Apsû to live with Ea, my lord' – Lambert suggests that this is not clear in all contexts, and 'one may suspect that it was assumed that Ea resided directly under the earth, while the Apsû in a sense extended to every sea-shore, but not as the very abode of Ea' (Lambert 2000, 77). Certainly Ea and his wife Damkina are referred to as 'Bewohner der Wassertiefe' in a Middle Babylonian text from Ur (Sallaberger 2003, 43).

Imagery of plenitude linking Enki/Ea and water can be found in many sources, two of which will suffice here. In *Enki and Ninhursag,* Enki says to his daughter Ninsikila (ll. 40-43),

When Utu steps up into heaven, fresh waters shall run out of the ground for you from the standing vessels (?) on/ Ezen's (?) shore, from Nanna's radiant high temple, from the mouth of the waters running underground.

(Electronic Text Corpus of Sumerian Literature,

see http://www-etcsl.orient.ox.ac.uk/section1/tr111.htm)

In a prayer to Ea, the god is called 'bringer of the high waters (that cause) abundance/ who makes the rivers joyful/ In oceans and in reed thickets you make plenteous prosperity' (Foster 1993/II, 552). It was no doubt literary imagery such as this which prompted Jacobsen to write, 'Enki is usually pictured with two streams, the Euphrates and the Tigris, flowing out of his shoulders or from a vase he holds' (Jacobsen 1976, 111), a feature confirmed by glyptic evidence of late 3rd and early 2nd millennium date as well (Braun-Holzinger 1996, 329).

The supernatural power of freshwater rivers is well-illustrated by the phenomenon of their deification. The deified river (Sum. ^{d}Íd, Akk. ^{d}*Narum*) was not a specific river but rivers in the broadest sense (Ebeling 1957-1971, 93; Edzard 1976-1980, 27), particularly in their role as *loci* of action in legal cases. As Bottéro has noted,

bodies of water (Nâru/Íd) were endowed with divine prerogatives: 'creative', purifying, and even judicial. A judge incapable of settling a case for lack of evidence submitted those concerned to the Ordeal… normally… accomplished through recourse to the discriminating power of a river.

(Bottéro 2001, 63)

In cases such as this, 'an appeal is made to the Rivergod (^{d}*Narum*) to judge whether the accused is guilty or not' (Günbatti 2001, 160). Attested in the laws of Ur-Namma (Roth 1995, 18; Wilcke 2002, 315) in an uncertain context (§13) and in an accusation of promiscuity directed at the wife of a young man (§14); in the Codex Hammurabi (Roth 1995, 81 and 106) in cases of witchcraft (§2) and suspicion of adultery (§132); and in the Middle Assyrian laws (Roth 1995, 159-160, 162) in accusations of promiscuity by a man's wife (§17), an unrelated man sleeping with another man's wife (§22), and of a householder knowingly harboring the runaway wife of another man (§24), the river ordeal has also been identified by a number of scholars in legal texts from Susa (Lieberman 1969, 28-43; cf. Klíma 1971, 1972; Hirsch 1973). These, however, have been re-examined by Frymer-Kensky who has concluded that rather than a river ordeal, the Susa sources bear witness to two different legal instruments involving water. In one group, the question is asked 'should X go to the water', followed by the answer 'may Šazi smite his skull (indict him?)' (Frymer-Kensky 1981, 117 and n. 12). Although Šazi was not an Elamite or Susian deity, he is known from Mesopotamian god-lists as the son of the river god ᵈÍd. The second group of texts from Susa state that a plaintif 'freely and voluntarily…took the waters', perhaps a reference to 'a drinking trial in which the litigant drinks a potion while avowing the legitimacy of his claim' (Frymer-Kensky 1981, 118-119). Possibly this is analogous to 'drinking a god' (in the sense of 'drink to' or 'toast' a god) in the Hittite sources (Güterbock 1998).

These examples suffice, I hope, to demonstrate that water in the cuneiform-using Near East was anything but unidimensional. In addition to (or, perhaps, because of) its very obvious function in sustaining all life on earth, water had a multitude of 'personalities' and incarnations – cosmogonic, magical, spiritual – which impacted on what might be termed 'practical religion'. In this, very broad sense, I do not believe one can divorce the interpretation of the Kurangun relief from its physical association with the Fahliyan river, particularly as the central male deity is shown with streams of flowing water emanating from his divine rod and ring, and the frieze of fish swimming in a stream supports, as it were, the entire scene. The problem is, how is one to interpret the very strong water associations in the Kurangun imagery and physical placement?

Ea/Napirisha and Inshushinak: A solution?

In discussing the objections one might raise to an identification of the deity of Kurangun with Inshushinak, de Miroschedji noted that one might well argue that it was Napirisha, rather than Inshushinak, who was represented at Kurangun because the deity in question 'est un dieu des eaux, dont l'iconographie rappelle celle d'Ea en Mésopotamie' and the incantation or exorcistic liturgy (Bottéro 2001, 116) known as Šurpu specifically identifies Naprushu (Napirisha) as 'Ea of Elam' (de Miroschedji 1981, 24). Furthermore, de Miroschedji observed, Na-pirisha was 'le dieu d'Anshan'. Nevertheless, in what can perhaps be described as the triumph of words over images, de Miroschedji continued to be swayed by the dedication to Inshushinak on the stele of Untash-Napirisha.

There can be no doubt that if one focuses on water and water imagery – whether it be the Apsû as the abode of Ea; freshwater brought by Ea as a manifestation of abundance and prosperity; or rivers as numinous places with an immanent, divine identity manifested in the notion of the river god – then the flowing streams, frieze of swimming fish (*viz.* their link to the Apsû) and the proximity to the Fahliyan river all combine to press the *interpretatio aquae* in this case. Even the fish at Kurangun could be interpreted in the light of Ea and the Apsû. That inter-communication by fish was possible between the cosmic Apsû and the 'clear water' of the Earth's surface is shown in several texts. A prayer text concerned with the expurgation of evil contains the observation, 'May a fish [take] it (the evil) to the Apsû', and a text of Esarhaddon concerning Marduk's destruction of Babylon refers to 'fish of the Apsû (Lambert 2000, 76).

Nevertheless, it seems highly unlikely, as de Miroschedji has argued, that a dedication to Inshushinak accompanies a representation of Ea/Napirisha on the Untash-Napirisha stela. Is there a satisfactory solution to the seemingly irreconcilable positions posed by the text of the Untash-Napirisha stela, which favours Inshushinak, and the imagery of the Kurangun relief, which favours Ea/Napirisha?

In fact, I believe there is. In a brief note published long after de Miroschedji, Seidl, Vanden Berghe and Trokay had struggled with the identity of the Kurangun deity, F. Vallat showed convincingly that a text from Susa which seemed to honour Inshushinak, Ea and Enzag (MDP 28, no. 7) was actually open to quite a different interpretation. Rather than seeing these three names as three different deities, Vallat has suggested that, in this context, Ea and Enzag should be understood as *epithets* of Inshushinak (Vallat 1997). If this is the case, then the water imagery of the Kurangun relief, and its obvious associations with Ea, do not represent an obstacle to de Miroschedji's interpretation of the central deity at Kurangun as Inshushinak. Moreover, Amiet's view that the deity in question was Napirisha becomes likewise correct, since, according to *Šurpu*, Ea = Napirisha. If the male deity at Kurangun is Napirisha, moreover, then the female deity is almost certainly Kiririsha, and thus we have a representation of the divine couple *par excellence* of Anshan. In this way, the interpretations of the major deity as Inshushinak/Ea/Napirisha are no longer in conflict. None of these insights, however, would have been reached without focusing, as I have tried to do here, on the water imagery of Kurangun which can hardly be unrelated to the impressive Fahliyan river which skirts the very mountainside below it. While Inshushinak had an undoubted role in the underworld, as attested by a group of funerary texts from Susa (Bottéro 1982, 392-400), that role seems nowhere in evidence at Kurangun.

I am aware that, from many points of view, this is a highly diplomatic solution to a problem which affirms, at least in part, the seemingly contradictory views held by Amiet, de Miroschedji and myself. Perhaps this is fitting, for as Jacobsen wrote of Enki, the Sumerian incarnation of Ea, this particular deity

exerts his will through diplomacy or guile' which 'may reflect the fact that he is the power in the sweet waters, for 'the ways of water are devious. It avoids rather than surmounts obstacles, goes around and yet gets to its goal'

(Jacobsen 1976, 112)

Can there be any more appropriate analogy for the waters of the Fahliyan river, the well-spring of Ea = Napirisha, epithet of Inshushinak, which head south the moment they reach the base of the Kuh-e Pataweh?

References

Amiet, P. 1973. 'Glyptique élamite, à propos de documents nouveaux', *Arts Asiatiques*, 26, 3-64.

Amiet, P. 1979. 'L'iconographie archaïque de l'Iran: Quelques documents nouveaux', *Syria,* 56, 333-352.

Amiet, P. 2000. 'Glanes élamites'. In: R. Dittmann, B. Hrouda, U. Löw, P. Matthiae, R. Mayer-Opificius & S. Thürwächter (eds.), *Variatio Delectat, Iran und der Westen: Gedenkschrift für Peter Calmeyer*. Münster: Alter Orient und Altes Testament 272, 1-8.

Atarashi, K. & Horiuchi, K. 1963. *Fahlian I. The excavation at Tepe Suruvan 1959*. Tokyo: Iraq-Iran Archaeological Expedition Reports 4.

de Bode, Baron C.A. 1843. 'Extracts from a Journal kept while travelling, in January, 1841, through the Country of the Mamásení and Khógilú (Bakhtiyárí), situated between Kázerún & Behbehan', *Journal of the Royal Geographical Society*, 13, 75-85.

Bottéro, J. 1982. 'Les inscriptions cunéiformes funéraires'. In: G. Gnoli & J.-P. Vernant (eds.), *La mort, les morts dans les sociétés anciennes*. Cambridge/Paris: Cambridge University Press & Editions de la Maison des Sciences de l'Homme, 373-406.

Bottéro, J. 2001. *Religion in Ancient Mesopotamia*. Chicago & London: University of Chicago Press.

Braun-Holzinger, E.A. 1996. 'Altbabylonische Götter und ihre Symbole: Benennung mit Hilfe der Siegellegenden', *Baghdader Mitteilungen*, 27, 235-359.

Calmeyer, P. 1994. 'Metamorphosen iranischer Denkmäler', *Archäologische Mitteilungen aus Iran*, 27, 1-27.

Ebeling, E. 1957-1971. 'Flußgottheiten', *Reallexikon der Assyriologie*, 3, 93.

Edzard, D.O. 1976-1980. 'Id', *Reallexikon der Assyriologie*, 5, 27.

Foster, B.R. 1993. *Before the muses: An anthology of Akkadian literature,* Vols. 1-2. Bethesda: CDL Press.

Frymer-Krensky, T. 1981. 'Suprarational legal procedures in Elam & Nuzi'. In: M.A. Morrison & D.I. Owen (eds.), *Studies on the civilization and culture of Nuzi and the Hurrians in honor of Ernest R. Lacheman on his seventy-fifth birthday, April 29, 1981.* Winona Lake: Eisenbrauns, 115-131.

Grillot, F. & F. Vallat 1984. 'Dédicace de Silhak-Insusinak à Kiririsa', *Iranica Antiqua*, 19, 21-29.

Günbatti, C. 2001. 'The river ordeal in ancient Anatolia'. In: W.H. van Soldt, J.G. Dercksen, N.J.C. Kouwenberg & Th.J.H. Krispijn (eds.), *Veenhof Anniversary Volume: Studies presented to Klaas R. Veenhof on the occasion of his sixty-fifth birthday.* Leiden: Nederlands Instituut voor het Nabije Oosten, 151-160.

Güterbock, H.G. 1998. 'To drink a god'. In: *XXXIVème Rencontre Assyriologique Internationale, 6-10/VII/1987 – Istanbul, Kongreye Sunulan Bildiriler.* Ankara: Türk Tarih Kurumu Basimevi, 121-129.

Herrmann, G. & Howell, R. 1983. *The Sasanian rock reliefs at Bishapur, Pt. 3. Sarab-i Bahram.* Berlin: Reimer [= Iranische Denkmäler Lieferung 11 enthaltend Reihe II, Iranische Felsreliefs G].

Herzfeld, E. 1926. 'Reisebericht', *Zeitschrift der Deutschen Morgenländischen Gesellschaft*, 80, 225-284.

Herzfeld, E. 1928. 'Drei Inschriften aus persischem Gebiet', *Mitteilungen des Altorientalischen Gesellschafts*, 4, 81-86.

Hinz, W. 1957-1971. 'Gott C. Nach elamischen Texten', *Reallexikon der Assyriologie*, 3, 546-547.

Hinz, W. 1972. *The lost world of Elam.* London: Sidgwick & Jackson.

Hinz, W. 1976-1980. 'Inšušinak', *Reallexikon der Assyriologie*, 5, 117-119.

Hirsch, H. 1973. 'Zum Fluß-Ordal in Elam', *Revue d'Assyriologie,* 67, 75-77.

Horowitz, W. 1998. *Mesopotamian cosmic geography.* Winona Lake: Eisenbrauns.

Huff, D. 1975. 'Nurabad, Dum-i Mil', *Archäologische Mitteilungen aus Iran*, 8, 167-209.

Jacobsen, T. 1976. *The treasures of darkness: A history of Mesopotamian religion.* New Haven & London: Yale University Press.

Kleiss, W. 1993. 'Kurangun, die Burganlage am Elamischen Felsrelief in Sudwest-Iran'. In: M. Mellink, E. Porada & T. Özgüç (eds.), *Aspects of Art and Iconography, Anatolia and its Neighbors. Studies in Honor of Nimet Özgüç.* Ankara: Türk Tarih Kurumu Basimevi, 357-360.

Klíma, J. 1971. 'Das Wasserordal in Elam nach den akkadischen Urkunden aus Susa und Huhnur (Malamir)', *Archiv Orientální*, 39, 401-424.

Klíma, J. 1972. 'L'ordalie par le fleuve en Élam (d'apres les documents akkadiens de Suse et de Huhnur-Malamir)', *Revue d'Assyriologie*, 66, 39-59.

Koch, H. 1986. 'Die achämenidische Poststrasse von Persepolis nach Susa', *Archäologische Mitteilungen aus Iran*, 19, 133-147.

König, F.W. 1965. *Die elamischen Königsinschriften.* Graz: Archiv für Orientforschung, Beiheft 16.

Lambert, W.G. 2000. 'The Apsû'. In: L. Milano, S. de Martino, F.M. Fales, G.B. Lanfranchi (eds.), *Landscapes: Territories, frontiers and horizons in the Ancient Near East, Pt. III. Landscape in ideology, religion, literature and art.* (History of the Ancient Near East/ Monographs, III/3). Padua: Sargon, 75-77.

Lieberman, A.I. 1969. *Studies in the trial by river ordeal in the Ancient Near East during the second millennium BCE*. (Unpubl. Ph.D. thesis). Brandeis University.

MacDermott, B.C. & Schippmann, K. 1999. 'Alexander's march from Susa to Persepolis', *Iranica Antiqua*, 34, 283-308.

de Miroschedji, P. 1980. 'Le dieu élamite Napirisha', *Revue d'Assyriologie*, 74, 129-143.

de Miroschedji, P. 1981. 'Le dieu élamite au serpent et aux eaux jaillissantes', *Iranica Antiqua*, 16, 1-25.

Mortensen, P. 1974. 'A survey of prehistoric settlements in Northern Luristan', *Acta Archaeologica*, 44, 20-48.

Mostafavi, M.T. 1978. *The land of Párs (The historical monuments and the archaeological sites of the Province of Fárs)*. Chippenham: Picton Publishing.

Potts, D.T. 1999. *The archaeology of Elam: Formation and transformation of an ancient Iranian state*. Cambridge: Cambridge University. Press.

Roth, M.T. 1995. *Law collections from Mesopotamia and Asia Minor*. Atlanta: Scholars Press.

Sallaberger, W. 2003. 'Die Entscheidung des Ordals erbitten: Zu den mittelbabylonischen Urkunden MBTU 11 und 73', *N.A.B.U.*, 2/39, 42-43.

Seidl, U. 1986. *Die elamischen Felsreliefs von Kurangun und Naqs-e Rustam*. Berlin: Reimer [= Iranische Denkmäler Lieferung 12 enthaltend Reihe II, Iranische Felsreliefs H].

Spycket, A. 1998. 'La baguette et l'anneau: Un symbole d'Iran et de Mésopotamie'. In: R. Dittmann, B. Hrouda, U. Löw, P. Matthiae, R. Mayer-Opificius & S. Thürwächter (eds.), *Variatio Delectat, Iran und der Westen: Gedenkschrift für Peter Calmeyer*. Münster: Alter Orient und Altes Testament, 272, 651-666.

Stein, Sir A. 1940. *Old routes of western Iran*. London: Macmillan.

Stronach, D. 1978. *Pasargadae*. Oxford: Clarendon Press.

Trokay, M. 1991. 'Les origines du dieu élamite au serpent'. In: L. de Meyer & H. Gasche (eds.), *Mésopotamie et Elam: Actes de la XXXVIème Rencontre Assyriologique Internationale, Gand, 10-14 juillet 1989*. Ghent: Mesopotamian History and Environment Occasional Publications, 1, 153-161.

Vallat, F. 1981. 'L'inscription de la stèle d'Untash-Napirisha', *Iranica Antiqua*, 16, 27-33.

Vallat, F. 1997. 'Inšušinak, Ea et Enzag', *N.A.B.U.*, 3/111, 103-104.

Vanden Berghe, L. 1984. *Reliefs rupestres de l'Iran ancien*. Brussels: Musées Royaux d'Art et d'Histoire.

Vanden Berghe, L. 1986. 'Données nouvelles concernant le relief rupestre élamite de Kurangun'. In: L. de Meyer, H. Gasche & F. Vallat (eds.), *Fragmenta historiae elamicae: Mélanges offerts à M.J. Steve*. Paris: Éditions Recherche sur les Civilisations, 157-173.

Wiggermann, F.A.M. 1997. 'Transtigridian snake gods'. In: I.L. Finkel & M.J. Geller (eds.), *Sumerian gods and their representations*. (Cuneiform Monographs, 7). Groningen: STYX, 33-55.

Wilcke, C. 2002. 'Der Kodex Urnamma (CU): Versuch einer Rekonstruktion'. In: T. Abusch (ed.), *Riches hidden in secret places: Ancient Near Eastern studies in memory of Thorkild Jacobsen*. Winona Lake: Eisenbrauns, 291-333.

A Palace Without Sealings?

ERIK HALLAGER

Open any book on the Aegean Prehistory and you will be presented with the information that Tiryns in the later part of the Aegean Bronze Age was a Mycenaean Palace. The reasons for calling Tiryns a palace are manifold. The site has the typical megaron found at the other palaces, with the central hearth, the columns and the decorated walls, and around this megaron we find the corridors from which there is access to isolated rooms. This central part of the palace is surrounded by a large settlement and it is completely protected by fortification walls, just as impressive as those of Mycenae. The careful German excavations have revealed a most impressive architecture and very many exquisite finds which fully justify the interpretation of the site as that of a lord or a king who is able to display a material culture expected in a Mycenaean palace. And on the top of that, at a relatively late stage in the excavation history of the site, Linear B tablets were also revealed,[1] which seemed to show that Tiryns was also an administrative centre like other palaces in the Late Helladic IIIB period.[2]

But is Tiryns really a palace in the full sense of the word? The question suddenly came to me when – last year – I started to study a distribution map and a table I had prepared for the conference 'Ariadne's threads' in Athens in 2003. The topic of my paper was on the uniformity in seal use and sealing practice during the Late Helladic/Late Minoan III period.[3] The conclusion of this paper, or rather what the evidence indicated to me, was that the use of seals and sealing types within the Mycenaean administration is profoundly different from that of the preceding Minoan period, but, on the other hand, that it was surprisingly consistent within the Mycenaean world regardless of geographical and possible chronological differences.

Basically there exist seven Mycenaean sealing types (fig. 1), but four are more dominant and – for the purpose of this paper – interesting than the rest. They are: the regular string nodules, the irregular string nodules, the combination nodules and to a certain extent the clay stoppers. The first three mentioned are new sealing types in the Mycenaean repertoire compared to the Minoan one and of the recognizable sealings they constitute 93% of the entire corpus.

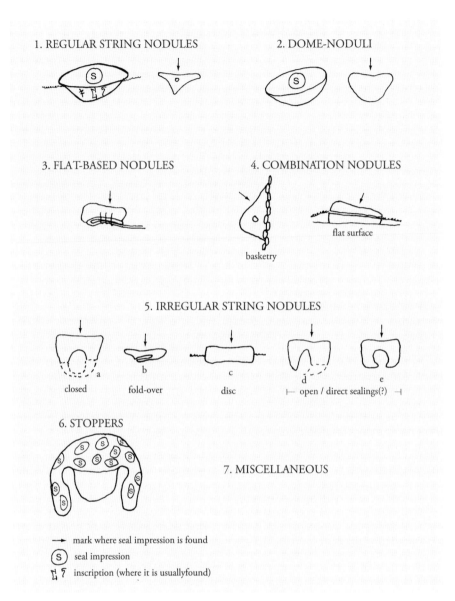

Fig. 1. The main types of Mycenaean sealed documents and their sub-types.

The regular string nodule is the Mycenaean sealing *par excellence*. This is the one which is known to most Mycenaean specialists, because it is the only one – with three exceptions[4] – which carry inscriptions in Linear B,[5] but it only constitutes c. 11% of the entire body. It is rather uniform wherever it is found. It is of an unmistakable gable-shaped section caused by the way it was held between the thumb and index finger while being impressed – it always has a very fine string with a knot inside the clay. These nodules do testify an unusually strong administrative practice geographically (and – if you prefer a high date for some of these documents – also chronologically). Obviously the Mycenaean bureaucrats learned one way to produce these documents whenever and wherever he lived. These nodules are very solid and may have been produced at any place within the boundary of the administrative area of the palace and they may without problem have followed the commodities often described upon them, as have, for example, the Thebes nodules of this type for which there is very convincing arguments.[6] Also the find circumstances of these nodules seem to confirm that they had no fixed place within the administration, since they have turned up in storerooms, workshops and archives within the palaces, close to entrance gates to cities and in private houses. In other words they have a wide, unpredictable distribution.

While the regular string nodules are very solid and in almost all cases were recovered as complete (or almost so) exactly the opposite is the case with the irregular string nodules. Other differences compared with the regular nodule is that the string hole is much larger and the nodule has no fixed shape. These irregular nodules constitute roughly two-thirds of the Mycenaean sealings and are thus by far the most common type. The irregular string nodules are not uniform as the regular ones, but what they do have in common is that they have impressions of strings and/or objects on the reverse, sometimes enclosing the string/object, but more often not. They were fastened to an object and all of those with a secure context were found in or close to magazines or workshops. The irregular string nodules, in contrast to the regular ones, thus seem to have a fixed physical position within the palaces. As mentioned, the irregular string nodules are with very few exceptions rather fragmentary and by far the majority of the recovered ones are probably discarded broken sealings which had served their purpose. Many scenarios can be imagined for the use of these irregular nodules. But one possible scenario is that 'someone' brings some sacks of wine to the wine magazines at the palace, some bring ordered pieces of wood to a workshop, or a pile of finished blankets to a storeroom. When received and/or stored, the shipment is provided with a nodule for security or for identification of the person responsible either for the delivery or for the storage.

While the regular string nodules were obviously produced by palace administrators inside and outside the palace, probably in order to accompany commodities, the purpose of the irregular string nodules was obviously quite different. In my opinion they could never have withstood transportation – they were too carelessly fastened to their object, and it seems to me the only tenable solution is that they were fastened to the object inside the palace once the commodities had been placed there.

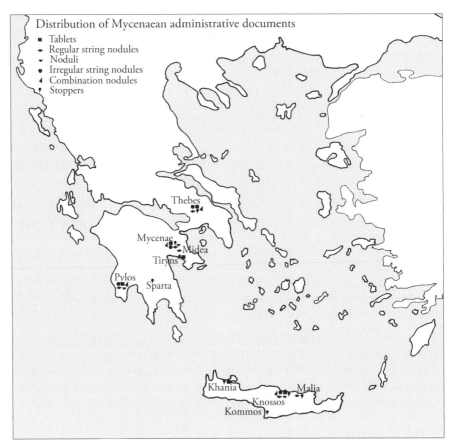

Fig. 2. Map of the Aegean with distribution of main types of Mycenaean administrative documents.

The combination nodule is a document which is both pressed against an object and at the same time secured with a string found inside the clay lump.[7] They exist in two main types: Nodules which were pressed against basketry[8] and nodules which were pressed against a flat object. The purpose of these nodules is obviously to secure different kinds of containers. They are invariably – both at the mainland and at Knossos – impressed with high quality seals, the majority of which are gold rings. These nodules are obviously the work of high officials within the Mycenaean administration. They seem to have no fixed find position, but they have only been discovered in the palaces, and at Pylos most of those found *in situ* came from the Archive Rooms 7 and 8.

We know of 36 clay stoppers or fragments of stoppers (3% of the entire Mycenaean population) and almost all of them were connected to stirrup jars. This is the most widespread 'document' in the Mycenaean period. The majority of

	Regular	Irreg.	Comb.	Label	*Nodulus*	Stopper	FB-nod.	Direct	?
Knossos	81 (15)	448	61	11	12	1	7	18	186
Pylos	57 (22)	76	8	2	8	4		3	24
Mycenae	14 (09)	3	4		1	34			
Thebes	62 (59)	2	3			1			1
Tiryns						2			
Khania		?				4			2
Midea	4 (3)								
Malia	1 (0)					2			
Kommos						5			
Sparta						2			

Table 1.   List of sites with Mycenaean sealings and their types. The numbers in ( ) are the inscribed nodules. Regular = regular string nodule; Irreg. = Irregular string nodule; Comb. = Combination nodule; Label (not shown in Fig. 1) is a string nodule with inscriptions, but without seal impressions; FB-nod = Flat-based nodule; Direct = direct sealings.

these are found on the Greek mainland (Mycenae) in LM/LH IIIB contexts and most of them proved to be of Cretan clay.[9]

When we consider the general distribution patterns of Linear B administrative documents (fig. 2 and Table 1) we first notice, that with the exception of the clay stopper the sealed documents are concentrated on the four palaces at Knossos, Pylos, Mycenae and Thebes. We note that four types are exclusively found at the palaces: the irregular nodule, the combination nodule, the *nodulus* and the label. The regular nodule has been found three times outside the palace boundary: In a private house, the Panagia House, at Mycenae, both inscribed and uninscribed, one uninscribed at Malia and three inscribed, and one uninscribed at Midea. Concerning Midea it has been suggested that the finds of inscribed nodules may indicate the presence of a palace as an administrative centre,[10] while another interpretation may also be possible. We know from Thebes that this kind of nodule was produced by the palace administrators outside the palaces to be shipped with commodities to the palaces. So one may also suggest that what we find in the private houses at Mycenae, in Malia and in Midea is actually nodules produced by palace administrators from Mycenae and Knossos respectively, and that the commodities with their nodules never reached their destination.

Most interesting is the fact that the most common and less conspicuous of all the Mycenaean sealings, the irregular string nodule, has only been found at the palaces. The reason why, is probably that the palaces were the places where wealth accumulated and where it had to be secured and registered and where responsible collaborators had to sign for the things for which they were responsible.

What the evidence of the Mycenaean sealings thus seem to suggest is that the presence of irregular string nodules are found at places where wealth is stored, accumulated and administrated. Furthermore the presence of combination nodules, being the work of high-ranking officials, seems to show a site of primary importance within the administrative sphere. The presence of regular string nodules, on the other hand, does not necessarily mean that we are dealing with a site of major importance within the administration of a boundary, and this is definitely not so with the clay stoppers which have been of importance only for the place of origin, and whose administrative function is as yet uncertain.

With these considerations in mind it may be worth while to ask where such sealings – especially the first two mentioned – have *not* been found. Here Tiryns springs to mind. It is a site which has been extensively and thoroughly excavated, but the only sealings as yet discovered are two clay stoppers. These stoppers and the Linear B tablets alone show that at least parts of Tiryns was destroyed by the fire necessary to transform sun-dried sealings into terracotta. Several storerooms and workshops have been identified, but no irregular string nodules to show that they may have been under a central supervision, and neither have the combination nodules been found – nodules which may have backed up the idea that high-ranking officials responsible for the stored items were present at the site.

It thus seems that if the evidence provided by the sealings at Knossos, Pylos, Thebes and Mycenae should be considered necessary to constitute a palace with a full central administration at work – Tiryns is not such a palace. Could John Chadwick, after all, have been correct, when he in 1976 (after the discovery of the first Linear B tablets) stated that 'Tiryns must have been a dependency of Mycenae.'?[11] Since the Linear B tablets are few, it is quite possible that they may have been the work of scribes from the main administrative centre of the Argolid: Mycenae.

The arguments which have been advanced above could, of course, also be applied to Khania, where Linear B tablets have been found, but where no palatial building of the Mycenaean period has been discovered and where the irregular string nodules and the combination nodules have not yet been found. But in the case of Khania it would be premature to insist. Many plots in the town have been excavated, but they constitute less than 2% of the LM III settlement.

Many pleasant archaeological surprises may, as yet, turn up in Khania and western Crete.

References

Chadwick, J. 1976. *The Mycenaean World*, Cambridge.

Führer durch Tiryns, 1975. Athens.

Hallager, E. forthcoming 1. 'Linear A and Linear B seal-administration', *The 11th International Mycenological Colloquium, Austin, 7-13 May 2000*.

Hallager, E. forthcoming 2. 'The uniformity in seal use and sealing practice during the LH/ LM III period' *Ariadne's Threads. Connections between Crete and the Greek Mainland in the Postpalatial Period (LM IIIA2 to SM)* (Tripodes 1), Athens.

Melena, J.L. & J.P. Olivier 1991. *Tithemy. The Tablets and Nodules in Linear B from Tiryns, Thebes and Mycenae* (Suppl. a Minos, 12). Salamanca.

Müller, W., J.-P. Olivier & I. Pini. 1998. 'Die Tonplomben aus Mykene', *AA*, 5-55.

Panagiotopoulos D. forthcoming. *Untersuchungen zur Mykenischen Siegelpraxis* I-II, Unpublished Habilitationsschrift, forthcoming.

Piteros, C., J.-P. Olivier & J. Melena 1990. 'Les inscriptions en linéaire B des nodules de Thèbes (1982): La fouille, les documents, les possibilités d'interprétation', *BCH*, 114, 103-184.

Tomlinson, J.E. & P. Day 1995. 'Comparison of petrographic and chemical results'. In: Tournavitou, I., *The 'Ivory Houses at Mycenae* (BSA Suppl. 24). London, 316-320.

Weingarten, J. 1988. 'The sealing structures of Minoan Crete: MM II Phaistos to the Destruction of the Palace of Knossos. Part II: The Evidence from Knossos until the destruction of the palace', *OJA*, 7, 1-25.

Notes

1 Melena & Olivier 1991, 15-16 with further references.

2 For example, Hartmuth Döhl in *Führer durch Tiryns*, 188-189.

3 Forthcoming in Hallager forthcoming 2. For more details on comparisons between the Minoan and the Mycenaean sealing practice see also Hallager forthcoming 1.

4 One odd exception to this rule is PY Wr 1327 from Room 98, which in shape should be characterised as an irregular two hole nodule. Perhaps the only 'sloppy' regular inscribed nodule? The other exceptions are two *noduli* from Knossos, *cf.* note below.

5 Few of the Mycenaean sealed documents are actually inscribed, – 114 regular string nodules (18 Ws from KN; 22 Wr from Pylos, 6 Wv from MI; 9 Wt from MY; and 59 Wu from Thebes), two noduli (2 Wn documents from Knossos) and a few nodules from Pylos (2 Wo documents) and Knossos (11 Wm documents) without seal impressions.

6 Piteros, Olivier & Melena 1990, 166-184.

7 Weingarten 1988, 6-7.

8 One subvariant of the basketry type-pressed against very fine basketry belongs to the irregular type.

9 Tomlinson & Day 1995, 320; Müller in Müller, Pini & Olivier 1988, 12.

10 Panagiotopoulos forthcoming.

11 Chadwick 1976, 14.

Seleukos Nikator and Syria

LISE HANNESTAD

Do not hurry back to Europe; Asia will be much better for you[1]

Recent years have witnessed a renewed interest in the individual, reflected in historical research and in, for instance, an increase in the number of biographies of historical personalities.

Another characteristic trend of the last couple of decades, in both the archaeology and history of the ancient Near East, is increased focus on a period which had until then either been considered virtually non-existent or as a brief interlude that left no imprint on the further development of the region, *i.e.* the period from the conquests of Alexander until the victory of Octavian over Anthony and Cleopatra in 31 BC.

The subject of this little contribution is the first king of the Seleucid dynasty, Seleukos I Nikator, not as politician and general,[2] but as a king whose reign brought decisive and long-ranging changes in the urban structure and material culture of Syria.[3]

In the first years of the tumultuous period following the death of Alexander, Seleukos had not yet come to the fore among the rivalling group of Macedonian generals who had taken over. But in an agreement drawn up after the murder of Perdikkas (the general to whom the dying Alexander handed his seal and who in the following period had supreme command in Asia) in 321/320 BC – a plot in which Seleukos had taken part – he was rewarded with the satrapy of Babylonia.[4] In the same agreement, Antigonos Monophthalmos the One-Eyed was appointed *strategos* of Asia, and in the following period he became the dominant figure among the Successors. Thus in the renewed power struggle Seleukos lost Babylonia to Antigonos, but regained it in 312 with the help of Ptolemy (who had taken solid possession of Egypt), an event which may be viewed as the starting point of the Seleucid empire. The importance of the event is reflected in the fact that 312 was reckoned as the beginning of the Seleucid era, a calendar which remained in use centuries after the last Seleucid king.[5] The following ten years were spent on the successful conquering of the 'upper satrapies', *i.e.* the Iranian satrapies, which after the death of Alexander had for the most part been held by Antigonos.

Seleukos reached his peak of power as a result of the battle of Ipsos in 301 BC in which Antigonos, his rival for power in Asia, was killed. Seleukos now became ruler of even vaster territories, from the Syrian coast to India.

The Greek historian Appian (*Syr.* 55) sums up Seleukos' personality and achievements in a few sentences:

Always lying in wait for the neighbouring nations, strong in arms and persuasive of diplomacy, he acquired Mesopotamia, Armenia, the so-called Seleucid Cappadocia, the Persians, Parthians, Bactrians, Arabs, Tapyri, Sogdiani, Arachotes, Hyrcanians, and all the other adjacent peoples that had been subdued by Alexander, as far as the river Indus, so he ruled over a wider empire in Asia than any of his predecessors except Alexander.[6]

This brief characterisation would probably have satisfied Seleukos, but there is actually much more to be said, not least as to how he set about controlling these vast areas and keeping his army of Macedonian and Greek soldiers content. That last element was important, since the outcome of the struggle for power among the Successors quite often depended on the fact that officers and soldiers changed their loyalties from one Successor to another.

The city-founder

In Babylonia Seleukos had founded his first capital, Seleucia-on-the-Tigris, but after his acquisition of Syria he decided to make this area the second centre of his realm. His motive for establishing this new base may have been, as J. Balty points out (1986/91, 205), that he wished to return to the Mediterranean 'theatre' from which he had been excluded for more than twenty years. One might perhaps say that the fascination of being a 'Persian king' gradually vanished in the years after the death of Alexander and that his successors, all born in Macedonia, saw the Mediterranean as the centre of their world. However, I do not agree with Balty that this was based on sentimental grounds. From Seleukos' point of view it was rather a decision made for 'real-political' reasons – the political focus of the world of the Successors being the Mediterranean and when all is said and done, the ambition for the Macedonian kingship had not yet ceased in this first generation of Hellenistic kings after Alexander.

Seleukos immediately began what had already become standard procedure during the campaigns of Alexander and was followed up by several of his successors when they had acquired new territory – the institution of a programme

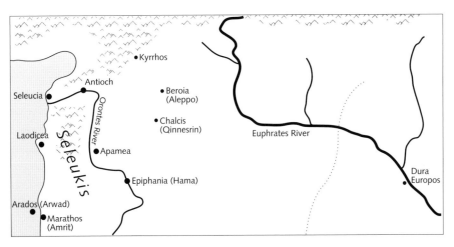

Fig. 1. Syria in the Hellenistic period. Only a number of major settlements are indicated.

of colonization. Colonies served various purposes: military, economic and political. Soldiers – reserve or retired – and their families, made up the majority of settlers in the colonies, which thus guarantied the necessary supply of soldiers.[7] The coastal region of Syria, with its Mediterranean climate and vegetation had been known by the Greeks for centuries. A very different ecological zone was to be found east of the mountain ranges and the fertile Orontes Valley, *i.e.* the steppe and desert zone. However, a substantial number of the men who became the citizens of the colonies probably already had a firsthand knowledge of the inland regions, being soldiers in the armies of Alexander and the Successors, with many years of campaigns in the Near East behind them. But others came directly from Greek Mediterranean cities, as is evidenced, for instance, by a decree from Antioch in Persis, stating that the city of Magnesia on the Maeander (in western Asia Minor) had, when king Antiochos I requested help in strengthening the population of Antioch in Persis, passed 'an honourable and glorious decree, offered a sacrifice and sent a sufficient number of men of great personal excellence, as they were anxious to help in increasing the people of Antioch'.[8] Some of the colonies were cities, others hardly more than fortresses. Some were also royal residences for a king always on the move, particularly in connection with wars (Austin 2001, 91).

Within a short period of time after the acquisition of Syria, Seleukos founded four major cities (the *Tetrapolis*) on the coastal plain and in the Orontes Valley: Seleucia in Pieria and Laodicea on the coast, and Antioch in the lower and Apamea in the upper Orontes Valley (fig. 1). Added to this huge effort a number of smaller cities were founded at strategic points, not least to secure the routes overland to the Euphrates and further to the first capital of the realm, Seleucia on the Tigris.[9] According to Appian (*Syr.* 57) Seleukos

founded cities throughout the whole length of his empire; there were sixteen called Antioch after his father, five Laodicea after his mother, nine Seleucia after himself, four called after his wives, three Apamea and one Stratonicea. Of these the most famous up to the present (Appian wrote his Roman history in the middle of the second century AD) are the two Seleucias, by the sea and by the river Tigris, Laodicea in Phoenicia, Antioch under Mt. Lebanon, and Apamea in Syria. The others he called after places in Greece and Macedon, or after his own achievements, or in honour of Alexander the king. That is why there are in Syria and among the barbarians inland many Greek and Macedonian place-names, such as Berroea, Edessa, Perinthus, Maronea, Callipolis, etc.[10]

A central issue when discussing this large-scale programme of city founding is the question of how these new cities were peopled? As already stated, the backbone must have been colonists, either soldiers of Seleukos' armies or people who came to seek a fortune in the vast new areas. Our written sources for Syria are seriously biased in that they are virtually all Greek, which means that they offer us only a few glimpses of the local people.[11] Also, the question arises of the habitation pattern of the area in the pre-Seleucid Persian period.

The settlement pattern of Syria during the Persian period

The extensive archaeological activities in Syria in recent years have mostly concentrated on earlier periods. Surveys seem to show that pottery and other material from the Hellenistic period are more numerous than from the Persian period. Grainger (1990b, Ch. I) has interpreted the scarcity of material from the Persian period as evidence for this period being one of few cities, indicating that the structure of society in Syria at the time of the arrival of Alexander was almost entirely of a rural type. He further assumes

that the boundary between sedentary and nomadic agriculture was moving north and east, so that more land was in use exclusively by the nomads – or not at all – (*i.e.* in the Persian period) than had been the case before

and refers to the fact that the Assyrian and Neo-Babylonian occupations of Syria both 'used imperial terror methods of destruction and deportation' and that this had resulted in a large-scale de-urbanization of Syria before the early period of Persian rule (539-404), which was peaceful and may have resulted in a partial recovery of the cities. The later Persian rule (404-333), however, saw no less than twelve military expeditions against Syria. Grainger sees this pattern as part of a larger similar pattern affecting the region from the Tigris to Egypt, and concludes that de-urbanization and the expansion of the uncultivated steppe zone together strongly suggest that the density of the total population of Syria during the Persian period was low. This scenario differs from that of many earlier studies, which have assumed that the life of the cities in Syria continued from earlier more peaceful periods.[12] However, it is quite possible that the changes which can be observed in the archaeological surveys are due mainly to a change in the utilization pattern of the steppe, *i.e.* how far east the land was cultivated by a sedentary population or to what extent the land was used for pastoralism, also in regions where agriculture was possible,[13] and that destruction and deportation did not play the role that Grainger assumes.

Though there is substantially more evidence from the Hellenistic period than from the Persian, there is less in the majority of surveys (and in many excavations) compared to material from the Bronze and Iron Age periods and from Roman and Byzantine times. A characteristic and clearly attested pattern is the diminishing importance of old urban centres, particularly in the marginal zones. An example is Tell Mardikh/Ebla. In the Persian and Hellenistic periods this site was reduced from a city to a fortress/rural village, occupying only the northeast part of the Hill with a villa or small palace as its central element (see Mazzoni 1986/1991).

Reduced habitations are recorded at many other important Bronze Age tells, such as Umm el-Marra in the Jabbul plain east of Aleppo,[14] and a similar settlement pattern appears in northern Mesopotamia. Here too, the old urban centres dwindled to smaller habitations, often on the summit of the tell.

These sites and evidence from surveys attest that the significant changes with long-lasting effects which took place during the early Hellenistic period, particularly during the reigns of Seleukos and his son, Antiochos I, did not mean a general revival of old urban centres but, as mentioned above, the foundation of a string of colonies, from cities to fortresses. Thus this colonization went hand in hand with large areas of Syria and northern Mesopotamia continuing a settlement pattern of small rural communities.

The Tetrapolis

Within a few years Seleukos founded the famous *Tetrapolis*: the four cities Antioch, Laodicea, Seleucia in Pieria and Apamea in the coastal region of northern Syria and the hinterland along the Orontes river, the region which came to bear the name *Seleukis*. Seleukos was not the first of Alexander's successors to have founded cities in the region. Thus we know that Antigonos the One-Eyed founded an Antigoneia in 307/306 (Diod. 20.47.5-6). According to Diodorus the city had only a short existence, and was dismantled by Seleukos and transported to his new Seleucia.[15] Seleucia and Laodicea were harbour cities, upholding vital access to the Mediterranean and harbour facilities for the Seleucid Mediterranean fleet. They also functioned as important emporia. Apamea in the hinterland was the main base of the Seleucid army in the region, as the rich pastures here could sustain a huge number of horses and the war elephants for which the Seleucid army was famous.[16]

Antioch was destined to become the capital of the Seleucids on the death of Seleukos, and one of the centres of the Hellenistic world, second only to Alexandria. The city continued – like Apamea – as a flourishing centre in the Roman period. Among the cities of the famous *Tetrapolis*, Laodicea and Antioch are still major cities today. A number of smaller cities were founded at strategic points, not least to secure the routes overland to the Euphrates and further to Seleucia-on-the-Tigris. Archaeologically by far the best known of these is Dura Europos – until the Parthian conquest of the region known only as Europos.[17] Further up the Euphrates yet another Seleucia (Zeugma) was founded at the main crossing point of the river. Other important cities founded by Seleukos on the two routes between Antioch and the Euphrates are Kyrrhos on the northern route, and Beroia (Aleppo, on the site of a much older settlement) on the southern (see fig. 1).[18]

Seleucia – the capital of Seleukos

Seleucia was undoubtedly intended to be Seleukos' new western capital, since it was probably the first of his foundations and was given the king's own name. Another indication that Seleukos considered this city his western capital is that the earliest Seleucid mint in Syria was situated here. A mint had existed in Antigoneia during its brief lifetime. Seleucia became its successor; tetradrachms of the Alexander type but in the name of Seleukos were produced here – apparently by the same die cutters who had worked in Antigoneia.[19] The fact that Seleukos was buried in Seleucia after being murdered in 280 BC is yet another argument that this was his capital.

The city[20] was situated north of the mouth of the Orontes on a mountain slope. The Greek historian Polybios (5.59.3) offers us a precious description of the city in his account of its reconquest by Antiochos III in 217 BC after the city had been occupied by the Ptolemies since 246 BC:

The situation of Seleucia and the nature of its surroundings are as follows. It lies on the sea between Cilicia and Phoenicia, and above it rises a very high mountain called

Coryphaeum, washed on its western side by the extreme waters of the sea separating Cyprus from Phoenicia, but overlooking with its eastern slopes the territories of Antioch and Seleucia. Seleucia lies on its southern slope, separated from it by a deep and difficult ravine. The town descends in a series of broken terraces to the sea, and is surrounded on most sides by cliffs and precipitous rocks. On the level ground at the foot of the slope, which descends towards the sea lies the business quarters (emporia) and a suburb defended by strong walls. The whole of the main city is similarly fortified by walls of very costly construction and is splendidly adorned with temples and other fine buildings. On the side looking to the sea it can only be approached by a flight of steps cut in the rock with frequent turns and twists all the way up.[21]

Seleucia still existed in the 6th century AD, but its harbour was by then blocked up by silt from the river mouth, and even though the site was still known by the Arabs and later by the Byzantine dynasty of the Comnenids (McNicoll 1997, 83) in the 12th century, it had by now dwindled to a mere shadow of the city it had once been.

The defensive walls are the best known part of Hellenistic Seleucia. The most recent study of them was made by the late McNicholl (1997). Fig. 2a shows McNicoll's plan, based on Athanassiou's map from 1936 (see Stillwell 1941). The surviving length of the walls are c. 5 km, from the harbour area in the south and up along the eastern slopes of the mountain. On the northern side the wall-line disappears (McNicoll 1997, 85) and a wall may actually never have existed here since the slope is very steep. On the western side nothing is preserved, though there must definitely have been a wall here. Some scholars have suggested the course of the wall *in toto* (see fig. 2b)[22] but McNicoll states that there is no longer evidence for this part of the wall. If this hypothetical course is correct the total length of the circuit would have been 12.5 km. Such enormous walls are characteristic of the Early Hellenistic period, the Successors having invested a substantial amount of their resources in splendid fortifications.[23]

The walls of Seleucia are built mainly of limestone. McNicolls has classified the masonry into six different types (McNicoll 1997, 86), something that does not necessarily – as has often been assumed – indicate different building periods. In Greek fortifications several types of masonry can be used simultaneously – possibly for aesthetic rather than functional reasons.[24] Isodomic ashlar, *i.e.* ashlars in courses of equal height, and polygonal (polygonal stones, used either hammer-faced or quarry-faced) are the most common types in the walls of Seleukia, and both types probably belong to the circuit built under Seleukos. According to McNicoll 'at least nine towers' varying considerably in size and construction technique can still be traced on the remaining part of the wall. Most of them (TT1-6a on fig. 2a) are of rectangular shape (the most common in Greek fortifi-

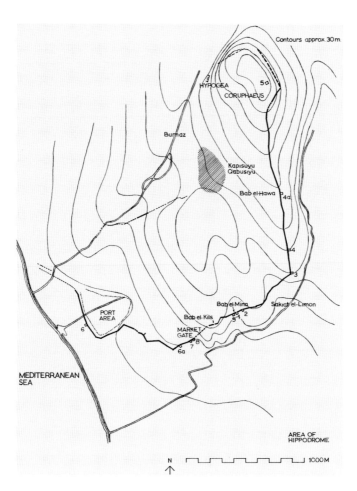

Fig. 2a. Plan of the walls of Seleucia (McNicholl 1997 Fig. 16).

cation building) and belong with the original circuit wall, whereas two (TT7-8) flanking the so-called market-gate are straight-sided with a semicircular front. Both the gate and the two towers are later additions and do not belong to the original layout, which had a gate without towers at this point (McNicoll 1997, 86), probably the main gate of the city. Another important gate must have been in the area at Bab el-Hawa where the road from Antioch entered the city. Construction remains on the top of the acropolis are probably to be identified as barracks of the garrison stationed there.

Though the slope on which Seleucia was built may have called for unorthodox solutions as to the layout of the city, to some extent it probably had similarities with the layout of the other three cities of the *Tetrapolis*, about which we are better informed.[25] One characteristic trait in the townscape, mentioned by Polybios, *i.e.* the staircase connecting the lower and the upper city, has been

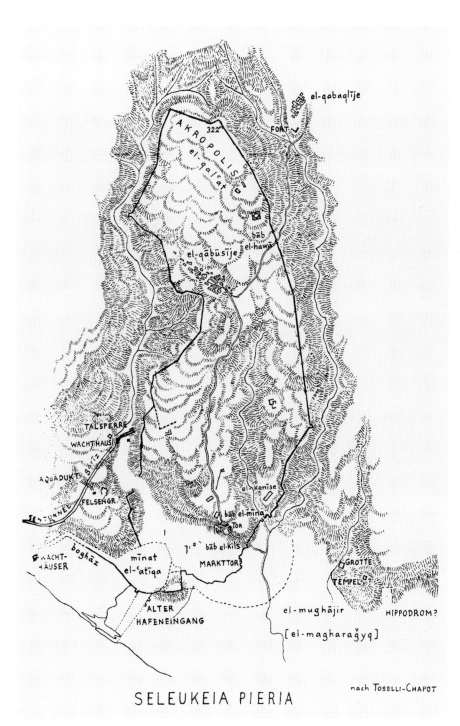

SELEUKEIA PIERIA

nach TOSELLI-CHAPOT

Fig 2b. Map of Seleucia made by Toselli (after *RE* Seleukeia in Pieria).

Fig. 3. The rock-cut stairway connecting lower and upper towns (Stillwell 1941 Fig. 4).

identified by the American Antioch Expedition (fig. 3). The grid plan identified in the three other cities of the Tetrapolis was probably also used in Seleucia. This type of city-plan had by then become a standard element in the foundation of new Greek cities, and Dura Europos offers us the best preserved example in Syria (see for instance Hoepfner & Schwandner 1994, 257 ff). The suggestion made by J. Balty that the same architect was responsible for the layout of all four cities seems highly probable. A very characteristic trait of at least both Antioch and Apamea is a main street oriented N-S, aptly called the spine of the city by Balty. In the map of Toselli (see fig. 2b) the road leading today from village to village inside the circuit of the ancient city and leading further north-east through the gate at Bab el-Hawa, *i.e.* the gate of the road to Antioch (see above) might reflect such a N-S oriented main street.[26] The longitudinal main street is also found in cities in other regions of the Seleucid empire, for example in Ai Khanoum in Bactria.

Polybios tells us of the splendour of the city. So far, only a large Doric temple has been identified from the Hellenistic period – until now the only Greek temple of the Seleucid period recorded in Syria (fig. 4).[27] The temple was situated on a high plateau in the upper city, and must have looked imposing. The size of the temple is almost 37 x 19 m, suggesting a peristasis of 6 x 12 columns (fig. 4).

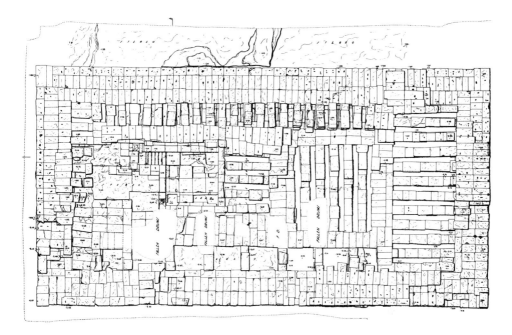

Fig. 4. The foundations of the Doric temple (Stillwell 1941 Pl. IX).

The cella opens to the east through a deep pronaos with two columns *in antis*, but there seems to have been no opisthodomos. The width of the foundations of the cella may suggest an interior order of applied columns. Behind the cella was an adyton, beneath which was a crypt reached by a flight of steps. Part of the floor of the crypt was still *in situ* when excavations took place in the 1930s and the excavators comment on the exquisite finish of the wall ashlars (fig. 5). A preserved fragment of a cornice suggests a date during the reign of Seleukos.

The building material is limestone, with ashlars of fine workmanship, fastened only with dowels in the typical Greek technique. The crypt under the temple is a most unusual feature, which so far finds parallels only in the two so-called heroa at Ai Khanoum in Bactria.[28] In Ai Khanoum two mausoleum temples have been excavated, one a temple with two columns *in antis* called the temenos of Kinneas, the other a peripteral temple. Under the cella of the temple of Kinneas were found a sarcophagus of limestone and three burials from later phases. The peripteral temple had a burial chamber, constructed of fine ashlars, underneath the adyton behind the cella. Though it must remain purely conjectural, the crypt under the temple in Seleucia is such an unusual feature that it is tempting to identify the building with the temple in Seleucia which Antiochos I built to his father after his death, the so-called Nikatoreion *temenos* (sanctuary) (App. *Syr.*

Fig. 5. The crypt under the Doric temple (Stillwell 1941 Fig. 42).

63). If the crypt was indeed the tomb of Seleukos, it was an urn with his ashes which was placed here. After he had been murdered by Ptolemaios Keraunos, a few months after the battle at Korupedion and just as he had returned to Europe, Philetairos, his vassal at Pergamon, bought his body from Ptolemy for a large sum of money, had it cremated and the ashes sent back to Syria (App. *Syr.* 63). The temple itself – if indeed identical with the Nikatoreion – was dedicated to the deified Seleukos by Antiochos, who for many years had been his father's co-ruler in the eastern part of the empire.

Among the 'other fine buildings' mentioned by Polybios must have been the *basileion*, the king's palace. In the years of Seleukos this building complex would probably have been similar to palaces in Macedon or at Pergamon, not like the later enormous palace complex at Antioch (see Nielsen 1994, 111 ff). As in Pergamon, the palace was probably situated high up on the slope in the upper city, and probably consisted of a number of large peristyle houses, a palace type that is also found in the capitals of Macedonia, Vergina and Pella, where such palaces are also situated in elevated positions on terraces or hills (fig. 6; see also Nielsen 1994, Ch. III).

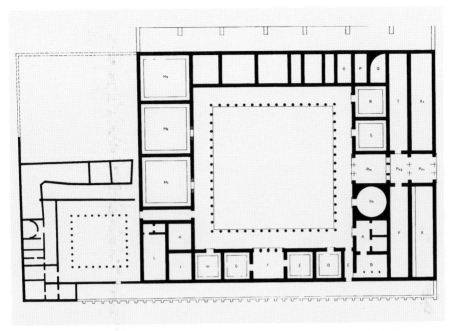

Fig. 6. Plan of the palace at Vergina (I. Nielsen, *Hellenistic Palaces, Tradition and Renewal*, 1994 Fig. 41).

Art in the early Seleucid empire

It has often been stressed that culture was not of great concern to the Seleucids, in contrast to the Ptolemies and the Attalids of Pergamon, (see Austin 2001, 103). There may be some truth in this, but at least Seleukos and his son Antiochos I emulated their rivals in other aspects than the acquisition of land, the founding of colonies or the building of huge defensive systems. The Tetrapolis cities with their splendour present clear evidence of that. That art was part of this splendour is evidenced for instance by the fact that under Seleukos one of the most influential statues of Antiquity was erected in Antioch: the famous Tyche of Antioch created by Eutychides, son of Lysippos, around 300 BC. Tyche, Fortune or Chance, was a notion of immense importance in Hellenistic times.[29]

The statue of Tyche is known only in Roman copies (fig. 7). She is depicted as a woman wearing a mural crown symbolising the city, and sitting on a rock from below which a personification of the river Orontes appears. Similar sculptures soon graced a huge number of Hellenistic cities, and its popularity continued into Byzantine times. Centuries after Euthychides created his Tyche, no less than forty-four cities in the eastern part of the Roman empire had adopted versions

Fig. 7. Roman marble copy of Tyche of Antioch (The Vatican inv. no. 2672, G. Lippold, *Die Skulpturen des Vatikanischen Museums* III,2, Taf. 143, 49).

of this sculpture for their temples and coins (Stewart 1990, 202). Tyche was not the only sculpture created for Seleukos to become famous in the ancient world. Another was the cult statue of Apollo for the temple of Apollon and Artemis at Daphne, the famous suburb of Antioch. This temple was founded by Seleukos, and the statue, of colossal size, was created by a sculptor named Bryaxis.[30]

From Pliny *NH* XXXIV, 73[31] we know that Bryaxis also made a statue of Seleukos. It has sometimes been suggested that this sculpture stood in the Nikatereion in Seleucia, but this is mere speculation, since statues of the first Seleucid must have been erected in all major cities of the kingdom.

Seleukos also copied Alexander's gesture of returning famous Greek sculptures that had been carried away as war booty by the Persians in the early fifth century BC. Where Alexander returned the early group of the Tyrant-Slayers to Athens, Seleukos returned to Didyma the cult statue of Apollon made by Kanachos, which had been taken by the Persians when they crushed the Ionian revolt in 494 BC. This gesture, however, was certainly a political gesture rather than that of a lover of art.

Portraits of Seleukos

Very few sculptural portraits (or painted ones, for that matter) of the Hellenistic kings have survived, though we know from literary sources and from inscriptions that they were erected everywhere, not only in the kings' own realms but also in such places as the most famous sanctuaries in Greece. Thus in Olympia there were statues of all the Successors, including Seleukos depicted as a victorious general on horseback (Pausanias 6.11.1). Some of the finest coin portraits ever created come from this period. In contrast to his rival in Egypt, Ptolemy I, for instance, Seleukos probably never put his own portrait on coins minted in his realm. There is perhaps one exception, a series of tetradrachms and drachms minted at Susa[32] by Seleukos as king, *i.e.* after he had assumed that title in 305/304. They show on the obverse a male head with a helmet covered with animal skin (usually seen as leopard skin) and adorned with the horn and ear of a bull (fig. 8). The face is that of a young man with features very similar to those of Alexander but the clear allusion to a bull rather suggests Seleukos. Whether this head portrayed Seleukos or Alexander assimilated to Dionysos the conqueror of India and master of leopards has been much debated. Most numismatists nowadays do not accept the identification as Seleukos. But the question arises of why Alexander should be portrayed in such an unusual fashion.[33] The horns of a bull are clearly associated with portraits of Seleukos. He was known for his physical strength, and according to Appian (*Syr.* 57): 'one day when a wild bull was brought for sacrifice to Alexander and broke loose from his bonds, he

Fig. 8. Tetradrachm. Obv. head of Seleukos (or Alexander). Probably Persepolis (Dr. B. Peus Nachf. *Auktion 376*, October 2003, no. 507).

Fig. 9. Tetradrachm. Obv. head of horse with two horns. Rev. a Seleucid war elephant. Pergamon c. 281/280 (O. Mørkholm, *Early Hellenistic Coinage*, 1991, no. 157 (New York)).

Fig. 10. Tetradrachm. Obv. head of Seleukos. Sardes ca. 277-272 (A. Houghton, *Coins of the Seleucid Empire from the Collection of A. Houghton*, 1983 Pl. 33,596).

resisted him alone and brought him under control with his bare hands. This is why his statues represent him with horns added'.[34] Could the portrait be an attempt to portray Seleukos, but still using facial features connected with Alexander? This is quite possible; Alexander's coin portrait was originally a Herakles portrait that came to be seen as that of Alexander, and in Roman times the earliest coin of a new emperor very often showed the features of his predecessor, until the emperor's own features became well-known in the capital from where portraits were distributed. At any rate this portrait is a unique occurrence; there are no other coin series with portraits of Seleukos on coins minted during his lifetime. Clear allusions to the king are, however, to be found on many coin issues where the horns play an important role, among them the reverse of a series of tetradrachms issued at Seleucia-on-the-Tigris after Seleukos had assumed the title of king, which shows Athena fighting from a chariot drawn by horned elephants (another Seleucid emblem), and exquisite tetradrachms struck at Pergamon after the victory at Korupedion, with an elephant on the reverse and a horned horse protome on the obverse (fig. 9).

Antiochos struck coins with portraits of the deified Seleukos. They show a very different portrait (fig. 10) from the helmeted head on the coins from Susa discussed above: a middle-aged man with strong facial features like most of the Successors. This physiognomy seems easily associated with a stalwart, strong general, a clever politician and an ambitious king – Seleukos Nikator. In a speech to his soldiers before the re-conquest of Babylon, Seleukos said:

Everything that is good and admired among men is gained through toil and danger.[35]

References

Austin, M.M. 1981. *The Hellenistic world from Alexander to the Roman Conquest. A selection of ancient sources in translation*. Cambridge.

Austin, M.M. 2001. 'War and Culture in the Seleucid Empire'. In: L. Hannestad & T. Bekker-Nielsen, (ed.) *War as a Cultural and Social Force, Essays on Warfare in Antiquity*. (The Royal Danish Academy of Sciences and Letters, *Historisk-filosofiske Skrifter* 22). Copenhagen.

Balty, J. 1986/1991. 'L'urbanisme de la Tétrapolis syrienne', *Ho Hellenismos stin Anatoli*, Athens, 203-229.

Bar-Kochva, B. 1976. *The Seleucid Army. Organization and tactics of the great campaigns*. Cambridge.

Cohen, G.M. 1978. *The Seleucid Colonies (Historia Einzelschriften*, Heft 30). Wiesbaden.

Cohen, G.M. 1995. *The Hellenistic Settlements in Europe, the Islands, and Asia Minor*. Berkeley.

Downey, G. 1961. *A History of Antioch in Syria from Seleucus to the Arab conquest*. Princeton.

Grainger, J. 1990a. *Seleukos Nikator*. London.

Grainger, J. 1990b. *The Cities of Seleukid Syria*. Oxford.

Hannestad, L. & D. Potts, 1990. 'Temple Architecture in the Seleucid Kingdom'. In: P. Bilde, T. Engberg-Pedersen, L. Hannestad, & J. Zahle (eds.), *Religion and Religious Practice in the Seleucid Kingdom*. Aarhus, 91-124.

Hoepfner, W. & E.-L. Schwander, 1994. *Haus und Stadt im klassischen Griechenland*. Munich.

Jones, A.H.M. 1971. *The Cities of the Eastern Roman Provinces* (2nd edition). Oxford.

Mazzoni, S. 1986/1991. 'The Persian and Hellenistic Settlement at Tell Mardikh/Ebla', *Ho Hellenismos stin Anatoli*, Athens, 81-98.

McNicoll, A.W. (revised by N.P. Milner,). 1997. *Hellenistic Fortifications*. Oxford.

Mehl, A. 1986. *Seleukos Nikator und sein Reich*. Louvain.

Millar, F. 1987. 'The Problem of Hellenistic Syria'. In: S. Sherwin-White & A. Kuhrt, (ed.), *Hellenism in the East*. London.

Mørkhom, O. 1991. *Early Hellenistic Coinage, from the Accession of Alexander to the Peace of Apamea (336-186 B.C.)*. Cambridge.

Nielsen, I. 1994. *Hellenistic Palaces, Tradition and renewal* (*Studies in Hellenistic Civilization* V). Aarhus.

OGIS – Dittenberger, W. 1903-1905. *Orientis Graeci Inscriptiones Selectae*. Leipzig.

RE – Pauly, A. & G. Wissowa, *Real-Encyclopädie der classischen Altertumswissenschaft*

Pollitt, J.J. 1986. *Art in the Hellenistic Age*. Cambridge.

Stewart, A. 1990. *Greek Sculpture, an Exploration*. New Haven & London.

Sherwin-White, S. & A. Kuhrt, 1993. *From Samarkand to Sardis. A new approach to the Seleucid empire*. London.

Shipley, G. 2000. *The Greek World after Alexander, 323-30 BC*. London.

Stillwell, R. 1941. *Antioch-on-the-Orontes* III. Princeton.

Weiss, H. 1997. 'Archaeology in Syria', *AJA*, 101, 97-148.

Notes

1   Appian (*Syr.* 56); an answer from the oracle at Didyma in Asia Minor to Seleukos I, when he inquired about his return to Macedonia.

2   Recent studies of Seleukos as politician and general are Mehl 1986 and Grainger 1990a.

3   Space allows only a brief presentation of some of the transformations that the region witnessed during the reign of the first Seleucid. Some scholars have seen the apparent lack of tangible evidence from Syria in the Hellenistic period as something that may reflect a real absence, not to be corrected by further discoveries, in an area dominated by war and political instability (thus Millar 1987). The aim of this paper is to give examples of how much is presently known of the large scale building activities etc. of Seleukos I. In short, to demonstrate that the picture drawn by Millar is too pessimistic, and his assumptions incorrect.

4   See Grainger 1990a, chapter 3. For a brief, lucid account of the history of the period of the Successors see Shipley 2000, chapter 2.

5   Thus the Seleucid calendar was still used in inscriptions in Palmyra from the second and third centuries AD and a mosaic found at Firkiye, now in the museum of Maarat al-Numan, carries an inscription dated to 822 according to the Seleucid era, *i.e.* 510 AD, with the emblem of the Macedonian star above one of the animals.

6   Translation Horace White, Loeb Classical Library.

7   For the Seleucid colonization see Cohen 1978. See also Cohen 1995.

8   *OGIS* 233. The translation is by Austin 1981, No. 190. Diodorus Siculus (XVIII, 7.1) offers a glimpse of the difficulties and frustrations felt by some Greek colonists: 'The Greeks, who

had been settled by Alexander in the upper satrapies, as they were called, although they longed for the Greek customs and manner of life and were cast away in the most distant part of the kingdom, yet submitted while the king was alive through fear; but when he was dead they rose in revolt' (translation R.M. Geer, Loeb Classical Library).

9   Sherwin-White and Kuhrt (1993, 20) aptly speak of 'a vast colonization programme' carried out by Seleukos and his son Antiochos I.

10   Translation H. White, Loeb Classical Library. Note that Appian in the middle of the second century AD considers Syria to be a completely integrated part of the Greco-Roman world, not barbarians as the peoples of the regions further inland.

11   For Babylonia we are in a much better position, with hundreds of cuneiform tablets dating from the Hellenistic period preserved. They attest continuities in Babylonian social, cultural and economic practices and traditions (Sherwin-White & Kuhrt 1993, 149 ff).

12   *E.g.* Jones 1971 who saw the later substitution of the Greek names of cities like Aleppo and Hama with their old names during the Roman period as evidence for continuity of existence. These two cities seem, however, to be exceptions rather than the rule.

13   This is a central theme in E. Wirth's important book *Syrien, eine geographische Landeskunde* (Darmstadt 1971), which deals with Syria in modern times.

14   See Weiss 1997, 147-148. The main aim of the excavations is the Bronze Age settlement, but the reports clearly show that there were also some Hellenistic and Roman remains on the tell, including on the acropolis a thick-walled rectangular building dating from the Hellenistic period.

15   Later authors, Libanius and Malalas, both citizens of Antioch (see Downey 1961, 59), state that the inhabitants of Antigoneia were transferred to Antioch.

16   In connection with his earlier campaigns to regain control of the 'upper satrapies' Seleukos had also waged war against the Indian ruler Chandragupta, but in the end was forced to make peace with him, surrendering some territories in exchange for a large supply of war elephants, for which the Seleucids became famous in the Hellenistic world, see Bar-Kochva 1976, 75-83.

17   Named after a city in Macedonia.

18   For a number of other settlements possibly founded during the reign of Seleukos, see Grainger 1990b, Ch. 2-3.

19   Mørkholm, 1991, 75. See also Downey 1961, 58-59 for arguments for Seleucia being the Syrian capital of Seleukos.

20   See McNicoll 1997, 81-89; *Princeton Encyclopedia of Ancient Sites* with references to older literature; Honigmann in *RE* 2, II (1921), 1198 (Seleukeia, Pieria).

21   Translation W.R. Paton, Loeb Classical Library.

22   See Honigmann with the map of Toselli (a map produced for Chapot, 1906, *Séleucie de Piérie*). Note that this map is also incorrect in details when it comes to the parts of the walls still preserved.

23   In the Archaic and Classical periods architectural rivalry among the Greek city-states was particularly expressed in temples; under the Successors fortifications took this place.

24   See Milner in McNicoll p. 221. The reason for the different types of masonry styles is much debated. From speculations about differences in time, a position often held by earlier experts on the subject of Greek walls (see Lawrence 1979, 235) – over functional reasons, not least the introduction of new siege weapons, and to Milner and McNicoll and others who consider that aesthetical reasons play a major role. Aristotle (*Pol.* VII. 11. 1331 12)

actually states that the walls of a city should be built so as to 'contribute to the adornment of the city'. The large-scale project of the large city circuits built by the Successors within a few years, and also the possibility of masonry crews working in different traditions should perhaps be taken into consideration.

25 For a short but informative article on the layout of Apamea and a general discussion of the layout of these three cities see Balty 1986/1991.

26 Alternatively, the grid system may have been used together with a serpentine main street to overcome the terrain, similar to what is seen in Pergamon. For this city see Radt 1999.

27 Most of the buildings recorded and excavated during the work of the American Antioch expedition are from the Roman period. There is a brief mention of an Ionic temple, but the drawings of the remains from this building were lost in the mail (Stillwell 1941, 4-5). This temple, which was built in marble, may have been Hellenistic or Roman.

28 For a brief account of these heroa, with further references, see Hannestad & Potts 1990.

29 For a brief and excellent discussion of *Tyche* see Pollitt 1986, 1-4.

30 Hardly to be identified with the well-known sculptor by that name who had worked on the Mausoleum at Halikarnassos around 350 BC, but a younger sculptor, probably from the same family.

31 Wrongly referred to by Honigmann as Pliny *NH* XXIV, 73.

32 Possibly also at Persepolis.

33 It is exactly in this period just before 300 that we find the earliest coin portrait of a Hellenistic ruler, Ptolemy I in Egypt.

34 Translation M.M. Austin 1981, 88.

35 Diod. XIX. 90.5

From Theatre to Temple

ROSS BURNS

One of the great pleasures of visiting the Danish Institute at Bayt al-Aqqad is to be at the heart of the living city of Damascus. Here life goes on much as it has done for centuries. In the multitude of impressions the visitor absorbs, it is not always easy to pick up all the many traces of the past that lurk in these *suq*s and alleyways. The present article seeks to dissect part of the area to show the role these streets have played over two thousand years and how the traces of that past are still very much part of the living city.

There is no need to go more than a few metres in Damascus to find yourself captive of its past. We take here only a short section (200 metres) of the route that lies between Bayt al-Aqqad and the Umayyad Mosque. The route (see fig. 1) is one that will often be taken by the visitor to the Bayt al-Aqqad. It links the busiest part of Straight Street not only to the Great Mosque of the Umayyads to the north but also to the main western axis leading to the Mosque, the Suq al-Hamidiye. The Hamidiye Suq is the most prestigious of the late Ottoman city's shopping precincts and still one of the most enticing thoroughfares of any Middle Eastern city.

History of the area

The route described below begins at the street running parallel to the north of the Suq al-Souf. This is the famous Straight Street (in Arabic, *Suq al-Tawil*; the Roman *Via Recta*), subject of Mark Twain's remark. The American traveller suspected the New Testament employed irony by referring to it as 'the street that is *called* Straight' and avoided any unqualified assertion of straightness.[1] The street is not the shortest distance between two points but takes a couple of distinct deviations along its route. The reason for these deviations was that like many Roman axes, it was the sum of its historical parts, having evolved across many centuries from what may originally have been a donkey track linking the Aramaean villages along the ridge that looked north across the rich meadows of the Barada. The Aramaeans, Greeks and later the Romans were all, to varying

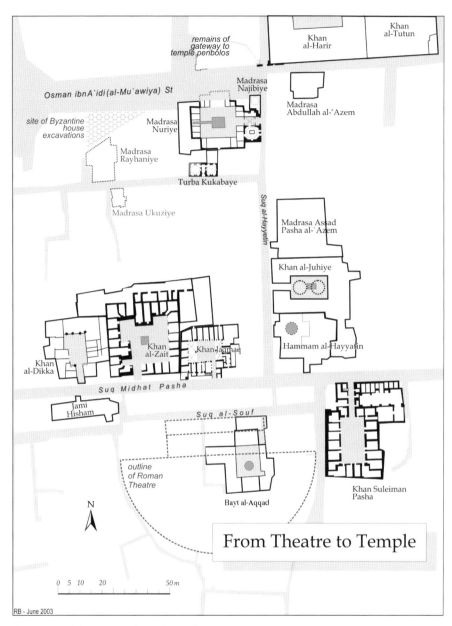

Fig. 1. Map of the area around Bayt al-Aqqad.

degrees, devotees of the straight line and did their best to take the kinks out
– not always with total success.

The focus of the Aramean settlements that joined together in the first version of Dimashq to serve as the capital of the Kings of Hadad-Rammon lay well

to the east of here, on the northern side of the mid section of Straight Street. Under the Greeks the town's focus shifted a little north. The Greeks preferred to settle on new territory lying between the temple (on the site of the present-day Umayyad Mosque) and the agora. From here they could easily replan and colonise the rich agricultural land to the north watered by the Arameans' Tora canal.[2] While the Greeks may well have attempted some straightening of the donkey track when they planned their grid-based 'new town', possibly in conjunction with the implantation of Greek colonial settlers in the second century BC, the full re-planning of the thoroughfare awaited the Romans.

The Roman need for new space naturally directed them towards the next available free land along the ridge, south of the temple. The area that lay south and west of the Great Temple to Jupiter now became the heartland of the Roman presence in the city. It was here that Augustus' great admirer, Herod the Great, did his bit for the spread of Hellenic culture by funding and constructing a theatre and a gymnasium, promoting those two touchstones of Greek culture, the body and the mind. It is that theatre whose location has now been confirmed by the restoration work on the Bayt al-Aqqad.

We know that probably in the later years of Augustus, the cross-city thoroughfare was replanned. The rear stage wall of the theatre was precisely aligned with the *decumanus* that soon strode in its splendid new dimensions across the full reach of the present-day walled city. The eastern starting point of the *decumanus maximus* was marked by a new freestanding gate that still exists following its reconstruction by the Syrian authorities in the 1960s – Bab Sharqi or the eastern gate. This improved axis crossed south of the old Aramaean and Greek quarters and continued west to form the spine of an extension of the city designed to mark the implantation of Rome's version of Hellenic civilisation. This re-vamped *decumanus,* the New Testament's Street Called Straight or *Via Recta*, was the scene of several of St Paul's experiences in the city in the mid 30s AD. Here Ananias was directed by his vision:

Get up and go to Straight Street and ask at the house of Judas for someone called Saul who comes from Tarsus. ... Go for this man is my chosen instrument to bring my name before gentiles and kings and before the people of Israel.

Ananias went and laid his hands on Saul. 'It was as if the scales fell away immediately from (Saul's) eyes and immediately he was able to see again.' Saul was then baptised as Paul and began his mission, spreading the message of Christ to the gentiles.

The colonnaded *Via Recta* echoed the east west axis to the north that joined the Greeks' *agora* (present-day Bab Tuma quarter) to the temple. The temple occupied a relatively flat expanse on the northern side of the ridge that had successively served as sacred space, passing from Aramaean to Greek to Roman hands. Along the way the city's patron god, Hadad-Rammon was transformed into Zeus and then Jupiter – or all three if you preferred, in a syncretistic environment that contrasted markedly with the rigid monotheism that caused so many problems to the south in Roman *Palaestina*.

Nothing remains of the *Via Recta*'s colonnaded shops, its shaded pedestrian thoroughfare and its wide central vehicular way. Nevertheless, some semblance of straightness has survived and the street pattern as a whole in the area south of the Mosque is reasonably orthogonal reflecting the grid adopted when the Romans extended the Greek city towards the west. We know that the theatre took many centuries to disappear altogether having served multiple uses into Arab times, including its use as a quarry (a handy source for nicely regular blocks) and as a prison (presumably in the bowels of the theatre's remaining sub-structure).

Following Roman times, the Byzantines probably used this area for more practical purposes than theatre and the cult of the body. The area seems to have been used for prestige housing in Byzantine times. On its northern limits, a Syrian excavation in the 1950s found remains of part of a Byzantine prestige residence southwest of the Umayyad Mosque, now covered by a modern building.[3] The house, originally constructed in the late fifth-early sixth century showed no sign of disturbance in the transition from Byzantine to Umayyad rule, bearing out Arab accounts of the taking of the city (Saliby 1997). The peaceful implantation of the Arab administration often drew on the remaining Byzantine educated class to provide the administrative cadre but in cases where the Byzantine upper class had fled, princely members of the new ruling house took up residence. At some stage in the Abbasid period, when Damascus' prestige had plummeted and it became only a relatively minor administrative centre, the area probably declined, the prestige housing giving way to more utilitarian uses.

Damascus' role was regenerated after the Fatimid period, its importance as a bastion against the Crusaders lifting the city to new strategic significance. This area southwest of the Great Mosque was again ripe for redevelopment. A number of madrasas founded as part of Nur al-Din's efforts to revitalise Sunni Islam were built here in the middle of the twelfth century. Around the same time, the commercial heart of the city – once focussed on the eastern axis leading to the Great Mosque and later on the middle stretch of Straight Street – gravitated to the west. Commercial structures then intermingled with new centres for the promotion of Islamic orthodoxy.

The Mamluk period saw the same mixed use of the area. New khans that reflected the Mamluk interest in promoting long-distance trade were built and the proximity of the area to the Mosque encouraged new religious projects. With the

Ottomans, the importance of the area to the city's commercial life became even more pronounced as the commercial heart of the city continued its swing from east to west. By the eighteenth century, the Ottomans – whose first building endeavours had favoured the area west of the walled city and the zone leading south west towards the pilgrimage route starting in the Midan – took a renewed interest in the zone outside the southwest corner of the Mosque. There they constructed great 'temples' to commerce that enshrined the eighteenth century Ottoman experiment in passing the management of the province of Damascus (and of the annual *hajj*) to the dominant representatives of commercial enterprise, the 'Azem family. Their major monuments lie in this quarter that became the prime commercial zone of the city. The creation of the Suq al-Hamidiye in the late nineteenth century, however, provided a new prestige shopping area leading along the western axis to the Mosque, one that was to dominate retail trade.

The Stroll

A stroll along the Suq al-Hayyetin will demonstrate all these themes in less than 200 metres. Any of the small laneways leading north from the Suq al-Souf will take you into the busy thoroughfare of Straight Street where the senses are bombarded with a mixture of noisy soundscape, spicy aroma and busy animation. This is still the busiest street in the old city, the only one taking traffic from one side of the city to the other. This is the role it has played for a good 3500 years since its origins as that country track along the Damascus ridge joining the small Late Bronze Age and Aramaean settlements.

On the northern side of Suq Midhat Pasha lie three of the oldest surviving khans of Damascus that span the early phases of the development of these commercial enterprises. The earliest in date is the *Khan al-Dikka*, an early Mamluk initiative. A tall broken arch marks its doorway in the continuous northern façade of the Suq Midhat Pasha. Most of its original structure has been radically altered over the centuries but one fascinating element persists, namely the ancient columns that were re-positioned here, apparently to form a colonnaded frame around the khan's courtyard. [4] In Roman times, the *Via Recta* ran immediately south of the site. The recent assumption that the colonnaded *decumanus maximus* was erected as early as the reign of Augustus is based on the style of embellishment applied to the Eastern Gate or *Bab Sharqi*, the first surviving monument in Damascus.[5] From the eastern gate to the western counterpart this grand 26 metre wide thoroughfare ran 1.8 kilometres to end at what is now the Bab al-Jabiya.

The *Via Recta* comprised a central carriage-way for wheeled vehicles and two arcaded and covered pedestrian thoroughfares with stalls or shops on the north and south sides along its length. The only direct evidence of this arrangement is the configuration of the inner face of Bab Sharqi and the remains of a gateway standing outside the Greek Orthodox Patriarchate, midway along Straight Street. Such configurations are the invariable rule in comparable cities of the Roman East, for example nearby Palmyra, Bostra or Gerasa (Jerash in Jordan). Over the centuries, beginning perhaps as early as the Byzantine period, this prestigious but wonderfully practical arrangement was encroached upon in order to cut down the space for vehicles (by then largely replaced by animal transport once the highpoint of Roman control passed) and to maximise the scope for small booths and multiple pedestrian thoroughfares. Whereas the *decumanus* or *Via Recta* had once spanned from the northern wall of the Bayt al-Aqqad to the northern side of Suq Midhat Pasha, it was now broken lengthwise into two or more smaller thoroughfares with pedestrians threading their way along cluttered alleyways between booths.

Many of the grand columns that once supported the colonnaded thoroughfare survived for many centuries, in fact were still noted by European visitors as late as the nineteenth century. They had, however, progressively been recycled or mined for their stone over the centuries. Enough must have remained by the thirteenth century for a selection to have been available to grace the new khan's courtyard since at least nine were repositioned here on the northern and southern sides of the open space. Most can still be identified in the modern khan though it preserves only in part the structure of its mediaeval predecessor. If you go across the courtyard to the northwest corner room you will find in among the warehouse clutter a beautiful intact Ayyubid-style broken arch sitting on one of the columns that once graced the Roman *decumanus*. The capital of the column bears exactly the same type of simple egg-and-dart decoration that you find on the columns on the inner face of Bab Sharqi, indicating that the whole length of the *Via Recta* was built to a single design and probably at the same time – a massive achievement for a city that had been under Roman rule for only a few decades. Note how the column height is considerably lower than they would have been in ancient times, indicating the steady rise in the ground level of the city.

The khan that borders Khan al-Dikka on the east, also accessed off Suq Midhat Pasha, is an example from the early Ottoman period (dated 1601-2). The *Khan al-Zeit*, as its name indicates, was built to service the olive or olive oil trade.[6] The khan survives in its original form, a fairly pristine example of the mixing of the practical with the elegant. Two levels of arcading, the lower with broken arches the upper with flatter, rounder examples surround a spacious square courtyard with a central pool. It has an airy and elegant feel.

Lying immediately east is another Mamluk example, the *Khan Jaqmaq*.[7] This time we have an attribution for the project. Emir Saif al-Din Jaqmaq al-Argun-sawi was Governor of Dam between 1418 and 1420 and was also responsible for the Madrasa Jaqmaqiye, now serving as the Museum of Epigraphy. The khan was substantially reconstructed in 1601 by Hasan Pasha Surbaza. A dilapidated central courtyard with pool has arched porticoes at the eastern and western ends. The façade indicates a project that closely related to contemporary examples in Aleppo and Cairo, not surprising given its sponsorship.

We now strike out northwards along the *Suq al-Hayyetin* ('Tailors' Suq') that originally joined this section of Suq Midhat Pasha to the outer perimeter of the Roman temple (*peribolos*). The street probably owes its strictly north-south orientation to the Roman grid plan in the area and may have been part of an axis joining the *peribolos* outer gate to the theatre. The street continued on this orientation into the Arab middle ages as we will see from the monuments that follow its alignment. The first three buildings on the right, however, date from the Ottoman period.

The first, the *Hammam al-Hayyetin*, now serves as a commercial establishment but the painted spandrels of the dome inside the western entrance off Suq al-Hay-yetin betray its origins as a bath. The tall domed dressing room dates from the bath's 1881 restoration. The hammam's origins probably go back to the previous century though no precise attribution has been established.[8] If the location of the bath is tracked against the underground water conduit system that dates to Roman times, it is evident that its location is no accident. The existence of this bath as well as the still-functioning Hammam of Nur al-Din in the next north-south street to the east, the Suq al-Bazuriye, reflect the existence of a main water channel in this area, probably intended to feed recreational facilities associated with the Roman administrative headquarters – baths and a gymnasium.[9] (The gymnasium donated by King Herod the Great is attested in Josephus though its location is not mentioned – Josephus *The Jewish War* I 422.)

The next khan, also east off the Suq al-Hayyetin, represents an important example of the development of the Damascus khan under the Ottomans – vari-ously known as the *Khan Juhiye*, the Khan al-Hayyetin or the Khan al-Qumush.[10] This is one of the earliest of the city's Ottoman khans (1565-6). The courtyard is now spanned by two yawning spaces – circular apertures supported on spandrels. Originally the courtyard was twin-domed but the structures fell, probably as a result of an earthquake, and were not replaced. Originally, however, the idea of roofing the courtyard of a khan, according to Stefan Weber's recent researches, may have originated in Damascus as a local development of the idea of a lock-able enclosed space for the storage of valuable goods (Weber 1997-8, 446-7).

The building immediately to the north now serves as a mosque (Mosque al-Hayyetin) but also bears the name *Madrasa As'ad Pasha al-'Azem* (Governor of Damascus, 1743-57).[11] The building was actually built earlier by the first 'Azem Governor of Damascus, Isma'il Pasha al-'Azem, but restored in 1749-50 as part of the ambitious program of works in this quarter by his son, the most illustrious of the 'Azem line, As'ad Pasha. The most magnificent example of his prestige is the great khan that bears his name one street to the east, immediately south of the Hammam of Nur al-Din. This is not on our route but the sheer scale and boldness of the enterprise underline As'ad Pasha's ambition to turn Damascus into a major centre of trade, building on its role as a base for the Mecca pilgrimage.

Continuing northwards look out for a cross street on the left which leads westwards towards the busy cloth markets of the Hariqa quarter. Thirty metres on the right look for a small Mamluk entrance along the narrow street – a central passageway that leads between two domed chambers. This neglected structure, often cluttered by street traders' wares, is the *Turba Kukabaye*, the tomb of Kukbay al-Mansuri the wife of the great Mamluk Governor of Damascus, Tengiz.[12] Tengiz ruled Damascus in the first half of the fourteenth century (governor 1312-40), largely coinciding with the third reign of Sultan al-Nasir Muhammed (1310-41). Tengiz was a great builder, both in Damascus and in Jerusalem, which at the time was under his jurisdiction. In Jerusalem he built the enormous complex centred on the Suq al-Quttanin that forms one of the western axes leading to the Haram al-Sharif and the Dome of the Rock. It includes several other facilities including two hammams, a khan and a madrasa. His major work in Damascus was the mosque built outside the western gate of the city. The mosque was often rebuilt and survives only in partial form on the northern side of Sharia Nasr. His beloved wife died ten years before the end of his governorship and was buried in this small complex that combined a tiny *ribat* or hostel for women (left) and a tomb chamber (right). Tengiz' funerary arrangements were much less orderly. He died in disgrace in Alexandria but his body was eventually returned to Damascus and entombed in the domed chamber to the right of the eastern-most entrance to the Tengiz Mosque.

Given this area's proximity to the Great Mosque – and, probably, the amount of neglected real estate available there after the uncertainties of the Abbasid and Fatimid periods – it is not surprising that it provided space for some early examples of the pious institutions encouraged under the Zengids and Ayyubids. The Madrasa Ukuziye (1141) and Madrasa Rayhaniye (1170) established along this same laneway have disappeared but the greatest of the twelfth century institutions is the next stop on our itinerary.

Return to Suq al-Hayyetin and head north again. Among the dark recesses on the left look out for a pair of windows with a water tap under the second. If you peer carefully between the bars of the window grilles you will see in the obscurity of the interior a simple cenotaph draped with a green cloth. This must be the most understated burial place of any great political or military leader. In this chamber, which you can access via the passage immediately to the north, lies the body of Nur al-Din. This was his funerary madrasa, the *Madrasa Nuriye al-Kubra* (1167-74).[13] Though it appears he may have changed his mind at the last moment and was starting planning for another place of interment closer in and immediately northwest of the Umayyad Mosque, death caught up with the great leader in 1174 before his new plans were realised (Allen 1996, part 2) (The second option was eventually to be appropriated to serve as the Madrasa al-'Adeliye, the resting place a half century later of the Ayyubid, al-Malik al-'Adil – north west of the Umayyad Mosque).

Whatever Nur al-Din's final intentions there could be no more fitting resting place than this sobre but dramatically under-stated chamber.[14] Above the sarcophagus, whose ends are elegantly but simply embellished in arabesques of carved plaster, one of the most marvellous *muqarnas* domes ever devised is suspended. It forms a beautifully proportioned cascade of light, seemingly suspended between heaven and earth. There can be few other examples that so successfully manage the transition from square base to dome so effortlessly. Two porphyry columns flank the mihrab of the funerary chamber. Yasser al-Tabba believes they were Byzantine and had possibly been removed from a ruined Damascus church (Tabba 1982, 124).

This was a pioneering building in many ways – first to combine a madrasa with the funerary chamber of the benefactor, and then first in Damascus to develop with such finesse the geometrical perfection of the *muqarnas* to cover an entire dome surface – and in brick, and not more easily worked plaster. Only the tomb chamber, the façade and the entrance *iwan* and passage survive from the original. The rest of the madrasa including the western *iwan* and the prayer hall are virtually new. The courtyard is thus only a sad memory of the original cruciform plan with a prayer hall replacing the usual south *iwan*. Most brutally, the northern *iwan* was chopped off during street widening in the 1960s, only one of the arch supports remaining to suggest its dimensions.

Before leaving, note the other original element of the complex, the entrance vestibule and passage. The doorway is recessed behind a vaulted space that leads under a monolith lintel (foundation inscription) into a second stone-vaulted passage. This suspended double cross vault was later given a retaining arch, a probably unnecessary attempt to support the hanging keystone (Sauvaget 1944-5, 218-9). Note the pioneering use of alternating ochre and white masonry on the street façade, the first extensive use of this *ablaq* technique. This was to become a Damascus speciality whose use with even more starkly contrasting stone would later spread to the major cities of the Mamluk realms and was employed with bold effect, particularly in Cairo.

Continue north a few metres to the intersection where the Suq al-Hayyetin meets the widened street coming in from the left, Osman ibn al-'Aidi Street. If you now look back to the south you will see the distinctive external form of the two muqarnas domes of the Madrasa Nuriye and the Madrasa Najibiye to its north. The Najibiye Madrasa was built by the first Mamluk governor of Damascus, Najib Jemal Aqush al-Najibi (Governor 1262-72, died in Cairo 1277-8). The dome over his funerary chamber is all that survives of the madrasa.[15] Al-Najibi directed the important restoration of the Umayyad Mosque under Baybars. Literary evidence suggests that the house of the tenth Caliph, 'Abd al-Walid Hisham ibn 'Abd al-Malik ibn Marwan (724-44), was located in this area (Moaz 1990, 111). Hisham had a long wait to succeed his three brothers, al-Walid, Suleiman and Yazid II, all sons of 'Abd al-Malik, as Caliph but his reign represented a prolonged period of prosperity before the demise of the Umayyads in the 740s. Like Walid, he was a great builder and his 'palaces' proliferated in the deserts of Syria, Jordan and Palestine.

From this corner, turn east along the laneway that is bordered by a stretch of wall to the north. A few metres on the right is the entrance to a charming madrasa now serving as a tourist bazaar (and from whose roof a good view of the Umayyad Mosque can be gained). This was originally another madrasa reflecting the 'Azem family's imprint on this area – the Madrasa 'Abdullah al-'Azem (1779). 'Abdullah Pasha was the last governor of the 'Azem line. The madrasa presents a compact three-storeyed shape rising from a central courtyard surrounded by colonnaded galleries. There is an uncompromising use of banding and the colonnades rise on elegant columns decorated with zig-zag patterns and topped by simple muqarnas capitals. A fine example of the late Ottoman style before the nineteenth century overwhelmed it with European affectations.

The area lay just outside the outer compound of the old Roman Temple (by then converted to a Byzantine church) surrounded by an extensive shopping complex, dubbed the *Gamma* after the Greek letter that described its shape – an inverted L enclosing the western and north-western edges of the temple-church inner compound. The outer gateway to the *Gamma* survives. Go back to the corner immediately north of the Suq al-Hayyetin. The suq's alignment is continued to the north by another suq, the Suq al-Haramein. Peering among the wares draped around the intersection, you should be able to find the remains of a grand doorway, the egg-and-dart topped lintel spanning the suq. On each side are stretches of regular classical masonry and the doorway is surrounded by a carefully rebated frame. When the first European researchers came this way at the beginning of the last century, the wall to the west stretched further and turned north to form the western outer wall of the *Gamma*. The *Gamma* gateway was probably inserted into the earlier Roman outer wall of the peribolos of the Jupiter temple. At this time the Byzantine or Late Roman authorities replanned the peribolos as a shopping complex complete with rows of well-spaced shops along the inner face of the walls to formalise the traditional use of the outer compound as a market area.

This concludes our dissection of a small part of old Damascus. It underlines the inexhaustible interest that its streets can unfold. The lack, until recently, of any scientific exploration of the levels under the city put the emphasis on deductive methods to peel back the layers of the city's past. Imagine how much more would be revealed if we could fossick in the five metres or so of rich past that lies under the present street level? But perhaps that would be spoiling the fun!

References

Allen, Terry 1999. *Ayyubid Architecture*. California: Solipsist Press, Occidental (published at http://www.sonic.net/-tallen/palmtree/ayyfront.html – June 2002).

Atassi, Sarab 2000. 'Von den Umayyaden zu den Mamluken: Aspekte städtlischer Entwicklung in Damaskus'. In: *Damaskus-Aleppo – 5000 Jahre Stadtenwicklung in Syrien*. Mainz am Rhein: Verlag Phillip von Zabern.

Braune, Michael 1999. 'Die Stadtmauer von Damaskus', *Damaszener Mitteilungen*, 11.

Degeorge, Gérard 1994. *Damas – des Ottomans à nos jours*. Paris: Sinbad.

Dodinet, M. *et al.* 1990. 'Le paysage antique en Syrie', *Syria*, LXVII.

Elisséeff, Nikita 1949-50. 'Les monuments de Nur al-Din', *Bulletin d'études orientales*, XIII.

Elisséeff, Nikita 1967. *Nur al-Din – Un grand prince musulman de Syrie au temps des croisades*, I-III. Damascus.

Freyberger, Klaus Stefan 1999. 'Das kaizerzeitliche Damaskus: Schauplatz lokaler Tradition und auswärtiger Einflüsse', *Damaszener Mitteilungen*.

Gaube, Heinz 1978. *Arabische Inschriften aus Syrien*. (Beiruter Texte und Studien). Beirut.

Herzfeld, Ernst 1942-8. 'Damascus Studies in Architecture', I-IV, *Ars Islamica*.

Kader, Ingeborg 1996. *Propylon und Bogentur*. Mainz am Rhein: Verlag Phillip von Zabern.

Meinecke, Michael 1992. *Mamlukische Architektur in Ägypten und Syrien – 1250 – 1517*, I-II. Glückstadt.

Moaz, Abd al-Razzaq 1990. *Les Madrasas de Damas et d'al-Salihiyya depuis la fin du V/XIe siècle jusqu'au milieu du VII/XIII siècle*. (Ph.D. thesis). Aix: Université de Provence.

Pascual, Jean-Paul 1983. *Damas à la fin du XVIe siècle*, I. Damascus: Institut français de Damas.

Rihawi, Abdulqader 1977. *Damascus*. (trans. Chevedden, Paul). Damascus.

Sack, Dorothée 1989. *Damaskus – Entwicklung und Struktur einer orientalisch-islamischen Stadt.* Mainz am Rhein: Verlag Phillip von Zabern.

Saliby, Nassim 1997. 'Un Palais Byzantino-Omeyyade à Damas'. In: *Les Maisons dans la Syrie antique du IIIe millénaire aux débuts de l'Islam.* Beirut: IFAPO.

Sauvaget, Jean 1944-45. 'Notes sur quelques monuments musulmans de Syrie a propos d'une étude récente', *Syria.*

Sauvaget, Jean 1932-50. 'Monuments ayyoubides de Damas I-IV', *Bulletin d'études orientales.*

Sauvaget, Jean 1932. *Monuments historiques de Damas.* Beirut: Imprimerie catholique.

Scharabi, Mohamed 1983. 'Der Suq von Damaskus und zwei traditionelle Handelslanagen: Han Gaqmaq und Han Sulaiman Pasha', *Damaszener Mitteilungen*, I.

Tabba, Yasser al- 1982. *The Architectural Patronage of Nur al-Din (1146-1174).* (Ph.D. thesis). New York: New York University.

Tabba, Yasser al- 1985. 'The Muqarnas Dome: Its Origin and Meaning', *Muqarnas*, 3.

Watzinger, Carl & Karl Wulzinger 1921. *Damaskus – die antike Stadt.* Leipzig: Walter de Gruyter & Co.

Wulzinger, Karl & Carl Watzinger 1924. *Damaskus – die islamische Stadt.* Leipzig: Walter de Gruyter & Co.

Weber, Stefan 1997-98. 'The Creation of Ottoman Damascus: Architecture and Urban Development of Damascus in the 16th and 17th Centuries', *Aram,* 9 & 10.

Will, Ernest 1994. 'Damas antique', *Syria*, LXXI.

Notes

1 Twain *Innocents Abroad* (1869) quoted in Yapp 1988. *Traveller's Dictionary of Quotations.* London.

2 Dodinet, M. *et al.* 1990 provides an interesting survey of Greek settlement patterns north of the city.

3 Location of excavations marked on map (fig. 1).

4 Hanauer 1924, 77-8; Watzinger & Wulzinger 1921, 46-7, Abb. 32; Wulzinger & Watzinger 1924, 80 (E 5.1). I am most grateful to Mick Godfrey for photos of the remaining columns.

5 Braune 1999, 78; Freyberger 1997-98, 127-128; Kader 1996, 167; Will 1994, 40; Watzinger & Wulzinger 1921, 65-77.

6 Scharabi 1983, 302; Weber 1997-98, 446; Wulzinger & Watzinger 1924, 80 (E 5.2).

7 Atassi 2000, 117; Rihawi 1977, 56; Scharabi 1983, 290-2; Weber 1997-98, 446; Wulzinger & Watzinger 1924, 81 (E 5.3).

8 Ecochard & le Coeur 1943 I, 111-2; Sack 1989, 111 (4.46); Wulzinger & Watzinger 1924, 81 (E 5.6).

9 The possible presence of Roman baths in this area and their link to the water-distribution system is a suggestion originally made by Tom Flemming Nielsen, consultant architect to the project.

10 Pascual 1983, 18; Rihawi 1977, 61; Sack 1989, 111 (4.45); Scharabi 301 (02); Weber 1997-98, 445-6; Wulzinger & Watzinger 1924, 81 (E 5.4).

11 Degeorge 1994, 75, n 303, 85, n 326; Gaube 1978, 69-70 (128); Sack 1989, 111 (4.44); Wulzinger & Watzinger 1924, 81 (E 5.4).

12 Meinecke 1992 II, 155 (9C/262); Toueir 1999, 47; Wulzinger & Watzinger 1924, 70-2 (E 4.14).

13 Allen 1996, chap. 2; Elisséeff 1949-50, 24 (54); Elisséeff 1967 III, 925; Herzfeld I 1942, 11-4, 40-1; Moaz 1990, 111-5; Rihawi 1977, 169; Sack 1989, 94 (1.40); Tabba 1982, 120-31, 189; Wulzinger & Watzinger 1924, 70 (E 4.13).

14 Best discussion is in Tabba, al- 1982, 120-31. For an interesting study on the philosophical 'meaning' of the muqarnas dome – Tabba, al- 1985. See also Elisséeff 1951, 24; Elisséeff 1961 III, 925-6; Moaz 1990, 111-5; Sauvaget 1932-50 II, 88-91.

15 Herzfeld 1942 I, 45; Sack 1989, 103-4 (3.43). Sauvaget 1932, 54 (22); Wulzinger & Watzinger 1924, 70 (E 4.12).

The Shaikh Zuwaydeh Mosaic
on the Border of Palestine and Egypt

MICHELE PICCIRILLO

In 1913, J. Leclant brought to light a perfectly preserved mosaic whilst digging on top of a dune at a site known to the Arabs as Shaikh Zuwaydeh, beyond a nearby valley, between Rafah and al-'Arish (Clédat 1915). A panel featuring a double mythological scene, Phaedra and Hippolytus in the top register and the Bacchic revel in the bottom one (fig. 1), decorated a hall paved with white mosaic tesserae, which the French archaeologist interpreted as part of a fortress of the Roman period. However, a closer examination of the structure suggests that it may actually have been a villa of the Roman period.

The mosaic, nowadays preserved in the Archaeological Museum of Ismailiyah, has been researched thoroughly and covers a wide range of aspects. The dating although absent from the inscriptions accompanying the two scenes has remained the same as that proposed by Leclant, namely, the second half of the 4th century AD. This dating was confirmed, on stylistic grounds, after the further study by D. Levi (1947). From an iconographic point of view, the two scenes have been compared with numerous parallels of the Antiquity; reliefs on sarcophagi, paintings and in mosaics known so far (updated bibliography in: Ovadiah et al. 1991). The inscriptions in verse as well as the captions identifying the characters, which do not present any particular epigraphic difficulties, have also been studied.

In my review of this well-known Palestinian mosaic, I intend to touch on two of the less investigated questions. The first pertains to the possible historical conclusions that can be drawn – from a religious point of view – from the presence of these two subjects in a mansion of the Late Roman period in the Palestinian south, also in light of parallel discoveries of similar motifs decorating the houses of the well-to-do in Jordan. The second question relates to the historical-geographical localization of Shaikh Zuwaydeh on the border of Palestine.

Fig. 1. The Shaikh Zuwaydeh mosaic.

Fig. 2. Snake fighting a bird.

The two mythological scenes

With thanks to the Egyptian Authorities for allowing us to photograph the mosaic again, we shall begin by describing briefly the two mythological scenes.

The mosaiced room, 7 m long and 6.60 m wide, is located in the southern sector of the excavated area. The entrance was through a door on the eastern wall. A second opening in the same wall led to a smaller enclosed area. A third door opened in the northern wall. The figured panel (4.75 × 3 m²) is set in a north-south direction next to the three entrances. On the northwestern corner it was accompanied by a rectangular panel, measuring 1.72 × 1.63 m, with a geometrical decoration. The rest of the floor was paved with white tesserae.

The figured panel is framed by a polychrome guilloche composed of three entwined bands, and is divided into three superimposed areas to be read from north to south. Next to the entrance was a swallow-tailed *tabula ansata* between two continuous series of birds, each facing a flower, in a west-east direction. The lower band begins with a snake fighting one of the birds (fig. 2) and ends with a bird facing a lotus blossom. The upper one begins with a sprig with two pomegranates and ends with a bird pecking a bunch of grapes spilling out of an overturned basket. Small palm trees and knotted wreaths accompany the two swallow-tailed handles of the *tabula*.

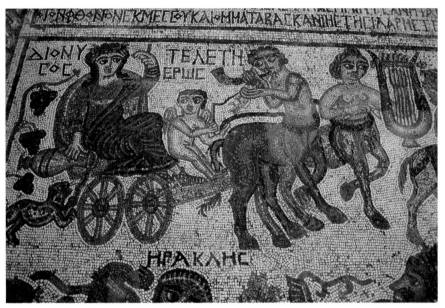

Fig. 3. The chariot of Dionysos.

The inscription in verse faces those entering the room[1]:

If you love me, gentleman, enter gladly into this grand hall
and then your soul will enjoy the works of art herein.
Cypris wove the splendid peplos of the Charites by a mosaic
of delicate cube stones, into which she put a lot of charm.

The middle area features the Bacchic procession in two superimposed registers. It begins in the top register with Dionysus seated in a chariot pulled by a pair of centaurs, male and female, playing respectively the flute and the lyre (fig. 3). Eros drives the chariot holding the reins in his left hand and a whip in his right. The god, dressed in tunic and himation, holds the thyrsus in his left hand and with his right pours wine from a *lekythos* to the panther that follows him. The scene is framed by a vine shoot. An old bearded Silenus follows, astride a donkey and dressed in a short tunic *orbiculata*, with a wine-skin thrown on his shoulder and a goblet in his right hand (fig. 4). Following him are a dancing satyr wrapped in a panther skin and a maenad playing a rattle whose dress has come apart in the frenzy of the dance, leaving her naked. Both accompany their progress with rattles and castanets. The captions refer to Dionysus, Eros, the *thiasos* or rite, and the dance.

Fig. 4. Silenus, dancing Satyr and Maenad.

Fig 5. Heracles and Satyr.

Fig. 6. Satyr and Maenad.

The bottom register is divided into two groups. The first group is introduced by an intoxicated Heracles, naked and partly wrapped in the skin of the Nemean lion; he is armed with a club and drags himself forward with the help of a satyr holding a rough shepherd's staff (pedum) in his raised left hand (fig. 5). Turned towards them is a dancing Pan with a rattle and a bunch of grapes. An isolated cantharus above and a panther near a vase below frame the scene of Heracles' drunkenness. Only Heracles is identified by a caption. A panpipe and a rattle separate this scene from the following one, which features a satyr wrapped in a panther skin with a pedum in his right hand, playing a horn, and a fully dressed maenad with a thyrsus in her right hand and a tympanum in her left, looking towards him (fig. 6).

The decoration – representing the Bacchic *thiasos* – of the hall discovered at Sepphoris, Galilee, in the vicinity of the theatre, adds a new interesting item for comparison with the lower panel of the Shaikh Zuwaydeh mosaic, more under the iconographic aspect than in terms of dating.[2] The 15 Dionysiac scenes of the Sepphoris mosaic are accompanied by captions that clarify their significance. The position of the mosaic, in the main hall of a wealthy palace, also helps in giving a context to the Shaikh Zuwaydeh mosaic, which must have decorated the dining hall of the Roman villa.

There follows a two-line inscription in verse set between the two scenes. This too faces the guest:

Fig. 7. Phaedra.

Friend, observe here with pleasure the charming things which art
has placed in the mosaic cubes petrifying

and repelling jealously and the eyes of envy. You are one who is
proud of the enjoyable art.

The third area of the carpet features the central episode of the myth of Hippolytus. Phaedra is represented on the left hand side, sitting in an aedicule with tympanum and acroteria, with the curtains raised and in a waiting attitude (fig. 7), while the nurse is giving Hippolytus the message of love sent her (*Phaedra*) (fig. 8). Eros

Fig. 8. Hippolytos.

glides above, armed with bow and arrow. The young man dressed in himation and a short tunic *orbiculata*, with boots and a spear in his left hand, is departing for the hunt accompanied by his tail-wagging dog set at a lower level, and by two hunters wearing short tunics and boots. The hunter in the foreground, armed with a shield, is holding the horse by its bridle. The second, in the background, is armed with a spear. All characters in the scene are identified by captions.

Outside the scene at the top, a brief inscription within a swallow-tailed *tabula ansata* held by two flying erotes, probably refers to the owner of the mansion who commissioned the mosaic:

You could see Nestor the builder, lover of beauty.

Parallels in Jordan

So far, among the mosaics uncovered in Jordan we have four parallels to the Bacchic procession and one parallel to the Hippolytus scene.

A very close parallel, from an iconographic point of view, to the Bacchic procession at Shaikh Zuwaydeh was discovered at the beginning of the 20th century in a house in Jerash and is dated to the 3rd century AD.[3] The mosaic of the Muses and Poets, contemporary to the mosaic uncovered in Sepphoris in Galilee, takes its name from the alternate series of portraits in a garland held by putti that forms the border of the carpet. Of the Bacchic *thiasos* in the registers of the central carpet only a few scenes survive; such as the drunken Silenus astride a donkey accompanied by a satyr, satyrs carrying the club and lion skin – the ensigns of Heracles, two satyrs and a maenad with a boy riding a panther, Dionysus and Ariadne in a chariot pulled by centaurs playing the lyre and the pan-pipe, Pan with a goat, a maenad with thyrsus, etc.

More interesting in relation to the problems that we proposed to investigate, are the other three mosaics in Jordan that feature both the Bacchic Procession and the Phaedra-Hippolytus scene, that were brought to light in Madaba and Jerash and are dated to the Byzantine epoch.

The Bacchic Procession, still preserved *in situ* at the Archaeological Museum of Madaba, was one of the first mosaics uncovered in the ruins of the city in the last two decades of the 19th century, after the reoccupation of the city in 1880.[4] The mythological character of the motifs and the nakedness of the figures were used as criteria for dating the work to the Roman era.

The Procession occupies the centre of the hall and of the decorative programme, which is mostly geometrical. At the time of discovery, it included three of the four figures of the thiasus: Ariadne, the Bacchant and the Satyr, while Dionysus was missing. Successively, the Ariandne figure was destroyed along with the vine shoots that separated the two dancers.

The surviving two figures, the Bacchant and the Satyr, give us the possibility to stylistically compare this work with the Achilles mosaic discovered in 1960, always on the southwest side of the tell (Piccirillo 1989, 136f.; Piccirillo 1993a, 76f). The Bacchic Procession develops in a second register above the frontal representation of Achilles between Patroclus and a young woman crowned by two erotes. The only remnant of the thiasus is a satyr playing a pan-pipe. He was followed by a maenad in a long tunic, of which only the left arm, holding a bell, remains. Then, towards the front of the procession, one can see the naked legs of a third person, very similar to those of the satyr in the Museum, and the front legs of the panther that usually accompanies Dionysus.

A third, much-damaged mosaic that used to decorate a house in the eastern quarter of Jerash, was brought to light in the spring of 1993 (Zu'bi I *et al.* 1994, pls. 27-30). The scene is surrounded by an acanthus scroll animated by running animals and develops in two superimposed registers. The captions help to complete those parts of the scene that were destroyed. The Bacchic Procession in the top register consisted of five characters. Pan with his pipe was followed by a female figure. The centre of the scene was occupied by Dionysus framed by a vine shoot with bunches of grapes and followed by a bacchant dressed in a long tunic, and by a satyr. The centre of the lower register was occupied by Aphrodite (the Cypris) preceded and followed by four characters, among which was probably Adonis, a peasant woman, and 'flower lovers', possibly *Eroti* and bees. The archaeological context is without doubt of the Byzantine era. This confirms the conclusions reached for the works in Madaba mentioned above, which are valid also for the Hippolytus mosaic we discovered beneath the Church of the Virgin in the centre of the city.

As in the previous scene, the myth of Phaedra and Hippolytus developed in two superimposed registers framed by an animated scroll, with the busts of the four seasons in the corners. It decorated a hall in the southern wing of a rich palace ('The Hippolytus Palace' in Madaba), located on the paved and colonnaded Roman road.[5] The top panel introduces the heavenly characters of Euripides' tragedy. On the left, Aphrodite – seated next to Adonis – punishes Eros with a sandal as he is being handed to her by a Grace after his unsuccessful attempt at hiding between the branches of a tree. The presence of a peasant woman places the scene in the countryside. The lower register introduces the earthly characters of the tragedy: the maidservants assist Phaedra, whilst her nurse delivers the love message to Hippolytus, who is ready to depart for the hunt, accompanied by fellow-hunters and by a servant holding a horse by the bridle.

Outside the acanthus border framing the Hippolytus mosaic are the Tychai of three cities (Rome, Gregoria and Madaba) holding staffs surmounted by *astile* crosses in their right hands. The presence of the Tychai is an additional confirmation for dating this mosaic, of a classical pagan mythological subject, to the Byzantine epoch (Piccirillo 1993a, 57). This discovery helped to correct the dating of the previously mentioned mosaics, which stylistically fit perfectly among the works of art of the 6th century.

The use of pagan mythological motifs in mosaics decorating Christian homes can be explained in two ways. Either it was the result of the classic culture and taste that imposed themselves in the capital Constantinople at the time of Emperor Justinian and from there imitated throughout the Empire, or it possibly indicates a pocket of pagan resistance among a population largely converted to Christianity. The dating, though based solely on stylistic ground, of the Shaikh Zuwaydeh mosaic to the 4th century (with Theodosius' reign as a *terminus ante*

Fig. 9a. A fragment of the Madaba mosaic. Note the 'reverse' orientation of North and South.

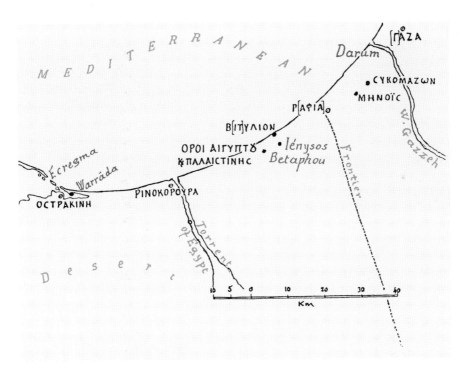

Fig. 9b. Sites on the Palestinian-Egyptian border shown on the Madaba Map.

quem, according to Leclant), leaves the second possibility open. Nestor may have been a member of the aristocracy still tied to paganism. The *Life of St. Hilarion* and the *Life of Porphyrius* bear witness to the persistence of pagan families in southern Palestine in the 5th century.[6] Sozomen in his *Historia Ecclesiastica* describes the inhabitants of Rafah as even more pagan than the inhabitants of Gaza (Ch. VII, 15, PG 67, col. 1457). The author of the *Life of Barsauma* writes that south of Gaza 'the pagans were powerful; they were the masters of the villages and towns of this region' (Dauphin 1998, 196).

On the other hand, the 6th century mosaics of mythological subjects discovered in Jordan can be better explained in the light of the first hypothesis, namely, that there was a cultural trend favouring the use of pagan motifs in the decoration of non-religious public or private buildings.[7] A further and more balanced examination of the literary works of the 5th century, such as the *Dionysiaca* by Nonnus of Panopolis or the *Life of Isidorus* by Damascius, as well as of other authors, attest to both the presence of pagan families, and still more the strength of the Hellenistic culture that survived thanks to its absorption by Christian rhetors and Christian artists (Bowersock 1990, Ch. IV and V). The above-mentioned literary works and the mosaics of the Dionysiac cycle discovered in Jordan are a clear testimony of the pagan heritage, but also of the symbiotic relationship between the pagan and the Christian worlds, who both indiscriminately used the same literary and iconographic schemes.[8]

On the border of Palestine

Leclant's discovery was an important occasion for focusing the interest of scholars in the Shaikh Zuwaydeh region.[9] Thanks to the Greco-Roman and Byzantine historical sources, that are rich with geographical details, it is possible to state that in the Ptolemaic epoch the border between Egypt and Palestine, was in the Shaikh Zuwaydeh area. During the Roman and Byzantine periods the border was purely an administrative matter, which survived until the Ottoman Period.[10]

A valuable document of the Ptolemaic period has reached us: it is the trilingual (hieroglyphic Egyptian, demotic Egyptian and Greek) Pithom Stele, dated to the time of Ptolemy IV Philopator, who was forced to fight against the expansionist aspirations of King Antiochus III of Antioch. The document describes the battle fought on 22 June, 217 BC, that was won by the Alexandrian king, as is told also by Polybius (*Histories* V, 79-86).

Ptolemy marched with his army from Alexandria to Pelusium, whence, after passing through Mount Casius and crossing the Sirbonis Lake, he established his camp after five days at fifty stadia (approximately 9 km) from Rafah 'that after Rhinocorura (al-'Arish) is the first of the cities of Coelesyria on the

Egyptian side'. From Gaza, Antiochus III came with his army to Rafah and set up camp at 10 stadia from the enemy (7.5 km west of the city). A few days later, he advanced his army up to five stadia from the enemy. A single kilometre separated the two armies.

The Pithom Stele specifies that the battle took place in 'Rph (Rafah) which is near the border of Egypt which is east of the sites of Bytyl and Paynofir'. The phonetic similarity allows us to identify Bytyl as Bitylion, where in the 6th century the Madaba Map places the border between Palestine and Egypt[11] (figs. 9a, 9b). This data is confirmed by Hierocles and Georgius Cyprius, as well as by the pilgrim Theodosius in the 6th century.[12] The latter places Bethulia (which he confuses with Bitylion) at 12 miles (17.7 km) from Rafah, which is consistent with the distance separating Rafah from Shaikh Zuwaydeh. The locality is therefore identified with ancient Bitylion.[13] Here, the traveller of medieval times would have found the Zaq'a station on the road to al-'Arish, which in the Mameluke period enjoyed the right of asylum (Alt 1940, 226).

The *Onomasticon* of Eusebius further specifies the point where the border post was located in the 4th century by fixing it at Betaphou 'which is a village beyond Rafah at a distance of 14 miles going towards Egypt, and it is the boundary of Palestine' (*Onomasticon*, 51, 18).[14] If the border was 14 miles from Rafah (20.7 km), the distance mentioned by Eusebius brings us to a point 5 km west of Shaikh Zuwaydeh. Bytyl-Bitylion was therefore on this side of the border, in Palestinian territory.[15]

Conclusion

The mosaic discovered on a dune at Shaikh Zuwaydeh near the sea, is evidence of the complex cultural contacts between paganism and Christianity in a transition period. At the same time, it is a reminder of the prosperity reached in the Roman and Byzantine periods in the border region, which armies as well as peaceful travellers were obliged to cross before venturing into the waterless land that divided Palestine from Egypt.

References

Abel, F.-M. 1931. 'Gaza au VIe siècle d'après le rheteur Chorikios', *Revue Biblique*, 9f.

Abel, F.-M. 1939. 'Les confins de la Palestine et de l'Egypte sous les Ptolémées', *Revue Biblique*, 207-236; 530-548.

Abel, F.-M. 1940. 'Les confins de la Palestine et de l'Egypte sous les Ptolémées', *Revue Biblique*, 224-239.

Alt, A. 1926. 'Bitolion und Bethelea', *ZDPV*, 49.

Barag, D. 1973. 'The Borders of Syria-Palaestina on an Inscription from the Raphia Area', *Israel Exploration Journal*, 23, 50-52.

Bowersock, G.W. 1990. *Hellenism in Late Antiquity*. The University of Michigan Press.

Clédat, M.J. 1915. 'Fouilles à Cheikh Zouède (Janvier-Février 1913)', *Annales du Service des Antiquités de l'Egypte*, XV, 15-47.

Daszewski, W.A. 1985. *Dionysos der Erlöser*. Mainz.

Dauphin, C. 1998. 'La Palestine byzantine. Peuplement et population', (BAR International Series 726, I). 190-213.

Figueras, P. 1999. 'The Road linking Palestine and Egypt along the Sinai Coast'. In: Piccirillo *et al.* 1999, 211-214.

Glucker, C.A.M. 1987, 'The City of Gaza in the Roman and Byzanine Periods', *BAR International Series 325*, 52f.

Honigmann, E. 1939. *Le Synekdémos d'Hiéroklès et l'Opuscule géografique de Georges de Chypre*. Bruxelles.

Joyce, H. 1980. 'A Mosaic from Gerasa in Orange, Texas and Berlin', *Mitteilungen des Deutschen Archäologischen Institus, Römische Abteilung*, 87, 307 f.

Klostermann, E. (ed.) 1904. *Eusebius, Das Onomastikon der Biblischen Ortsnamen*. Leipzig.

Kriseleit, I. 1984. 'Ein Fussbodenmosaik aus Gerasa', *Forshungen und Berichte*, 24, 75-97.

Levi, D. 1947. *Antioch Mosaic Pavements* I. Princeton, 72f.

Meyers, C.L., E.M. Meyers, E. Netzer & Z. Weiss 1996. 'The Dyonisos Mosaic', *Sepphoris in Galilee, Crosscurrents of Culture*, North Carolina Museum of Art, 1996, 111-113.

Meyers, E.M., E. Netzer & C. L. Meyers. 1992. *Sephoris*. Indiana.

Ovadiah, A., C. Gomez de Silva & S. Mucznik. 1991. 'The Mosaic Pavements of Sheikh Zouède in Northern Sinai'. In: *Tesserae, Festschrift für J. Engelmann*, (*Jahrbuch für Antike und Christentum, 18*). 181-191.

Piccirillo, M. 1989. *Chiese e Mosaici di Madaba*. Jerusalem.

Piccirillo, M. 1993a. *The Mosaics of Jordan*. Amman.

Piccirillo, M. 1993b. *Kanais wfusaifasa*. Jerusalem.

Piccirillo, M. & E. Alliata, (ed.) 1999. *The Madaba Map Centenary (1987 – 1997)*. Jerusalem.

Roberts, C.H. & E.C. Turner, 1952. *Catalogue of the Greek and Latin Papyri in the John Rylands Library* IV. Manchester.

Tsafrir, Y., L. Di Segni & J. Green 1994. *Tabula Imperii Romani, Judaea -Palaestina*, 91.

Weiss, Z. 1993. 'Sepphoris', *The New Encyclopedia of Archaeological Excavations in the Holy Land*, IV. Jerusalem, 1326f.

Zu'bi, I., P.-L. Gatier, M. Piccirillo & J. Seigne 1994. 'Note sur une mosaïque à scène bachique dans un palais d'époque byzantine à Jérash', *Liber Annuus*, 44, 539-546.

Notes

1 We give here the translation by Ovadiah *et al.* 1991, 182f.

2 Weiss 1993; Meyers E.M. *et al.* 1992, 38-59; Meyers C.L. *et al.* 1996, 111-113. An updated bibliography on the representations of myth in: Ovadiah *et al.* 1991, 184, fn. 21.

3 Parts of the mosaic composition are preserved at the Pergamon Museum in Berlin and at Orange in Texas (Joyce 1980, 307f; Kriseleit 1984, 75-97; Piccirillo 1993, 20.)

4 Piccirillo 1989, 134f (see Piccirillo 1993b, 134); Piccirillo 1993a, 68-70, 76.

5 'The Hyppolitus Hall' in Piccirillo 1989, 50-66 (the same pages in Piccirillo 1993b); Piccirillo 1993a, 49-67.

6 The problem is further investigated by C. Dauphin in: Dauphin 1998.

7 Procopius of Gaza, in one of his works describes the mosaic with Phaedra and Hypollitus that decorated a palace within the city (Abel 1931, 9f; Glucker 1987, 52f)

8 See the study of the mosaics forming part of the Dionysiac cycle discovered at Paphos on the island of Cyprus (Daszewski 1985).

9 For a brief survey of the monuments along the road that linked Egypt to Palestine see Figueras 1999, 211-214.

10 Cyril of Alexandria could write: 'Palestinians and Egyptians are once again neighbours and no space separates them; but on the Egyptian border, I mean those to the east and the sea, there starts the first points of penetration into Palestine' (In Isaiam XIX, 18). Father F.-M. Abel dedicated a long study to the subject (Abel 1939; Abel 1940)

11 Oroi Aigyptou kai Palaistines, (Piccirillo *et al.* 1999, 93). For an updated bibliography on the site see: *Bitulion* in Tsafrir *et al.* 1994, 91.

12 The episcopal seat of Bitulios is set among the cities of the Palestina Prima, whereas Rinocorura (Al-'Arish) in the Egyptian Province of Augustamnica I (Honigmann 1939, 42, 719, 11; 67, 1023).

13 Abel 1940, 224f. The identification of Bitylion with Shaikh Zuwaidah was proposed by A. Alt (1940, 236-242, 333-335).

14 '*Bethaffu in tribu Iudae, vicus trans Rafiam milibus quattuordecim euntibus Aegyptum, qui est terminus Palaestinae*' (Klostermann 1904). The toponym is remembered in the Papyri of Theophanes as Boutafis (Roberts *et al.* 1952, Nos. 627-8 ([*apo Bou*]*taphiou eis Rapheya*[*n milia*] *g*). The text, according to Barag, could be further *amended with 1g miles*, that is 13, and that does not correspond perfectly with the Onomasticon (Barag 1973). The scholar published an inscription from the Roman era, unfortunately mutilated, in which the distance was indicated starting from 'the Syria-Palestine border' (*apo oron Surias Palai*[*stines milia*…]).

15 In the Ptolomaic epoch it was in Egyptian territory, west of the border (Abel 1939, 547f.)

Muhammad's Letters

JØRGEN BÆK SIMONSEN

Muslim historians provide information of letters written and sent by the prophet Muhammad to a number of important persons in the region, among others to the Byzantine emperor and to the ruler of Sasanid Iran. We have the letters transmitted differently in a number of medieval historical works. Thus, Abu Ubayd al-Qasim ibn Sallam (died 838) gives the full text of a letter sent by Muhammad to Heraclius (reigned from 610 to 641).[1] Abu Ubayd also gives the full text of the response sent by Heraclius to Muhammad (Abu Ubayd 1935, 22), while the historian Ibn Sa'd (died 845) only informs the reader that a letter was sent followed by a summary of the contents of the letter (Ibn Sa'd, Vol. I, 258). The Muslim sources also mention letters sent by Muhammad to local rulers in the vast area to be conquered by the caliphs during the 630s and 640s. In all letters the recipient is invited to embrace Islam.

The Qur'an was revealed during a period of 22 years. According to the classical Muslim tradition, Muhammad received the first revelation around 610 and after a short break continued to receive revelations until shortly before he passed away in the summer of 632. Scientific research of the text of the Qur'an has proved how important core ideas pertaining to the faith developed gradually and step by step, and since the publication of Theodor Nöldeke's pioneering book *Geschichte des Qurans* researchers have vested a great deal of effort in uncovering the cronology of the Qur'an.[2]

The scientific approach of researchers from the West and their critical work with the sources has been looked at with scepticism by Muslim scholars. Traditional Muslim scholars claim with some right that a critical and source-based approach to the text of the Qur'an does not display the respect expected *vis á vis* the revelation from God the Almighty to mankind. No compromise seems possible, however, as a scientific approach has to abide to the principle that history in the final analysis is the result of man's enterprise alone. Any idea of a God interfering at random in the historical course of events has to be rejected. Scientific research is based not on belief but on the presumption that everything pertaining to Islam can be analyzed as all other social, cultural, religious or political subjects or matters. A number of recent publications have expressed deep and profound respect for Islam and Muslims, but, at the bottom line, such an enterprise does not provide a more scientific analysis![3] The Orientalistic tradition castigated by Edward Said in his now classical analysis from 1978 (*Orientalism,* 1978) was actually based on a scientific approach, despite its many defects and inadequacies.

Orientalism is not alone with its interest for a greater knowledge of the chronology of the Qur'an. Ever since the birth of Islam, Muslim scholars have been interested in getting a clear understanding of the chronology of the many different revelations contained in the Qur'an. Needless to say the prime motive behind the Muslim interest in the chronology is anchored differently compared to the Oriental tradition (Ayoob 1984).

When Muhammad died in 632 the Qur'an was not available in any final form. The Muslim sources offer different names of the person(s) who took the initiative to supply the *umma* with a complete edition of the revelations and why such a codified edition was necessary at all (Watt 1970; Burton 1977). In the Muslim sources disagreement is also visible when it comes to the historical context in which a specific revelation was received by Muhammad. Information pertaining to this is part and parcel of the two genres established very early that focus on the life of the prophet (the *sira* literature) and on the many conflicts and struggles Muhammad and his followers had with different tribes and different cities prior to the conquest of Mecca in 630, and Muhammad's final ascent to the position as *de facto* ruler of the Eastern part of The Arabian Peninsular (the *maghazi* literature). The oldest *sira* work transmitted to us dates back to Ibn Ishaq (died 767), and the oldest complete *maghazi* work we have dates back to the historian al-Waqidi (died 823). In both works we can trace a number of sources now lost. The same goes for a specific genre developed by Muslims scholars with a special interest in achieving knowledge of when the different revelations were received by Muhammad (the *tafsir* literature). The medieval works on *tafsir* contains an enormous amount of information not yet sufficiently analyzed either by Muslim scholars or by researchers in the West (Rippin 1985).

The theological and dogmatic reasons for the painstaking work done by Muslim scholars through the ages in af effort to uncover the chronology of the revelation is intimately linked to a number of verses in the Qur'an referring to the need for abolishing verses during the time between the first revelation in 610 and the death of Muhammad in 632. The best example is Sura 2, 142-145, where the Muslims are told to perform their prayers facing the Ka'ba in Mecca. Prior to the revelation of Sura 2, 142-145, Muslims were facing Jerusalem. In the *Tafsir* works, the revelation of the verses prescribing Muslims in the future to face the

Ka'ba is dated to 624, *i.e.* a few years after Muhammad and his few followers had migrated from Mecca to Medina (Ibn Kathir 2000, Vol. 1 p 434ff).

In the theological and dogmatic works this is known as *naskh* and *mansukh*. The Arabic verb *nasakha* can be translated *to abrogate, to repeal* or *to revoke* and is used in a technical meaning in the *tafsir* literature as well as in the legal literature for Qur'anic stipulations of an early date changed or altered later by a new revelation. In this way the older revelation is abrogated by a younger revelation. As the Qur'an in Sura 45,18, claims to represent a revelation embracing all aspects of human life, it is no surprise to notice how Muslim scholars have been interested in knowing what early revelations have been abrogated or altered by later revelations (Al-Sadusi 1985).

The many alleged letters written by Muhammad to a number of important rulers in the Middle East in the early 7th century, referred to in the Muslim tradition, are concrete examples of how early Muslim scholars tried to define Islam. The letters are not original letters written by Muhammad,[4] but are examples pertaining to the discussion of the early Muslim scholars trying to interpret the revelation and its repercussions for those who accepted Islam.

Muhammad perceived the religion of Islam not as a new religion but as a confirmation of the one true religion revealed during the course of history to a number of prophets and messengers sent to mankind by the One and Only God. The contents of Islam is in agreement with the message revealed earlier by other prophets like Abraham, Isaac, Jacob, Moses and Jesus to mention only a few of those prophets Islam claims to share with the Jews and the Christians. This idea is to be found in many revelations in the Qur'an (see *e.g.* Sura 6, 83-86) expressing the idea upheld by Muhammad all through his life from 610 onwards. When Islam's prophet in 610 received the first revelation in a cave in the mountains outside his native town of Mecca he was shocked and fell into a deep crisis. He finally decided to interpret the event as a sign from God that he had been chosen as the last prophet, the last *rasul* or *messenger* to convey to mankind the final revelation. God had chosen him as he previously had chosen Abraham, Moses and Jesus. Muhammad, however, was the final messenger, the seal of the prophets as indicated in Sura 33, 40. The definition of Muhammad as the seal of the prophets gave way to vehement clashes with the Arabs who had converted to Judaism or Christianity. For obvious reasons they could not accept the interpretation developed by Muhammad.

In a historical work entitled *The Conquests of the Countries (Futuh al-Buldan)* Ahmad ibn Yahya al-Baladhuri (died 892) has collected information about the expansion of the caliphate during the first century after the death of the prophet. His work begins with a description of the *hidjra*, the migration of Muhammad and his few supporters from Mecca to Medina. In this way Baladhuri is interpreting the ensuing expansion as a result of the *hidjra* and the establishment of the Islamic *umma* in Medina based as it was on the rules and regulations contained in the final revelation from the One and Only God.[5] The composition of Baladhuri's work is of course a construction in the modern anthropological sense of the word being an interpretation of the course of history embedded in a religious belief. From a modern historical point of view the question can be posed if Muhammad actually had perceived an idea of an expansion of Islam beyond the borders of the Arabian Peninsular into the rest of the world. We know it happened, but a historical interpretation of history must reiterate that the ensuing expansion in no way was a result of *manus Dei* but a consequence of initiatives and possibilities decided by men acting in their specific historical setting. The course of history is a result of human endeavours, not of divine interference!

The interpretation of Islam formulated during the first century rests on an assumption that Islam was a monopoly for the Arabs and not a matter for non-Arabs. Accordingly the caliphate did not arrange any systematic effort to force the conquered peoples to convert to Islam. The conquering Muslim Arabs for their part settled in a limited number of cities in the conquered provinces. Where they settled, they founded, as a general rule, new cities secluded from the population. This was the case in Iraq (Kufa and Basra), in Egypt (al-Fustat), and to a certain extend in Syria (Qinnisrin and al-Djabiya). In all the new *amsar* detachments of the caliphal army were stationed, and from these newly established cities the conquered provinces were taxed and politically controlled. The conquered population had to pay what was needed, and as time passed the amount and the kind of levies demanded from the population expanded.

The turbulent social development during the Umayyad caliphate – when conversion increased from the early 8th century – is intimately related to different and opposing interpretations of Islam. The Qur'an in several cases points to the fact that Muhammad was an Arab messenger (*e.g.* Sura 42, 7 and in a more direct way Sura 43, 31) and in a number of cases the Qur'an is referred to as an Arab revelation (*e.g.* Sura 12, 2 and Sura 13, 37). In the *tafsir* works it is common to find hints to an early interpretation of Islam along the follwing lines: with God's choice of Muhammad as the final prophet, the Arabs were finally included into the group of chosen peoples who was offered insight into the plan of God with his creation. In the early parts of the Qur'an we can see how the Arabs converted to Judaism and Christianity prior to Muhammad's revelation questioned this interpretation. Arab Jews and Arab Christians had great difficulties in accepting the Muslim interpretation of their revelation as linked in *any* way to the revelation passed on to Muhammad. Quite a number of the early revelations circles around this. The intensity of the debate can also be seen in the language used, not least in the many verses about *djihad* and the call to contribute and participate in the cause of God (*cf.* Malik 1979, Firestone 1999).

At a later stage Sura 7, 158 is offered as proof of the universel message of Islam. According to this revelation Islam is for all mankind and not only for the Arabs. But at this stage the historical context had changed dramatically compared to the beginning of the 7th century when Muhammad was still alive. Islam was now present outside the Arabian Peninsular, and a growing number of persons who earlier had adhered to other religions were now converting to Islam. The conversion in other words exposed the rights of later Muslim converts compared to the rights of the original Arab Muslims. Were they to be equal, or were the converts only to enjoy some of the rights granted to the original Arab Muslims?

If we take Muhammad's alleged letter to the Byzantine emperor Heraclius as an example, the message is clear and unambiguous: Christians converting to Islam will enjoy the same rights as the Arab Muslims. In case they do not convert they will have to abide in a place in society where religious affiliation was a determinant for the payment of taxes to the caliphate. In the early caliphate the privileged position of the Arab Muslims was intimately linked to an interpretation of Islam as a revelation passed on to the Arabs. Back in time the Jews and Christians were offered the revelation and were invited to organize their life in accordance with the wishes of God. But both Jews and Christians chose to manipulate the contents of the revelation in order to secure for themselves certain privileges (*cf.* Sura 3, 23-25 and Sura 4, 46). With the revelation passsed on to Muhammad this deception became clear to all (*cf.* Sura 6, 154-157). Even so, Jews and Christians were recognized as *ahl al-kitab*, People of the Book (*cf.* Sura 2, 101 and 105 and Sura 98) and granted the right to sustain their own religious and legal traditions. The autonomy offered had to be paid by *djizya*, a poll tax legitimized with rerference to Sura 9, 29. When *ahl al-kitab* recognizes the duty to pay this levy they obtain *dhimma*, *i.e.* protection from the Muslim polity to persue and uphold their own religious and legal traditions.

In this respect all the alleged letters of Muhammad are in accordance: all members of the *ahl al-kitab* who convert are granted equal rights with the Arab Muslims. The principle is traced back to Muhammad by way of alleged letters describing the way the prophet of Islam *intended* to treat Jews and Christians who converted to Islam. The alleged letters of Muhammad are relics of the debate among the Muslim scholars of the first century. The scholars tried to strengthen their arguments and their points of view by presenting sources presumably dating back to the prophet himself. The argument was inevitable as the Qur'an states

Muhammad to be an example for all other Muslims (*cf.* Sura 33, 40). Anyone acting in accordance with the *sunna* of the prophet was considered to be right, while those acting with no basis in his *sunna* could be dismissed as illegitimate or even apostates.

When conversion began to gain momentum from the early 8th century onwards the newly converted Muslims demanded the same privileges and the same rights as the Arab Muslims. This in itself was a challenge to the administrative praxis established when the various provinces were conquered in the 630s and 640s. When the caliphal army conquered the provinces formerly belonging to the Byzantine Empire or the Sasanid Empire, they took over the local administration and left it unchanged. The Arab conquerors demanded what they needed in cash and in kind from the population and left the actual work of collecting the taxes to the local administration. As new needs surfaced these were demanded from the local population as well.

During the first century after the conquest we can follow in the papyri from Egypt how the Arab-Muslim administration extended the demands from the local population. The great mosques build in Jerusalen, *i.e.* The Dome of the Rock and The al-Aqsa Mosque, demanded a workforce far bigger than the one that could be supplied from Palestine alone, and accordingly skilled craftsmen from Egypt were demanded to come to Jerusalem or to other places, where the caliphal administration found reason to build new official buildings. Likewise, a number of papyri indicate how the attacks by sea on Byzantium during the 7th century were organized by way of the forced conscription of a number of young men from different small villages along the Nile (*cf.* Eickhoff 1954, Bæk Simonsen 1988).

The Arabic historians offer scattered references to the *mawali*, *i.e.* the non-Arab converts. Very often the *mawali* were active in social uprisings and the sources seem to indicate a close link between these uprisings and the converts' claim to be placed on equal terms with the Arab Muslims (Wellhausen 1902, Sharon 1983). The question of the *mawali* still needs thorough analysis and many questions pertaining the question of conversion remain unanswered and await further research (Dennett 1950; Bulliet 1979; Levtzion (ed.) 1979).

The early caliphal administration was based on a tight hierarchy. In the case of Egypt, the Arab Muslim governor was placed in al-Fustat, and he passed on demands (*entagia*) to the various administrative areas throughout Egypt headed by the local *pagarchos*. Demands covered everything from large amounts of money needed when the Arab Muslim army was to be paid, to minor demands for a local guide for an Arab Muslim passing this or that village along the Nile. In general terms the demands from the Arab Muslim governor in al-Fustat were increasing as the bureaucracy expanded. This context is mirrored in the many letters from one *pagarchos* to another, left over from Egypt. In quite many examples the single *pagrachos* tries to keep the population inside his administrative area in order to avoid a decreasing number of taxpayers (Rémondon 1953). The debate between the local population in charge of the early caliphal administration sheds light on some of the many coherent problems pertaining to the administration of the early caliphate. So does the information to be deducted from the early books on legal questions collected by the early Muslim scholars (Conrad 1994; Motsky 2002).

The passages in the Qur'an defining Islam as the final revelation provides the textual point of departure for the classical definition of Islam as a revelation for all mankind and not a revelation for the Arab only. In the later classical interpretation of Islam, Muslim scholars spread the message of Muhammad out to include everyone everywhere. This new interpretation became necessary as Islam had, by way of the conquests, made itself known outside the Arab Peninsular. The debate embedded in the Qur'an between Muslims and Arabs who had converted to Judaism and Christianity prior to the revelation of the Qur'an was repeated in the conquered provinces.[6]

In this respect it was necessary to find out how non-Arab converts were to be socially included in the *umma*. The Qur'an emphasizes that all Muslims are equal no matter what position they had had prior to their conversion. The strong sense of egality was extended to include also the growing number of non-Arabs who had become Muslims from the early 8th century onwards (Gruber 1975; Marlow 1997). They were granted the same rights as other Muslims. On the other side of the coin were the Jews and the Christians who did not convert to Islam. They were obliged to pay a special tax in response to the autonomy they were granted by way of an interpretation of the Qur'an along the following lines: Islam being the final revelation was needed because the Jews – and then the Christians – had manipulated the revelation from God. By way of letters claimed to date back to the prophet, Muslim scholars in the early 8th century were able to legitimize the administrative praxis as being part and parcel of the *sunna* of the prophet. The letters are claimed to have been sent to the emperors of the Byzantine Empire and the Sasanid Empire *prior* to the conquests. In this way the administrative praxis of the early caliphate is legitimized as being in compliance with the ideas and principles formulated by the prophet himself.

References

Abu Ubayd, al-Qasim ibn Sallam 1353/1935. *Kitab al-Amwal.* Cairo.

Baladhuri, Ahmad ibn Yahya al- (no year indicated). *Futuh al-Buldan.* (Ed. Salah al-Din Munadjdjid). Cairo.

Bennett, Clinton 1998. *In search of Muhammad.* London. Cassell.

Bæk Simonsen, Jørgen 1988. *Studies in the Genesis and Early Development of the Caliphal Taxation System.* Copenhagen: Akademisk Forlag.

Bulliet, Richard W. 1979. *Conversion to Islam in the Medieval Period. An Essay in Quantitative History.* Cambridge, Mass.: Harvard University Press.

Burton, John 1977. *The Collection of the Qur'an,* Cambridge: Cambridge University Press.

Conrad, Gerhard 1994. *Die Qudat Dimasq und der Madhab al/Auza'i. Materialen zur syrischen Rechtsgeschichte,* Beirut: Beiruter Texte und Studien, Band 46.

Dennett, Daniel C. 1950. *Conversion and the Poll Tax in Early Islam.* Cambridge, Mass.: Harvard University Press.

Eickhoff, E. 1954. *Seekrieg und Seepolitik zwischen Islam und Abendland 650 – 1040,* Saarbrücken.

Firestone, Reuven 1999. *Jihad. The Origin of Holy War in Islam,* Oxford: Oxford University Press.

Gaudeul, J.-M. 1995. *Riposte aux Chrétiens par 'Ali al-Tabari,* Rom.

Goddard, H. 2000. *A History of Christian-Muslim Relations.* Edinburgh: Edinburgh University Press.

Gruber, Ernst August 1975. *Verdienst und Rang: Die Fada'il als litterarisches und gesellschaftliches Problem im Islam,* Islamkundliche Untersuchungen, Bd. 25. Frieburg in Breisgau.

Ibn Kathir 2000. *Tafsir al-Qur'an,* Riyadh: Dar al-Salam, 8 Vols.

Ibn Sa'd, Muhammad (no year indicated): *Kitab al-Tabaqat al-Kubra,* Beirut: Dar al-Sadir, Vols. I – IX.

Levtzion, Nehemia (ed.) 1979. *Conversion to Islam.* New York: Holmes and Meier.

Malik, S.K. 1979. *The Quranic Concept of War,* Lahore: Wajidalis.

Motzki, Harald 2002. *The Origins of Islamic Jurisprudence: Meccan fiqh before the classical schools,* Leiden: Brill.

Marlow, Louise 1997. *Hierarchy and Egalitarianism in Islamic Thought,* Cambridge: Cambridge University Press.

Nöldeke, Theodor 1860. *Geschichte des Qurans,* Göttingen, Vols. I-III.

The Holy Qur'an. English translation of the meanings and commentary, King Fahd Holy Qur'an Printing Complex.

Rémondon, R. 1953. *Papyrus grecs d'Apollos Ano.* Documents de Foilles de l'Institut francais d'Archeologie Orientale de Caire. Publié sous la Dirction de Ch. Kuentz. Le Caire.

Rippin, Andrew 1985. 'Literary Analysis of Qur'an, Tafsir and Sira: The Methodologies of John Wansborough'. In: Martin, Richard (ed.): *Approaches to Islam in Religious Studies,* Tucon: University of Arizona Press.

Rippin, Andrew 2001. *The Qur'an and its Interpretavie Tradition*, Ashgate: Aldershot.

Robinson, Neal 1996. *Discovering the Qur'an: A Contemporary Approach to a Veiled Text,* London: SCM Press.

Sadusi, Qatada ibn Di'ama al- 1998. *Kitab al-Nasikh wa-l-mansukh fi kitab Allah ta'ala.* Beirut: Mu'assasat al-Risala.

Sahas, Daniel K. 1972. *John of Damascus on Islam, the 'Heresy of the Ishmaelites'.* Leiden: Brill.

Said, Edward 1978. *Orientalism.* New York: Vintage Books.

Sharon, Moshe 1983. *Black Banners from the East: the Establishment of the Abbasid State.* Jerusalem: Magnes Press, The Hebrew University.

Thomas, David 2002. *Early Muslim Polemic against Christianity. Abu 'Isa al-Warraq's 'Against the Incarnation'.* Cambridge: Cambridge University Press.

Wansborough, John 1977. *Quranic Studies.* Oxford: Oxford University Press.

Watt, W. Montgomery 1970. *Bell's Introduction to the Qur'an,* Edinburgh: Edinburgh University Press.

Wellhausen, Julius 1889. *Skizzen und Vorarbeiten IV,* Berlin: Georg Reimer.

Wellhausen, Julius 1902. *Das arabische Reich und sein Sturz,* Berlin: Georg Reimer.

Notes

1 Abu Ubayd 1935, 21f.

2 Nöldeke 1860; Wansborough 1977; Robinson 1996 and Rippin 2001.

3 *E.g.* Bennett 1998.

4 Underlined already by Wellhausen 1899, 89.

5 Baladhuri, ed. Salah al-Din Munadjdjid, Cairo, 2ff.

6 Sahas 1972; Gaudeul 1995; Goddard 2000; Thomas 2002.

Three Eastern Islamic Leather Wallets and Three Related Stone Press-moulds in the David Collection

KJELD VON FOLSACH

In an article from 1997, Ralph Pinder-Wilson published a leather wallet and four stone press-moulds from Khurasan now in the Nasser D. Khalili Collection (Pinder-Wilson 1997). This profound study has in all respects shed light on the topic and the following remarks are mainly some supplementary notes prompted by the examination of the unpublished, related pieces in the David Collection, that is three wallets (figs. 3-5) and three double-sided stone moulds (fig. 8, 10 and 11).

In his article, 'Foundation-moulded Leatherwork – a Rare Egyptian Technique also used in Britain', Richard Ettinghausen published what probably was a leather wallet from the early Islamic world (Ettinghausen 1965, fig. 12). It is a lyre-shaped fragment and only one side is preserved (fig. 1). The technique employed for

Fig.1. Fragment of wallet (?) Painted and foundation-moulded leather. H: 17.2; W: 13.4 cm. Egypt, late 7th century (?) Walters Art Gallery, Baltimore. After Ettinghausen, Richard 1965.

Fig. 2. Wallet. Press-moulded leather. H: 10.5; W: 9.5 cm. Khurasan, late 12th or early 13th century. MXD 286, The Nasser D. Khalili Collection. After Pinder-Wilson, Ralph 1997.

its decoration is quite rare and different from the one used on the other wallets discussed in this article. Strings were glued to a coarse linen backing, forming a floral design over which the thin leather was placed, and this was then tooled, causing the design to protrude in low relief. The leather itself was dyed red and additionally painted in yellow, green and black, giving it a very lively appearance (Baltimore 1957, cat. no. 32). Ettinghausen places the fragment in Egypt since it was acquired there and dates it to the end of the 7th century. While this might be correct, in the eyes of the present writer the design could be somewhat later (Ettinghausen 1965, 68-69).

The second published leather wallet is the one in the Khalili Collection (fig. 2). Ralph Pinder-Wilson has convincingly attributed it to Khurasan – that is, present-day north-eastern Iran, southern Turkmenistan, southern Uzbekistan and Afghanistan – in the late 12th or early 13th century (Pinder-Wilson 1997, 341). According to Pinder-Wilson's description the flap, back and front of the wallet are made from one continuous piece of leather sewn together on the sides with separate gussets. The inside is lined with thinner leather and the two layers are separated by a layer of paper. A wooden button is fixed to the flap. To close the wallet, a leather loop running from the top to the bottom inside the front catches the button.

The decoration is made on a press-mould like the ones shown on figs. 7, 8, 9, 10 and 11, or perhaps on pottery moulds.[1] The leather would have been placed over the mould and pressed into the carved cavities of the stone, making the design stand out in relief on the finished piece. Because of wear and tear and deterioration of the surface, the design of the Khalili wallet has nearly disappeared today, but one can faintly see scrollwork, knots, roundels, etc.

Pinder-Wilson mentions another unpublished wallet in the Al-Sabah Collection in Kuwait.[2] It has lost its flap, but on the other hand the partly figurative partly floral decoration is well preserved.

The wallet first acquired by the David Collection (3/2001, fig. 3) was made from two pieces of rather thick leather, one making up the flap and the back, the

Fig. 3. Wallet. Press-moulded leather. H: 9.5; W: 8.5 cm. Probably Afghanistan, late 12ᵗʰ or early 13ᵗʰ century. 3/2001, The David Collection, Copenhagen. Photo: Pernille Klemp.

other the front. On the outside, the hard and brittle leather is partly covered with an orange-red pigment, which again in a few places has traces of a brownish layer reminiscent of lacquer on top of it. The orange is mainly seen on the background of the protruding relief decoration, which might imply that the colour was applied to the surface of the mould while the intaglio-cut design was void of pigment. The missing pigment on the highest level of the moulded design could, however, also result from wear. The inside of the wallet is lined with thinner leather tinted dark brown. No attempt has been made to determine from which animal the two types of leather might originate, but in the case of book-bindings, goatskin was often used for the covers, while softer sheepskin was preferred for the doublures with moulded designs.[3] A rather thick layer of reused paper with Arabic letters was put between the inside and the outside of the wallet. This is clearly visible on the front of the flap, where most of the leather has disappeared. The sides and the bottom were sewn together with sometimes green/ sometimes red lamella of leather or gut. These can be seen intact in many places, but the wallet was repaired coarsely back in the medieval period with a thick, uncoloured cotton thread.

This wallet is the only one in the group with a fairly complicated iron closing mechanism. A small hook is pinned to the front panel while the corresponding part with a movable closing device is pinned to both sides of the flap. The back is furnished with an iron loop intended for suspending the wallet from the owner's belt.

The design of the wallet is quite impressive though part of the moulded leather is missing from the back and most of it from the flap. The main decoration would have consisted of twelve interlaced medallions with the signs of the zodiac. Of the twelve, three are missing but they were probably placed in the following order. Back: Libra (top left), Scorpio (middle left), Sagittarius (bottom left), Capricorn (bottom right), Aquarius (middle right), Pisces? (top right). Front: Aries? (top left), Taurus? (top right), Gemini (middle left), Cancer (bottom left), Leo (bottom right) and Virgo (middle right). The logic of the sequence on the back is broken on the front, where Taurus should have followed Aries in the central medallion to the left, but this is not the case. On both sides, the medallions are placed within and connected to a frame, which on the back follows the edge but on the front also follows the shape of the flap, leaving the space under it blank. In addition, the front also shows six birds, of which the two central ones have long intertwined necks. The back has rather unusual scrolls or arabesques and in addition one (originally two) birds related to the ones on the front. In the centre is a bigger bird – an eagle? – with spread wings and legs recalling heraldic depictions. Apart from the slightly unusual birds and arabesques, the decoration is related to the one seen in metalwork from the east Iranian world from

Fig. 4. Wallet. Press-moulded leather. H: 9.8; W: 8.2 cm. Probably Afghanistan, late 12ᵗʰ or early 13ᵗʰ century. 14/2001, The David Collection, Copenhagen. Photo: Pernille Klemp.

the 12ᵗʰ and mainly 13ᵗʰ century, and the depiction of the zodiac corresponds equally well.[4]

The second wallet acquired by the David Collection (14/2001, fig. 4) was, like the first, made from two pieces of rather thick and hard leather, one making up the flap and the back, the other the front. The outside of the flap and the back is tinted dark brown leaving most of the design light beige – the colour of the leather. The front, like the wallet just described, is coloured with an orange pigment, which again in areas is covered by a brownish lacquer-like layer. The inside of the wallet is lined with a material that probably is thin, felt-like deteriorated leather, but because of the brittleness of the wallet, it is difficult to open the flap. Again in this wallet, paper was placed between the two layers of leather. About four millimetres of the brown back was folded over the red front and then sewn with lamella of leather or membrane. At some point in the medieval period this wallet was also repaired with a coarse uncoloured cotton thread.

Set in between the two layers of the flap is a leather strap ending in a knotted button in the shape of a trefoil. This would have been caught by a loop formed by a double leather string running through the four holes made for it in the front. Close to the top of the back are remnants of a leather cord intended for suspension.

The design that adorns the front (including the flap) of this wallet is closely related to that on its back but they are not identical. Built up the same way, they consist of a double medallion contained within a frame having additional decoration in the corners. On the front the centre of the medallion displays two addorsed rabbits in the lower part and a scroll in the upper part. In the surrounding band there are four birds in small medallions and four dog-like quadrupeds. The top corners contain flying harpies on a background of scrolls while the bottom left corner has a quadruped on a similar background. In the centre of the back is the well-known motif with three running hares connected through their ears. In the surrounding band we again have four birds in small medallions and four quadrupeds – perhaps jackals or foxes. In the top corners are sphinxes against a scroll background and in the bottom corners are quadrupeds that might be griffins. On the edge between the top of the back and the flap a clearly visible cross hatching can be observed.

All the motives of this press-moulded wallet are well known from engraved and silver inlaid metalwork of the 12th-13th century: the running – at times pursuing – quadrupeds, the hares, the little birds, the harpies, the sphinxes and the griffins.[5]

The third wallet in the David Collection (15/2001, fig. 5) came together with the one just described above, but is in several respects different from it and the other wallets discussed so far. The shape – rectangular with concave sides – is the same, and like the one in the Khalili Collection, it is made of relatively soft leather sewn together from one continuous piece. However, it has no gussets on the sides; instead, the back was a bit wider than the front and the two extra pieces were folded over the front before they were sewn with lamella of leather or membrane tinted red and green. The wallet is lined with undyed tabby-woven cotton cloth while the leather itself is tinted dark brown.

Hardly anything is left of the original closing system. The flap has remnants of a leather strap probably ending in a knot similar to the wallet shown on fig. 4. Like that wallet, it has also got four holes or slits made in the front for a double string ending in a loop meant to catch the knot.

The biggest difference between it and the other wallets, however, is the way the decoration has been applied. The design is very simple: a rectangle, a number of 'eye' ornaments and a frieze of teardrop ornaments. Instead of protruding, as seen on the foundation-moulded or press-moulded wallets, it is stamped into the leather, forming a negative impression. The technique of blind tooling with simple or complicated stamps was widespread among the craftsmen producing book-bindings since the decorative variation that could be obtained by means of relatively few stamps was impressive. Book-covers were also meant to be used and to last, and therefore a decoration sunk into the binding was preferred, being much more durable than one protruding in relief. This was probably not

Fig. 5. Wallet. Blind tooled leather. H: 9.8; W: 8.5 cm. Probably Afghanistan, late 12th or early 13th century. 15/2001, The David Collection, Copenhagen. Photo: Pernille Klemp.

so important when it came to wallets, which would have been thrown out when they were out of fashion or worn. The crude reparation of two of the David Collection wallets and of the one in the Al-Sabah Collection shows, however, that they must have had some second-hand value attached to them.

Of the six wallets mentioned here, the fragment published by Ettinghausen differs from the rest in many respects. First of all it is not completely sure that it is a wallet. Technically it is the only one that is foundation-moulded, the leather is dyed red and has three additional colours, it is lyre-shaped, it is dated to the 7th century and it was bought in and ascribed to Egypt.

Though there are certain differences, the last five wallets seem to form a much more homogeneous group.[6] They all have the same basic squarish shape with concave sides. The decoration on four of them is press-moulded while one (15/2001, fig. 5) is blind-tooled. The same four are lined with paper while the blind-tooled wallet is lined with cloth, and the same four share a related artistic and iconographic language while the blind-tooled wallet is simpler. At least two of the press-moulded wallets have two colours – a dark brown and an orange-red (figs. 3 and 4). The one in Kuwait might also have had two colours while the Khalili wallet and the blind-tooled one are brown. The two last ones are also much softer than the first two.

Partly on the basis of stylistic analysis, Ralph Pinder-Wilson has pointed to 12th – 13th century Khurasan as the period and area of origin for the Khalili wallet (fig. 2). His arguments are also valid for the three other press-moulded

Fig. 6. Mural in the audience hall at Laskhari Bazar. Afghanistan, first half of the 12ᵗʰ century. After Sourdel-Thomine, Janine 1978.

wallets and this attribution is further substantiated by Afghanistan being mentioned as the putative provenance for the Al-Sabah wallet as well as for the three in the David Collection. It is therefore likely that the entire group – including the somewhat different blind-tooled wallet – should be ascribed to Khurasan, as suggested by Pinder-Wilson or perhaps even more precisely, to the area constituting present-day Afghanistan. This slightly more precise attribution is supported by the surviving depiction of such a wallet in use, namely one worn by a guardsman painted on the wall of the audience hall at Lashkari Bazar southeast of Herat (fig. 6). One cannot see the decoration on the wallet, but at least the mural shows that this type and shape were in use in the area as early as the first half of the 12ᵗʰ century (Sourdel-Thomine 1978, 36 and pls. 120-124).

An Afghan provenance for these wallets is also supported by the stone-moulds that were produced for the manufacture of most of them. Again Ralph Pinder-Wilson studied this group in depth when he wrote about the wallet and the four moulds in the Khalili Collection.[7] The purpose here is not to discuss the designs of the stone-moulds but rather to publish pictures of the three moulds in the David Collection and sum up the information on provenance and manufacture that can be deduced from the group now published.

As mentioned above, the decorative motifs of the wallets are fully in accordance with those found on metalwork from the eastern Islamic world in the 12th and 13th centuries, and the same can be said of motifs on the moulds. Some display the typical mixture of humans, animals, fabulous beasts and plants, others are more restricted and some are more or less abstract reflections of a floral world. A third element is inscriptions. Most of these express the usual good wishes for the owner of the moulded object and some provide information about the maker but unfortunately not about provenance. However, in one case – on one of the Khalili moulds – we find the name of Izz al-Din Husayn ibn Kharmil, who Ralph Pinder-Wilson has identified as a Ghurid general and governor of Herat who died in 1210 or 1211 AD (Pinder-Wilson 1997, 343-344 and cat. No. 215). From this information, it can pretty safely be deduced that the mould was produced for, or by, a local leatherworker in Herat while ibn Kharmil was governor of this town at the beginning of the 13th century. Additional support for this provenance is that the light grey, greenish grey and at times more charcoal grey, soft, flaking limestone which was used for most of these moulds is found in the mountains north of Herat (Pinder-Wilson 1997, 344). To complete the picture it should be mentioned, however, that L.I. Rempel has published a fragmentary mould with a wallet design which is 'from Afrasiyab' (Samarkand) and probably excavated there (Rempel 1978, 76, fig. 36).

In 1954 Richard Ettinghausen published a fragmentary stone-mould that he dates to the early 12th century (fig. 7).[8] On the side of it – outside the design – there is an inscription in positive stating, 'work of Bandar the saddle-maker'. In the border of the design itself there is a scroll and an inscription in negative

Fig. 7. Fragmentary press-mould. Carved greenish-grey limestone. Approximate H: 28; W: 13.6 cm. Iran 12th century. 31.374, Museum of Fine Arts, Boston. After Ettinghausen, Richard 1954.

Fig. 8 a+b. Double sided press-mould. Carved greenish-grey limestone. H: 33.5; W: 18.5 cm. Probably Afghanistan, late 12ᵗʰ or early 13ᵗʰ century. 4/2000, The David Collection, Copenhagen. Photo: Pernille Klemp.

expressing good wishes. This last inscription would of course come out in positive on the finished leather object whatever it might have been. If one takes the first inscription at face value, then it actually means that Bandar not only was a saddle-maker but also made/carved his own moulds.

One of the moulds in the David Collection (4/2000, fig. 8) also has inscriptions in positive and negative – the first outside the design, the others inside. The positive inscription placed in the centre of fig. 8a reads, 'Its owner is Isfarin.' On the same side two of the designs have inscriptions in negative, and the one on the smaller ends, '…. the work of Isfarin'. This means that Isfarin on his finished leather products appears as the maker. In positive – directly readable – it is stated that the mould belongs to Isfarin but not necessarily that it was carved by him. However, the 'hand' looks very much the same on this very well-designed mould, so it is tempting to believe that Isfarin either carved it all, or that the carver knew that Isfarin would be the future owner of the mould and wrote his name on it.

The last mould with a name is one from the Khalili Collection (fig. 9). The design in question is for a wallet intended to be moulded in one piece. As expected, most of the framing inscription is in negative, but on the flap it is positive! On the back, the usual blessings end with, 'the work of Muhammad' in negative. However, as if this information was not sufficient, the empty space on the front – intended to be covered by the flap – is inscribed in negative, 'made by Muhammad ibn Yusuf'. This is engraved with a less elegant hand. Though we clearly understand that Muhammad was the leather-worker, we have no indication whether he made the mould himself. The person who did was not very careful when it came to the inscriptions – some of the letters on the front are actually upside down – and perhaps he just tried to copy a given design without being able to read and write himself.

Though the mould for Muhammad ibn Yusuf's wallet (fig. 9) has problems with regard to its inscriptions, it must have worked well as a moulding tool. It was intended for one continuous piece of leather, which would have been folded and then sewn together only on the sides. Between the three designs – where the finished wallet would have been folded – fine hatchings are engraved in the mould. Similar hatchings can actually be observed on the top between the flap and the back of one of the David Collection wallets (14/2001, fig. 4). The wallet in the Khalili Collection (fig. 2) is the only one of the press-moulded wallets that is made of one continuous piece of leather; the others have a separate

Fig. 9. Double sided press-mould. Carved greenish-grey limestone. H: 29.8; W: 26.5 cm. Khurasan, late 12th or early 13th century. MXD 97, The Nasser D. Khalili Collection. After Pinder-Wilson, Ralph 1997.

Fig. 10 a+b. Double sided press-mould. Carved greenish-grey limestone. H: c 20.5; W: 12.4 cm. Probably Afghanistan, late 12th or early 13th century. 9/1994, The David Collection, Copenhagen. Photo: Pernille Klemp.

Fig. 11 a+b. Double sided press-mould. Carved dark grey limestone. H: c 11; W: 21.5 cm. Probably Afghanistan, late 12th or early 13th century. 10/1994, The David Collection, Copenhagen. Photo: Pernille Klemp.

front, while the back and the flap are in one piece. This fact might reflect the somewhat curious phenomenon that can be observed on some of the other designs for wallets (figs. 8a, 9, 10 and 11). Whatever shape they have, they have one feature in common: the flap and the lower part of the front are part of the same design. From the point of view of moulding the leather, this requires a more complicated working procedure, though it can be done. On one piece of leather, the back could be moulded and then turned around to mould the flap. Hereafter the outline and lower part of the front could be moulded on another piece of leather, and finally the back and the front could be sewn together. From the point of view of designing and carving the moulds, this way of doing it was preferable since the artisan was better able to judge what the finished wallet would look like with the flap in place. As on fig. 11a, some of the moulds have designs for both the front and the back of a wallet, while others – like the one on fig. 10a – only have the front. This might indicate that the back was engraved on another stone mould, but it might also suggest that some wallets were simpler – with no decoration on the back.

The use of moulds normally indicates some level of mass production. This would also seem valid here especially since the moulds were carved in relatively hard stone, in comparison to pottery moulds. Many of the objects that were produced were also small and relatively common, for example wallets, scabbards, belts, etc. On the other hand – whether the object was mass produced

or a unique piece – there was probably no other way to make finely moulded, relief-decorated leather objects. Foundation moulding was much coarser and blind tooling with stamps, as seen on the wallet on fig. 5, had a different effect because the design was sunk into the leather. In any case, 'mistakes' like the ones in the inscription on the Khalili mould (fig. 9) seem unacceptable if the wallet was produced *en masse*. The mould with the name of Izz al-Din Husayn ibn Kharmil, which in the present author's opinion probably was made for a saddle front, would not have been for a mass-produced object but rather for one made to order.[9]

Though there seems to be some support for the idea that the same craftsman, or at least the same workshop, produced both leather objects and the moulds to decorate them, nothing can be said for sure. And what about the designs that were at times very beautiful and intricate? Were they produced by the individual leather workshops, were they ordered from local artists or were they circulated in pattern books similar to those found in the later Diez album?[10] Time might tell.

References

Baer, Eva 1983. *Metalwork in Medieval Islamic Art.* New York: State University of New York Press.

Baltimore 1957. *The history of Bookbinding 525-1950 A.D. An Exhibition held at the Baltimore Museum of Art November 12, 1957 to January 12, 1958.* Baltimore: The Trustees of the Walters Art Gallery.

Bosch, Gulnar, John Carswell & Guy Petherbridge 1981. *Islamic Bindings & Bookmaking. A Catalogue of an Exhibition, The Oriental Institute, The University of Chicago May 18 – August 18, 1981.* Chicago: University of Chicago Printing Department.

Ettinghausen, Richard 1954. 'The Covers of the Morgan Manafi Manuscript and Other Early Persian Bookbindings'. In: Dorothy Miner (ed.), *Studies in Art and Literature for Belle da Costa Greene.* Princeton: Princeton University Press, 459-473.

Ettinghausen, Richard 1965. 'Foundation-moulded Leatherwork – a Rare Egyptian Technique also used in Britain'. In: *Studies in Islamic Art and Architecture In Honour of Professor K.A.C. Creswell.* Cairo: The American University in Cairo Press, 63-71.

Ettinghausen, Richard, Oleg Grabar & Marilyn Jenkins-Madina 2001. *Islamic Art and Architecture.* Yale University Press.

Folsach, Kjeld von 2001. *Art from the World of Islam in The David Collection.* Copenhagen: The David Collection.

Lentz, Thomas W. & Glenn D. Lowry 1989. *Timur and the Princely Vision. Persian Art and Culture in the Fifteenth Century.* Los Angeles: Los Angeles County Museum of Art.

Pinder-Wilson, Ralph 1997. 'Stone press-moulds and leatherworking in Khurasan'. In: Emilie Savage-Smith, *Science, tools & magic.* (The Nasser D. Khalili Collection of Islamic Art, vol. XII, part two). London: Oxford University Press, 338-355.

Rempel, L.I. 1978. *Iskusstvo srednego vostoka* [Art of the Middle East]. Moscow: Sovetskij Chudoznik.

Sourdel-Thomine, Janine 1978. *Lashkari Bazar. Une résidence royale ghaznévide et ghoride. 1 B: Le décor non figuratif et les inscriptions.* (Mémoires de la délégation archéologique Francaise en Afghanistan, tome XVIII + tome XVIII Planches). Paris: Diffusion de Boccard.

Notes

1   Pinder-Wilson 1997. In note 12 on page 345, Pinder-Wilson mentions 5 pottery moulds in the Al-Sabah Collection, one of which has a design for a wallet.

2   Pinder-Wilson 1997, 340. LNS 21. I am grateful to Sue Kaoukji for mailing me a photograph of the wallet without a flap and a loose flap LNS 23. The two are supposed to come from Afghanistan, but not with the same provenance. However they seem extraordinarily related and are also quite similar to one of the wallets in the David Collection (14/2001, fig. 4).

3   See for example Bosch *et al.* 1981, Cat. Nos. 3, 4, 9 and 12.

4   See for example Baer 1983, fig. 205, and von Folsach 2001, Cat. Nos. 483 and 487.

5   See for example Baer 1983, figs. 146 and 154 and von Folsach 2001, Cat. Nos. 484, 487, 495.

6   Another wallet that seems to belong to this group was sold at Christie's London, *Islamic Art, Indian Miniatures, Rugs and Carpets* 17 October 1995 as lot number 267. Since there was no illustration and it was not seen by the present writer, it has not been taken into consideration.

7   Pinder-Wilson 1997, Cat. Nos. 215-218. In note 11 on page 345, Pinder-Wilson enumerates the published moulds. The two mentioned as being sold from Bonhams, 27/4-1994 lot No. 100, were acquired by the David Collection as 9/1994 (fig. 10) and 10/1994 (fig. 11). The mould acquired later, 4/2000 (fig. 8), is obviously not on Pinder-Wilson's list, and neither is a big mould sold at Christie's, 17/10-1994 lot. No. 266. Another mould is published in Ettinghausen, Grabar & Jenkins-Madina 2001, fig. 282. Several unpublished moulds are in The National Museum of Qatar.

8   Ettinghausen 1954, 472-473 and fig. 359.

9   Pinder-Wilson 1997, Cat. No. 215. The catalogue text mentions that there is no way of knowing what the designs were made for. Both the inscription bearing the governor's name and the shape seem to me to suggest a saddle.

10   Lentz & Lowry 1989. For example, pages 192-198.

Saone – Sahyûn – Qalaat Saladin

OLAF OLSEN & RIKKE AGNETE OLSEN

The title above presents three different versions of the name of a magnificent castle, one of Syria's most important and attractive monuments from the dramatic age of the Crusades in the 12th century when waves of Franks – *i.e.* Christian warriors and settlers mainly from Western and Central Europe – overran the Middle East and for a time managed to conquer most of the Holy Land and its neighbouring areas along a narrow strip of the East coast of the Mediterranean. *Saone* is the Frankish term, *Sahyûn* the Arab, while *Qalaat Saladin* (Saladin's Castle) is today the official Syrian name for the site, introduced by a governmental decree in 1957 and used everywhere in guidebooks, on maps and on road signs. This name is slightly misleading however, as Saladin, the great Arab warlord, neither built nor improved the castle, and never lived there, except perhaps for the very night after he conquered it from a Frankish seigneur in 1188 AD. In this paper we will stick to *Saone*, since it was the Franks who gave the castle its most impressive structures and spectacular appearance.

The castle of Saone is situated in the mountainous area c. 30 km East of the harbour town Latakia. The access to the site has recently been much improved by the construction of a partly new road, leading directly to the castle from a major road between Latakia and the Orontes Valley. Advancing on this road the visitor will soon find himself in the middle of nowhere, making his way through valleys and ravines in an uninhabited and crude landscape, surrounded on all sides by hills and rocks dressed only with prickly scrub and dwarf trees, nourishing a few stray goats. And then suddenly the contours of the mighty castle appears high up above, at the end of a large mountain ridge, with stone walls flanking the top of the ridge over a stretch of more than 700 metres. Indeed an impressive view.

At the foot of the mountain, the eye is caught by an even more breathtaking feature. A great fosse with high vertical sides is cut – or should one say hewn – in the massive rock all the way across the mountain ridge, protecting the castle against surprise assaults from advancing foes who had taken the highway to the castle over the unfortified part of the ridge. The fosse or ditch is dry and

Fig. 1. Saone. Seen from the Northwest. Rikke Agnete Olsen photographer. 1974.

c. 150 m long and 18 m broad. This in itself is not so remarkable, but its depth is no less than 28 metres and the almost perfectly shaped vertical sides would make it absolutely impossible for intruders to climb from one side of the fosse to the other. The only entrance to the castle over the fosse was by a drawbridge, which has disappeared long ago. Due to the great span of 18 metres, this bridge had to be supported midway. The castle builders solved this problem in an unusual and brilliant fashion. When cutting the fosse through the solid rock of the mountain, they simply left a slim, obelisk-like pillar of untouched rock, more than 20 metres in height, in the middle of the fosse and added it with a few courses of masonry on top (fig. 2).

Except for the side towards the great fosse, the outer walls of the castle faithfully follow in all detail the contours of the mountain ridge, in this way permitting the defenders to gain full advantage of the steep rock sides as an important strengthening of the fortification. This explains the oblong and very irregular shape of the plan (fig. 3). Inside, a transverse fosse or ditch divides the castle into two parts: A higher and heavily fortified Eastern court and a lower and less built-up court to the West. The total area inside the walls amounts to c. 5.5 ha, which is considerably more than the two other giant crusaders' castles in Syria, the impressive Margat on its high cliff near the Mediterranean South of Latakia, and the most famous of them all, the well preserved (and almost too well restored) compact fortress Crac des Chevaliers in the inland.

Fig. 2. Saone. The great fosse with the 'needle' for the drawbridge. After Fedden *et al.* 1957, pl. 16.

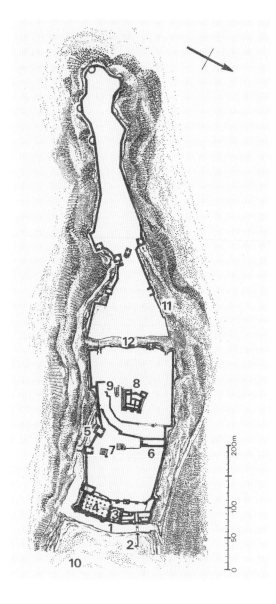

Fig. 3. Saone. Plan with contours of the mountain ridge. 1. The great fosse. 2. The drawbridge. 3. The donjon. 4. The pillar hall. 5. The main entrance. 6. A cistern. 7. The mosque. 8. The Byzantine citadel. 9. The Romanesque church. 10. Saladin's and 11. Zahir's position during the siege 1188. 12. The secondary fosse. After Eydoux 1982, 68.

In modern times, Saone was until 1936 a distant place far from civilization, and it could only be reached on foot or horseback. This – and the vast extent of the castle with scattered ruins covered by impenetrable vegetation – explains why the archaeological knowledge of the site still is insufficient. Few scholars have stayed here for more than a few days, and only minor parts of it have been subjected to thorough archaeological examination and excavation. The first professional eyes to be cast upon Saone were those of Guillaume Rey, a French archaeologist, who published his observations in the pioneer work *Étude sur l'architecture militaire des Croisés* in 1871. Another early visitor was T.E. Lawrence, later to be famous for his role in the Arab revolt during the First World War. He came here in 1909 as an energetic young Oxford undergraduate studying Medieval castles, making his way through most of Syria on Shanks' mare (at this stage in his life he detested all four-legged animals). Lawrence stayed for two days in Saone, loved it all and sent an enthusiastic description of the castle to his mother in England. For him, he wrote, the 'needle' for the drawbridge in the fosse was the most sensational thing in castle-building he had ever seen (Lawrence 1936, 220).

By far the most important contribution to the understanding of Saone has been provided by the outstanding French scholar Paul Deschamps, who won his fame in Crac des Chevaliers in the 1920s and worked on and off with the architecture of the crusader castles in the Holy Land during most of his life. He first came to Saone in 1928, returned to the site several times and could, furthermore, supply his own observations with the results from exhaustive studies of the masonry and excavations in small but significant areas inside the castle, which were carried out in his absence by his close collaborator and favourite architect Pierre Coupel between 1939 and 1944. Deschamps' final account on Saone from 1973 is the indispensable tool for everyone who wants to immerse in the history of the castle (Deschamps 1973, 217-47).

Saone is to-day administered and well looked after by scholars from the Syrian Antiquities Department who understandably have concentrated much of their scholarly work and restoration efforts on the remains of buildings from the Arab habitation in the castle after the conquest in 1188, a theme that was only of secondary interest to the European students of crusader architecture. This work has proved very successful, revealing important traces of refined Arab art and architecture of high quality.

Nobody knows when Saone was first occupied for military purposes. Both its secluded position in the mountains and its suggested, almost nearby, command of one of the major traffic routes between the Mediterranean coast and the Orontes Valley have led to speculations that sometimes claim a very early origin of the castle, perhaps even from Phoenician times. There is no documentation of this, but it cannot be excluded that some of the many aggressors who harassed the tormented Syria during the following thousand years, be they Ptolemies, Romans, early Byzantines or the conquering Arabs, now and then have taken advantage of the strategic possibilities of the site. This suggested prehistory of the castle would have been easier to clarify if there had been a large archaeological activity inside the castle. Up till now however, less than one per cent of the total area of the site has been subjected to meticulous archaeological excavation with systematic collection of casual finds in the ground.

Almost all investigations on the site have been restricted to studies of the visible masonry. These studies are also full of problems, as the building history of the castle is long and complicated. There are many phases in its development and habitation, and in the course of time much masonry has been pulled down and reused in the next phase, sometimes on the same spot, sometimes in new structures elsewhere in the castle. The use of local architects and craftsmen, of which the crusaders were often dependant when building, makes it even more complicated. Therefore, it is often difficult to determine the time of origin and the proper age of parts of the surrounding walls and of the buildings inside the castle.

Written sources indicate the possibility that the Arab Hamdanid dynasty of Aleppo at some stage in the middle of the 10th century used the mountain ridge as a military post. This is not yet confirmed by archaeological observations on the site, where all visible remains seem to be later, belonging either to the later Byzantine, the Frankish or the post-conquest Arab periods. Evidently, the first to fortify the mountain ridge of Saone in a great scale were the successors of the mighty Byzantine emperor Johannes Tzimiskes, who successfully expanded his large empire both in the North and South and restored Byzantine power in some of the regions lost to the Arabs more than 300 years earlier. He conquered most of Syria in the year 975 when fighting the weak Hamdanid rulers. Johannes Tzimiskes died the year after, but the Byzantines managed to keep possession of their conquests in Northern Syria and secured their power by stationing contingents of soldiers in old and new strongholds in the area. One of the new strongholds, and surely the mightiest, was Saone.

It has been questioned whether all the large area inside the present walls was fortified by the Byzantines, but all such doubts were put to shame when Pierre Coupel could demonstrate the presence of hitherto unnoticed Byzantine masonry in many places all over the castle, even in the remains of the westernmost tower in the wall of the lower court at the very end of the mountain ridge. Also, at least the most important of the three rectangular towers protecting a postern in the Southern wall of this court have a Byzantine past. Although little is known about the buildings in the lower court – due to the large size and the unfriendly vegetation, meaning that most of it has not yet been examined properly – there are remains of two small Byzantine chapels, leaving no doubt about the former presence of Byzantine habitation here. The buildings were probably dwellings for the lower ranks and common soldiers and servants of the garrison.

The higher Eastern court was the important one. The heart of the Byzantine castle was the citadel, domineering the highest point of the ridge, 439 metres above sea level. By now it is very ruined, but it is evident that it has been an impressive building, strengthened by protruding corners, perhaps in the shape of small rectangular towers. However, the walls of the citadel are fairly slim, and its defence depended largely on an elaborate system of secondary walls inside the castle area, a common feature in Byzantine military architecture. Towards the lower court there was a wall along the edge of the fosse dividing the two parts of the castle, and just 25 and 40 metres East and South of the citadel two almost concentric walls have blocked the way for intruders.

The strongest outer defences of the whole castle were already in Byzantine times concentred in the East end, behind the great fosse. In many places the outer wall along the fosse contains Byzantine masonry in the lower courses. The edge of the fosse follows exactly the line of the wall, also where this was built with slightly protruding towers. As defensive walls cry for protection from a ditch at their front, it is most likely that the fosse itself is of the same age as the wall and not a Frankish addition, as it is sometimes suggested. It is not in any way certain, however, that the fosse had its present overwhelming depth from the very beginning. This seems much more in proportion with the Frankish extension of the defences. A solution could be that the fosse in Byzantine time was not 28, but c. 8 metres deep, with the bottom corresponding with the level from which the obelisk-like pillar was later created as a monolite during a Frankish deepening of the fosse. The fosse could also have been narrower in its first phase. A dating of the pillar to the Frankish period could perhaps be supported by the presence of a similar (though much smaller) carved-out pillar in the fosse of the 12th century crusader castle Nephin, near Tripoli in Lebanon (Deschamps 1973, 300; pl. LXII B), but the phenomenen is actually also known from elder Byzantine fortifications, *e.g.* the citadels in Edessa and Gargar (Smail 1956, 238. The impressive rock-pillar in Edessa is depicted in Lawrence 1936, 56).

Another transverse Byzantine wall, also strong but without towers, is running inside the castle parallel to the outer Eastern wall and at a distance of only 30 metres from it. It survived both the Frankish and Arab alterations to the castle, and there are still considerable remains of it. Surprisingly, however, archaeological excavations have revealed traces of a third parallel wall between the two, strengthened by at least four protruding round towers (fig. 4). Two of these towers stand so near to each other that one must suppose that the entrance to the castle was here. It is possible that this wall was the original outer Eastern wall of the Byzantine castle. If so there must have been a c. 15 m broad berm between the wall and the fosse.

We can conclude that Saone was an extremely large and strong castle already in the Byzantine period, raised in order to house a large garrison and in expectation of the possibility of severe attacks. This is in some ways in contradiction to a widespread belief, according to which Byzantine castles of this period were not much more than fortified camps, claiming that their Arab rivals did not

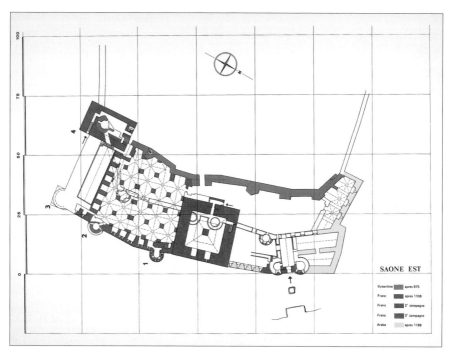

Fig. 4. Saone. The Eastern front with the postern, the donjon, the pillar hall, a cistern and the remains of Byzantine walls. After Paul Deschamps 1973.

possess sufficient siege-machinery to conquer them (*e.g.* Runciman 1971, 369). The Byzantine builders of Saone evidently knew better than that.

Nothing is known about the history of Saone during the Byzantine occupation. It must have been considered of great importance when built, but the Byzantine power was not very consistent in the border areas of the empire, and Saone might have been lost to an enemy or at least deserted by the garrison some time in the later part of the 11th century when the empire was under severe pressure from the Seljuq Turks who conquered most of Syria.

Whatever happened, Saone fell an easy prey to the first wave of crusaders when they conquered the Latakia area in 1108 and incorporated it into the Frankish principality, newly established in Antiochia. Saone came into the hands of one of the most prominent barons of the principality, Robert, son of Foulques, with the nickname *le Lépreux,* a man – maybe – of Norman descent. He was mentioned in 1118 as Robert of Saone and acquired also at least two other important castles in the area, Balaton and Sardone.

Robert did not live long to enjoy the fruits of his vast possessions. During a campaign in 1119 he fell off his horse, was captured by Arabs and handed over to the atabeg of Damascus, Togdekin, who personally decapitated his captive when he refused to convert to Islam. Robert was succeeded by his son Guillaume, but also he had only a limited time as seigneur of Saone. He died in war in 1132, not in combat with Moslems, as one would have thought, but while fighting other crusaders. It cost him his life when he, together with other Northern barons, tried in vain to resist the troops of the king of Jerusalem who had intervened in order to pacify fatal internal strifes between the barons that threatened to undermine the crusading communities.

After Guillaume's death his brother Jarenton took over Saone. The castle stayed in the hands of the family until the Arab conquest in 1188, but neither Jarenton nor any of the later Frankish seigneurs of Saone possessed anything like the wealth and power of Robert and Guillaume. Therefore, it is beyond reasonable doubt that the impressive Frankish remodelling of the mountain castle must be ascribed to one of these two mighty men or to both of them, *i.e.* between 1108 and 1132 AD.

What they did was first of all to move the cardinal point of the fortification of the castle from the citadel on the top of the ridge in the middle of the higher court to the very Eastern end of the court. The immense deepening of the great fosse has been already mentioned. At the same time the Byzantine wall along the fosse was strengthened, heightened and partially rebuilt with a front of carved, bossed blocks. This kind of masonry in Syria is in itself a strong indication of competent crusaders' work. The round mural towers or turrets of the old wall survived the rebuilding and were built upon without changing their shape. This is a feature otherwise not known in early crusader castles, where all towers are square or rectangular. Only the Southeastern corner tower has been transformed into an almost square shape, but this might have been done by the Arabs much later.

However, the most striking improvement of the East front of the castle was the introduction of a magnificent donjon with its Eastern side built into the wall. The donjon is still in good shape and preserved almost from top to bottom (fig. 5). Its bossed ashlars are of exceptional quality and much of the masonry of remarkable size, with blocks measuring up to 4 metres in length. The dimensions of the donjon are 24.5 metres square with a height of 23 metres, so that the distance from the merlons on the top terrace of the donjon to the bottom of the fosse right below is as much as 51 metres. The thickness of the East wall is the impressive 5.40 metres, to the other sides a bit less. The building has two floors, both of them covered by heavy vaults supported by a massive central pier. The room in the lower floor is high, c. 11 metres, but in spite of this it appears sinister, only lit from two narrow embrasures in the Eastern wall. A staircase built into the thickness of the wall connects the two floors and the terrace.

The outer appearance of this massive edifice is clearly modelled on the donjon, the favourite type of major contemporary castles in Western Europe. There are certain dissimilarities however, the most important concerning the inner lay-out. The European donjon normally contains a comfortable dwelling for the lord of the castle and his family. This was not the case in Saone, where the daily life of the lord probably took place in the Byzantine citadel, while the rooms in the donjon exclusively served military purposes, as illustrated by its narrow apertures and by the thickness of the walls – more or less the double of the usual size in Europe at the time. A weak point is the position of the entrance to the donjon from the court. In Europe it is always from a wooden outside staircase several metres above the ground, here it is through a doorway in the ground floor on the West side, only protected by the secondary Byzantine wall and a beam in the jambs of the door. A missing feature is a well inside the building. This would have been difficult to establish in the hard rock underneath the high ground of Saone. Instead a small indoor cistern was hewn out under the floor.

It is interesting to note that there is no entrance into the donjon from the rampart walks on the adjoining stretches of the wall. This could be awkward during an attack, preventing the defenders on the rampart to move quickly from one side of the donjon to the other. On the other hand it strengthens the position of the donjon as 'the last resort'. This is considered a heritage from Byzantine fortification tradition. A similar lacking connection to the rampart walk occurs by two solid towers in the Eastern part of the South wall, somehow giving them the status of secondary mini-donjons.

These two towers are definitely Frankish in their present state, but like most other towers on the long sides of the outer wall – there have been at least nine towers on the South side and two in the steeper North – it is not yet ascertained whether they also have a Byzantine past.

In Byzantine times the main entrance to the castle might have been over the fosse in the East front where the narrow gate was protected by the two flanking turrets. This gate was preserved by the Franks, but probably meant as a postern, due to the stenous ascent from the valleys to the adjoining part of the mountain ridge. It is generally believed that the preferred access to the Frankish castle was through a tower on the South side (fig. 3, n. 5). This tower might have had a Byzantine predecessor, as the passageway inside the tower, according to Byzantine practise, does not follow a straight line, but turns 90 degrees. Due to the uneven nature of the terrain, aggressors would have to follow a steep and narrow path and would meet many obstacles when approaching from here, and both outside and inside the castle they could, furthermore, risk a hot welcome from the other solid tower that is flanking this entrance.

Fig. 5. Saone. The Eastern (see fig. 4) front from the inside with the secondary Byzantine wall and the donjon. Michael Fuller photographer. 2001. http://users.stlcc.edu/mfuller/Medieval/Saone.html

There are also two entrances to the lower court, one to the North and one to the South, both to be considered as posterns. The Northern postern has its entrance through a Frankish tower, while the more vulnerable Southern postern is well defended by a system of towers, mainly built or at least strengthened by the Franks. Except for the testimony of the towers almost nothing is known to-day about the appearance of the lower court in Frankish time, and it is tempting to suggest that the habitation here must have been of a flimsy character, perhaps not dominated by men, but by domestic animals and provisions.

In contrast, there is evidence of men in abundance in the higher court of the castle. Most striking in the Southwestern corner where a large hall, c. 32 × 30 metres, with vaulted ceiling, carried by 30, almost cyclopic, pillars (fig. 4) have given shelter to the garrison of the castle. This hall was built shortly after the donjon and more or less at the same time as a large and deep cistern in the very corner of the castle. The great demand of water for hundreds of men and their livestock, living in a dry climate with long spells of drought, is emphasized by the presence of another giant cistern, 30 metres long and 10 metres deep, built in the North side of the court. Most of the water must have been brought to the castle in barrels from far away, and it has been a laborious and never-ending task for a large number of men and mules to secure a high water level in the cisterns. Large stores of foodstuffs were also needed, and a multitude of covered underground pit silos – Deschamps has registered at least 24 of these – were established for this purpose in the open areas of the court.

South of the Byzantine citadel, excavations have revealed traces of a modest, but well proportioned Romanesque church, vaulted and with a rounded apse, but smaller than any of the two cisterns. As was generally the case in crusader castles, the religious demands of the dwellers were subordinated to the military necessities.

There are several other traces of Frankish edifices in the higher court. Altogether, the character, mass and quality of the buildings show that the castle was a baronial settlement of great importance, built with great care and meant to house a military force of considerable size. In times of trouble a large garrison was needed here because of the awkward shape of the site, bringing about almost 1800 running metres of outer wall to be defended.

The Frankish seigneurs who took over Saone at the beginning of the 12th century and strengthened the castle, possessed that power. Their successors, weakened by the interior squabbles among the crusaders, could not muster so many troops, and this turned out to be disastrous for the fate of the castle. In 1187 Saladin, the great restorer of Moslem power, had beaten the Christian army by Hattin in Galilee and three months later he shocked the Christian world by conquering almost the whole kingdom of Jerusalem, including The Holy Town itself. In the spring next year he turned towards the North where he bypassed both Crac des Chevaliers and Margat, deciding that these two strong crusader fortresses, owned and manned by the mighty Hospitaller brethren, were too much of a handful, and concentrated his attention onto the coastal towns and baronial castles in Northern Syria. Having taken Tortosa (except for the Templar citadel in the town), Jeble, and on the 23 July, Latakia, his great army went straight to Saone, arriving there already on the 26 July, 1188.

The conquest of Saone is well documented in contemporary Arab chronicles, partly written by eyewitnesses (Sa'ade 1968. We have not managed to get hold of this important paper, but have relied on the account of it in Deschamps 1973, 229f). Saladin divided his army in two main corps. He took position himself on the outside of the great fosse, bombarding the wall fiercely with mangonels on both sides of the postern behind the drawbridge. The Franks responded with their mangonels from inside the castle, but suffered hard and could not drive the enemy away. At the same time Saladin's son al-Malik Zahir, sultan of Aleppo, attacked the weakest point of the lower court from the South (fig. 3, no. 11) with mangonels that were placed on the opposite slope of the ravine and supported by other siege machinery and sappers. And already on the second day of the siege he managed to breech a hole in the wall, allowing the superior Arab troops to swarm into the lower court and force their way over the secondary fosse and the wall behind it into the higher court. Here, the panicked Franks took refuge in the donjon, while the conquerors settled in the court and relaxed there, eating the hot food which the defenders had prepared for themselves moments before. Realizing their total defeat and hopeless situation, the Franks in the donjon surrendered more or less at once, being granted free departure with their household goods for a ransom of ten pieces of gold from each man, five from each women and two from children (A copious extract of one of the main sources is given in Boase 1967, 50f).

This was the end of the crusaders' epoch in Saone. Unlike several of Saladin's other conquests, the castle was never recaptured by the Franks, but stayed in Moslem hands. For a couple of centuries Saone became a residence for various noble Arab rulers and Mameluke sultans, sometimes fighting each other, and in 1287 the castle once more experienced a siege.

At that time the interior of the castle had undergone great changes. The damage to the walls from Saladin's mangonels was repaired by the new owners soon after the conquest, and inside the castle the church was pulled down and replaced by a mosque with a grand minaret, while refined palatial buildings of great beauty were erected in the higher court. This story will not, however, be told here. It belongs to the Syrian archaeologists of today who are busy just now with their spades and spoons, eliciting fascinating new knowledge from the Arab ruins on the mountain ridge.

In light of the quick and sudden collapse of the crusader possession of the castle of Saone, it is tempting to consider the enormous investments in the building and upkeep of the great fortress a complete failure. This would be absolutely wrong. Before this defeat, during most of the turbulent 12th century, when the first wave of crusaders settled in the Near East, Saone served the knights from the West as a awe-inspiring and paralysing expression of their power in Moslem Syria. Their possession of the castle had to come to an end, but the giant fortress did its job while it lasted.

References

Boase, T.S.R. 1967. *Castles and Churches of The Crusading Kingdom.* London.

Deschamps, Paul 1973. *Les châteaux des croisées en Terre Sainte III. La défense du Compté de Tripoli et de la Principaute d' Antioche.* Paris.

Eydoux, Henri-Paul 1982. *Les Châteaux du Soleil, Forteresses et Guerres des Croisés.* Paris.

Fedden, Robin & John Thomson 1957. *Crusader Castles.* London.

Lawrence, T.E. 1936. *Crusader Castles.* London. Reprinted 1992 with preface by Michael Haag.

Rey, Guillaume 1871. *Étude sur l'architecture militaire des Croisés.*

Runciman, Steven 1971. *A history of the Crusades*, III. London: Penguin Books.

Sa'ade, Gabriel 1968. 'Histoire du Château de Saladin', *Studi Medievali*, Spolète, 3.ser., IX, 2, 1968, 980-1016.

Smail, R.C. 1956. *Crusading Warfare 1097-1193.* Cambridge.

The Architecture of Hospitality
A *madâfâh* in Northern Jordan

ALISON MCQUITTY

> Behold, a companion on the road, a guest, and thirdly a neighbour
> Like a prayer are protected by Allah's law and tradition.
> Ours the shame if a shot should hit our guest
> As long as our right arms can lift our swords.
> If we yield our guest, no work is left in our hand for us,
> We shall then sit behind a heap of branches instead of in a fine tent.[1]

The obligations and benefits of hospitality are familiar to anyone who lives, travels and works in the Middle East. While the above lines refer to a Bedouin community living in tents, another feature of traditional society that soon becomes apparent is that the traditions and customs of hospitality apply equally in settled rural communities. In much of Bilaad as-Sham both societies are tribal and it is on tribal law and custom rather than *sharia'a* law that the requirements of hospitality are based (*Encyclopedia of Islam* 1965, 100). The requirements are two-fold:

1. To offer protection to the guest.
2. To provide food and lodging for the guest.

The poem concentrates on the first aspect and both oral history and ethnographic accounts abound with the obligations surrounding the requirement of protection (Jaussen 1948, 80-90). Musil describes the obligation as offering shelter and protection without question, even to a known enemy, for 'three days and one-third of the fourth day' (1928, 455). In effect, the rules of hospitality provide a method of offering asylum. Just as other points of tribal law and custom survive into the 21st century so too does this.

The second aspect of providing food and lodging can be examined in material terms: the building in which the guest was lodged and hosted was the *madâfâh*. While the custom of lodging a guest in the *madâfâh* is no longer common, strangers to the village are often welcomed into the *madâfâh* to give

Fig. 1. Early 20th century house in Barha district of Irbid. By McQuitty.

an account of their purpose in visiting, their intentions and background to the male elders of the tribe. Not surprisingly, given the patriarchal nature of the traditional society, these buildings are overwhelmingly a male domain. *Madâfât* are tribally based so that in a village of several tribes, there will be a corresponding number of *madâfât*. While the name of the building is obviously derived from the Arabic word for guest (*dayf*), another, arguably more significant role for the *madâfâh* and one still important today, is as a venue for facilitating and negotiating the day-to-day interactions of tribal society and between tribe and state.[2] Echoes of one of the functions of the so-called 'Desert Castles' spring to mind (Gaube 1979, 206 ff.). In addition, as Barghouti recorded in 1924, the building retains its use as 'a public meeting place for daily gatherings where people vie with each other in boasting of good deeds and in relating the history of their ancestors and their valiant deeds' (1924, 179). The tribal memory and identity is reinforced. Such functions are also suggested for the earlier *andron* or men's meeting-houses found in Classical and Late Antique cities, *e.g.* Serjilla in Syria (Tchalenko 1953-8, II). Barghouti makes a distinction between the *dawâwîn* (sing. *diwan*) and the *madâfât* (1924, 182). The former is either owned by one man or the man and his extended family. As discussed below the building in Hartha may more accurately be a *diwan* according to this classification, but it is certainly never referred to as anything but a *madâfâh,* as are the guest-rooms found in any large residential complex.

Hartha is located in northern Jordan close to the major town of Irbid. The village lies in fertile land where cereals, legumes and summer-vegetables are cultivated with a very significant tree-crop of olives grown both for their fruit and

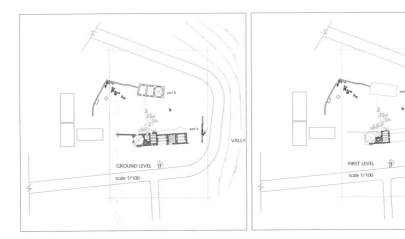

Fig. 2. Ground plan of Hartha *madâfâh*. By JUST students.

oil (Palmer 1998, 157). The village is inhabited predominantly by the Obeidat tribe who accumulated their wealth by oliculture and tax-collection. Hartha is one of five villages reckoned to 'belong' to the Obeidat. The nearby site of 'Abila accounts for the earlier settlement of the area (Mare 1984) and the modern village seems to owe its roots to the 15th century AD. It is mentioned in the Ottoman *defters* as having a typical Mediterranean mixed-farming economy of cereal and summer-crop production, goats and beehives with a very sizable amount of taxable production coming from olives (Hütterhoth & Abdulfattah 1977, 199). By the end of the 19th century the nearby town of Irbid had become the seat of the Ottoman governor (*kaymakam*) and its architecture reflects this new-found importance. The proportions and façades of the buildings and in particular the detail around doors and windows (fig. 1) point to the adoption of a regional urban style that is paralleled in Salt and southern Syria and to some extent in Madaba and Amman (Denton & St Laurent 1996; al-Asad 1997).

The *madâfâh*[3] is part of a larger farmstead complex (fig. 2) that at the time of construction would have been located on the edge of the village. The range of rooms on the back-wall (Part B)were used for family residence, animal stabling and storage of both agricultural equipment and produce (fig. 3). Each unit opened onto a central courtyard where much of the daily domestic cycle – food preparation, cooking, family socialising – would have taken place. There is a separate entrance into the courtyard. The main façade opens onto the street (fig. 4) and from left to right comprises the *madâfâh,* an entrance into a lower room that itself opened onto the courtyard and stairway leading up to the *aliyeh* and a range of rooms that opened solely onto the courtyard (Part A). The *aliyeh*

Fig. 3. Range of buildings built onto the rear wall of the *madâfâh* complex. By McQuitty.

is the name given to the upper room used particularly in summer for family socialising when the cool breezes can be enjoyed. The roof of the *madâfâh* was supported by a cross-vault while the other rooms were spanned by iron girders, in a few cases supported by arches, covered with a flat roof of reeds and mud. The construction throughout is of dry-laid machine-dressed limestone laid in two-skin walls filled with large amounts of rubble and mud mortar. There is no indication of a construction spanning several phases. Inside the *madâfâh* was a central hearth for the preparation of coffee, cupboards along the walls for the coffee equipment and a shelf on which mattresses could be stored. All of these features are entirely in keeping with the *madâfâh*'s function for receiving guests and public socialising.

The most striking feature of this building is the façade and more particularly the attention given to the decoration of the entrance surround (figs. 5 and 6). The date-stone above the entrance records that the complex was constructed in 1918 AD/AH 1337 for Quaider Obeidat who was a wealthy man although not the *shaykh*. The basic impression of the entrance is of references to Classical themes in the use of columns, capitals, vegetal relief and decorated architraves, although the decoration itself has been simplified, for example the vine-scrolls or acanthus leaves directly above the door. Such trends are also evident in the urban architecture of Salt where the street façades and entrances show similar rich decoration. The same arrangement of an upper arch over the doorway flanked by columns is common, as are the simplified capitals. These buildings date to the early decades of the 20th century AD (Al-Asad 1997, 28; Royal Sci-

Fig. 4. Main façade of the *madâfâh* complex. By McQuitty.

entific Society 1990). By the 1930s such attention to architectural decoration has given way to even greater simplicity and emphasis on horizontality in the treatment of façades. Another distinctive feature of the Hartha building is the use of the cross-vault which was common in the village architecture of Palestine but rarer in Jordan where it is concentrated in the north of the country. Most of the houses of the late 19th century AD village of Umm Qays include vaulted rooms and it is here that the closest parallels in the arrangement of units and courtyards and inclusion of features such as the *aliyeh* can be seen (Daher 1999; Shami 1989). Here the façades are plainer and if decorated incorporate real Classical elements from the earlier city, Gadara, on which the village was built. The introduction of iron girders into the construction repertoire can be dated very precisely to the coming of the Hijaz railway (that used iron girders) in the first decade of the 20th century AD, but this is a fairly early use of the technique. In the villages further south in Jordan on the Kerak Plateau, iron girders are not routinely employed in roof construction until the 1940s (Kana'an & McQuitty 1994, 145). Other *madâfât* are less splendid than the Hartha example; often free-standing but distinctive for being so, since most villages were composed of courtyard complexes and they stand alone. It is this question of access that is a distinguishing feature: even in the Hartha example which *is* part of a complex, the access is to the public street, not through the private family area.

The splendid entrance to the *madâfâh* signals *its* functional importance to the community and tribe. It should also be remembered that it signals the importance of its proprietor, Quaider Obeidat. The builder of the Hartha *madâfâh* is

Fig. 5. Entrance to the *madâfâh*. By McQuitty.

Fig. 6. Detail of the columns and architraves of the *madâfâh* entrance. By McQuitty

not known but he was obviously well-acquainted with the urban architectural repertoire of that time. In Jordan, not since the Byzantine/Early Islamic period had there been such incursions of urban style into a rural context and this trend is repeated throughout the wealthier villages. Several factors that contributed to this trend can be suggested. In the late 19th century rural Jordan, particularly the north, was being re-incorporated into the Ottoman Empire and urban world as land-registration was initiated (Mundy 1996, 82-83) and the Ottoman government retained a physical presence with the presence of officials and the establishment of garrisons in the towns of Irbid, Salt and latterly Karak. The down-side of this incorporation was conscription and taxation. But some individuals were able to benefit and accumulated significant wealth through tax collection on behalf of the government and through the sale of surplus agricultural produce to a wider trade network that could be reached with new forms of transport, for example the Hijaz Railway. New building techniques, for example the machine-dressing of stone, and new construction materials, for example the iron girder, and window-glass, became available. Urban style was accessible to the rural community but it did not change the fundamental requirements of the community. A *madâfâh* was part of those requirements, sitting firmly as it does within the traditions of hospitality. The building's form *i.e.*, its access from the public rather than private world, did not alter; what did was the way in which its presence was signified architecturally.

Acknowledgements

Many of my first experiences of Jordanian village life were gained through frequent weekends spent in Hartha with the families of Abu Walid Obeidat and Umm Ra'ad Obeidat. For their hospitality, knowledge, openness and welcome, I am forever grateful. More recently the individuals mentioned in footnote no. 3 have benefited from background information given by the mayor Shlash Saleh Obeidat, his mother Thuriah al Saleh, 'Ali Mahmoud Quaider Obeidat (grandson of the original owner) and Ra'ad al Sarough. I am also much indebted to Dr R. Daher and Dr D. Obeidat for their assistance in producing this article.

References

Al-Asad, M. 1997. *Old Houses of Jordan: Amman 1920-1950*. Turab.

El-Barghouti, O.S. 1924. 'Rules of Hospitality', *The Journal of the Palestine Oriental Society*, IV(4), 175-203.

Daher, R. 1999. 'Gentrification and the Politics of Power, Capital and Culture in an Emerging Jordanian Heritage Industry', *Traditional Dwellings and Settlements Review*, X(II), 33-46.

Denton, B. & B. St. Laurent. 1996. 'Early Twentieth Century Architecture'. In: P.M. Bikai & T.A. Dailey (eds.), *Madaba: Cultural Heritage*, 47-89. Amman: American Center for Oriental Research.

Dunn, E. 1998. *Evaluation of Hartha Guest House*. Archive conservation proposal.

Encyclopedia of Islam. 1965. E.J. Brill and Luzac and Co.

Jaussen, A. 1948. *Coutumes des Arabes au Pays de Moab*. Paris: Librairie d'Amérique et d'Orient.

Kana'an, R. & A. McQuitty. 1994. 'The Architecture of al-Qasr on the Kerak Plateau: an Essay in the Chronology of Vernacular Architecture', *Palestine Exploration Quarterly*, 126, 127-51.

Gaube, H. 1979. 'Die syrischen Wüstenschlösser: Einige wirtschaftliche und politische Gesichtspunkte zu ihrer Entstehung', *Zeitschrift des Deutsche Palästina-Vereins*, 95, 182-209.

Hütterhoth, W-D & K. Abdulfattah. 1977. *Historical Geography of Palestine, Transjordan and Southern Syria in the Late 16th Century*. Erlangen: Frankischen Geographischen Gesellschaft.

Mare, W.H. 1984. 'The 1982 Season at Abila of the Decapolis', *Annual of the Department of Antiquities of Jordan*, 28, 71-9.

Mundy, M. 1996. '*Qada* 'Ajlun in the Late Nineteenth Century: Interpreting a Region from the Ottoman Land Registers', *Levant*, 28, 77-95.

Musil, A. 1928. *The Manners and Customs of the Rwala Bedouins*. Oriental Geographical Society No. 6, American Geographical Society.

Obeidat, D. & A. 1998. *Architectural Documentation Project for the Town of Hartha*. Archive proposal in Arabic.

Palmer, C. 1998. '"Following the plough": the Agricultural Environment of Northern Jordan', *Levant*, 30, 129-166.

Royal Scientific Society. 1990. *Salt: A Plan for Action* (Arabic). Amman: Salt Development Corporation.

Shami, S. 1989. 'Settlement and Resettlement in Umm Qeis: Spatial Organisation and Social Dynamics in a Village in North Jordan'. In: J.P. Bourdier & N.A. Sayyed (eds.), *Dwellings, Settlements and Tradition*. New York: American Universities, 451-76.

Tchalenko, G. 1953-8. *Villages antiques de la Syrie du nord: le massif de Belus à l'époque romaine*. 3 vols. Paris.

Notes

1 These lines are by an unknown poet but recited at the turn of the 19th century by two members of the Rwala tribe (Musil 1928, 466).

2 This subject is explored by Abdel Karim Hesban *Tribe and State: Madâfât in Irbid*. Unpublished M.A. dissertation (in Arabic). University of Yarmouk.

3 The *madâfâh* was first recorded by the author in 1983 as part of a study of the vernacular architecture of Northern Jordan funded by the then British Institute at Amman for Archaeology and History and the Palestine Exploration Fund. The photographs date from this original recording while the drawings were prepared by Dr Daher's students. Subsequently further study has been undertaken by an *ad hoc* group of concerned individuals: Ms Rowan Attour (Turath: Heritage Conservation Consultants), Dr Rami Daher (Jordan University of Science and Technology), Ms Edith Dunn (University of Minnesota), Mr Asem Obeidat, Dr Daifallah Obeidat (Ahl al-Bayt University), Ms Nawal Obeidat and the author. The whole complex has suffered great damage and is unlikely to survive for much longer.

An Egyptian *qa'a* in 16th Century Damascus

Representative Halls in Late Mamluk and Early Ottoman Residential Architecture in Syria and Lebanon

STEFAN WEBER

Historical houses from the Ottoman (1516-1918) and Mamluk (1260-1516) periods are the real treasure of Syrian cities. Damascus and Aleppo contain hundreds of these very valuable monuments. Some of them are outstanding monuments but their importance becomes even more evident in their setting as an 'urban ensemble' in connection with the old *suqs*, mosques, *hammams*, bakeries, coffee houses, and other elements of architecture.

During the last decade, more attention has been given to this urban heritage by both scholarly circles and the general public. Many houses were changed into restaurants and renovated according to their new functions. Private money has also been invested in fixing old family houses or in providing homes for people who have consciously discovered this heritage. This private initiative is very much needed and welcomed, however the restoration of some of the residences has not always been beneficial for the structure: some houses were literary rebuilt and destroyed in the name of restoration. For numerous years the old living culture has been neglected in the public consciousness and this, together with daily practices and modern education, have all contributed to destroying the traditional know-ledge of space, its characteristics and its usage. Saving these treasures from decay, neglect, or from some fancy commercial 'restoration' is one of the very urgent tasks in the heritage conservation of modern Syria. The spirit and characteristics of these houses should be communicated to the public and different models of how to save them must be developed and made known. The restoration of the Bayt al-Aqqad, that houses the Danish Institute, has played a pioneer role as a model for scientific restoration. It was Peder and Inge Mortensen who had the idea, the spirit and the energy to plan and carry out this project.

Being one of the most striking and important houses in Damascus, the Bayt al-Aqqad has various rooms containing masterpieces of Syrian craftsmanship in residential architecture, mainly from the 15th, 18th, 19th and early 20th centuries. Its importance is not only evidenced by the few Roman theatre remains in the

Fig.1. Damascus, Qasr al-'Azm, dated 1163/1749-50, picture of the *qa'a* before the fire of 1925.

walls of the house, but also by the fact that the Bayt al-Aqqad, with the *iwan* and the *qa'a*, contains two large building units from the Mamluk period. Only few Mamluk rooms are known in Damascus, among them the most spectacular is preserved in the Bayt al-Aqqad. The *qa'a* of the Bayt al-Aqqad was rebuilt twice in the 18th century but its original Mamluk shape allows us to form hypotheses about how it may have looked in the past. This article should therefore provide some information for further speculation.[1]

Fig. 2. Damascus, Bait al-Hawraniyya, built and decorated between 1202/1787-88 and 1218/1803-04, plan of the *qa'a*.

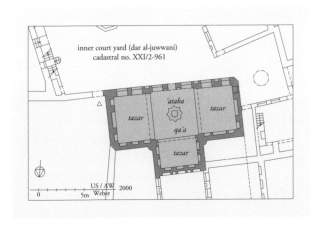

Until the middle of the 19th century living rooms in the Ottoman period had a very formalized layout: When entering a room one came first into a lower part, the so-called *'ataba* (threshold), which often took up one-fifth to one-third of the space and was the entrance area of the room. The second part of the room, called *tazar*, or depending on the regions and times – *diwan* or *majlis*, rises 40-50 cm from ground level like a platform, and is separated by a high rising arch (*iwan*). In the reception rooms (*qa'a*) of the houses of wealthy families, the *'ataba* could lead to two or even three *tazars*. In some cites the *'ataba* is domed or the whole room is covered by cross vaulting. All *qa'as* known in Damascus so far are roofed by beams covered by a thick layer of compressed mud and fibre. The ceiling of the *qa'as* in the Syrian capital (also found in many houses in Aleppo, Hama and Sidon) is normally decorated with painting or even lacquer work on light mouldings called *'ajami*. Normally the ceiling on the *tazar* is panelled, while the ceiling of the *'ataba* is higher and the *'ajami*-painting is directly fixed on the beams.

The shape of the Damascene *qa'a* in the 18th century is well known but we have difficulties in establishing a clear genealogy of the *qa'a*; in every city of Bilad al-Sham a different mix of influences shaped the layout of *qa'as* and often different concepts were applied during the same time. In Damascus no Mamluk *qa'a* survived in its original form and the oldest known examples date from the 16th and 17th centuries. The *qa'a* of the Bayt al-Aqqad, which is found in structures from the Mamluk period, was fundamentally reshaped during the 18th century (we were able to establish at least five building phases).[2]

Domed *qa'as* and free-standing *qa'as*

Since material evidence is missing about the appearance of *qa'as* at the transition from Mamluk to Ottoman rule, we must depend on written sources for the reconstruction of early *qa'as*. As mentioned sometimes in Mamluk sources, we have no written indication of the shape of *qa'as* in the Mamluk period. Different endowment deeds (*waqfiyya*) and court records from the early Ottoman period, held at the Syrian National Archive for Historical Documents, give descriptions of houses that were sold, bought or added to a foundation or personal property. Here we find the existence of domed *qa'as* (!) and of single *qa'as* without being constructively an integral part of a courtyard structure. The existence of free-standing *qa'as* (not being constructively united with the rest of the house as we know it today) will be dealt with in a later stage of this article.

However, the relevant sources will be given at this point regarding the question of domes. In the year 991/1583 Niqula ibn Yuhana al-Mawardi rented one *qa'a* with two *tazars/iwans* in the city quarter of Qaymariya.[3] The arrangement of the rooms resembles an entrance *qa'a* from 1155/1742 found during our documentation and restoration study of Bayt al-Quwatli in al-Naqqashat. This kind of construction can be found twice in 992/1584 next to the Siba'iya-Madrasa, where in one house two *qa'as* are mentioned, one of them with a dome and each of them possessing two *iwans/tazars* facing each other. Also a year later a Jew named Sulayman ibn Yusuf bought, according to the document, a house with a *qa'a* that contained two *iwans*, one of them (as written in the document) had a *tazar*. Even more unusual and appealing must have been the *qa'a* that Hasan Jawish ibn Khudrawardi bought (in 993/1585) from the Mufti Isma'il al-Nabulsi. His *qa'a* with a large and small *iwan* (*tazar*) had two upper floors, which were similar to those in Aleppo, *i.e.* accessible by a stone staircase from inside the *qa'a*.[4] The *waqfiyya* of Ahmad ibn Sinan al-Qaramani mentions, for example, several houses that were turned into a *waqf* in 1011/1603. His house, built in 999/1590-91 southeast of the famous Bimaristan Nur al-Din (north to the Madrasa al-Khatuniyya al-Juwaniyya), borders on an independent *qa'a* also owned by him. Another house that he bought in 986/1578-79 is said to have a *qubba* (dome) in the outer courtyard (*barrani*), and another dome of wood, 'which has two windows'.[5] In the early 18th century one can still find descriptions of houses in court records that mention domed *qa'as*, for example the house in the west of Suq al-Buzuriyya that the governor Isma'il il Pasha al-'Azm bought in 1140/1727 from Khadija bint Abd al-Rahman ibn Ahmad al-Mufti. In the *barrani* the records describe a *qa'a*, which is 'topped by a dome' and contains two *iwans/tazars* (a southern and a northern). The house contained different shaped *qa'as* and included – next to the domed *qa'a* mentioned above – the *qa'a* of the

Fig. 3. Homs, Bait al-Zahrawi (Korn 1996, 266).

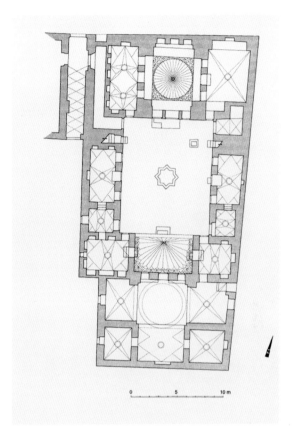

Fig. 4. Aleppo, Bait Janbulat (David 1998, 55).

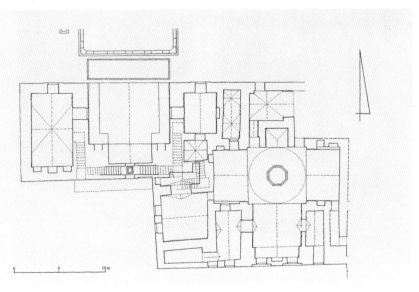

Fig. 5. Tripoli, Khan al-'Askar, *qa'a* western part, ~17th ct.

Fig. 6. Tripoli, Khan al-'Askar, *qa'a* western
part, 17th ct. (1:400)

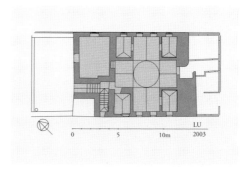

juwwani, which had a painted wooden ceiling (*musaqqafa bi-l-saqf al-'ajami al-madhun*), as known from other *qa'as* of that time.[6]

The evidence in sources is surprising because during recent surveys of several hundreds of houses by the French and German Institutes in Damascus no single domed *qa'a* was found. Domed *qa'as* are well known in other cities and might have deep historical roots. Well known is the green dome on top of the palace of Mu'awiyya (40/661), the centre of Umayyad rule in Damascus (Ibn 'Asakir 1954 II, 125, 133, 138; al-Rihawi 1972, 32 ff.; Sack 1989, 19 f.). The great Umayyad reception hall on the citadel in Amman has four *iwans* that might have had a similar function to later *iwans* in *qa'as*. But so far it has not been proven whether the reception hall was domed or not (Northedge 1992, 71). Also in Ottoman architecture domed reception halls with *tazar/iwan*-like like wings on the four sides are known. The Çinli Köşk in Istanbul is the most famous pavilion with this layout (Eldem 1969). But these examples are far-fetched and too scattered to establish a clear link.[7]

Fig. 7. Tripoli, Khan al-'Askar, Left to right: *khan* (east), connection hall (ex stables of *khan*), *khan*-like residential building topped by the domed *qa'a* (west) (Lebanese University).[8]

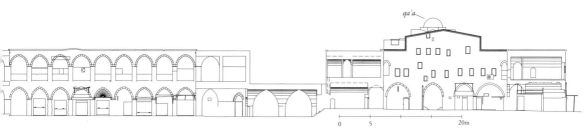

More interesting are examples that are closer in time and geography. The Bait al-Zahrawi in Homs was built or rebuilt in 945/1538-39 and contains on its southern side, behind the *iwan*, a full developed T-shape *qa'a* and a domed *qa'a* with two *iwans/tazars* in the North (Korn 1996). If these elements – especially the T-shape *qa'a* – do belong to the early 16th century or even earlier, it would prove that the shape was already developed when the Ottomans arrived in this region. Jean-Claude David mentions the Matbakh al-'Ajami and a building next to it as examples of the Mamluk domed *qa'as* of Aleppo (David 1998, 34 ff). He dates the development of the T-shape *qa'a* (one *'ataba*, three *tazar/iwans*), with a dome on the *'ataba*, to the 16th century. Indeed the *qa'a* of the Bait Janbulat (reconstruction David 1998, 55) from the middle of the 16th century and the *qa'a* at the Khan al-Jumruk dated 1574 (David 1996), with its cross shaped *qa'a* (central dome on the *'ataba* and four *tazar/iwans*), seem to be the predecessors of the T-shaped domed *qa'as* in Aleppo a few decades later. Similar cases of domed *qa'as* with three or four *tazars/iwans* could be found in Tripoli and Sidon.

The – as yet – undated Khan al-'Askar in Tripoli includes a room that responds to the shape of a cross *qa'a*. The domed *qa'a* is located on the 2nd floor in the western part of a composite structure consisting of a *khan* (east, cadastral-No. TZ60-553), a *suq* with a dome to the entrance of the *khan*, the *khan*-like living structure with the cross *qa'a* to which I am referring (west, cadastral-No. TZ60-14), and a connection hall (stables) between them (fig. 7).

During our recently started survey on the *suqs* and historical sources of Tripoli no information on the Khan al-'Askar has yet been found; however the *muqarnas* ribbon on the entrances to both structures in the west and east allows for a dating between the late 16th and early 18th century. The whole western structure of the Khan al-'Askar is an impressive building topped by a domed *qa'a*, which was – in analyzing its layout – not a commercial structure but most probably a residential complex. The building only consists of living units and does not indicate any commercial use; storage space and shops are missing. It may have been built next to the northwestern city gate to host travellers or military troops.[9] The *qa'a* on the top floor is the most important room and is marked on both the street façade and courtyard façade by a gable that serves no architectural purpose. The interpretation that the domed *qa'a* with four *tazar/iwans* belongs to a residential complex is supported by another important residential complex, the Bait Kastanflis – 'Adra in the Rammane Quarter (cadastral-No. TR2-41). This late Mamluk or early Ottoman house was rebuilt twice during the 19th century but still preserves a domed *qa'a* with four *tazar/iwans* topping the house on the third floor.

In Sidon, during our research for the Debbané History Museum (www. museumsaida.org) we have so far identified three houses with domed *qa'as*.

Fig. 8. Sidon, *qa'a*, house of French consul, southern façade.

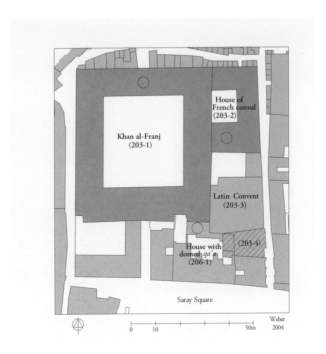

Fig. 9. Sidon, surrounding
Khan al-Franj (1:1500).

The most important one is located on top of a house (cadastral-No. 203-2) attached in the East to the Khan al-Franj (cadastral-No. 203-1) and shows four *tazar/iwans*. Consular records in the French National Archive give evidence that this house was administered by the provincial treasury in Damascus (AE/B1/1019, 1712-15 p. 169) and was rented out to the French consul in the early 18th century by Mustafa and Ali Agha al-Hammud. It was Mustafa who gave permission in 1711 – and at later phases – to repair and change the

Fig. 10. Sidon, *qa'a*, house of French consul.

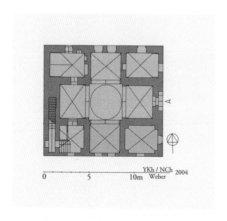

Fig. 11. Sidon, *qa'a*, house of French consul.

building.[10] The consul writes: '…mais ici que P.P. a obtenu d'Agi Moustafa, procureur du trésorier de Damas, propriétaire de la maison occupée par mon dit sieur le consul, la permission par l'écrit du 15 fev. dernier de faire bâtir une grande arcade…'[11] The Chevalier D'Arvieux, who visited Sidon between 1658 and 1665, attributes the building to Fakhr al-Din al-Ma'ni (1590-1633), saying that it served as a residence for his wives (D'Arvieux 1982, 44f). This seems quite doubtful, since residences for women only, and attached to a *Khan*, are not known. D'Arvieux, who gives detailed descriptions of places he visited, generally tends to attribute buildings to Fakhr al-Din (like the Khan al-Franj, see below). D'Arvieux arrived 25 years after the death of Fakhr al-Din, whose influence was still very palpable. However, after the historian, Abdel Nour, this house belonged to the Ma'ni family and was confiscated in 1633 with the other properties of the Ma'nis. It was then being incorporated into the *waqf* for Mekka and Medina (D'Arvieux 1982, 41, note 63).

This house was built in local construction and layout techniques during the impressive building activity around the Saray Square in the late 16th and early 17th centuries. A terminus post quem is given by the Khan al-Franj, which was founded in 1560 by the famous Ottoman politician Sokullu Mehmet Pasha (d. 1579), Grand Vizier from 1565 to 1579.[12] The joints between the two buildings show that the *khan* is older than the house, hence the house was built between 1560 and 1633/1658. Today the building serves as a school and has been changed and restored during the last years. It is not possible to see any remains of *tazars* in the *qa'as'* four arms, and neither is it possible to detect if any has been built and removed at a later phase. D'Arvieux gives a detailed description of the room:

De la première terrasse on entre dans la chambre consulaire. Elle est en forme de croix, dont les bras à droite et à gauche sont percés chacun de deux grandes fenêtres, avec des grilles de fer. Les unes regardent la mer, et les autres donnent sur la basse-cour. Le bras du fond opposé à l'entrée, est occupé par deux grandes armoires. Les quatre cantons de la croix forment quatre petites chambres fort propres, dont les deux du côté de la mer, servent de chambre et de cabinet au consul; le deux opposées lui servent de garde-robes; et dans la dernière est un passage et un escalier, qui conduit sur la dernière terrasse, c'est-à-dire, sur la plus élevée, sur laquelle on a bâti une chambre ouverte de tous côtés, qui sert de belveder, d'où l'on découvre bien loin à la mer du côté de Sour. (D'Arvieux 1982, 45).

Like the Khan al-'Askar or Bait Kastanflis – 'Adra in Tripoli, this domed *qa'a* is meant to serve as a belvedere and to be seen from afar as well. When D'Arvieux entered the consulate via the Khan al-Franj and a small courtyard to the south

Fig. 12. Deir al-Qamar, Saray Yusuf al-Shihabi.

of the *qa'a* he noticed: 'La maison consulaire est au nord de cette cour; c'est un gros corps de logis de six toises en carré, couvert d'un fort beau dôme' (D'Arvieux 1982, 44). Without doubt the domed *qa'as* mentioned here were built to be the most prominent feature from both the inside and the outside of the buildings. The T-shaped *qa'a* of the Saray of Amir Yusuf al-Shihabi (ruled 1770-88) from the second half of the 18th century, in Deir al-Qamar, is a good example of this wish to be conspicuous. Its dome is not only visible from within the courtyard but also from the outside, where the *qa'a* is indicated in the clear standing façade by a *tazar/iwan* that juts out, and is marked by a wooden köşk.

To recall: unlike Aleppo, Hama, Tripoli, Sidon or even Deir al-Qamar, no single domed *'ataba* is known in Damascus. This seems quite logical, because public and residential architecture in all the mentioned cities is mainly based on stone, while Damascene craftsmen used much more wood and clay. Normally the ground floor and arches are made of stone, while the walls of the upper floor are built of a grid of half timber, its compartments filled with unburned clay bricks carrying a roof of wooden beams covered with a mud-fiber roof system. The absence of domed *qa'as* in Damascus must partly be seen as an outcome of the building materials that are used. Why construct a heavy, expensive and difficult vaulted or domed structure when wood can be borne more easily by half

Fig. 13. Hama, Qasr al-'Azm (1153/1740).

timber walls and can then be painted lavishly in the *'ajami* technique. The material seems to determine some aspects of the shape of the *qa'a*. But as previously mentioned, written sources indicate clearly that Damascus also had domed *qa'as* at some time. The reason for the absence of domed *qa'as* in Damascus in the existing residential architecture from the 17th to the 19th centuries is a bit more complicated however, and cannot be solely explained by the building materials. In fact strong evidence indicates that Egyptian residential architecture may have had an influential role to play.

An 'Egyptian' *qa'a* in Damascus

A large hall in the Bab Tuma quarter could serve as a key monument for investigating the shape of *qa'as* in late Mamluk and early Ottoman times. The hall strongly squattered and subdivided by modern additions of concrete walls is hidden today in a large compound of small shops and workshops. A fire that broke out around 1980 in one of the workshops ruined the original ceiling and caused further damage to the structure. The eastern part was already separated in the early 20th century and has, since 1996, served as the well-known night-club/restaurant Marmar (compare fig. 14).

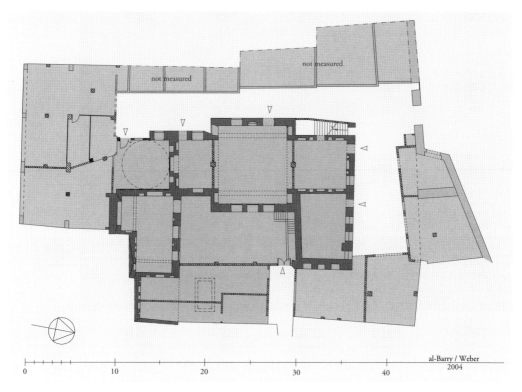

Fig. 14. Damascus, Qa'at al-'Imadi, present-day situation without the secondary elements in the centre of the hall (original walls highlighted, recent additions hatched/ dashed, 1:400).

Fig. 15 gives a preliminary reconstruction of the original position of the building based on observation results made on site. The main hall consists of four large arches (height 9.16 m, width 7.56 m/east-west and 5.28 m/north-south) that lead on the western and the eastern side to 1.2 m deep aisle-like sections, and in the north (6.52 m depth) and south (4.37 m depth) to *iwan/tazar*-like rooms. In the south, a chamber is attached to a –now – lost dome of 2.62 m diameter. This setting is highly unusual in Damascus and could have only served as a reception hall in a residential complex since no grave or *mihrab*/apse was found. The niche in the western wall is a normal niche/*kutubiyya* in the centre of the *qa'a*-wall facing the entrance. For a school – a possibility in view of the typology of the building (see below) – it would need a *mihrab*-niche in the south, since the *qibla* in Damascus is oriented in this direction. The original entrance from the east with a courtyard, fountain and attached rooms supports this reading of the building. I will hereafter name the complex as Qa'at al-'Imadi due to the closeness of the 'Imadi Mosque located to the west.

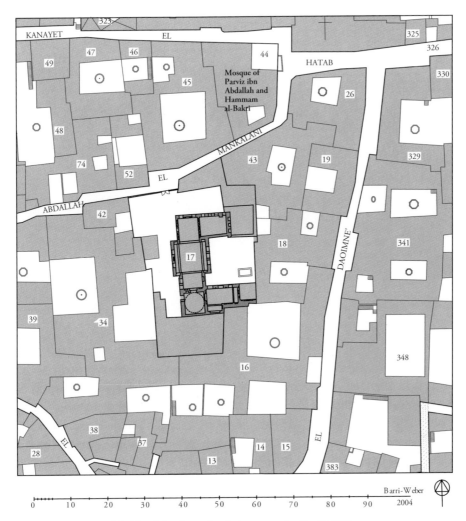

Fig. 15. Damascus, Bait al-Imadi, location and preliminary reconstruction (1:1000).

The *qa'a* lay south of the Hammam al-Bakri (1026/1617) and the small mosque (restored in 1069/1658-59) of the Amir al-Umara Barawiz (Parviz) ibn 'Abdallah (d. 1015/1606-07), and could possibly be ascribed to one of these two buildings.[13] We know from sources that members of the Bakri family, which was very prominent during the 16th and 17th centuries, lived in the Bab Tuma quarter of the city and this enormous residential hall may have belonged to the Bakri household. It is, however, more likely that another very important figure of the second half of the 16th century and very early 17th century was the patron of this *qa'a*. Barawiz

Fig. 16. Damascus, Qa'at al-'Imadi, (outside) Nightclub Marmar.

(Parviz) ibn 'Abdallah (d. 1515/1606-07) was as Amir al-Umara one of the most prominent notables in the city during the second half of the 16th century.[14] He had built the mosque for himself close to his home next to the Hammam al-Bakri; after leaving his official position he became the Muazzin and Imam of the mosque. In different court records the house is mentioned as located next to the mosque, but I could not identify the mentioned buildings directly with this *qaʿa*.[15] Another court record states that the buildings of Parviz were all restored in the year 1130/1717-18, among them seven houses (*dar*) and one palace (*qasr*). Three of the houses with an enclosed piece of land (*hawsh*), situated in Bab Tuma, were connected to each other.[16] The Qa'at al-'Imadi is the only building in the neighbourhood and vicinity of the mosque that fits the mentioned buildings in function, date and importance. The Bait Mishaqa (cadastral-No. XIV-315) in the north of the mosque has two rooms dating from the same period (16th/17th centuries). But, by the middle of the 19th century, this house was the property of Mikhail Mishaqa (1800-1888) and could not therefore have been referred to in 19th century sources as the *waqf* of Parviz. However, the *qaʿa* described here could have been part of the residential complex of Parviz, but this assumption must remain hypothetical.

An analysis of its architectural decoration remains the only way to date the building. But this undertaking is quite complicated, since we find features that could be dated to the 15th/16th and 17th century in the same area. One should

Fig. 17. Damascus, Qa'at al-'Imadi, (inside) southwest corner.

mention that the building decoration of the 15th and 16th centuries in Damascus contains similar single elements and overall arrangements. It is not always possible to distinguish a late 15th from a middle 16th century building and there are some cases where doubts remain. Such a case is that of the Qa'at al-'Imadi, which shows elements that cannot have been applied before the late 16th century, and some other elements seem to be relicts from the local Mamluk past (not necessarily from Cairo).

For example, one finds in the building the same sequences of serrated medallions (the large ones 36.5 cm long and 15.8 cm wide, figs. 18 and 19), which are extremely rare for buildings of the 16th century, and it would thus be an argument to attribute the *qa'a* to the Mamluk period. The same is true for some of the *muqarnas* camphor, where one finds the exact same design of camphor in Mamluk buildings. Other *muqarnas* camphor in the *qa'a* are typical for the late 16th/early 17th century. The interwoven ribbons (15 cm wide) are quite usual in 15th and 16th century Damascene architecture. At all four intersections of the four larch arches, the plinths with *muqarnas* camphor sit at right angles to each other showing some irregularities. They may have been changed at a later point of time. Different building phases between the early 16th and middle of the 17th century cannot be excluded, but the overall homogeneous layout and decoration of the *qa'a* indicates an overlapping of two styles, which occurred in a period of transition.

Fig. 18. Damascus, Madrasa al-Sibaiyya, (915/1509-921/1515).

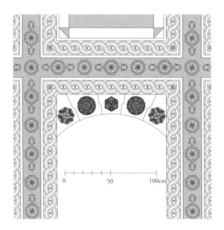

Fig. 19. Damascus, Qa'at 'Imadi, east elevation, detail, (al-Barry, not to scale).

The above mentioned 'relics' of Mamluk architecture makes a dating back to the Mamluk period tempting, but, as mentioned previously, there are some elements that date the *qa'a* to the end of the first Damascene Ottoman century. The first of these elements are medallions (see fig. 19, middle) and ribbons in the colour paste technique.[17] This technique developed in the late 14th century. However, small elaborated medallions in lintels and arches of doors and windows (between 8 and 10 cm diameter), like those in the Qa'at al-'Imadi, can only be found from the late 16th century onwards. Another feature in colour-paste technique makes the dating to the late 16th and early 17th century even more certain. Two buildings from the turn of the 16th/17th century, the Khan al-Sanawbar/al-Fawqani (cadastral-No. XXI-756) and the Bait al-Sa'ada (cadastral-No. XII-179),

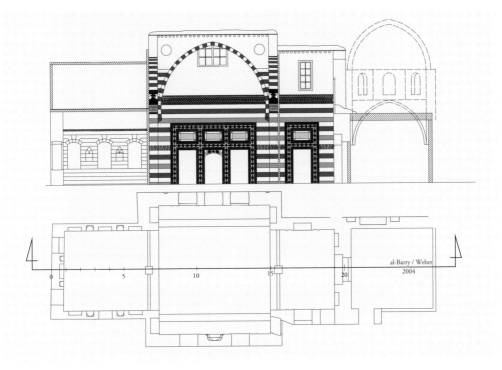

Fig. 22. Damascus, Qa'at al-'Imadi, elevation east façade (modern structures in blue, reconstruction dashed lines; 1:250).

have a depiction of small facing pigeons worked in black colour paste on the surface of one of the arch segments that divide the rooms. This motive is slightly enriched by a centred cup on one stone segment (33.8 cm x 60 cm) of the arches in the *qa'a*. The dating to the second half of the 16th or early 17th century would also correspond with the assumed patronage of Parviz ibn Abdallah.

Mamluk *qa'as*

The most interesting feature of the building is its plan, which is rare for a Damascus layout but known from Cairo in the Mamluk and Ottoman period. The Mamluk *qa'a* (in Cairo called *mandara*) has two large rooms on the shorter sides and not very deep, but high, rising niches or flat *tazar/iwan*-like sections on the longer sides. These elements of the room known from the public and private architecture of Mamluk Cairo, are marked by wide spanning and high rising arches as we know them from *tazar/iwans*, or later from Ottoman *qa'as*.[18] Examples of Mamluk *mandaras* are found in the houses of Ahmad Kuhya, Muhibb al-Din Yahya, Shakir ibn al-Ghannam or the palace of Tashtimur in Cairo (fig. 23).

Fig. 23. Cairo, *qa'as* (Maury / Garcin / Revault / Zakariya 1982, 179, not to scale).

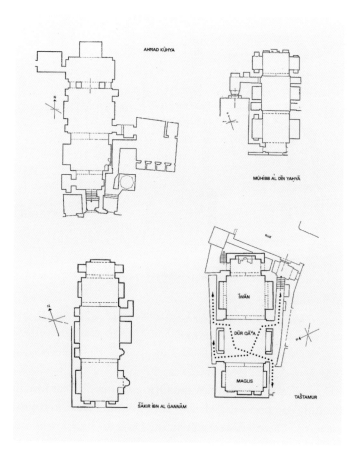

Fig. 24. Damascus, Bait al-Muradi (Reuther 1925, 210, 1:400).

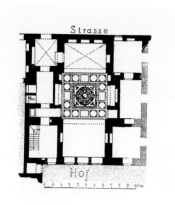

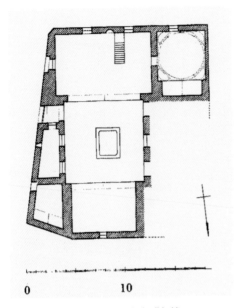 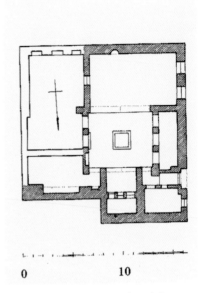

Fig. 25. Damascus, Madrasa al-Shadhbakliyya (857/1453), Meinecke 1992, I, 191 (1:400).

Fig. 26. Damascus, Madrasa al-Haidariyya (878/1473-74), Meinecke 1992, I, 191 (1:400).

They continue throughout the Ottoman period, but lose their small *iwan*-like flanking components and are reduced to the *'ataba* (in Cairo called *dur qa'a*) and two larger *iwans* (*diwan/tazar*). The Qa'at al-'Imadi, with two large *tazar/iwans*, and two smaller flanking ones, corresponds more to the Cairene Mamluk *qa'as* and can be considered an heir of the Mamluk *qa'a*.

Subsequently the question of the possible appearance of the Mamluk Damascene *qa'a* comes up. Our research on the *qa'a* of the Bayt al-Aqqad, the Qa'at al-'Imadi and of the written sources shows that *qa'as* were quite often free standing, situated in a larger complex of buildings, but not formalized with the courtyard as we know it from later structures.[19] This corresponds well to David's theory of the 'pavilion' character of Mamluk and early Ottoman *qa'as* in Aleppo (David 2004). Some pavilion-like *qa'as* from Mamluk Cairo have survived. Also the early Aleppine *qa'as* show partial parallels in plan with the Cairene models, but they differ from the surviving examples in Damascus and Cairo by their domed structure. Another house published by Oscar Reuther in 1925 and dated by him to the 16th century proves that the Qa'at al-'Imadi is not an exception (fig. 24). The *qa'a* of the recently destroyed Bait al-Muradi in Damascus shows a very similar plan to our *qa'a* with the same main elements as the Egyptian Mamluk *qa'as*: one central part (*dur qa'a/'ataba*) and two large and two small flanking sections (*tazar/iwan/diwan*) – no dome.

Fig. 27. Damascus, Madrasat and Turbat Afridun al-Ajami/ Fardawsiyya (744/1343-44) Wulzinger/Watzinger, 1924, 88 (1:400).

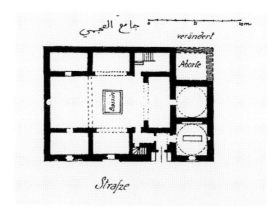

Fig. 28. Cairo, Madrasa and Mausoleum of Qaytbay (877/1472 – 879/1474) Meinecke 1992, I, 166 (1:800).

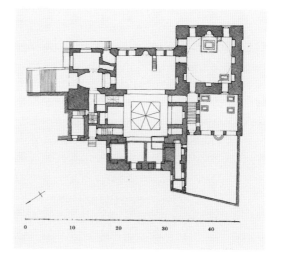

The parallels between Cairo and Damascus are not reduced to residential architecture only. Fifteenth century school buildings show a close parallel between the Mamluk capital and the second city of the Empire, Damascus. From the 15th century onwards the same layout of a covered hall (*qa'a*) with four *tazar/iwans*, two larger ones and two smaller ones – also became very frequent in *madrasas*, where the most known example in Cairo is that of the Madrasa of Qaytbay (877/1472 – 879/1474). This plan is quite known and developed from the *iwan-madrasas* but its courtyard was covered and the yard turned into a hall at a later stage, such became the type of *qa'a* discussed here. The Madrasa al-Shadhbakliyya (857/1453) and the Madrasa al-Haidariyya (878/1473-74) are two examples from 15th century Damascus. If the present ceiling of the Madrasat

Afridun al-Ajami/Fardawsiyya (744/1343-44, fig. 27) had a Mamluk predecessor, *iwan madrasas* in the *qa'a* style with a flat roof would have been known in Damascus since the 14th century.

Conclusion

Given that some of the decoration of the Qa'at al-'Imadi is a continuation of local Mamluk decoration, the shape of this *qa'a* could quite easily be a continuation of the local layout of reception halls. As previously mentioned, no Damascene Mamluk *qa'a* is preserved in its original shape. In Cairo the plan of late Mamluk madrasas and *qa'as* are quite close to each other. The same could be true for Damascus. The two 16th century *qa'a* plans ('Imadi/Muradi) are very close in plan to those of some Mamluk madrasas in the town. It is most likely that residential *qa'as* of the same type existed in Mamluk Damascus. On the other hand it would be misleading to state that Mamluk *qa'as* in Damascus looked like the Qa'at 'Imadi. The Qa'at 'Imadi is an outstanding reception hall and, as such, not representative of all the *qa'as* in Damascus. But it is this Mamluk tradition, which makes Damascus closer to Cairo than any of the other Syrian cities. It is most probably this connection to Mamluk Cairo that, on the background of local construction techniques, has formed the Damascene *qa'a* without domes as we know it from numerous examples of the 18th century.

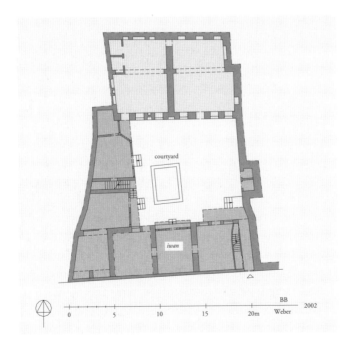

Fig. 29. Damascus, Bait al-Sa'ada, ground plan (1:400).

Fig. 30. Damascus, Bait al-Sa'ada, eastern *qa'a* from entrance.

A good example of a transitional *qa'a* shape, with one *'ataba* and only one *tazar*, is that of the Bait al-Sa'ada (cadastre XII-179, Fig. 29 and Fig. 30). This house was rebuilt several times, but still preserved large parts of its original late 16th or early 17th century structure.[20] Among them are two parallel rooms on the northern side of the house with the described *'ataba – tazar* layout. The *'ataba*

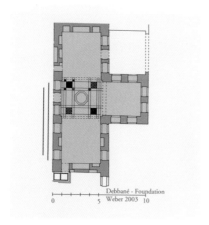

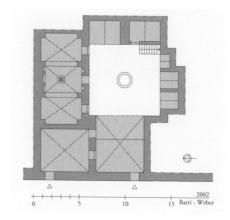

Fig. 31. Sidon, Qasr Debbané (1134/1721-22), *qa'a*, (1:400).

Fig. 32. Sidon, Bait Baraka, ground floor (1:400).

today is filled to the level of the *tazar* but the elements of these two rooms are the same. There is only a slight difference in the arrangements from all the rooms we know from the 17th, 18th and early 19th century (compare fig. 1 and fig. 2).

Fig. 33. Sidon, Qasr Debbané, *qa'a* (1134/1721-22).

But one should be cautious not to read into these connections a linear and absolute evolution. As seen above some *qa'as* in Damascus had domes. The overlapping and intermingling of different types and fashions is one of the major characteristics of urban residential architecture. Tripoli, Aleppo, Damascus or Sidon have not always adhered consistently to local schools of architecture. Residential architecture is especially open to changes and influences brought about by changing needs, fashions and techniques.

A good example of this is Sidon in the 18th century where, at the same time, one finds a continuation of the local style of cross-vaulted *qa'as*, domed *qa'as* similar to the buildings described above (like the building used today as Restaurant Istiraha), or *qa'as* in an imported Damascene style. The *qa'a* of the Qasr Debbané with a wooden ceiling in *'ajami* is an example of the latter.

Foreign construction and decoration workshops were very prominent in 18th century Sidon. Interestingly, one finds a mixture of north Syrian construction techniques and Damascene decoration techniques. A possible reason for this may be that governors from Syria – the most prominent members of the 'Azm family – often served as governors in Sidon in the first half of the 18th century. Hama or northern Syria might be the place where those who built the 'Istiraha', or the

Fig. 34. Sidon, Bait Baraka, *qa'a*.

house to the south of Khan al-Franj (see fig. 8) or the Saray Yusuf al-Shihabi in Deir al-Qamar (see fig. 12) originated. But it is absolutely sure that a Damascene workshop was employed to design the rooms and *qaʿas* of the Hammud family, one of the city's main tax farmers and the most influential family in the first decades of the 18th century. The *qaʿa* of the house of ʿAli Agha Hammud (cadastral-No. 166-1), built in 1134/1721-22 and – in the 19th century –becoming the Qasr Debbané, employed the colour paste techniques and *ʿajami* ceiling made by a Damascene workshop. This *qaʿa* has a great resemblance to the very important Damascene *qaʿas* (fig. 2).

The difference in style becomes very clear in comparison with the oldest house we found so far in Sidon. The Bait Baraka (cadastral-No. 248-2) could have been built between the 15th and the middle of the 17th century. However, due to the lack of comparable examples from that period in Sidon an accurate dating is not possible, but derivation from the 16th century seems likely. This *qaʿa* shows no colour paste or *ʿajami*, few stone carvings, but stucco ornaments, and cross vaulting over the *ʿataba* and *tazars*. It is a completely different style than the 18th century *qaʿas* of the Hammud family. Even in the 18th century, cross-vaulted main rooms of houses were to be seen, quite often next to domed rooms with *ʿajami* wood ceilings. Different ways of building a reception hall or a residential unit were applied at the same time in the same place.

What is true for Sidon in the 18th century could also be true for Damascus in the 15th century. There are different ways of building a *qaʿa*. While buildings like the Qaʿat al-ʿImadi or al-Muradi, with domed *qaʿas* and normal *ʿataba/tazar* arrangements could have existed next to each other in 15th and 16th century Damascus, domed *qaʿas* never really caught on there, so wooden roofed *qaʿas*, as those known in Cairo, became more dominant. Judging from material evidence and written sources one could state that the *qaʿa* of Bayt al-Aqqad in Damascus may, or – most probably – may not have had a dome, as would have been the case in Aleppo, Homs, Sidon or Tripoli. The reason might be that different building techniques were applied, or that Damascene residential architecture was more interrelated with Egyptian Mamluk architecture than other cities.

References

Abdel Nour, Antoine 1982. *Introduction à l'histoire urbaine de la Syrie Ottomane (XVIᵉ-XVIIIe siècle)*. Beirut.

al-Ansari, Sharaf al-Din Musa 1991. *Nuzha al-Khatir wa-Bahjat al-Nazir. 946 – baʾd 1002*, Vol. I-III. Edited by ʿAdnan Muhammad Ibrahim. Damascus.

Barbir, Karl K. 1979/80. 'From Pasha to Efendi: The Assimilation of Ottomans into Damascene Society, 1516-1783', *International Journal of Turkish Studies*, 1, 68-83.

Behrens-Abouseif, Doris 1989. *Islamic architecture in Cairo. An introduction*. Cairo.

D'Arvieux, Laurent. *Mémoires par Laurent D'Arvieux.* (Extracts published by Antoine Abdel Nour from Mémoires du Chevalier D'Arvieux). Beirut. Vol. I, 251-463; Vol. II, 324-471; vol. III, 341-370.

David, Jean-Claude 1996, 'Le consulat de France à Alep sous Louis XIV. Témoins architecturaux, descriptions par les consuls et les voyageurs', *Res Orientales*, VIII, 13-24.

David, Jean-Claude 1998. *La suwayqatʿAli à Alep*. Damascus.

David, Jean-Claude forthcoming. 'La qaʿa de la maison Wakil à Alep: origine d'un nouveau modèle d'espace domestique.' In: Julia Gonnella & Jens Kröger (eds.): *The 'Aleppo-Zimmer' Symposium in Berlin*. 12.-13. April, 2002. Kunst des Orients.

Deguilhem, Randi 1995. 'Le Khan des Français à Sidon: un waqf ottoman loué par la France'. In: Daniel Panzac 1995. *Histoire économique et sociale de l'Empire ottoman et de la Turquie (1326-1960)*. 133-144.

Eldem, Sedad Hakkı 1969. *Köşkler ve kasırlar*. Istanbul.

al-Ghazzi, Kamil al-Bali al-Halabi 1926. *Kitab Nahr al-Dhahab fi Tarikh Halab*. 2 vols. Aleppo.

al-Ghazzi, Najm al-Din Muhammad 1981. *Lutf al-Samar wa-Qatf al-Thamar. Min Tarajim Aʾyan al-Tabaqa al-Ula min al-Qarn al-Hadi ʿAshr*. Edited by Muhammad al-Shaykh. 2 vols. Damascus.

Ibn ʿAsakir 1954. *Tarikh Madinat Dimashq*. Edited by Salah al-Din al-Munajjid. Damascus.

Korn, Lorenz 1996. 'Das Bait az-Zahrāwī in Homs: Ein Stadtpalast und seine Stellung in der syrischen Wohnarchitektur', *Damaszener Mitteilungen*, 9, 263-280.

Maury, B., J.-C. Garcin, J. Revault & M. Zakariya 1982. *Palais et Maisons du Caire. I Epoque Mamelouke (XIIIᵉ – XVIᵉ siècles)*. Paris: Éditions du Centre National e la Recherche Scientifique.

Maury, B., A. Raymond, J. Revault & M. Zakariya 1983. *Palais et Maisons du Caire. II Epoque Ottomane (XVIᵉ – XVIIIᵉ siècles)*. Paris: Éditions du Centre National e la Recherche Scientifique.

al-Muhibbi, Muhammad Amin 1970 (1868). *Khulasat al-Athar fi Aʾyan al-Qarn al-Hadi ʿAshar*. 4 vols. Beirut.

Northedge, Alastair 1992. *Studies on Roman and Islamic ʿAmman*. (Vol. 1: History, Site and Architecture). Oxford.

al-Rawwaz, Muhammad Hasan Hilmi 2003. *Tarikh Sayda al-ʾUthmani*. Sidon.

Reuther, Oscar 1925. 'Die Qaʿa', *Jahrbuch der Asiatischen Kunst*, 205-216.

Revault, Jaques 1984/5. *Le fondouk des Français et les consuls de France a Tunis 1660-1860*. Paris.

al-Rihawi, ʿAbd al-Qadir 1972. 'Qusur al-Hukkam fi Dimashq I', *Les Annales Archéologiques Arabes Syriennes*, 22, 31-71.

Sack, Dorothée 1989. *Damaskus, Entwicklung und Strukturen einer orientalisch-islamischen Stadt.* Mainz.

Sidky, Ahmed 1997. 'The development of the Cairene Qaʾaʾ, *Alam Al-Benaa*, 191, 6-9.

Weber, Stefan 1997-1998. 'The Creation of Ottoman Damascus. Architecture and Urban Development of Damascus in the 16th and 17th centuries', *ARAM*, 9 & 10, 431-470.

Weber, Stefan 2004 (in print). 'Walls and Ceilings.' In: John Carswell (ed.): *The Future of the Past.* The Robert Mouawad Private Museum.

Weber, Stefan, Peder Mortensen & Marianne Boqvist (in preparation). 'A Period of Transition: Bait al-ʾAqqad between the 15th and the 18th Century', In: Peder Mortensen (ed.), *Bait al-ʾAqqad: History and Restoration of a House in Old Damascus. Proceedings of the Danish Institute in Damascus.*

Notes

1   The material for this article was collected during my surveys on Damascus, Sidon, Tripoli and the Lebanese Mountains. The Damascus Survey is based at the German Archaeological Institute in Damascus. The Tripoli Survey is based on a co-operation between the Municipality of Tripoli and the German Orient Institute in Beirut (OIB) located in the Qasr al-Nawfal. The Sidon Survey is carried out for the Debbané Foundation in co-operation with the OIB for the Debbané History Museum in Sidon. I would especially like to thank Beshr al-Barry, Youssef al-Khoury and Nathalie Chahine for their work in the measuring campaigns in Sidon and Damascus. Many thanks to Lana Chehade and Geraldine Zimmermann for their critical reading and Ustadhna Akram Ulabi for his supporting work on the records.

2   The southern section of the Bait al-ʾAjlani/Bani Manjak (Qasr Jirun) in the northeast of the Umayyad Mosque could be from the 15th century. On the other hand it might be the *qaʾa* which was after al-Muhibbi (1651-1699) built by the Amir Muhammad ibn Manjak (d. 1032/1622) around 1007/1598-99 between Bab al-Jirun and Darb al-Silsila (al-Muhibbi 1970 III, 230f). The *iwan* and the fountain and parts of the northern section of the Bait al-Quwatli (as-Samman/al-Muradi – north of the Umayyad Mosque) date from the 15th century. The Bait al-Misri/an-Nasiri in the north of the Bait Nizam has a Mamluk *iwan*, and the Bait Sallum, south west from there, contains a Mamluk *qaʾa*-façade. For more details and the Mamluk elements in Bayt al-Aqqad and examples of Damascene *qaʾa*s in the 16th and 17th centuries see Weber, Mortensen & Boqvist.

3   Syrian National Archive (Markaz al-Wathaiq al-Tarikhiyya / MWT) S1/W5 (991/1583).

4   For these records: MWT S1/W264 (992/1584); S1/W11 (993/1585); S1/W594 (993/1585). Further mentioning of domes in houses: 991/1583 in al-Qanawat [S1/W30] and 1046/1636 north to the ʿAdiliyya Madrasa [S4/W438]. One *qaʾa* from 992/1584 with two domes in Bab Jirun in [S1/W494] and one dome on a *qaʾa* in Uqayba in 1036/1627 [S2/W211].

5   Syrian National Archive (Markaz al-Wathaiq al-Tarikhiyya/MWT) in Damascus: Waqfiyya al-Qaramani. Also the Waqfiyyat al-Ghazzi (Ramadan 935) mentions domes and *qaʾa*s.

6   Court records MWT S40/W458 (1140/1727). The term *qubba* was used next to proper
    domes maybe also for important vaulting systems. Toilets and passages next to it are
    sometimes covered by elaborate cross vaults. A quite detailed description in 1127/1715 of a
    toilet in the house of Hamida bint Muhammad al-Amin, the wife of Abd al-Muhsin ibn
    Muhammad Halabi al-Safarjalani, mentions a dome build of burned bricks (*qubba ma'quda
    min al-ajurr*). The house was in the northwestern corner of what became three decades later
    Qasr al-Azm. MWT al-Hujja 26 b.

7   More detail on the historical roots of domed *qa'a*s: David, *maison Wakil à Alep*
    (forthcoming). I would like to thank Jean-Claude David for sending me his article before it
    was published.

8   Fig. 6 and 7: Centre for Restoration of the Lebanese University (Khoury, Rihan, Haddad
    and Abu Assaly), slightly changed by me for this article.

9   The name Khan al-'Askar (the soldier *khan*) is most probably not the original name of the
    building and might not refer to its first function. In the Ottoman provinces, *khan*s were
    frequently used as barracks and often received their name due to that function. Khan al-
    Hummus (cadastral-No. 29-1) built in 1132/1721 by Ali Agha Hammud in Sidon was named
    Khan al-Qishla (*qishla* – Turkish for barrack) after it was turned into a military barracks.

10 For the house see among other: Archives Nationales (Paris) Affaires étrangers B1 1019,
    1712-15, p. 168 f., 292, 498; 1021, 1719-25 p. 159; Deguilhem 1995. The neighbourhood of
    this house is extremely interesting. Directly south of the house one can find on the first
    floor a courtyard with doors to the Khan al-Franj and the church of the Latin Covent
    (1856, cadastral-no 203-3). The substructures of the church are made out of a large living /
    kitchen complex (cadastral-no 203-4) dated through a Latin inscription on the door to the
    western courtyard 1726. Based on stylistic features of its decoration, this house in the west
    (cadastral-no 206-1), which also contains a domed *qa'a* can be dated back to the late 16th or
    17th century. Consulates in khans were quite common, see for the French consuls: Revault
    1984/5 for Tunis, David 1996 for Aleppo, Deguilhem 1995 for Sidon.

11 AE/B1/1019, 1712-15, p. 498.

12 This Khan is generally attributed incorrectly to Fakhr al-Din al-Ma'ni and was first
    known by the name of Ibrahim Khan (al-Rawwas 2003, 161 ff; Abdel Nour 1982, 351,
    Deguilhem 1995, 138). Ibrahim Khan (d. after 1031/1621-2) the son of Sultan Selim II's
    daughter Esmakhan Sultan (d. 993/1585), and Sokullu Mehmet Pasha was the *mutawalli* of
    his father's *waqf*s. This also identifies the Muhammad Basha ibn Jamal al-Din Sinan and
    Ibrahim Khan of the famous *waqfiyya* in Aleppo (Khan Kumruk et al.), cited by al-Ghazzi
    (friendly hints by Stefan Knost). Sokullu Mehmed's father, who was administrator of a
    waqf in Bosnia was called Jemal ül-Din Sinan Beg after he converted to Islam. Al-Ghazzi
    (1926, II 415 ff) translated parts of the *waqfiyya* in Aleppo (dated 982/1574) and after this
    '*a new khan on the shore in the quarter of the sea in Saida*' belonged to the *waqf* of Sokullu
    Mehmed Pasha.

13 All relevant sources for this mosque given in Weber 1997-1998, 436.

14 See for Barawiz ibn 'Abdallah: Barbir 1979/80, 72; al-Ghazzi 1981, I, 340; al-Muhibbi 1970,
    I, 451. After al-Ansari 1991, II, 169 was Parwiz in 961/1553-54 *qadi*.

15 His houses next to the mosque and his *waqf* are also mentioned in: MWT (MSh) S407/
    W27 (1264/1848); S471/W48 (1270/1854); W471/W219 (1270/1854); S676/W181 (1293/1876);
    S676/W182 (1293/1876).
16 MWT (MSh) S36, S49 and 73 (1130/1717-18).
17 See for this technique Weber, Mortensen & Boqvist; Weber 2004.
18 See for those *qa'a*s Behrens-Abouseif 1989, 20; Maury/Garcin/Revault/Zakariya 1982, 75-90,
    101-105, 176 -187, Sidky 1997. For the Ottoman ones: Maury/Raymond/Revault/Zakariya
    1983.
19 See above and compare note 2 and the above-mentioned *waqfiyya* of Ahmad ibn Sinan al-
    Qaramani. See for the Bayt al-Aqqad Weber, Mortensen, Boqvist. I would like to thank
    Sarab Atassi (IFPO) for giving me this idea first.
20 For further details see Weber, Mortensen & Boqvist.

Illustrations of Islam

Reflections on the Historical Role of Muslim Mass Media

JAKOB SKOVGAARD-PETERSEN

It is an often stated fact that we live in the age of the image. Wherever we turn, we are met with pictures and illustrations. But, as the idea of an age implies, it has not always been like that. In earlier ages, pictures and images were expensive and rare. In certain places they were even prohibited. How did these places make the leap into the age of the image? This question has, as it were, not really been investigated. A particularly instructive example may be the Muslim World where the prohibition against images, the iconoclasm, was grounded in religion. This religion has by no means lost its significance. In fact, millions of Muslims seem to take their religion much more seriously than their parents or grandparents did. And quite often, they even claim to subscribe to a particularly literalist and rule-bound understanding of religion and blame previous generations for not having done that. How does this religious resurgence deal with the traditional iconoclasm? And how does it square with living in an age of the image among the rest of us?

Whenever Islam and the image is discussed, it is worth looking at how Muslim jurists have viewed the legality of pictures. There may be good reason for nuancing the perception of Islam as an iconoclast religion. On the other hand, the Islamic iconoclasm is a historical fact, and it has definitely left its mark on Islamic culture, even in a modern world saturated with images.

This essay will take a look at how the new image culture developed, and the response to it in religious circles. It will concentrate on Egypt, from the first mass produced pictures of the 1860s and up until today. In particular, it will seek to follow the Egyptians' depictions of their own – including their Muslim – identity, which like all other collective identities today has acquired its own iconography. In this way, it aims at being a media- and identity-historical portrait of modern Egypt. I shall begin by discussing the introduction of public images, and the response to them, in relation to the appearance of a public sphere in Egypt, and the erection of statues in Cairo and Alexandria. The statues are also a good introduction to the theme of national identity and mediated self-representations through pictures. I shall discuss the Islamic component in this self-representation and briefly take it up to our day, following the issue of Islamist aesthetics. But prior to that, some initial reflections on the traditional use of images in the study of religion, and the curious lack of interest in mass culture.

Great and small tradition

The point of departure of this essay is, as mentioned, an apparent paradox: on the one hand, the Muslim world of today is full of pictures. On the other hand, as most people know, there is a long tradition of Islamic theological and juridical writing opposed to the representation of human figures.

A popular way of dealing with this and other paradoxes has been to distinguish between the great and the small tradition. That is to claim that Islamic culture was really two rather opposed cultures: a theological and juridical normative tradition, saying one thing, and a popular tradition happily ignorant or indifferent, doing something else. This distinction between a great and a small tradition, between a *Juristenislam* and a *Volksislam*, dates back more than a hundred years in the study of Islam. It is very convenient, and also quite plausible. But there are certain problems.

For one thing, this distinction clearly has its roots in Romanticism and 19th century anti-clericalism, which would always stress the spontaneity of living people in contrast to the scholastic and barren speculations of priesthoods seeking to submit life to their stiff categories. Such claims are standard in early 20th century descriptions of Islam and met with little resistance in the Muslim world because not many Muslim scholars would ever come across these writings, and those who did were typically anti-clerical themselves. Unsurprisingly, whenever the authors sympathized with a phenomenon they would place it squarely within the small, popular tradition, or at least stress its tensions with the dogmatism of the great tradition. Sufism is a case in point.

Secondly, it seems clear that so-called popular and juridical positions have co-existed and known each other well, at least in the major cities in the Muslim world. They have been integrated into the same society and related to each other. And in dealing with them we should take this relationship into account. Let us look at the great tradition. The term itself dates back to the anthropologist Robert Redfield's studies in Yucatan, Mexico, where he identified the great tradition with the hierarchical, orthodox Catholic Church. But quite such a formal and hierarchical church never existed in the Muslim world (even if modern international Muslim organizations such as the Muslim World League bear some resemblances to the early councils in the history of the church). The closest we get is the state-organized Islam of the Ayatollahs in Iran – but here pictures and images are widely used, even in the ritual arenas of the Husseiniyyas.

Throughout history, the Sunni Muslim world has been much more loose and fragmented: a dynamic juridical tradition, *fiqh*, held together not by authoritative dogmas, but by the training and method of the individual scholar, linked to others through networks of apprenticeship, travelling and a common ethos. Their positions and squabbles have often been ignored by ordinary people and rulers alike. To claim that the *fiqh* tradition was generally adverse to Sufism and vice versa is a simplification; many great Sufis were also great lawyers and theologicans, and major institutions of the scholars, such as the al-Azhar in Cairo, were suffused with Sufism. It would be fair to conclude that instead of a great and a small tradition, we do have a normative tradition, but this tradition is characterized by a great variety of positions and a remarkable flexibility when it comes to local lifestyles and attitudes; not coincidentally, local practice, *'urf*, is a significant category and source of law in Muslim jurisprudence.

Instead of making a distinction between great and small tradition, or elite and popular culture, this essay will try to focus on mass culture; the images in mass production and mass circulation in the Muslim world today, taking Cairo as its reference locality. What is important in the study of mass culture is often not the individual detail, but the serial theme; the properties of pictures and images seen and absorbed by many people. Hence, this study will trace the development of a repertoire of Egyptians' representations of their own identity, as a nation, as citizens, as Muslims, and as impersonated by politicians or symbolic figures.

Iconoclasm

Those who will be most severely punished on the Day of Judgment are the murderers of a Prophet, one who has been put to death by a Prophet, one who leads men astray without knowledge, and a maker of images or pictures

This *Hadith* (saying attributed to the Prophet Muhammad) from the collection of al-Bukhari is one of a number condemning the making of pictures, and similar condemnations are found in the literature of *fiqh*, Islamic jurisprudence. Ever since a 1915 article by Henri Lammens on Islamic iconoclasm, however, European Islamic studies have been aware that this attitude may not date back all the way to Muhammad himself. Based on the study of coins and early mosques, Oleg Grabar has dated the iconoclastic attitude to around 690, or some sixty years after the death of Muhammad (Grabar 1973).

In a modern Egyptian context, the debate among Muslim scholars has been raging while in the meantime pictures and images spread ever wider. Each new development – such as illustrated magazines, statues, academies of art, photography and film – has prompted pious Egyptians to petition for fatwas (a normative statement by a legal scholar) on their legal status.[1] The classical definition of the prohibition as covering any living being with a soul, or any image casting a shadow, has come under severe strain.

Just prior to his death in 1905, the well-known theologian and jurist, Muhammad Abduh, states in a fatwa that the above Hadith about the punishment of those who make pictures was directed at those among the heathen Arabs who produced idols. This kind of picture was still forbidden. On the other hand, drawings of human beings for the purpose of science or pedagogical instruction could be allowed in this modern age, because the threat of idolatry had disappeared (Rida 1931, 445-46). Hereby, allowance had been made for all sorts of illustrations. Abduh's permissive view was, however, contested by numerous other scholars (Ahmad 1963, 23-31).

Be that as it may, a result of the classical iconoclasm has been a lack of tradition in a country like Egypt for depicting humans and animals, or rather an association of such production with the Coptic Christians, and later with European culture. This has made artistic production appear as a foreign import and made those who ventured into art look like, if not cultural traitors, then at least cultural innovators and modernists.

Fig. 1. Cordier's statue of Ibrahim Pasha, Cairo.

Fig. 2. Lions on the Kasr an-Nil Bridge, Cairo.

The Statues

The touchstone – literally speaking – of iconoclasm has been the statues. The introduction of statues into the Muslim world has its own fascinating history; as images casting a shadow they were a patent threat to the classical prohibition.

In the Middle East, the honour of introducing the public statue must go to Ismail Pasha, the ruler of Egypt (1863-79) who is famous for his admiration of France and major construction works in Cairo. In 1867, not long after his ascendance to the throne he succeeded in adopting the title of *Khedive* and a more formalized degree of independence from the Ottoman Sultan in Istanbul. In this connection he invited two European sculptors to make statues of his grandfather Muhammad Ali and his father Ibrahim Pasha. These statues were erected in Cairo and Alexandria and marked the (retroactive) creation of a proper dynasty (Kreiser 1997, 106). The statue of Ibrahim Pasha, its side panels depicting Egyptian victories over the Ottomans at Akka and Konya in 1832, was set up in 1872 in front of the Cairo Opera (fig. 1). The following year, the giant lions were added to the Qasr an Nil Bridge (fig. 2).

Fig. 3. Aronco's telegraph monument, Damascus.

These statues are still in place. In 1882, in the religious and anti-European fervour of the Urabi Revolt, they were torn down by the mob, but they were duly placed in the cellar of the Egyptian Museum and later re-erected (Schölch 1972, 244). The man behind the action was the Maliki Mufti Shaykh Illish who considered it a pious act of purification. Muhammad al-Mahdi, the Hanafi Mufti and the prime religious authority of the country, was asked for a fatwa on the statues. In his question to the Mufti, Urabi states that the statues are idols (*sanam*), and that Egypt has been haunted by mischief ever since they were erected. Al-Mahdi answers that the books of *fiqh* make it clear that it is not allowed to procure a large image of a being with a soul, and that it is correct to remove it. In a small and highly unusual appendix to the fatwa, he adds that the government must remove everything that is reprehensible, and that this includes banks and bars. The implication being that the removal of the statues is no more than a publicity stunt, and that the real test of the religious intentions of the Urabists lies elsewhere, in the prohibition of similarly reprehensible, but more indispensable and lucrative institutions such as banks (Peters 1996).

In the Ottoman Empire itself, the Sultan had a collection of minor statues that were kept in the Palace in Istanbul. He did not set up public statues of human beings, but as the erection of public monuments was considered an important display of state order and power, other types of statues were favoured, some of them with Islamic motives. A well-known example is the telegraph monument on Marje Square, Damascus, from 1907, executed by the Italian Raimondo d'Aronco (1857-1932) and set up to commemorate the opening of the telegraph line to the holy cities of the Hijaz (fig. 3). It depicts the telegraph poles and

Fig. 4. The Mustafa Kamil statue, Cairo.

lines, and on top of this monument is a replica of the newly-erected Hamidiya Mosque in Istanbul (Kreiser 1997, 111).

The Ottoman reticence in setting up statues of human beings did not survive the Empire, as anyone traveling through Turkey today can attest. Mustafa Kemal was a great believer in the edifying role of the public statue of the head of the Republic, and throughout his reign he himself was in fact the only person depicted. He stated that it was demeaning to suppose that Muslims, 1300 years after the death of Muhammad, would still commit the error of worshipping a stone as soon as they were presented with one (Kreiser 1997, 114). Similarly, the former Ottoman provinces of Syria and Iraq have taken with a vengeance to erecting statues of the head of state, as we all know.

The Modern National Self-Image

Returning to Egypt, the British occupation and the loss of power of the Khedives put an end to grand-scale royal self-promotion through the means of statues. But, interestingly, popular sentiment towards the erection of statues was no longer negative. On the contrary, the next statue to be set up in Cairo was to be

Fig. 5. Mukhtar's 'Reveil de l'Egypte', Cairo.

of a young 'man of the people', the deceased leader of the national movement, Mustafa Kamil (fig. 4). After his early death and massive funeral in 1908, leading nationalists decided that he deserved a statue. Only 25 years after the Urabi revolt, statues had become a national and popular enterprise. Even if a fatwa by the well-known reformist Rashid Rida denounced them as an expression of European culture (Kreiser 1997, 114; Ahmed 1963, 23-31).

'The striking thing about monuments is that nobody notices them' said the author Robert Musil.[2] Well, that does not include their inauguration. In fact, a modern history of Egypt could be written around the inaugurations of the grand monuments of their day. This, of course, is due to their durability, visibility and symbolism. They are expressions of the local – mostly national – ideological order and priorities. When, twenty years later, the Egyptians inaugurated their next important statue, it was once again a popular celebration on a major scale, with representatives of Cairo high society present at the square in front of the central station (fig. 5). This time the motive was significantly different though, as it was Egypt herself, portrayed as a young peasant girl who, with her right hand resting on the head of the Sphinx, draws her veil aside and gazes towards the future. The modernist aesthetics and ideology is evident, but so is the incorporation of the nationalist theme, the Sphinx symbolizing the ancient greatness of Egypt. The statue bore the title 'Reveil de l'Ègypte' and is the major sculptural expression of what is known today as the nationalist Pharaonocism of the 1920s. Most suitably, it was finally the work of a local artist, Mahmud Mukhtar.

Due to their nature, statues are rarely the first expression of new tendencies. 'The awakening of Egypt' was preceded in poetry, plays, journalism and speeches, if only because it had been ten years in the making. There were also cheap prints and newspaper drawings, a much cheaper mass-produced commodity that gave a first visual expression of what many people had come to perceive as their Egyptian and Muslim identity. Indeed, there were embarrassing charges made that the motive of 'Reveil de l'Ègypte' had been taken from a British war poster from the First World War (Skovgaard-Petersen 2001, 306). To identify the pictorial repertoire that became the building stones of this national imagination, we shall have to take a closer look at printed images.

Printed images

It is a well-known fact that the printing press arrived late in the Middle East. In Egypt, a viable commercial press appeared around 1870, and it soon benefitted from an influx of talent from the Levant, fleeing the Ottoman censorship after 1876. Of the numerous periodicals which appeared and disappeared in the last decades of the 19th century, a few have Islamic sounding names, and in some

Fig. 6. *Al-Hilal*: George Washington.

of these cases the name points towards a theme in the mass-produced collection of symbols that gradually emerges. These are names like 'The Islamic Flag' (*al-'alam al-islami*), 'the Crescent' (*al-hilal*), 'The Wisdom' (*al-'irfan*), 'Paradise' (*al-janna*), 'The Warner' (*al-nadhir*), 'The Direction of Prayer' (*al-qibla*), 'The Straight Path' (*al-sirat al-mustaqim*), 'The Mother of Towns' (*umm al-qura*) and 'The Firm Grasp' (*al-'urwa al-wuthqa*). But these are the exception. By far the most, and the biggest, periodicals and newspapers do not have a religious name. And among those that do, the content is not necessarily Islamic in practice; a famous and still existing magazine is *al-Hilal* ('The Crescent') from 1894, published by the Syrian Christian Jurji Zaydan and not Islamic in its content. *Al-Hilal* was among the first magazines to introduce images, although they were few and of poor quality. Still, these pictures had great impact, as they – and *al-Hilal* in general – introduced the Egyptian public to a world culture hitherto beyond their horizon: During the first years of publication, the Egyptians could read about Konfutse, Benjamin Franklin, Augustus and Dante, and even learn what they looked like (fig. 6).

An even earlier example, which was for part of the time produced in Paris, was the famous satirical magazine 'The Man with the Blue Glasses' (*abu nadhara zarqa*), published by the Egyptian Jew Ya'qub Sannu'. It even introduced photographs and colors before it was closed in 1910 (Ostle 1997, 154). In his satirical comments, Sannu' makes use of his 'man with the blue glasses' to comment upon events, also in drawings.

The nation as a woman

With Sannu' we see an early example of a feature that we also met in the statue of 'Le reveil de l'Ègypte': in the new culture of illustration, Egypt is depicted as a woman. This is an established feature of 19th century European iconography where figures such as Brittania, Germania and Marianne become standard impersonations and references to the major powers. In the Egyptian case, this is still somewhat more *risqué* and controversial, as can be seen (fig. 7).[3] Sannu' has found an elegangt solution here, as it is the point of the illustration that Egypt is a female slave, a commodity fought over by the powers of the world. It is only from around 1910 that Egypt will be depicted without a veil – or with a chic little one (fig. 8) – and this obviously enlarges the artistic possibilities, not to mention the assumed interest of the male readers. One might say that Mukhtar's statue of Egypt drawing her veil aside, describes well the historical development of the illustration of Egypt.

Fig. 7. *Abu Nadhdhara* (Sannu').

ILLUSION DÉTRUITE

Fig. 8. A veiled girl. From *Rethinking Nationalism in the Arab Middle East,* Gershoni & Jankowski 1997, 120.

Fig. 6.9   Egypt and England. [*Al-Kashkul* 5, no. 250 (1926), 1]

With Mukhtar's statue, Egypt moves from being a slave girl or a harem girl to becoming a peasant girl, a tried and tested symbol in territorial nationalist ideology, for instance in Scandinavian nationalist iconography. Moreover, the Sphinx is a further step away from Islam: the Sphinx not only fits the picture of an ancient idol – worshipped instead of the one God – but the statue is also an expression of an idea of continuity, often referred to in the history of religion as cult continuity, which was highly popular among the nationalists, *e.g.*, the assumption that Pharaonic rituals, expressions, attitudes and world views had survived in particularly authentic parts of the population, such as the Copts or the Upper Egyptian peasants.

Fig. 9. 'The Fighting Egypt'.

In a later example dated 1951, 'The Fighting Egypt', she has developed further from being a commodity and a passive object, and is also more lovely and lively (fig. 9). Note the combination of a nationalist symbol with the crescent, which may also be the crown of Isis.

8   Introduction

العلم نور

(وزير المعارف) : مبسوط مني دلوقت ؟ ... زى ما انت شايف كل يوم بازور مدرسة أو دار لتتعلم ...
(المصري افندى) : طيب إياك على الله تتعلم لك حاجة ...

Fig. 10. *Ruzz al-Yusuf*: Misr Effendi ('Mr Egypt').

The citizen

Now, the nation may be a woman, but the citizen is a man. In media iconography the Egyptian is a man. But, significantly, that does not make him a Pharao, rather he is more a Muslim. There is less idealism and more realism here.

He does not appear right away. It was only following the introduction of a parliament and elections in the 1920s that he turns up as a political man in the liberal magazines of the time. The still important cultural magazine *Ruzz al-Yusuf* (1925) introduces the character Misr Effendi ('Mr. Egypt'), a representative of the reading, but not well-to-do urbanized and perhaps somewhat lax effendi class – just the audience the magazine addressed (fig. 10). A rival magazine, *Kashkul*, (1921-45) which satirized the corruption of the Wafd Party and government, had its own Misri Bey ('Sir Egypt'). In 1941 the *Hilal* magazine introduced yet another competing figure, *ibn al-balad* ('son of the country' – denoting an upright, but also unimpressed national character) as a poorer, more plain man than the effendis (Gershoni & Jankowski, 1995, 7-11).

While these figures are introduced as points of identification for the reader, and have a negligible Islamic content, yet another standard character makes his appearance in the 1930s. He is definitely more Islamic, but he is not intended as a person for the reader to identify with: *Shaykh al-ʿyun* ('The shaykh with the eyes').[4] Contrary to the man with the blue glasses, this is not an observing and commenting figure, this is an acting man. And the focus is on the eyes, rather than the object (fig. 11). The humorous point, or rather the polemical point, is in the revelation of his simplistic moralizing aggressivity, combined with the spark of interest in his eyes, he capacity to discover anything reprehensible. This is the response of the liberal press to the rise of Islamic moralism and censorious public behavior. When Islam is finally personalized in a standard character, the intention is not for the reader to identify with him, but to distance himself from him.

Fig. 11. Shaykh al-'Uyun ('The Bathing Law" 1934).

Fig. 12. Book cover: The massacre of Hama.

The self-image of Islamism

The period 1925-40 may be called the formative period of Islamism in Egypt. My material for this Islamism is quite limited, and I do not dare draw any definitive conclusions, but it seems that the prohibition against pictures is taken seriously. The Muslim Brotherhood, by a long chalk the most important Islamist organization, published a weekly periodical with no illustrations. Also, with regard to books, calligraphic embellishment of the title is the only illustration used. But, as Brynjar Lia has described, the Brotherhood is quite capable of staging demonstrations, parades and the like with the waving of Korans and similar ways of building up a repertoire of images around the organization.

Fig. 13. Zaynab al-Ghazzali's autobiography.

Fig. 14. Sketch from *al-I'tisam*

Today, books from the publishers associated with the Brotherhood may well have dramatic covers with human beings, as evidenced in the examples of the massacre of Hama in Syria 1982 (fig. 12) or the memoirs of the famous Muslim sister Zaynab al-Ghazzali (fig. 13). But even today the magazines of the Brotherhood are characterized by a certain hesitancy in the use of illustrations; overall, they concentrate on photos, sometimes portraits, and small vignettes. This typical sketch (fig. 14) of a veiled girl in front of Cairo University was the symbol of the woman's page of the Brotherhood's magazine in the 1980s – edited by the same Zaynab al-Ghazzali. This, by the way, is also clearly an illustration of the citizen; instead of depicting the woman at home or with her children, she is placed in the public domain and given a higher education.

By the standards of classical *fiqh*, even a drawing like this would be forbidden, as it is a depiction of a being with a soul. The Brotherhood, like everybody else, has departed from the classical iconoclasm. And how could it not, given the prevalence of pictures and images in modern society. But it could be argued that iconoclasm plays a peculiar aesthetical role. This seems to be affirmed when one compares the Islamic and non-Islamic part of a modern Arab bookstore; the Islamic publications are characterized by few photos, sketchy and semi-abstract drawings, and a generally limited use of illustrations, except for calligraphy. It is as if unadorned pages with writing signify seriousness and moderation, but somehow also purity and Islamicness. One could perhaps say that the religious prohibition has been transformed into a certain 'puritan aesthetics'.

References

Ahmad, Muhammad 1963. *Die Auseinandersetzung zwischenal-Azhar und der modernistischen Bewegung in Ägypten*. Hamburg.

al-Fatawa al-Islamiya min Dar al-Ifta. Vol. 10, 3453. Cairo. 1980.

al-Fatawa al-Islamiya min Dar al-Ifta. Vol. 10, 3525. Cairo. 1979.

al-Fatawa al-Islamiya min Dar al-Ifta. Vol. 4, 1279-80. Cairo. 1921.

al-Fatawa al-Islamiya min Dar al-Ifta. Vol. 4, 1297. Cairo. 1950.

Armbrust, Walther 2001. 'Colonizing Popular Culture or Creating Modernity? Architectural Metaphors and Egyptian Media'. In: Korsholm Nielsen & Skovgaard-Petersen: *Middle Eastern Cities 1900-1950: Public Spaces and Public Spheres in Transformation*. Aarhus: Aarhus University Press, 20-43.

Baron, Beth 1998. 'Nationalist Iconography: Egypt as a Woman'. In: Gershoni & Jankowski 1997. Cambridge, 105-24.

Gershoni, I. & J. Jankowski 1995. *Redefining the Egyptian Nation 1930-45*. Cambridge: Cambridge University Press.

Gershoni, I. & J. Jankowski (eds.) 1997. *Rethinking Nationalism in the Arab Middle East*. New York: Columbia University Press.

Grabar, Oleg 1973. 'Islamic Attitudes towards the Arts'. In: Grabar: *The Formation of Islamic Art*. New Haven: Yale University Press, 75-103.

Kreiser, Klaus 1997. 'Public Monuments in Turkey and Egypt 1840-1916', *al-Muqarnas*, 14, 103-17.

Ostle, Robin 1997. 'The Printing Press and the Renaissance of Modern Arabic Literature'. In: Skovgaard-Petersen (ed.), *The Introduction of the Printing Press in the Middle East*. (Culture & History 16). Copenhagen, 145-57.

Peters, Rudolf 1996. 'The Lions of Qasr an-Nil Bridge'. In: Masud, Messick & Powers (eds.), *Islamic Legal Interpretation*. Cambrigde & London: Harvard University Press, 214-20.

Rida, Rashid 1931. *Tarikh al-ustadh al-imam Muhammad Abduh*. Vol. II. Cairo.

Schölch, Alexander 1972. *Ägypten den Ägyptern*. Zürich.

Skovgaard-Petersen, Jakob 2001. 'Ægypternes genfødsel – ægyptomani i 1920ernes Ægypten'. In: Erik Christiansen (ed.), *Arven fra Ægypten*. Vol. 2. Aarhus: Aarhus University Press, 305-18.

Notes

1 Examples of such fatwas are found in the published official records of the office of the State
   Mufti of Egypt: *al-Fatawa al-Islamiya min Dar al-Ifta*, vol. 4, 1279-80 (on photographs,
   dated 1921); vol. 4, 1297 (on the appearance of prophets in films, dated 1950); vol. 10, 3453
   (the establishment of museums and exhibitions of statues, excavations, and statues next to
   mosques, dated 1980); vol. 10, 3525 (on the drawing of nudes, dated 1979).
2 Musil, Robert: *Essay on Monuments* (1927). Here quoted from Kreiser 1996, 103.
3 This whole argument draws on Baron 1998.
4 Armbrust 2001, 35.

Archaeology and Islamic studies
The development of a relationship

ALAN WALMSLEY

The intention of this paper is to present a brief review and assessment of Islamic archaeology as it is practised in parts of the Middle East today. It is, primarily, an individual appraisal based on 25 years of experience in the region and, perhaps more significantly, very fruitful discussions with a number of colleagues. One of the most satisfying features of Islamic archaeology as a relatively new discipline is its collegial nature, and much of the rapid development in the field during recent years can be attributed to the spirit of cooperation amongst practising Islamic archaeologists and other supportive parties. Hence it is fitting that this paper is offered with great respect to Peder Mortensen, whose early interest in and support for Islamic archaeology has done much to preserve Denmark's international profile in this field.

As already implied, this paper ranges widely over the field of Islamic archaeology, and in particular as undertaken in the Levant today (fig. 1). Some of the main points to be covered in this paper include: the recent origins of and developments in an archaeology specifically dealing with the Islamic periods and Islamic lands; what the subject can offer the broader field of Islamic studies; what Islamic archaeology can do and, perhaps more importantly, what it cannot do; and finally the prospects for the discipline and the way ahead. The paper focuses on the Levant due to the considerable advances made in Islamic archaeology during the last two decades, much of the credit for which must go to the all-important 'interface' between the various national governments and international missions: the departments of antiquities. The level of support has been, and continues to be, a crucial factor in the development of the discipline, especially in a situation where institutional support in Western nations is, regrettably (although with notable exceptions), not always as positive as it could be. Islamic archaeology continues to be the 'poorer' cousin of other archaeologies in the Middle East, specifically Prehistoric, Biblical, Classical and early Church studies.

Islamic archaeology in the Levant stands at the terminus of two fruitful decades of significant development (Walmsley 2001; Whitcomb 1995 and 2001).

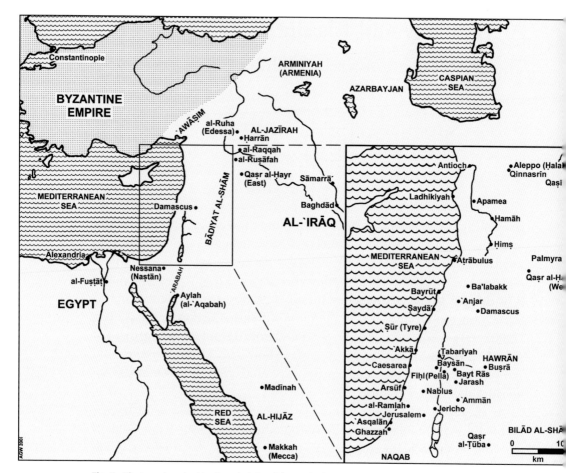

Fig. 1. The Levant: major Islamic-period sites (Alan Walmsley).

Over this period we have seen for the first time and with increasing clarity the creation of a clearly identifiable and adequately defined field of archaeological study concerned with the world of Islam and Muslim societies of the past. Meant is here an archaeology that is not simply preoccupied with the recovery of monumental architectural remains, or the acquisition of art objects. As with nearly all branches of archaeology, such practises have existed for much of the twentieth century, but with Islamic archaeology they have, regrettably, persisted unreformed longer. However, this is generally true for the whole of the Middle East, so is not a criticism that can be specifically levelled at Islamic archaeology in the region.

Rather, these formative decades have seen the establishment of an archaeology that, drawing from a wider source base, seeks to understand more deeply the development of the many aspects of Islamic society. Greater thought is being applied to the suitability of the tasks being applied to archaeological data. The focus has been, and continues to be, towards an understanding of the processes by which early Islamic societies were formed and developed. Yet on another level, Islamic archaeology has been increasingly concerned with identifying points of commonality and diversity within the Islamic world, and the formation of Islamic identities at the local, regional and interregional level.

In that sense, Islamic archaeology as it exists today stands somewhat separate from, although alongside, the study of two well established, and more well-known, companion fields. These are the subjects of the history of Islamic art and Muslim architecture. Connections between the three fields – that is, art history, architecture, and archaeology – remain particularly strong and this, surely, is to be encouraged. Each field can, and does, make valuable contributions to the other, and clearly the exchange of information and cross fertilisation of ideas is mutually beneficial to all three. Nevertheless, recent shifts within Islamic archaeology are having the effect of drawing the discipline away from art history and, to a lesser extent, traditional architectural studies, although the latter field is also in a state of flux, including profitable advances in the analysis of the built environment (see especially, Tonghini & Vannini 2003).

From another perspective, Islamic archaeology is quite different from other archaeologies in the Middle East, for Islam is still a living, vibrant religious and cultural entity in the region, and increasingly so. This situation is unlike many other societies that are the subject of archaeological research, which are long extinct or radically disconnected from an ancient past. Accordingly, the related disciplines of cultural anthropology and ethnographic studies have a crucial role to play in Islamic archaeology. These fields, however, have been little explored or utilized by Islamic archaeologists.

An important issue that needs addressing from the outset is whether the discipline of Islamic archaeology is a legitimate field of study or simply another Eurocentric intellectual construct by which Western standards and conceptions are imposed upon the Islamic world. Such a bias in other fields of academic endeavour has been brilliantly exposed by Edward Said (1978), but the question has been little debated in archaeological circles. The issue, however, is real, especially as some aspects of early work in the field seem deeply influenced by European colonial attitudes, for instance French studies of the 'Oriental City' in North Africa and the Levant (see further below). It could also be argued that Islamic archaeology is conceptually too broad and all-encompassing, and runs the risk of becoming unintelligible. However, as Timothy Insoll has stressed in his book *The Archaeology of Islam*, there are clear unifying features across the Islamic world today, as in the past (Insoll 1999). Particularly unifying are: a place of prayer, the mosque, which is clearly identifiable; burial of dead including orientation, the manner of burial and a general absence of grave goods; and dietary practices, for instance the prohibition of certain foods (which should be clearly represented in the faunal remains from excavations).

Yet it has to be conceded that there was, and still is, enormous diversity within the Muslim world in cultural practises and beliefs, and the level of observance by the individual. Certainly in the archaeology of private, domestic quarters, one is dealing with the way of life of individuals – their domestic arrangements, their types of food, how they decorated their houses, levels of personal wealth, hygiene and so on. Yet how individuals varied from the norm is just as revealing as the norm itself.

Having diverted a little from the main subject of this paper, it is perhaps necessary to return to a consideration of the current state of Islamic archaeology and where it stands in Islamic studies more generally. It is, probably, an appropriate moment to consider these topics, for it could be argued that Islamic archaeology has reached a developmental plateau, and perhaps a plateau after which there are many challenges ahead. The options are simple: stagnation or even oblivion, or a new ascent to a higher level of competence and clarity. Clearly, we need to strive for the latter.

As stated at the start of this paper, the last 20 years has seen the recognition of a distinct branch of archaeology concerned with the study of the cultural heritage of the Islamic world. Yet, where do we go now; in other words, what is the way forward for the discipline? Indeed, does Islamic archaeology currently exist as a separate entity with its own, clearly defined identity? Is there, by implication, a group of 'archaeological practitioners' (for want of a better term) who identify themselves as working together in a common field, seeking a generally common goal, with broadly agreed objectives and principles? The approach in this paper is to address those central issues from a number of approaches, drawing on some examples of recent archaeological work. Not surprisingly, there will be a bias towards known areas of research to this writer, which is, broadly, economic and cultural transformations in the Arab-Islamic world over half a millennium, c. AD 600-1100.

The choice of these dates is fairly easy to justify. On the eve of the disastrous Crusader intervention, many aspects of cultural, political and economic life in the Middle East had changed considerably compared to five centuries earlier, yet there was still great social variety and fluidity. For instance – and much to the surprise of Baldwin (ruled 1100-18) and the Crusaders – a Greek monastery with a history supposedly hundreds of years old kept vigil over the reputed tomb of Aaron, brother of Moses, on a mountain top in south Jordan. The Crusader occupation of the Levant, although their effective rule lasted less than a century,

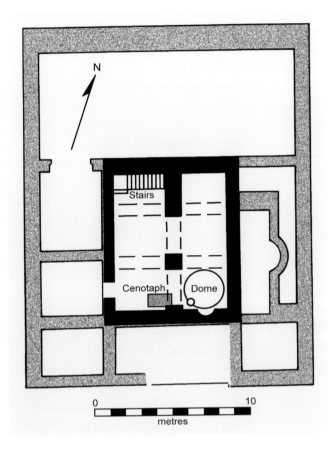

Fig. 2. Plan of the Mamluk shrine on the summit of Jabal Harun (black lines), which was built over the site of an earlier monastery (depicted as underlying grey lines). It was probably that monastery in which the monks lived at Baldwin's visit in AD 1100.

had the disastrous effect of substantially reducing the earlier plurality of eastern Mediterranean society. Five centuries of change that had gone before was permanently locked into place, but most notably the Crusader presence completed the significant political and cultural developments of the eleventh century as a permanent feature in the cultural landscape. The impact was spread over many aspects of social life, such as settlement, commerce, architecture and material culture (Walmsley 2001). The Harun monastery, for instance, disappeared with the 1187-88 defeat of the Crusaders, a victory that in this area of south Jordan was marked by the surrender of the castles at Karak and Shawbak. Today, the hilltop is marked by an Islamic shrine to Harun (fig. 2), which is of Mamluk date (1338-39) with the monastic ruins, currently under investigation, situated nearby. What followed, historically termed the Ayyubid and Mamluk periods, opened a new chapter in the history of the Middle East that was built upon, and in reaction to, the changes and traumas of the eleventh and twelfth centuries.

One of the most difficult issues facing Islamic archaeology is finding common ground between it and the related fields of historical studies and art history, and reaching an agreement on a suitable academic home for the subject. To date, the placement of Islamic archaeology in universities has reflected the personal preferences of the individual archaeologists, and that of their discipline supporters. Accordingly, no particular pattern can be noted, although institutes of Oriental studies teaching a wide range of cultural, historical and language subjects have, above all, favoured appointments to Islamic archaeology, for instance the Oriental Institute in Chicago, The School of Oriental and African Studies in London, The Carsten Niebuhr Institute, Copenhagen, and the Oriental Institute, Oxford. Centres of archaeology and art have also hosted Islamic archaeology, for instance The Institute of Archaeology and Art, Paris, the Department of Archaeology in Nottingham, and the Department of Art and Archaeology at Princeton.

The historical origins of Islamic archaeology have been a major determinant in the placement of the discipline. Where Islamic archaeology is to be found today has influenced attitudes towards it by other archaeologies, as did a possibly undue reliance on architecture in the early years. The prevalence of architectural studies can be easily traced back to pioneering work in the field, notably (but by no means exclusively) by K.A.C. Creswell and Jean Sauvaget. Creswell, of course, should require no introduction. In addition to his monumental *Early Muslim Architecture* in two volumes (Oxford, 1932, 1940; volume 1 revised in two parts, 1969), and *The Muslim Architecture of Egypt* also in two volumes (Oxford: Clarendon, 1952, 1959), his most enduring and influential legacy has been *A Short Account of Early Muslim Architecture* (Penguin, 1956), subsequently reprinted and, more recently, revised and updated by James Allan (Creswell & Allan 1989). All three publications are acknowledged masterpieces, ranging wide in their analysis, yet thorough and influential. Only in the last decade or so have questions arisen as to the value of persisting with such scholarship (Allan 1991), or major challenges been presented questioning some of Creswell's basic tenets, such as seeking the origin of the mosque in the Prophet's house in Madinah (Johns 1999).

Also concerned with architecture was the pioneering French scholar Jean Sauvaget, remembered especially for his work in the first part of the twentieth century on the Syrian cities of Aleppo, Ladhikiyah and Damascus, and especially for his widely quoted model on the development of the 'Medieval suq' (Sauvaget 1941; Sauvaget 1949). In this model, Sauvaget argued that the conversion of the broad colonnaded streets of the Classical city into an enclosed and covered market – a *suq*, found in every major city of Syria – occurred during a period of political upheaval in the tenth and eleventh centuries (figs. 3 and 4). The enclosure of public space, that is encroachment on once wide open streets,

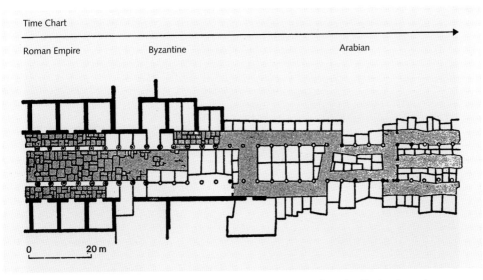

Time Chart

Roman Empire   Byzantine   Arabian

0   20 m

Fig. 3. Schematic drawing in E. Wirth, 2001, *Die Orientalische Stadt im islamischen Vorderasien und Nordafrika* (Mainz: Philipp von Zabern), figure 14, redrawn from Sauvaget and depicting this proposed three-stage transformation from a colonnaded street to an enclosed *suq*, based on Sauvaget's work at Ladhikiyah.

was viewed as the reawakening of an anarchic 'oriental' mentality after a millennium of Classical civic 'order'; that is, this process was seen as an entirely Islamic phenomenon and, in some way, represented the cultural reassertion by an 'Oriental' East over an ordered, Hellenized urban environment. His underlying social theory was one that equated political disorder with social chaos – a colonial view, and one that championed iron rule over a subject people and their unruly society. His model has been often repeated as evidence for urban, and indeed cultural, change in the Islamic period.

As Sauvaget was dealing with still operating towns, he relied upon historical rather than archaeological evidence to date the formation of the *suq* in the Syrian cities. However, by drawing on another body of evidence – archaeology – Hugh Kennedy has concluded that the process of suq formation began considerably earlier, principally in the mid-sixth century (Kennedy 1985a). To Kennedy, the process was a reflection of the political, economic and demographic collapse of towns, resulting in a weakened Syria in the decades before the Islamic Conquest (Kennedy 1985b; 1992).

Parallel with these early architectural and urban studies, the first significant archaeological excavations of Islamic sites were undertaken in the east Mediterranean, although some of the work was more accidental or simply incidental than intentional. Khirbat Mafjar ('Hisham's Palace') at Jericho is a clear case. The large field of ruins, thought at first to be Hellenistic or Herodian in date,

Fig. 4. The *suq* of Aleppo: such 'Orientalist' images intrigued early European Islamic scholars (Alan Walmsley).

was excavated between 1934 and 1948 by the Palestine Department of Antiquities (Hamilton 1959; 1988). The excavations revealed a monument built in four clear parts: a forecourt with a fountain, a *qasr*, a mosque and a reception hall with

Fig. 5. Khirbat Mafjar (Hisham's Palace), c. 743. View of the mosaic floor (photo courtesy of Ross Burns).

a huge floor area of mosaics and adjoining baths (fig. 5). Yet, a crucial but less spectacular part of the complex has been largely ignored: a caravanserai located immediately to the north of the princely complex. Surface artefacts reveal occupation in the ninth century, and perhaps into the tenth. Identifying a major commercial element at the site completely changes our understanding of the site. Khirbat Mafjar is not simply, if at all, a 'pleasure palace'. Not only was 'Hisham's Palace' initially misdated, the site has been subsequently misinterpreted.

Excavations of major *tell* sites additionally brought Islamic remains to the attention of archaeologists. At Baysan (Beth Shan), a major complex of early Islamic date was cleared and almost totally removed from the summit of Tell Husn. Only scantily published (Fitzgerald 1931), the similarity of the structure's plan with the administrative complex on Amman Citadel would suggest a similar function for the Tell Husn building, although on a less grand scale than Amman's complex (Almagro 1983; Northedge 1992). The Danish excavations on the tell of Hamah in Syria likewise uncovered extensive Islamic remains, and the recent publication of these levels has demonstrated the great difficulty faced by the excavators due to the very mixed nature of the deposits (Pentz 1997). In Jordan, excavations at the major tell sites of Dhiban and Hisban exposed major

Islamic deposits, with those at Hisban forming the basis of a doctoral thesis by Jim Sauer, one of Jordan's pioneering archaeologists of the Islamic periods (Sauer 1973). However, although most tell excavations are undertaken by large university-based teams, few such projects have produced university-tenured Islamic specialists – surely a reflection of project (and university?) priorities.

Other early archaeological work had the objective to expose elite architecture and define architectural decoration (*e.g.* stucco, mosaics); perhaps a reasonable objective, but little attention was paid to the contents of the excavated rooms, or the wider context of the monuments. For instance, at the behest of Creswell, the governor's residence adjacent to the Kufah mosque in Iraq was excavated in the 1950s, recovering interesting architecture but seemingly little else. In north Syria, the mudbrick and stuccoed palaces at Raqqah were excavated (B, D and G) between 1950 and 1954 by the Syrian Department of Antiquities. In Lebanon, excavations commenced in 1953 at 'Anjar in the Biqa' valley as a show piece project for the new Lebanese Antiquities service, and research on this enigmatic site has continued on and off ever since, but with little improvement in clarity (Chehab 1993; Hillenbrand 1999). The emphasis was on cities and monuments, and a clear architectural purpose – or at least results – was paramount and intended. Nevertheless, projects such as these did establish and draw attention to Islamic archaeology as a legitimate field of study. The Raqqah and Mafjar excavations also established a reference corpus of early Islamic ceramics, especially plain (unglazed) wares, but misdating of the finds was a common problem (Whitcomb 1988).

From another direction, Islamic archaeology has been partnered – sometimes uncomfortably – with art history and the collection of artefacts. The outcomes have not always been favourable, for instance with the excavations at Nishapur in Iran which, while producing a fine collection of glazed ceramics and metalwork, were unfortunately followed by extensive looting of the site to supply the art market (Wilkinson 1975). Of course, the partnering of archaeology with art is not only to be found is Islamic studies; most famously, this partnership can be seen in traditional approaches to Classical archaeology, with an emphasis on stylistic analyses of painted Greek vases and so on. Yet, contemporary Classical archaeology, especially of the Greek Archaic period, has progressed well beyond a conventional art historical approach, in which social processes and city-state formation are of greater importance. Similarly, a major part of Islamic archaeology has in the last decade moved in the same direction.

In an endeavour to identify a discipline home for Islamic archaeology it is necessary to ask, what is the intellectual objective of such archaeology? Is it simply an historical 'gap filler' to provide interesting and curious details not available in the written sources, thereby supplementing an historical framework already mapped out? Or perhaps as an adjunct to the study of the history of architecture, in which standing monuments are fully documented and the ruins of others, mostly unknown, exposed and recorded. Alternatively, Islamic archaeology could be viewed as an adjunct to antiquarian studies, in which artefacts are retrieved and their chronologies refined.

It should be obvious that such objectives are quite inadequate, and although Islamic archaeology can offer valuable information for the historian, architectural studies and art history, the goals of archaeological research need to be much more ambitious than this. Islamic archaeology (as with all archaeologies) must reach beyond being simply and slavishly an historical gap filler, but rather an elaborator, offering depth, complexity and new dimensions and understanding not even hinted at in historical sources. Archaeology can also serve as an independent arbitrator, for historical sources were commonly written to an agenda with a point to prove. Archaeology produces a category of evidence that, when adequately interpreted, is a first hand record of things as they were. While the interpretation of the discoveries can be disputed, the data cannot be denied, for instance the production, trade and consumption of wine as revealed by the discovery of amphorae' or the presence of pig bone in Islamic levels. There are many variables in viewing the significance of such finds, but the material evidence is unquestionable.

This role for archaeology is not a new idea, but only in recent years have Islamic archaeologists, at least in the Levant, sought to identify intellectual objectives beyond the immediate. Regrettably, Islamic archaeology has also failed to present research results in a useable manner for scholars in related fields of academic research, although this is a problem which has plagued the subject in general. Often data is presented with little analysis or interpretation, or naively so, which discredits the results and even the discipline as a whole (this is particularly the case with Islamic archaeology). Furthermore, there never seems to be any consensus amongst archaeologists what particular discoveries actually mean; take, for instance, the thorny problem of pig bone in Islamic levels or modification of church architecture after the Islamic conquest. Not surprisingly, then, historians have avoided dealing with archaeological sources, especially when they seem to contradict historical data. The need to find common ground is still a pressing issue, even after two decades of advances (see, for instance, Shboul & Walmsley 1998).

There can be no question that Islamic archaeology today has firmly established a place as a legitimate area of independent research. It has shared interests with, and has much to offer the history, architecture and art history of Islamic periods, and needs to further develop profitable links in all three fields. Yet archaeology can do – and must do – much more than this, especially in the area of writing

Islamic social histories from the perspective of retrieved material culture. Islamic history has been described as 'princely' and 'male', and early archaeological studies reflected this bias, especially with an emphasis on monumental architecture and elite art objects. Other, sub-elite social groups have been largely ignored, while the social role of women has been generally invisible, a failing common to all historical studies but further 'justified' in this case by male, Western, concepts of Islam. Archaeology offers new, reliable and an almost unlimited supply of data with which to tackle Islamic social history from a non-elitist and post-colonial perspective, and while it has the potential of broadening our perspective of the Islamic world, archaeological research will also provide support for and expand the capabilities of erstwhile 'traditional' fields of research.

Note: This paper is a revised version of an address first given at a meeting of the Orientalsk Forum, Copenhagen, in 2002.

References

Allan, J.W. 1991. 'New Additions to the New Edition', *Muqarnas,* 8, 12-22.

Almagro, A. 1983. *El Palacio Omeya de Amman 1. La Arquitectura.* Madrid: Instituto Hispano-Arabe de Cultura.

Chehab, H.K. 1993. 'On the Identification of 'Anjar ('Ayn al-Jarr) as an Umayyad Foundation', *Muqarnas,* 10 (Essays in Honor of Oleg Grabar), 42-48.

Creswell, K.A.C. & J.W. Allan. 1989. *A Short Account of Early Muslim Architecture.* London: Scolar Press.

Fitzgerald, G.M. 1931. *Beth-Shan Excavations 1921-23. The Arab and Byzantine Levels.* Philadelphia: University of Pennsylvania.

Hamilton, R.W. 1959. *Khirbat al Mafjar: an Arabian mansion in the Jordan Valley.* Oxford: Clarendon Press.

Hamilton, R.W. 1988. *Walid and His Friends. An Umayyad Tragedy.* (Oxford Studies in Islamic Art 6). Oxford: Board of the Faculty of Oriental Studies/Oxford University Press.

Hillenbrand, R. 1999. "Anjar and Early Islamic Urbanism'. In: G.P. Brogiolo & B. Ward-Perkins (eds.), *The Idea and Ideal of the Town between Late Antiquity and the Early Middle Ages.* (The Transformation of the Roman World). Leiden: E.J. Brill.

Insoll, T. 1999. *The Archaeology of Islam.* Oxford: Blackwell.

Johns, J. 1999. 'The "House of the Prophet" and the Concept of the Mosque'. In: J. Johns (ed.), *Bayt al-Maqdis: Jerusalem and Early Islam.* (Oxford Studies in Islamic Art IX.2). Oxford: Oxford University Press.

Kennedy, H. 1985a. 'From *Polis* to *Madina*: Urban Change in Late Antique and Early Islamic Syria', *Past & Present,* 106, 3-27.

Kennedy, H. 1985b. 'The Last Century of Byzantine Syria: a reinterpretation', *Byzantinische Forschungen*, 10, 141-84.

Kennedy, H. 1992. 'Antioch: from Byzantium to Islam and back again'. In: J. Rich (ed.), *The City in Late Antiquity*. London: Routledge.

Northedge, A. 1992. *Studies on Roman and Islamic Amman, Volume 1. The Excavations of Mrs C-M Bennett and Other Investigations*. (British Academy Monographs in Archaeology 3). Oxford: British Institute at Amman for Archaeology and History/Oxford University Press.

Pentz, P. 1997. *The Medieval Citadel and its Architecture*. (Hama: fouilles et researches de la Foundation Carlsberg 1931-1938, 4.1.). København: Nationalmuseet.

Said, E. 1978. *Orientalism*. London: Routledge & Kegan Paul.

Sauer, J.A. 1973. *Hesbon Pottery 1971. A preliminary report on the pottery from the 1971 excavations at Tell Hesban*. (Andrews University Monographs 7). Berrien Springs, MI: Andrews University Press.

Sauvaget, J. 1941. *Alep*. Paris: Librairie Orientaliste Paul Geuthner.

Sauvaget, J. 1949. 'Le Plan Antique de Damas', *Syria*, 26, 314-358.

Shboul, A.M.H. & A.G. Walmsley. 1998. 'Identity and Self-image in Syria-Palestine in the Transition from Byzantine to Early Islamic Rule: Arab Christians and Muslims'. In: G. Clarke (ed.), *Identities in the Eastern Mediterranean in Antiquity*. (Mediterranean Archaeology 11). Sydney: Mediterranean Archaeology.

Tonghini, C. & G. Vannini. 2003. 'The Contribution of "Light" Archaeology to the Study of Fortified Sites in Northern Syria'. In: I. Thuesen & A. Walmsley (eds.), *Proceedings of the Second International Congress on the Archaeology of the Ancient Near East, Copenhagen 2000*. Winona Lake: Eisenbrauns.

Walmsley, A. 2001. 'Fatimid, Ayyubid and Mamluk Jordan and the Crusader Interlude'. In: B. MacDonald, R. Adams & P. Bienkowski (eds.), *The Archaeology of Jordan*. (Levantine Archaeology, 1). Sheffield: Sheffield Academic Press.

Whitcomb, D. 1988. 'Khirbat al-Mafjar Reconsidered: The Ceramic Evidence', *Bulletin of the American Schools of Oriental Research*, 271, 51-67.

Whitcomb, D. 1995. 'Islam and the Socio-Cultural Transition of Palestine – Early Islamic Period (638-1099 CE)'. In: T.E. Levy (ed.), *The Archaeology of Society in the Holy Land*. London: Leicester University.

Whitcomb, D. 2001. 'Umayyad and Abbasid Periods'. In: B. MacDonald, R. Adams & P. Bienkowski (eds.), *The Archaeology of Jordan*. (Levantine Archaeology, 1). Sheffield: Sheffield Academic Press.

Wilkinson, C.K. 1975. *Nishapur: Pottery of the Early Islamic Period*. New York: Metropolitan Museum of Art.

Contributors

Ross Burns has recently retired from the Australian Foreign Service after a career that included several Middle East postings. He studied history and archaeology at the University of Sydney, just enough to turn him into a frustrated archaeologist. After an assignment in Damascus in the 1980s, he prepared *Monuments of Syria – An Archaeological Guide* (IB Tauris, London and New York University Press, New York), which has appeared in two editions (1993 and 1998) and was translated into French. He is currently completing a history of Damascus to be published by Routledge, London.

Kjeld von Folsach, Dr. phil., is a historian and art historian. His original area of research was European architecture and decorative arts of the 18th-19th century. Since 1985 he has been Director of the David Collection in Copenhagen. His present field of research is Islamic art. [Peder Mortensen has been a member of the board of trustees of the David Collection since 1986].

Hans Georg K. Gebel, Dr., specialised in Near Eastern Early Holocene/ Neolithic research, i.e. in palaeoenvironmental reconstructions and chipped stone analysis. Director of the Ba'ja Neolithic Project, the previous PIGPA-Project in Southern Jordan, and Mazyad Project in Abu Dhabi Emirate; participated in various capacities in many other projects in Jordan (Basta, 'Ain Rahub), Abu Dhabi, Oman, Turkey, Iran, and Syria; co-editor of *Neo-Lithics*, the *Studies in Early Near Eastern Production, Subsistence, and Environment*, and the *bibliotheca neolithica Asiae meridionalis et occidentalis*; Chairman of ex oriente, Berlin. [First introduced to chipped lithic analysis by Peder Mortensen in 1978].

Ernie Haerinck is Professor of Near Eastern Art and Archaeology at Ghent University, Belgium. In the 1970s participated in several expeditions in the Pusht-i Kuh, Luristan, Iran. Organised nine expeditions in the United Arab Emirates (1987-1995), particularly excavating at the 1st century AD coastal site of ed-Dur, in the Emirate of Umm al-Qaiwain, and three on Bahrain (1998-2000). Editor of the international journal *Iranica Antiqua*.

Erik Hallager, Dr. phil., was appointed Honorary Professor in 2001 at the Department of Classical Archaeology at the University of Aarhus. From 1972-73 was Assistant Director at the Swedish Institute in Athens, and since 1972 field director for the Swedish part of the Greek-Swedish Excavations at Kastelli in Khania, western Crete. Since January 2004 has been Director of the Danish Institute at Athens. Has written a number of scientific papers and monographs, including books on the final destruction of the Palace at Knossos, a unique seal impression from Khania and the Minoan administrative system based on the use of seals.

Lise Hannestad is Reader at the Department of Classical Archaeology, University of Aarhus. She has written extensively on the Hellenistic period in the Near East, the focus being on interaction between Greek and non-Greek cultures. At present she is working on a book on the Seleucid kingdom.

Frank Hole is currently C.J. McCurdy Professor of Anthropology at Yale University and Head, Anthropology Division, Yale University Peabody Museum. His archaeological research has focused primarily on the Near East, from Iran to Syria where he has conducted numerous reconnaissance surveys and excavations, mostly concerning the early stages of agriculture and animal husbandry, and regional settlement history. In 1973 he travelled in Luristan, Iran, with a group of tribal nomads on their annual spring migration. In Iran he also carried out several small excavations in palaeolithic caves and rockshelters in the Khorramabad Valley. The Iranian research has been published in two monographs, one edited book and numerous articles. His most recent research has been in northeastern Syria.

ALISON MCQUITTY read European Archaeology at Durham University and has an M.A. in Middle East Area Studies from the School of Oriental and African Studies. She was Director of the British Institute at Amman for Archaeology and History (later the Council for British Research in the Levant – CBRL) from 1990-91 and 1994-99. She is CBRL Visiting Research Fellow and Visiting Research Associate, Centre for Tourism & Cultural Change, Sheffield Hallam University. Currently she lives in the Netherlands and is completing the final publication of her excavations of a rural settlement, Khirbat Faris, on the Karak Plateau in Jordan (jointly conducted with Dr J. Johns of the Oriental Institute, University of Oxford). Her main research interests are the archaeology of the Byzantine-modern rural landscape and vernacular architecture.

SULTAN MUHESEN is Professor of Prehistory, Head of the Department of Archaeology at Damascus University; former Director General of Antiquities and Museums in Syria; director or co-director of several prehistoric excavations in Syria; author or co-author of several publications on prehistory and archaeology; researcher; visiting scholar at several European, American, and Japanese institutions and universities.

HANS J. NISSEN, Prof. Dr., studied law between 1955-63 and subsequently studied Ancient Near Eastern Languages and Archaeology, Comparative Semitic Languages, and Prehistory at the Free University of Berlin and the Universities of Vienna and Heidelberg. Doctoral Thesis: *Zur Datierung des Königsfriedhofes von Ur* from Heidelberg University (with Professor Adam Falkenstein). After positions with the German Archaeological Institute (Baghdad) and the Oriental Institute of the University of Chicago, was appointed (Full) Professor of Ancient Near Eastern Archaeology at the Free University of Berlin in 1971; retired in 2000. Since 1964 has worked on the decipherment and edition of the Archaic Texts from Uruk (five volumes to date).

JOAN OATES, Dr., is an archaeologist who has excavated extensively in northern Iraq and Syria on sites of prehistoric through Roman date (Nimrud, Ain Sinu, Tell al Rimah, Choga Mami, Tell Brak). Her early research was on the Ubaid period in Mesopotamia, with particular reference to Eridu. She is a Fellow of the McDonald Institute for Archaeological research and a Life Fellow of Girton College in the University of Cambridge, and is currently Deputy Director of the Tell Brak Project (NE Syria).

OLAF OLSEN was Curator of the National Museum of Denmark from 1958-1971. He was Professor of Medieval Archaeology at the University of Aarhus from 1971, and Keeper of National Antiquities and Director of the National Museum from 1981-95.

RIKKE AGNETE OLSEN became Curator National Museum of Denmark in 1966. From 1971 has been a free-lance author and lecturer and has specialised mainly in Medieval castles and warfare.

BRUNO OVERLAET, Dr., studied Near Eastern archaeology at Ghent University with the late Louis Vanden Berghe and participated in excavations in the U.A.E. and Siberia. He teaches art history at Vesalius College (Free University Brussels) and works on the Iranian collection of The Royal Museums of Art and History, Brussels. He made his Ph.D. on the Early Iron Age in Luristan and is co-author of the final excavation reports of the Belgian Luristan expedition.

MICHELE PICCIRILLO is an archaeologist at the Studium Biblicum Franciscanum in Jerusalem. The author of a number of works on the archaeology of Jordan, he has directed excavation and restoration projects since 1973, mainly at the Memorial of Moses on Mount Nebo, at Madaba and Umm al-Rasas.

DANIEL POTTS is the Edwin Cuthbert Hall Professor of Middle Eastern Archaeology at the University of Sydney, where he has taught since 1991. Prior to that appointment he was an Associate Professor at the Carsten Niebuhr Institute, University of Copenhagen from 1986-1991, and Wissenschaftlicher Assistant at the Free University in Berlin from 1981-1986. He has worked extensively in Iran, Saudi Arabia and the United Arab Emirates.

JØRGEN BÆK SIMONSEN, Dr., is a historian and a historian of religions, and has specialised in Arab and Muslim history. He holds a chair at the Carsten Niebuhr Institute, from which he is presently on leave to be Director of the Danish Institute in Damascus.

ROSE L. SOLECKI is a Research Associate in the Department of Anthropology, Columbia University in the City of New York. For the past forty years she has been engaged in research in the prehistoric cultures of the Near East.

RALPH S. SOLECKI is Professor Emeritus at Columbia University, New York. His fieldwork in the Near East began in 1950 in Kurdistan, Iraq, where he discovered Shanidar Cave. Notable finds in Shanidar Cave included the recovery of the skeletal remains of nine Neanderthals.

HENRIK THRANE, Dr.phil., is Professor of Prehistoric Archaeology at Moesgård, University of Aarhus. Among his main research interests are Bronze Age in Denmark and Europe, and Bronze and Iron Age in Luristan. Henrik Thrane has participated in the EU-project "Tomba" – a database for tombs of the elites in Bronze Age and Early Iron Age Europe – and in the Danish "War and Society"-project.

INGOLF THUESEN is an archaeologist specialising in the urbanisation process and early state formation in West Asia. He has carried out field work in Iraq, Syria and Jordan since 1978. At present he is engaged in field work in Jordan, the Neolithic site Shaqarat Meziad in the Petra region, and in the Nebo region. Since 1998 he has been the head of the Carsten Niebuhr Institute.

ALAN WALMSLEY is an archaeologist specialising in the East Mediterranean during the first millennium AD, with a particular focus on social and economic continuity and change in Late Antique and Islamic Syria-Palestine (*ca*. 6th–11th centuries). Currently Associate Professor of Islamic Archaeology and Art at the University of Copenhagen, he has worked in the Middle East for over 25 years, directing four major field projects. In 2002, he instigated the Danish-Jordanian Islamic Jarash Project with the intention of revealing Jarash's Islamic heritage, discovering a large Congregational Mosque in the process.

STEFAN WEBER has been a postdoctoral research fellow of History and Art History at the Orient-Institute Beirut since 2001. He is coordinating the research projects on Mamluk-Ottoman Tripoli and Sidon. As a member of ICOMOS he is involved in several restoration projects. Between 1996 and 2001 he was a Junior Research Fellow at the German Archaeological Institute in Damascus for History of Islamic Art and Architecture. His dissertation on city, architecture and society of late Ottoman Damascus at the Free University of Berlin was entitled *Zeugnisse Kulturellen Wandels: Stadt, Architektur und Gesellschaft des spätosmanischen Damaskus im Umbruch (1808-1918)*. The Danish Institute in Damascus will publish an English translation of this dissertation.